NARRATOLOGY

16

1

LONGMAN CRITICAL READERS

General Editor:
STAN SMITH, Professor of English, University of Dundee

NARRATOLOGY: AN INTRODUCTION

Edited and Introduced by

SUSANA ONEGA
AND
JOSÉ ANGEL GARCÍA LANDA

LONGMAN
LONDON AND NEW YORK

Addison Wesley Longman Group Limited
Edinburgh Gate,
Harlow, Essex CM20 2JE, England
and associated companies throughout the world.

*Published in the United States of America
by Longman Publishing, New York.*

First published 1996

ISBN 0 582 25542 2 CSD
ISBN 0 582 25543 0 PPR

British Library Cataloguing-in-Publication Data

A catalogue record for this book is
available from the British Library

Library of Congress Cataloging-in-Publication Data

Also available

Phototypeset by 20 in 9½/11½ Palatino
Produced by Longman Singapore Publishers Pte.
Printed in Singapore

Contents

PART FOUR: NARRATOLOGY AND FILM

PART FIVE: POST-STRUCTURALIST NARRATOLOGY

General Editors' Preface

The outlines of contemporary critical theory are now often taught as a standard feature of a degree in literary studies. The development of particular theories has seen a thorough transformation of literary criticism. For example, Marxist and Foucauldian theories have revolutionised Shakespeare studies, and 'deconstruction' has led to a complete reassessment of Romantic poetry. Feminist criticism has left scarcely any period of literature unaffected by its searching critiques. Teachers of literary studies can no longer fall back on a standardised, received methodology.

Lecturers and teachers are now urgently looking for guidance in a rapidly changing critical environment. They need help in understanding the latest revisions in literary theory, and especially in grasping the practical effects of the new theories in the form of theoretically sensitised new readings. A number of volumes in the series anthologise important essays on particular theories. However, in order to grasp the full implications and possible uses of particular theories it is essential to see them put to work. This series provides substantial volumes of new readings, presented in an accessible form and with a significant amount of editorial guidance.

Each volume includes a substantial introduction which explores the theoretical issues and conflicts embodied in the essays selected and locates areas of disagreement between positions. The pluralism of theories has to be put on the agenda of literary studies. We can no longer pretend that we all tacitly accept the same practices in literary studies. Neither is a *laissez-faire* attitude any longer tenable. Literature departments need to go beyond the mere toleration of theoretical differences: it is not enough merely to agree to differ; they need actually to 'stage' the differences openly. The volumes in this series all attempt to dramatise the differences, not necessarily with a view to resolving them but in order to foreground the choices presented by different theories or to argue for a particular route through the impasses the differences present.

The theory 'revolution' has had real effects. It has loosened the grip of traditional empiricist and romantic assumptions about language and literature. It is not always clear what is being proposed as the new agenda for literary studies, and indeed the very notion of 'literature' is questioned by the post-structuralist strain in theory. However, the uncertainties and obscurities of contemporary theories appear much less worrying when we see what the best critics have been able to do with them in practice. This series aims to disseminate the best of recent criticism and to show that it is possible to re-read the canonical texts of literature in new and challenging ways.

RAMAN SELDEN AND STAN SMITH

The Publishers and fellow Series Editor regret to record that Raman Selden died after a short illness in May 1991 at the age of fifty-three. Ray Selden was a fine scholar and a lovely man. All those he has worked with will remember him with much affection and respect.

Notes on Editors

SUSANA ONEGA is Professor of English Literature at the University of Zaragoza. She is also the president of the Spanish Association for Anglo-American Studies (AEDEAN), and represents Spain on the board of the European Society for the Study of English (ESSE).

She has published numerous articles on English and American literature or literary theory and is the author of *Análisis estructural, método narrativo y 'sentido' de* The Sound and the Fury, *de William Faulkner* (Zaragoza, 1989), and another entitled *Form and Meaning in the Novels of John Fowles* (Ann Arbor, 1989). She is also the editor of *Estudios Literarios Ingleses II: Renacimiento y Barroco* (Madrid, 1986) and of *Telling Histories: Narrativizing History, Historicizing Literature* (Amsterdam, 1995). She also belongs to the editorial boards of several journals.

JOSÉ ANGEL GARCÍA LANDA (Ph.D. Zaragoza, M.A. Brown University) is Senior Lecturer in English Literature and Literary Theory in the English and German Department at the University of Zaragoza. He has published numerous articles on English literature and on literary theory. He is the author of *Samuel Beckett y la narración reflexiva* (Zaragoza, 1992) and the editor of *Miscelánea: A Journal of English and American Studies*.

The editors are members of a research team which has been doing work on narratology since 1989. Several research projects carried out by this team have been financed by the University of Zaragoza (Vicerrectorado de Investigación) and the Spanish Ministry of Education (DGICYT).

Acknowledgements

Our interest in narratology goes back to two team research projects financed by the University of Zaragoza in 1989 and 1990–1, and further developed in two wider research projects financed by the Spanish Ministry of Education (PS90–0117 and PS94–0057).

We are grateful to the authors and other copyright holders of the articles reprinted here for permission to reproduce copyright material, and to Stan Smith, who suggested the topic of this reader. We would also like to thank Celestino Deleyto for specialized advice on film studies, Beatriz Penas and Tim Cooper, who read the introduction, and the Longman copy-editor, who has been most helpful and efficient.

Susana Onega
José Angel García Landa
1996

The publishers are grateful to the following for permission to reproduce copyright material:

The Editor of *Atlantis* for an edited version of 'Focalisation in Film Narrative' by Celestino Deleyto in *Atlantis 13* (November, 1991) pp. 159–77; Blackwell Publishers Ltd/Cornell University Press for an edited version of 'Voice' by Gérard Genette: *Narrative Discourse: An Essay in Method*. Translated from the French by Jane Lewin. Copyright © 1980 by Cornell University Press; Cambridge University Press/ Vandenhoeck & Ruprecht for an edited version of 'A New Approach to the Definition of the Narrative Situations' by F. K. Stanzel in *A Theory of Narrative*. Translated by Charlotte Goedsche, pp. 46–78 and diagram p. xvi (Translation of *Theory des Erzahlens* Gottingen: Vandenhoek, 1979); the author, Teresa de Lauretis for an edited version of her 'Desire in Narrative' from *Alice Doesn't: Feminism, Semiotics, Cinema*. (Bloomington, Indiana University Press, 1984); HarperCollins Publishers Ltd/Farrar, Strauss & Giroux Inc. for an edited version of 'An Introduction to the Structural Analysis of Narrative' by Roland Barthes in *Image, Music, Text*. Edited & translated by Stephen Heath. (New York, Hill & Wang, 1977, pp. 79–124). Translation of Roland Barthes' 'Introduction à l'analyse structurale due recit' in *Communications 8* (1966) pp. 1–27; the author, Linda Hutcheon for an edited version of her 'Modes and Forms of

Narrative Narcissism: Introduction of a Typology' in *Narcissistic Narrative: The Metafictional Paradox*. (New York, Methuen 1984, pp. 17–35); International Thomson Publishing Services/the author, Edward Branigan for an edited version of his 'Story World and Screen' in *Narrative Comprehension and Film*. (London, Routledge, 1992, pp. 33–86, notes 230–46); Johns Hopkins University Press for edited versions of 'The Logic of Narrative Possibilities' by Claude Bremond, translated by Elaine D. Cancalon in *New Literary History* 11 (1980) and 'Introduction to the Study of the Narratee' by Gerald Prince, translated by Francis Mariner in *Reader Response Criticism. From Formalism to Post-Structuralism*. Edited by Jane P. Tompkins. First published in *Poétique* 14 (1973); Alfred A. Knopf Inc. for an edited version of 'Reading for the Plot' by Peter Brooks from *Reading for the Plot: Design and Intention in Narrative*. Copyright © 1984 by Peter Brooks; National Council of Teachers of English (NCTE) for an edited version of 'Authors, Speakers and Mock Readers' by Walker Gibson, first published in *College English 1* (February, 1950); Tel Aviv University, Porter Institute for an edited version of 'Fabula and Sjuzhet in the Analysis of Narrative', by Jonathan Culler, first published in *Poetics Today* 1:3 (Spring, 1980) pp. 27–37; University of Chicago Press and the authors/editor Hayden White, W. J. T. Mitchell, Wayne Booth & Paul Ricœur for edited versions of 'The Value of Narrativity in the Representation of Reality' by Hayden White in *On Narrative* edited by W. J. T. Mitchell. (Chicago, University of Chicago Press, 1980, pp. 1–23. First published in *Critical Inquiry* 7:1 (Autumn, 1980)), 'Types of Narrative' by Wayne Booth in *The Rhetoric of Fiction*. (Chicago, 1961, pp. 149–65), 'The Time of Narrating (Erzählzeit) and Narrated Time (Erzählte Zeit)' by Paul Ricœur in *Time and Narrative 2*. Translated by Kathleen McLaughlin and David Pellauer. (Chicago, University of Chicago Press, 1986, notes 182–6). Translation of *Temps et recit 11. La configuration dans le recit de fiction*); University of Nebraska Press for an edited version of 'Reflections on Actantial Models' by A.-J. Greimas in *Structural Semantics: At Attempt at Method* by A.-J. Greimas. Translated by Daniele McDowell, Ronald Schleifer & Alan Velie. Copyright © Librairie Larousse, 1966. Translation copyright © 1983 by the University of Nebraska Press; University of Toronto Press Inc. for an edited version of 'Focalization' by Mieke Bal in *Narratology: Introduction to the Theory of Narrative*. Translated by Christine van Boheemen. (Toronto, Buffalo, London: University of Toronto Press, 1985, pp. 100–18). Translation of *Theorie van vertellen en verhalen*. (Muiderberg, Countinho, 1980); Yale University Press for an edited version of 'Line' by J. Hillis Miller in *Ariande's Thread: Story Lines*. Copyright © 1992 by Yale University Press.

Introduction

Preliminaries

Definition of narratology

Narratology is, etymologically, the science of narrative. The term was popularized, however, by such structuralist critics as Gérard Genette, Mieke Bal, Gerald Prince and others in the 1970s.[1] As a result, the definition of narratology has usually been restricted to structural, or more specifically structuralist, analysis of narrative.

The post-structuralist reaction of the 1980s and 1990s against the scientific and taxonomic pretensions of structuralist narratology has resulted in a comparative neglect of the early structuralist approaches. One positive effect of this, however, has been to open up new lines of development for narratology in gender studies, psychoanalysis, reader-response criticism and ideological critique. Narratology now appears to be reverting to its etymological sense, a multi-disciplinary study of narrative which negotiates and incorporates the insights of many other critical discourses that involve narrative forms of representation. Consequently, while our selection of texts in this reader gives ample representation to the original structuralist core of the discipline, it also includes samples of approaches which are narratological in the wider if not in the strict formalist sense of the term.

Wider and narrower definitions

Is Aristotle's *Poetics* the first narratological treatise?[2] Although Aristotle's work focuses on one specific genre, tragedy, it offers extraordinary narratological insights which are applicable to all genres that use plots. For Aristotle, plot (*mythos*) is the central element in a literary work, a narrative structure which is common to dramatic and narrative genres proper. The conceptual ambivalence of 'narrative' is present, then, from the very beginning of the discipline. A wider Aristotelian definition of 'narrative' might be 'a

1

work with a plot' (e.g. epic poetry, tragedy, comedy); a narrow one would be 'a work with a narrator' (epic poetry, but not, in principle, drama or film). Today, narratology studies the narrative aspects of many literary and non-literary genres and discourses which need not be defined as strictly narrative, such as lyrical poems, film, drama, history, advertisements.

Narrative as mediated enunciation

The difference between narrative in the wider sense (as 'a work with a plot') and narrative proper has a parallel in the distance between the poles of dramatic narrative and mediated narrative ('showing' and 'telling'). Linguistic narrative (history, the novel, short stories) would be narrative in what we have called the narrow sense of the term, that is, narrative mediated in this case by the discursive activity of a narrator. Still, there may be other forms of mediacy: in film, the camera is a mediating device, albeit non-verbal (the use of the word 'enunciation' in this case is therefore a new, analogical development). Drama itself, of course, is a mediated presentation which uses a variety of linguistic and non-linguistic strategies, some of which may be more 'narrative' than others (e.g. the chorus in classical Greek tragedy, the device of the messenger who reports offstage events or, at the extreme, Brecht's 'epic' theatre).

The specificity of each narrative medium

Each medium and each genre allows for a specific presentation of the fabula, different point-of-view strategies, various degrees of narratorial intrusiveness and different handlings of time. Consequently, each narrative medium requires a specific analytical approach to narrative structures and levels (see, for instance, chapter 14).

The novelistic tradition is one of continuous redefinition of the narrative voice, from fake memoirs and letters, to intrusive and omniscient narrators, to modernist experiments with objective presentation or a limited point of view. Some critics have argued that innovative novel-writing is inherently reflexive: the discourse of the novel is simultaneously a reflection on past and present ways of telling a story. This reflexivity leads both to a defamiliarizing foregrounding of technique and to experimental variations on the specific areas of narrative structure exploited by a given novelist (e.g. temporal structure, perspectival control). It should be stressed, however, that defamiliarization is not necessarily a characteristic of narrative (or the novel, or literature, for that matter): there are also eminently ritualistic genres in which narrative pleasure derives from strict adherence to generic conventions (e.g. jokes, neoclassical tragedy, or *noh* drama in Japan).

One of the main differential traits of the novel is its ability to mix reflection and narrative (thence, in part, its reflexivity). The classic novel became the genre which revealed the inner life of characters, showing not just their behaviour but the relationship between action and character. By contrast, drama, in general, is much more directly focused on action. It is easy to see that the foregrounding of action in drama and of character in narrative leads to a whole array of consequences for the treatment of such aspects as time or psychological representation. Drama generally tends to focus on a significant and clearly defined action, with a strong plot based on cause and effect. The 'unity of time' of neoclassical drama, which of course was not meant by neoclassicist critics to apply to written narrative, was a recognition of this difference. It was also a recognition, albeit an exaggerated one, of the specificity of dramatic illusion.

The theatrical element of drama involves a further difference: the written, verbal text of a play is only the basis for the actual performance, which is a different and constantly changeable interpretation of that text and in fact on every occasion a new text for the audience. In film, unlike drama, the visual/aural presentation becomes a fixed text, which nevertheless remains subject to the viewer's perceptual activity. Drama and film, like narrative paintings, comic books, and so on, have a visual element in common. Images may be used to narrate just like words; it is here perhaps that narratology shows most clearly that it is not just a subsection of *literary* theory, but rather of a *general semiotic* theory.

Definition of narrative

A narrative is the semiotic representation of a series of events meaningfully connected in a temporal and causal way. Films, plays, comic strips, novels, newsreels, diaries, chronicles and treatises of geological history are all narratives in this wider sense. Narratives can therefore be constructed using an ample variety of semiotic media: written or spoken language, visual images, gestures and acting, as well as a combination of these. Any semiotic construct, anything made of signs, can be said to be a text. Therefore, we can speak of many kinds of narrative texts: linguistic, theatrical, pictorial, filmic. Any representation involves a point of view, a selection, a perspective on the represented object, criteria of relevance, and, arguably, an implicit theory of reality. Narrative structuring may become most elaborate in literary texts, but narrativization is one of the commonest ways of applying an order and a perspective to experience.

The term 'narrative' is, then, potentially ambiguous. As we have seen, it has at least two main senses: the broad one, which we have just defined, and the narrow one, according to which narrative is an exclusively linguistic phenomenon, a speech act, defined by the presence of a narrator or teller and a verbal text. This definition would restrict the area of analysis to oral or written narrative, and in the case of literary studies, to such literary genres as the novel, the short story, epic poetry, ballads, jokes. Here we shall be concerned mainly with the narrower sense, with the study of verbal narrative, and specifically with fictional/artistic narrative. The contributions we have selected deal in the main with the narrative element in the literary genres, although a few items deal with non-verbal narrative media such as film.

Narratological analysis concentrates on those aspects of textual production, structure and reception which are specific to narrative: for instance, the study of plot, or the relationship between action and character portraiture. Narrative may of course be approached in other ways: historically, thematically, stylistically, archetypally, deconstructively. In fact, most of the structures studied by narratologists do not exist exclusively in narrative works, but in narrative they are central and noticeably distinct. This is the case with regard to point of view or enunciation, for example, which may be found in a meditative sonnet as well as in a novel.

The analysis of narrative structure

Narratology in the strict sense of the word is usually associated with structuralism. Thus, in selecting relevant contributions for this reader we have assumed that structuralist approaches constitute the core of the discipline. The work of Saussure and the Russian formalists early in this century prepared the ground for structuralist thought. The formalists argue that words in poetry do not function only as signifiers: they are also *signifieds*. Literature is defined as a functional system, as a set of devices whose value is determined by other devices which are played off against them (those of other genres, past styles, and so on). A work presupposes conventions, other works, styles, genres, structures of meaning which go beyond the work itself. Literature is for these early structuralists a kind of *langue* of which each specific work is an instance of *parole*. French structuralists carried these linguistic analogies further during the 1960s and 1970s.

Structuralists often hesitate, however, when it comes to deciding the level at which the analogy should work: is it literature as a whole that works as a language, or is it the individual work that does so? Each work may be argued to constitute to some extent a *langue* of its own, may be seen as a self-regulating structure, since it creates, up to a point, the conditions for its own meaning and helps define the language in which it is interpreted. When the structuralists opt for this second alternative and seek to analyse the functioning of individual works, they are closer to the New Critical analysis of works as 'organic wholes'. If, on the other hand, they choose the first, that is, the analysis of general literary mechanisms, the individual work comes close to disappearing. It becomes a mere crossroads of different codes, the codes being the real object of analysis. A kind of turning-point away from this tendency is represented by Barthes in *S/Z* (1970), which rejects the idea that a work can be reduced to the codes that enable its existence.[3] *S/Z* is often considered as the opening statement of the post-structuralist analysis of narrative, which tends to emphasize the reader's active manipulation of semiosis.

The initial question a narratologist would try to answer is: in what sense can we analyse the structure of narrative? How can we begin? The very definition of narrative we propose – 'the representation of a series of events' – assumes that narratives are composite entities in a number of senses, that a narrative can be analysed into the events that compose it, and that these events can be studied according to their position with respect to each other. In a series of events some are at the beginning, some in the middle, some at the end. A narrative therefore consists of a number of successive parts: it has a longitudinal structure of time and actions. This 'horizontal' approach to narrative description is analogous to syntactic analysis in linguistic studies. We shall call it the *syntagmatic* axis in analysis.

A narrative, then, is in one sense a succession of elements. But it is a compound in other senses, too, and can be analysed in more ways than one. In our definition, it should be noted, a narrative is not 'a series of events', but '*the representation* of a series of events'. Here the composite nature of narrative appears not as a number of successive parts, in length or horizontally, but, as it were, vertically, in *depth*: the narrative is not what it seems to be; it is a sign which represents a state of affairs. This 'vertical' direction in analysis leads us from the sign to its signification. The basic activity in this sense is interpretation, and therefore we shall call this the *hermeneutic* direction in narrative analysis. What we get in a narrative text are not events as such, but signs, the representations of events. Here an infinite complexity may arise. In what way are the events represented? In what way is the narrative similar to or different from the events it represents? Narratological theories will largely consist in the formulation of possible answers to these questions.

We see, then, that the very definition of narrative leads us to the beginning of analysis, and in several directions at once. We shall examine different theories which analyse narratives either horizontally, or vertically, or both. As far as horizontal analysis is concerned, we have spoken so far of beginning, middle and end. Other concepts will complicate this simple account of parts. As far as vertical analysis is concerned, we may speak of *levels of analysis*. Our definition distinguishes at least two basic levels. If narrative is a semiotic representation of a series of events, one level of analysis will examine the events represented. Another level of analysis will examine the structure of the representation. We shall find that narratological theorists often differ when it comes to defining these levels of analysis: some distinguish two, while others speak of three or four. Mieke Bal tells us that there are three basic levels of analysis of narrative: fabula, story and text; Tomashevski only speaks of two, fabula and *siuzhet*.[4] In fact, this problem arises in all areas of literary study. Theories which appear to be similar often turn out to originate in entirely different critical projects. For the purpose of this discussion, we assume a framework of three levels of 'vertical' or hermeneutic analysis of the narrative text: text, story and fabula (see e.g. Bal, *Narratology*). Thus, if we take a work such as *Robinson Crusoe*, we will say that the *text* is the linguistic artifact that we can buy and read, written *de facto* by Defoe and supposedly by Robinson. The *fabula* is whatever happened to Robinson in his travels and on his island. The *story* is the precise way in which that action is conveyed, the way the fabula is arranged into a specific cognitive structure of information.

Bal has defined these concepts as follows:

1. A TEXT is a finite and structured set of linguistic signs.
1.1. A *narrative* text is a text in which an agent *relates* a story . . .
2. A *story* is the signified of a narrative text. A *story* signifies in its turn a *fabula*.[5]

We may represent these levels of signification by means of the following diagram:[6]

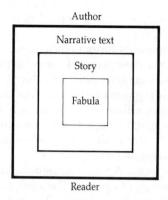

Figure 1

The fabula is, according to Bal, a bare scheme of narrative events which does not take into account any specific traits that individualize agents or actions into characters and concrete events. A description of the fabula (or action) would also omit any temporal or perspectival distortions: there are no flashbacks or variations in point of view at this level of analysis. In other words, in Bal's conception the fabula is actually an action-scheme: it is a synthetic abstraction, not the concrete, full-blown action that we construct when reading or watching a narrative. It may be confusing that other theorists (Ingarden, Martínez Bonati, Ruthrof) use the other concept of deep structure (concrete action and world, not abstractive fabula). We shall retain both concepts, since both are analytically significant: the full-blown or concretized action can be meaningfully opposed to a more abstract and reduced fabula or action-scheme.

It is also possible to draw up schemes of the story and the text (the 'reduced' version of the text being best called a *summary*). By this method we obtain the following critical tools:

Text	Summary
Story	Story-scheme (plot)
Action	Action-scheme (fabula)

The term 'plot' as used in everyday language often designates a story-scheme or an action-scheme, or a structure in between, mixing traits of both. Here we shall use it to refer to a scheme consisting of the structures of action and perception which shape the story. However, 'plot' is a tricky word because of its rich meaning, and several theories take into account other phenomena implicit in the everyday use of the word.[7]

The concept of *story* needs further elucidation. A story is a fabula which has been given a presentational shape: a specific point of view and temporal scheme have been introduced. We could say that a story is *a fabula as it is presented in a text* – not the fabula as such. The text is not the story, either: 'story' is still a synthetic abstraction we produce from the text, taking into account only its narrative aspects, considering it only in so far as it represents an action. We may recall that for Aristotle *mythos* was merely one of several 'aspects' of a literary work. A text is a linguistic construct, while a story is a cognitive scheme of events. The same story can give rise to a number of texts: for instance, when Kafka wrote *The Castle* in the first person and then rewrote it in the third person, the story remained essentially the same, but the text became a different one. The same story could in principle be told by means of different texts: a film, a comic book or a novel. But film adaptations of novels usually tell very different stories, even if the basic elements of the action are preserved. The story, then, can be looked on as a further structuring of the action. It may be ideally defined as the result of a series of modifications to which action is subjected. These modifications can be relative to time or to informational selection and distribution (Genette's 'mood', *Narrative Discourse*). Telling a story from a single character's point of view is one of many possible modalizations of the action.

A narrative text is also an instance of discourse, of linguistic action. *Discourse* is the use of language for communicative purposes in specific contextual and generic situations, called *discourse situations*. These can be described at different levels of specificity: there is written discourse in general, but also specific *fictional* written discourse. Increasing specificity would take into account historical or generic considerations. Of the infinite number of discourse situations which could be defined in this way, we may draw attention to a few: the writing of narrative discourse which is intended to be read as literature, the 'naive' reading of the same, the critical (academic) discourse on literature, writing factual narratives such as reports, or more personal narratives such as diaries and memoirs.

A text cannot be reduced to its linguistic codification, especially if by 'linguistic' we mean 'relative to the abstract system of language'. From the standpoint of linguistic pragmatics there are many cultural codes, apart from the Saussurean *langue*, structuring discourse (including narrative discourse). For instance, the social interaction rituals which allow speakers to position and identify themselves in conversation remain active when social interaction is represented in a text. An author uses a multiplicity of codes in shaping a narrative, with various degrees of deliberateness or consciousness. Many of these codes are to be recognized and used by a receiver in interpreting the text, if the interpretation is to be shared and accepted by other speakers. This retrieval of the author's meaning can happen with various degrees of awareness. There are no doubt many codes organizing the meaning of texts which have not yet been identified by theoreticians, although readers will use them intuitively. Not all the codes used by the author need to be identified or retrieved, even in this intuitive way. A portion of the meaning of the text is usually enough for the purposes of most readers and critics, who may, moreover, interpret the text according to codes which were not used by the author, and in this way construct new meanings. The legitimacy and value of these or any other meanings are defined in a specific discourse situation – they cannot be determined *a priori*.

The intrinsic context of a work is a communicative context. It can be conceived as a virtual communicative situation, in which a *textual author* communicates with a *textual reader*. The concepts of 'textual author' and 'textual reader' derive from Russian and German formalism,[8] and more immediately from Walker Gibson's 'mock reader'[9] and Wayne Booth's 'implied author' and 'mock reader'.[10]

The textual author is a virtual image of the author's attitudes, as presented by the text. The textual reader is a virtual receiver created by the author in full view of the actual audience he or she presumes for his or her work. The textual reader need not coincide with the author's conception of the audience: this reader-figure may be a rhetorical strategy, a role which the author wishes the audience to assume (or even to reject). Likewise, the reader's textual author and the author's textual author need not coincide any more than the meaning of the work for author and reader. But if communication is to occur these figures must have elements in common.

The levels of analysis just mentioned can be conceived as a series of semiotic strata, in which each level is the result of the application of a set of transformational rules to the previous level. A reader will consider the (verbal) text as a given, and will use it to construct the story. In its turn, the fabula is constructed on the basis of the story, by 'undoing' the transformations which gave rise to the latter.

The complexity of this enunciative structure can be exploited aesthetically in literature. A variety of displacements are possible. The subject required by the narrative act, the narrator, need not coincide with the subject of the fictional statement, the textual

9

author. The narrator may be an entirely fictional figure, as in most first-person novels, or may coincide formally though not ideologically with the textual author – an unreliable third-person narrator (Booth, *Rhetoric*).

Many combinations are possible, and the differences between the various textual subjects may be clear-cut or extremely shady. This is to be expected, since the textual author, like the narrator, is not a substance but a discursive role. Discursive selves, permanent or provisional, proliferate in literature as much as in other modes of discourse. When we speak in our professional capacity, for instance, we use a set of discursive conventions to fashion an official persona, a provisional self designed for use in a given sphere of action. Irony is another way a speaker may modulate the presentation of self. Through the use of irony, a textual author creates a provisional, evanescent enunciator (subject) which does not coincide with the author's overall discursive self. More sustained irony will produce something like a hypothetical character, and by pushing this a bit further we can create a fictional narrator consistently differentiated from the author by means of ironic distance. Such narrators may use first- or third-person narrative strategies; they may write a (supposedly) factual narrative – letters, memoirs, a diary – or an explicit fiction.

The narrator's utterance is addressed to a hearer (reader) located at the same structural level: the narratee.[11] Just as the various fictional narrators merge gradually into the textual author, the various narratees shade into the textual reader. This means that in some tales the differences between the narratee and the implied reader are crucial and clear-cut, while in others they are only latent.

So far we have identified a variety of textual figures, roles or subject-positions. They each perform an activity which has a direct object (if it is transitive) and an addressee:[12]

Subject	Activity (Verb)	Direct object	Addressee (Indirect object)
Author	Writing	Lit. work	Reader
Textual author	Literary enunciation	Literary text	Textual reader
Narrator	Narration	Narrative	Narratee
Focalizer	Focalization	Focalized (story)	Implied spectator
Agent	Performance	Action	(Agent)

We can also represent the structure of fictional narrative diagrammatically:

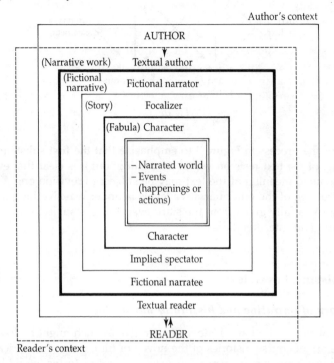

Figure 2

From the surface level of the linguistic text the reader constructs two kinds of interpretive scheme: the discursive schemata (the fictional speech situation, the textual senders and receivers) and the narrative deep structures (the narrative and the story). An interpreter will usually end by constructing some kind of literary statement or interpretation, which becomes for him or her the meaning or significance of the story.

Figure 3 represents this process of construction in a schematic way. The vertical and slanting double arrows indicate that the process of interpretation is not linear; it does not proceed neatly from one level of the textual structure to the next. Instead, there is a constant feedback between interpretation of the action, of the narrative structure and of the textual subjects. Differences in construction of the implied authorial attitude therefore often result in different constructions of the action. We have used one-way arrows in the first

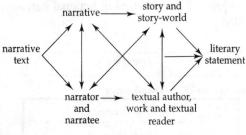

Figure 3

step of the process in Figure 3 to emphasize that the first substantial contact of the text rests on verbal denotation; but it is clear that even the denoted meaning of the text may be subject to revision once construction of the other narrative levels is under way. Nothing in the work is fully given from the start: everything is subject to revision and interpretation.

An historical overview

History of narrative and history of narratology

It is not clear yet what a history of narrative as such might be like. There are of course histories of the novel, of film, even of historical study itself; but a more general history of narrative forms would have to be an interdisciplinary achievement. Most work in narratology consists of synchronic formal analysis, and the discipline still needs to develop a comparative and historical perspective on narrative genres and structures. The history of the discipline of narratology itself is also largely unwritten. What follows sketches its development through the early prescriptive poetics of specific genres, through formal and structural analysis, to recent trends which stress the relationship between representation and specific ideological or cultural forms. A study in depth of the historical development of narrative genres would result in a cultural narratology, the study of narrative forms in their relationship to the culture which generates them. Cultural studies, derived from neo-Hegelian, Marxist, feminist or Foucauldian sources, open up a new speculative area for narratology that lies beyond the classification of formal devices and the purpose of this book.

Narrative theory before 1950

Classical and post-classical

In Plato's *Republic* we find the groundwork of genre theory and of
the analysis of literary enunciation.[13] After expounding a theory
of art as mimesis, Plato's spokesman Socrates discusses the *style* of
poetic compositions: 'All mythology is a narration of events, either
past, present or to come. . . . And narration may be either simple
narration, or imitation, or a union of the two' (p. 27). That is, the
poet may speak in his own voice (simple narration) or may speak
through the voice of a character (imitation, mimesis). Tragedy and
comedy are wholly imitative, while in dithyramb, lyric poetry and
similar genres the poet is the sole speaker, 'and the combination of
both is found in epic, and in several other styles of poetry' (p. 28).
From a narratological viewpoint, this is the first theoretical approach
to the problem of narrative *voice*, preceding a pragmatic approach to
the text as utterance.

Aristotle's *Poetics* further develops the formal approach to
literature. Aristotle apparently takes for granted that 'serious'
literature (of which tragedy is the highest form) is narrative – in the
wider sense of 'telling a story'. He roughly preserves the Platonic
classification of genres on the basis of enunciation, distinguishing the
wholly imitative form of dramatic performance from the mixed
presentation of epic narrative. Within the genres based on incident
and event (narrative proper and drama), the *mythos*, 'plot', or
'structure of the incidents' is for him the basic infrastructure; it is
foremost among the aspects of tragedy (plot, characters, diction,
thought, spectacle, song):

> The most important of these is the arrangement of the incidents,
> for tragedy is not a representation of men but of a piece of action,
> of life, of happiness and unhappiness, which come under the
> head of action, and the end aimed at is the representation not of
> qualities of character but of some action. . . . And furthermore, two
> of the most important elements in the emotional effect of tragedy,
> 'reversals' and 'discoveries', are parts of the plot. . . . The plot is
> then the first principle and as it were the soul of tragedy: character
> comes second.
>
> (*Poetics* VI, pp. 25–7)

The *mythos*, the plot of the tragedy, is defined as 'the arrangement of
the incidents', so, strictly speaking, 'it is the plot which represents

the action' (*Poetics* VI, p. 25). We therefore have two possible ways of
looking at a tragedy, two possible levels of analysis of the story
which is being represented. On the one hand, it is an *action (praxis)*,
just as our daily activities may be described as actions. On the one
hand, it is a *plot (mythos)*, an artistic structure which the poet builds
out of the action. That is, on the one hand we find mere incidents,
on the other, the *disposition* of incidents. The poet is the maker not of
verses or of incidents but of this important intermediate structure,
the plot. We may note that Aristotle did not include action as a
separate constituent of tragedy; he probably felt that the presence
of plot in that list of parts accounted for both of them.

Critical traditions in any cultures usually begin with foundational
texts which, as Miner has noted, normally take one specific literary
genre, most frequently 'lyric' poetry, as the model or epitome of all
literature.[14] In spite of the centrality of narrative to all cultures, we
find that only one major critical tradition (the Japanese one, deriving
from Murasaki Shikibu's *Tale of Genji*) takes narrative as the central
literary genre. Significantly, Aristotle's *Poetics* is based on drama,
specifically tragedy. Many aspects of the analysis of narrative form
sketched in the *Poetics* remained largely undeveloped until the
twentieth century, when they were taken up by the formalist and
structuralist critical schools.

The classical discipline of rhetoric was not primarily concerned
with narrative. Nevertheless, it provided many insights into the
mechanism of style and composition which were gradually
incorporated into the analysis of narrative. The most influential
treatises on rhetoric follow a standard development of the discipline,
concentrating on:

1 The possible kinds of discourse, the genres of rhetoric (*genera*).
2 The structure of discourse, the way it divides into sections, its
   internal organization (*ordo, materia* or *res*). Aristotle had already
   introduced the syntagmatic analysis of narrative at two
   differentiated levels: that of the text (the sections of a tragedy,
   for instance) and that of the story (*mythos*) – the complication,
   turning-point and unravelling of the plot.
3 The steps we must follow in order to compose a discourse (*opus*).
   Concepts such as *inventio, dispositio* and *elocutio* would eventually
   be applied to narrative as well as to oratory.[15] The study of
   dispositio, for instance, afforded the distinction between *ordo*
   naturalis, the natural and chronological presentation of events, and
   ordo artificialis, the artistically intended distortion of the
   chronological arrangement of events. A typical statement of this

distinction is found in Geoffrey of Vinsauf's *Poetria nova*.[16] The classical distinction between simple, complex and mixed narrative is preserved in post-classical rhetoric, and the study of narrative voice also benefited from systematic study of the resources of *elocutio*. Notions such as the levels of stylistic treatment (the *rota Virgilii*), and the differentiation of characters' voices (*sermocinatio*), were to lay the foundations for the structural study of literature.

The Renaissance and Enlightenment periods developed their own literary systematics often through a re-reading and expansion of classical treatises. The Aristotelian theories of Robortello, Scaliger and Castelvetro constitute a gigantic step forward in terms of the detailed discussion of formal issues.[17] Countless other treatises discuss the poetics of tragedy, epic poetry, romance, and so forth. Although we may disparage the neoclassical obsession with generic laws and rules, as well as the prescriptive nature of these treatises, we should not overlook their increasing analytical power. For example, debates on the famous 'three unities' of drama helped to refine such basic concepts as the opposition between represented and representational time, narrative ellipsis and compression, the use of physical space to signify fictional space, or the relationship between dramatic illusion and convention. G. E. Lessing's *Laokoon*, for instance, remains within the neoclassical and prescriptive *episteme*, but its analytical subtlety and its wealth of conceptual abstraction foreshadow later developments in aesthetics and semiotics. Lessing defines literature as an art intrinsically conditioned by the temporal sequentiality of linguistic signs (while the plastic arts use spatial signs). This abstract definition is the starting-point for practical analysis of such issues as the immediacy effect, dramatization and the use of point of view.[18]

The theory of the novel was neglected during the emergence of the genre in the seventeenth and eighteenth centuries. Novels or 'romances' are not to be found in the classifications of Boileau or in the criticism of Dryden. In the eighteenth and early nineteenth centuries such critical statements as do exist are usually far behind the criticism of poetry in theoretical development. Nevertheless, the appearance of the novel leads to a qualitative step forward in analysis. From the point of view of theory, the new form invites a new paradigm, asking new questions and demanding new answers. Novelists are among the first to make significant statements about their craft. Innovative works themselves were such statements: the novel is an intrinsically parodic genre, and the best novels are very often a parody of, or at least a commentary on and interpretation of, previous modes of fiction writing. *Don Quixote* is often defined as a satire on romances, and this implied critique can be read everywhere in fiction, more explicitly than in drama or poetry. Great novels have always been to some extent metafictions, or anti-novels.

Henry Fielding, the great heir of Cervantes in the British scene, integrates commentary and fictional writing, most obviously in *Tom Jones*, where each book is headed by one introductory chapter of commentary. Fielding calls himself 'the founder of a new province of writing' with independent laws,[19] the 'comic epic poem in prose'[20] – a deliberately paradoxical formulation, stressing both that the novel is born out of the convergence of diverse genres and that it is essentially parodic in nature: a way of setting previous conventions of writing against one another. More specifically, the novel is the parodic genre which results from setting the conventions of epic and romance against prosaic reality.

Additional valuable insights are provided by Samuel Richardson and Laurence Sterne.[21] Drawing on the classical distinction between pure, imitative and mixed narrative, Richardson distinguishes between first-person narration (in which the writer tells of his own adventures), epic narration (controlled by what we would call an authorial narrator) and a technique which is more dramatic, introducing dialogue and direct speech. Richardson especially values this dramatic mode, clearly with his own epistolary technique in mind. Sterne pushes narrative experiment to a limit: *Tristram Shandy* can be read as an entertaining and often teasing commentary on the way narrative expectations are created and frustrated.

German critics, such as Friedrich Schlegel and G. W. F. Hegel, provided some of the earliest theoretical approaches to the novel. In his *Brief über den Roman*, Schlegel voices in an explicit way the notion of the novel as a medley or convergence of all previous literary genres. For Hegel, the novel is the modern version of the epic: both bourgeois and subjective – a result of the turn of romantic literature towards subjectivism and reflexivity. Hegel's theories were developed in the twentieth century by the young Lukács, one of the main theorists of narrative realism, who sees the novel as the product of bourgeois demythologization of aristocratic ideals.[22]

The aesthetics of realism

The early theory of the novel was formulated for the most part under the realist aesthetics of the nineteenth century. While in this century the theory of the lyric is expressive, the theory of the novel remains largely mimetic. That is, the lyric is defined as an expression of the poet's feelings, and its representative element is subordinated to this expressive function (hence the 'pathetic fallacy', the projection of subjective passions on to the landscape). Victorian theorists of fiction often drew an opposition between the genres of the romance and the novel. Romance was light entertainment, making free use of fantasy and stirring adventure. The novel, on the other hand, was on the way to becoming 'serious' narrative, through its aesthetics of verisimilitude. This theory often originated with the novelists themselves, such as Balzac in France. In England we find an eloquent defence of realism in the essays of George Eliot and George Henry Lewes, who attack popular fiction and contend that realism is a novelist's moral responsibility.[23]

Among the basic terms of analysis in the realist aesthetic are *plot, character, setting, theme, moral aim* and *verisimilitude.* For realist critics, a novel should have a good construction, starting with a coherent plot. The distinguishing trait of the novel, however, is not the plot but its mimetic aim in the depiction and characters and setting. Many realist critics see deliberate plotting as a somewhat extraneous element which may distort the spontaneous revelation of character. In the Victorian age, the term 'novel of character' is often used as a hallmark of narrative quality: the novel of character is privileged over the simple-minded 'novel of action' or romance. Sometimes it is the regional specificity of the characters and setting that is emphasized, as in the late nineteenth-century school of 'local colour'. The realist novel, in any case, should be a psycho-social study, one that reveals new truths about human feelings and relationships. Such a novel has a theme and is linked to a well-defined moral intention, an authorial stance towards that theme, which is easily identified, whether it is conveyed by direct or by indirect means. It is this moral intention that makes realism something more than an attempt at copying nature.

Bulwer Lytton's essay 'On Art in Fiction' is a typical nineteenth-century approach to the narrative specificity of the novel.[24] Lytton gives great weight to the author's intended effect and deliberate manipulation of the materials. It is essential to have a plan in a novel: an artistic shape, although this shape does not coincide with that of drama. For instance, the novelist uses description, not used by the playwright, which as Lytton notes is integrated with plot and character. He also argues that since the plot of a novel is less tight and less guided by cause and effect than that of a play, the new genre should be understood to have its own autonomous poetics. The novelist has interests other than those of the playwright: in character study and range of intimate emotions.

One of the most influential nineteenth-century approaches to narrative construction is found in Edgar Allan Poe's theory of the short story. Poe identifies the unity of a work not so much in the structure of the work itself as in its effect on the reader: the unity of the reading experience is essential for the unity of the work. He sees the novel as a genre devoid of a true unity of impression, while the short story is for him the most artistic prose genre, because the unity of effect on the reader can be calculated and preserved.[25] Poe advocates a hyper-conscious theory of writing: everything is controlled by authorial intention. The end of the work must be complete in the writer's mind before actual composition begins: there is to be no improvization or change of plan during the writing. Thus, Poe situates himself in opposition to novelists like Dickens or Trollope, who often worked without a pre-established plan and improvised their plots in the making. Poe's conception of narrative is centred on its closure: 'It is only with the *dénouement* constantly in view that we can give a plot its indispensable air of consequence, or causation, by making the incidents, and especially the tone at all points, tend to the development of the intention.'[26]

We have seen that early theorists like Lytton placed some emphasis on defining the conventions of the novel as such, and on distinguishing the narrativity of fiction from that of drama. However, many novelists have praised narrative techniques which approach the effects of drama. Certain comments on narrative technique by Richardson, Stendhal or Dickens are interesting forerunners of Henry James's theories of fictional form because of the value they set on the dramatic elements of the novel: writers should not tell the whole of the story in their own person, but should show it – make their characters tell it by means of dialogue and action. Stendhal proudly notes that all other novelists tell the story, while only he shows it to the reader.

Studies of narrative technique developed piecemeal, in Switzerland with Edmond Scherer and in Germany with Friedrich Spielhagen.[27] Spielhagen adumbrated a fully-fledged theory of 'dramatic' narrative technique especially suited to psychological realism.

With Henry James, likewise, we witness the evolution of realism towards subjectivism and perspectivism, in part because of James's psychological bent. According to James, the novel (unlike drama) can reveal to us the inner life of characters, and this is the essence of the genre, which otherwise must follow, in his opinion, a dramatic ideal of concentration.[28] But the novel is a free form, he says. It has no grammar which can be defined, no rules that can be taught, because it is 'a personal, a direct impression of life' (p. 664). Execution and intensity of impression are the grounds of its value, and they cannot be defined. They stem directly from the personal way each novelist sees life. In James's essays and prefaces to his own novels we find some of the clearest and most influential statements of the period on point of view and narrative voice, as well as on action and character.

James makes a distinction between voice and point of view in his novelistic practice as well as in his rhetorical statements. This distinction arises from his concern with the novel's ability to depict experience and psychological life. First-person narrative is not adequate for his purposes, because he is not looking for a conscious revelation of character, or for a novel based on recollection of past experience, which is what first-person narratives are most suited to reveal. His novels are usually written in the third person, which is less 'intrusive', more 'dramatic'. The story should in any case unfold in a transparent way without the writer stepping in to make his own comments. Rather than being simply 'told', we are 'shown' action and character as they develop through significant scenes. And there is an ideal way of 'showing' in third-person narration which is at once dramatic and psychologically immediate. This is what James calls narration through 'centers of consciousness' (Preface to *The Portrait of a Lady*), 'vessels of sensibility' or 'reflectors' (Preface to *The Wings of the Dove*), which many narratologists now call focalizers. The scenes usually act on a perceiving character, a reflector or focalizer, whose psychological reaction, the development of his or her understanding of the action, contributes to the organic unity of the plot. This is the role of Strether in *The Ambassadors*, or of Maisie in *What Maisie Knew*. James does not consider it necessary, as do some of his followers, to avoid changes of perspective during the narrative, but he does seek to cut the story into perspectival blocks that are internally coherent. For instance, in *The Wings of the Dove*, the story of Milly Theale is seen mainly through the eyes of two characters, Merton Densher and Kate Croy, as well as through Milly's own eyes. Every change of point of view, James says, has its aesthetic justification, its dramatic coherence, but it is essential for a novel to establish a 'register', a set of perspectival rules to which it consistently adheres.

Just as Aristotle argued that an action or *praxis* had to be treated artistically before it became the plot or *mythos*, James distinguishes between the 'subject' and the 'wrought material' or novel, thus prefiguring the Russian formalists' opposition between *fabula* and *siuzhet*. The 'register' defines the relationship between the material and the finished novel. Form and psychology converge: the dramatic form allows the reader a new insight into the characters' perception and interiority. James conceives of the rules governing point of view as organic and internal, springing from the very nature of the psychological material of the novel.

19

The influence of James's ideas is readily apparent in most important twentieth-century writers on fictional technique and point of view: Percy Lubbock (*The Craft of Fiction*, 1921), Cleanth Brooks and Robert Penn Warren (*Understanding Fiction*, 1943), Jean Pouillon (*Temps et roman*, 1947), F. K. Stanzel (*Typische Erzählsituationen*, 1954), Norman Friedman ('Point of View in Fiction', 1955); Wayne C. Booth (*The Rhetoric of Fiction*, 1961), Gérard Genette (*Figures III*, 1972), Mieke Bal (*Narratologie*, 1977).[29]

Since the early phase of modernism (James, Conrad), theoretical reflection on narrative has consistently been opposed to experimental, avant-garde or at least 'highbrow' narratives. The various genres of popular fiction continue to rely heavily on the classical narrative devices of plotting and stereotyped characters. Still, critics have often valued the pleasures provided by narratives of action (as opposed to narratives of character, of point of view or of linguistic experimentation). R. L. Stevenson's defence of the romance, an answer to James's defence of psychological fiction, is a case in point.[30]

Early modernism

As we have seen, Henry James helped theorize the transition from Victorian realism to modernism. Critics like Joseph Warren Beach and Percy Lubbock were to systematize and popularize these ideas.[31]

Beach coined the phrase 'exit author' to describe the new dramatic autonomy of the novel, whose action was to unfold directly under the eyes of the reader, without the mediating value judgements of the narrator. Percy Lubbock's book *The Craft of Fiction* was something of an unofficial textbook of the modernist aesthetics of indirection. Lubbock draws an opposition between two methods, 'showing' and 'telling': 'The art of fiction does not begin until the novelist thinks of his story as a matter to be *shown*, to be so exhibited that it will tell itself.'[32] The aim of the novelist is to create a whole and full impression, to produce a controlled effect on the reader through the careful arrangement of form and subject matter. The aim is still to tell a story which is morally or metaphysically relevant, but the point now is that the reader must perceive and feel the story together with the character – as an experiential process, not as a finished product seen from the outside. Related to this aesthetic position is Dos Passos' and Hemingway's concept of impersonal fiction, as well as Lawrence's injunction to 'trust the tale' instead of the teller or Joyce's image of the author standing apart from his creation, 'paring his fingernails'.

According to Lubbock, what makes the story be shown rather than

told is a matter of composition, of the adequate treatment of the
story material through the use of subjective point of view and scenic
presentation. The novelist must use a coherent style: a consistent
narrative mode. If the subject matter requires transitions between
different modes they must be made smoothly: the seams must be
invisible. Nothing must remind us of the novelist's presence.
Everything that is told in a story must be motivated; that is, it must
be there on account of some character's experience. Of course, in
calling for a limited point of view Lubbock is also assuming a subject
matter that is psychological in nature: some kind of personal drama,
instead of the vast social frescoes of the Victorians. His model is
Henry James's *The Ambassadors*. Lubbock calls for conscious
craftsmanship, an attention to composition, and the development of
an adequate critical vocabulary to describe it. Similar ideas, the stress
on character, point of view and composition rather than on plot, are
also found in Ortega y Gasset's theory of the novel, and in various
other modernist critics.[33]

Other valuable aesthetic approaches to the genre in the English-
speaking world are E. M. Forster's ever-popular *Aspects of the Novel*
and Edwin Muir's *The Structure of the Novel*.[34] Forster studies the basic
narrative elements of realist fiction, under such headings as 'story',
'plot', 'people', 'pattern and rhythm'. His emphasis, following what
is perhaps the mainstream British tradition, falls on the depiction of
'people'; that is, of character. His classification of characters into 'flat'
(based on one trait and therefore predictable) and 'round' (complex
and lifelike) became universally accepted (incidentally, this
conception was far from new – the essentials can be found in
neoclassical critics, such as Dryden). Edwin Muir's work, less popular
with later readers, tries to establish different types of novel on the
basis of their experiential treatment of time, action and point of view:
the character novel, the dramatic novel based on conflict, or the
chronicle, the wide-ranging multiplot novel of social panorama.

High modernism and New Criticism

Henry James's ideas (as well as those of Lubbock, Forster and Muir)
were representative of the transition between the classical realist
novel, with its emphasis on story, setting and character, and the
modernist novel with its stress on writing and composition. In
the 1920s and 1930s there was a widespread critical revolution
against the aesthetics of late Romanticism. In literature this
revolution is called modernism and is identified with a self-conscious
avant-garde; in critical theory it was identified as New Criticism or
as formalism. The modernist/formalist revolution had deep

consequences for the writing and criticism of all literary genres. The New Critics moved further away from mimetic considerations. They dismissed the Romantics and favoured lyric poetry that was complex, ironic and intellectualized. They criticized literature in terms of its structural complexity, not in terms of its immediate fidelity to life. That is, the aesthetic judgements of the New Critics tend to be intrinsic rather than extrinsic. A work is above all a pattern of words, a self-sufficient entity which constructs and manipulates emotions and thoughts that have only an analogical relationship to reality. It is a self-enclosed structure, meaning that any element has to be judged within the pattern, taking its function into account, rather than being identified in an immediate way with its equivalents in the historical world. Originally the New Critics did not pay much attention to fiction, although later we find readings of fiction in terms of tone, pattern, irony and balance.[35] With the 'close reading' developed by William Empson and F. R. Leavis, the novel suddenly became a 'dramatic poem' – its language became significant in terms of tension and image, like the language of poetry.[36] Virginia Woolf claimed that modern fiction would assume the quality of a poem, and opposed fiction modelled on fact or report (like that of the naturalists). For her, as for other modernists, fiction must work through poetic suggestiveness rather than through narrativity.[37]

Plot and character as critical terms seemed to fade into the background, all emphasis falling on language and imagery, and on the overall pattern woven by all these elements. This intrinsic turn in critical thought eventually favoured the development of a reflexive theory of fiction, although it took some time for this to be explicitly formulated in the Anglo-Saxon world. For the time being, mimetic concerns still occupied the foreground, but mimesis had become internalized (Erich Kahler spoke in this respect of an 'inward turn' of the novel).[38] Critics from the 1930s to the 1950s paid particular attention to the modes of representation of inner life developed by the modernist novel, by Joyce, Woolf or Faulkner. Terms such as 'free indirect style', 'interior monologue', 'camera eye' narrative or 'stream of consciousness' occupy the centre of the critical stage.[39] We shall not dwell long on this phase; our main concern here is with the next stage of theoretical development: the theory of the novel as it stood in the 1960s and 1970s. It was with the second wave of formalism, in other words with structuralism, that narratology underwent a wholesale expansion. But first we need to consider additional formalist approaches which prepare the ground for this development.

Formalisms

Continental criticism witnessed an increase in formalist analysis of fiction, with the advanced work of German and Polish critics and the work of the Russian formalists in the 1920s. It is true that aesthetic studies simultaneously appeared in the English-speaking world,[40] but in general theoretical speculation was more common in continental Europe. The tradition of theoretical reflection descending from Schlegel to Spielhagen and Walzel includes such interesting practitioners as Käte Friedemann. Her book *Die Rolle des Erzählers in der Epik* is a fully-fledged narratological treatise written many years before the appearance of mainstream narratology.[41] She analyses the technique of early modernist 'dramatic' narration as formulated by Spielhagen (whom we could usefully compare to James in the Anglo-Saxon sphere) and contends that other types of narrative voice which allow for the narrator's intrusions or commentary are equally 'artistic' and useful for the novelist.

While German aesthetics is one of the main influences on the Russian formalist school, the systematic and functional approach to form developed by Shklovski, Propp or Tomashevski is considered by many as the inaugural statement of narratology proper.[42] The formalists react against both impressionist and historicist approaches to literature, and supplement their aesthetic background by rethinking Aristotelian insights, which they enrich with concepts borrowed from the new developments in theoretical linguistics (Baudouin de Courtenay, Saussure, Jakobson). Key narratological concepts inherited from the Russian formalists are the opposition *fabula/siuzhet* (the source of the opposition fabula/story/text mentioned above), or the concept of pseudo-oral narrative voice, *skaz*. Such concepts are not to be applied in a mechanical way: the aim of the formalists is to account for the organic effect of the work and the interaction of all its elements. For instance, in their discussion of 'realistic motivation' they argue that a technique such as epistolary narrative has a specific informative function *vis-à-vis* the reader, while it is simultaneously 'justified' or motivated by the story, therefore acting as a sign of realism. The work of Vladimir Propp on the Russian folktale, influential in both anthropology and literary theory, introduced such key analytical tools as the concept of 'narrative functions' and their organization into 'sequences'. Propp's work is a grammar of narrative which identifies the basic 'deep' structure underlying any number of 'surface' manifestations.

The most important contribution of the formalists, then, is one of general method: they aim at devising a general science of literature (narrative) capable of describing the systematics of literary forms and also of literary evolution. Form and function are intrinsically related: literary forms, for instance, may become worn and give rise to new forms (parody) while their previous social function is taken up by originally minor forms that evolve and come to the fore.

The systematic study of literary forms is characteristic of twentieth-century criticism. The systematics may derive from linguistics and aesthetics, but also from philosophy as well as from comparative studies of anthropology, religion and myth.

Although there are a variety of philosophical approaches relevant for the study of narrative, we may single out phenomenology as the most akin to narratology *stricto sensu*. Phenomenology is a systematic study of experience. It approaches reality as a formal system of relationships, so leading naturally to the problem of additional subsystems such as literary works and fictional objects, and converging with semiotics in the study of sign systems and representations. Roman Ingarden's *The Literary Work of Art*, which applies Husserl's phenomenology to the description of literary works, is a foundational text in this line,[43] usefully complementing structuralist descriptions of narrative form. In his later work Ingarden antedates many aspects of the reader-response approaches of the 1960s and 1970s.[44] Critics such as Wolfgang Iser have further developed the phenomenological study of reception and reading in closer convergence with the structuralists.[45] There is, in addition, a rather well-defined phenomenological approach to narrative which is associated with existentialist philosophy, represented by the work of Jean-Paul Sartre or Jean Pouillon.

Like literary phenomenology, 'myth-and-ritual' studies of narrative have a formal (narratological) dimension. Many literary critics have drawn inspiration from Sir James Frazer's *The Golden Bough*, Carl Jung's studies on collective psychology or Joseph Campbell's *The Hero with a Thousand Faces*.[46] Frazer's book is an attempt at finding a common narrative structure beneath a wide range of myths and rituals. Campbell's book identifies the basic stages of archetypal narratives similar to those studied by Propp. A comparison of these books reveals striking similarities not only in the object of study but also in the abstractive nature of their approaches, although each is grounded in a totally different discipline and intellectual tradition.

Northrop Frye's *Anatomy of Criticism* is yet another major treatise on archetypal plot structures.[47] Indeed, Frye constructs a complex interpretation of all literature in which the different genres and modes are organized as phases in a narrative structure associated with the cycle of life. The creativity, learning and subtlety evinced in this work have been rewarded by its immense influence. Like many other works not strictly narratological, Frye's *Anatomy* is essential reading for any student of narrative.

Myth criticism is often combined with early psychoanalytic approaches. Sigmund Freud himself devoted some attention to the psychoanalytical interpretation of narrative literature as well as to the narrative dimension of psychoanalysis.[48] Early analyses based on Freud's work lay more emphasis on the former, that is, on mechanisms of identification in reading, the writer's fantasies of sexuality and power, or the 'pathological' origin of plot structures and patterns of images or motifs. By contrast, present-day psychoanalytic criticism often privileges the second perspective, that is, the fantastic element in the analyst's (or the critic's) interpretive activities, the formal and institutional constraints of the diagnosis, and so on.

Contemporary narratology

Comparative narratology

Interdisciplinary studies of narrative afford a promising area for future development. A 'comparative narratology' – in the sense of 'comparative literature' – addresses such matters as the structural differences of given narrative genres or sub-genres, the phenomenological difference between narrative and other literary and artistic phenomena, and the comparative poetics of different cultures and traditions. Interdisciplinary narratological studies also try to strengthen the ties between narratology and other critical endeavours, such as the theory of interpretation or reception, women's and gender studies, deconstruction. The interdisciplinary direction offers the most interesting avenues for development, although it often leads beyond narratology proper.[49]

From a strictly narratological perspective, we may classify theories of narrative according to their main object of study within the narratologically defined structure of the text. A theory is always a limited model which isolates or gives preference to certain features of the object of study. Most theories of narrative, therefore, privilege either narrative as process or narrative as product, the level either of the fabula, of the story, or of textual representation.

Theories of authorship

Authorship and literary production have been a traditional area of literary research. In the nineteenth century, historical scholarship developed alongside the bourgeois conception of the writer as a detached observer of society. The historicist orientation, together with an individualist conception of writing, are still largely dominant today. Roughly speaking, we can distinguish two tendencies. One is towards impressionistic criticism, often biographical in tone and interested in the personality of the authors, their lives and at best the quality of their imagination and style, the comparison of different works and the study of influence. This kind of criticism had its academic heyday in the work of Walter Raleigh or David Cecil,[50] and is perhaps the tone most often associated nowadays with journalistic reviews and interviews. The other is more concerned with literary history: the demarcation of literary periods and their defining characteristics, the study of schools and movements, the interplay between literature and other cultural phenomena (from Saintsbury, Ker and Lanson to contemporary theorists of postmodernism.)[51] French, German and often American critics are more prone than the British to grounding literary scholarship on contemporary theories of history, whether positivist (Taine), evolutionist (Brunetière), classicist (T. S. Eliot), Hegelian (the early Lukács), Marxist (the later Lukács, Weimann), Weberian (Watt) or structuralist (White).[52] The specifically narratological aspect of these theories often lies in the links they establish between the narrative process and the 'master narrative' of history they use as their basic framework.

Psychoanalysis is another major source for theories of authorship. We should keep in mind here that Freudian theories, too, provide a master narrative of the development of the self. The critic's aim is usually to relate stylistic or thematic patterns in the work to the structure of an author's personality, evaluating the interplay between conscious and unconscious influences. The influence of psychoanalysis on studies of narrative is too pervasive to attempt even a limited overview. There is, besides, the closely related issue of psychoanalytic treatment considered as a narrative process whose patterns and symbolism can be approached much like those of a literary text.

Theories of enunciation

Theories which foreground the study of enunciation and its protocols are related to twentieth-century formalist criticism (stylistics, Russian formalism, New Criticism, the Chicago school, structuralism and literary pragmatics). They try to identify different strands or levels in the voice of the text: it is no longer, or not only, the voice of the author which is analysed, but also a number of fictional masks of personae which mediate between the authorial voice and the characters. Such theories differentiate the historical author from the narrator and the implied author; Wayne Booth's *The Rhetoric of Fiction* is a seminal text in this respect. Linguistic theories studying the articulation of subjectivity in language (Benveniste, Austin, Bakhtin) are often applied to the analysis of narrative enunciation.[53] Narrative pragmatics may also focus on the enunciative pecularities of fictional and non-fictional narrative. The specific rhetorical devices of each of the textual voices help define the style of the text.

From the point of view of literary pragmatics, fictional narrative is a second-degree discourse activity (or complex speech act), whose understanding presupposes the understanding of more primitive or literal discourse situations from which it derives. In the early classifications of speech acts there was no place for fictional narrative. This is not surprising, since these classifications were not really concerned with actual speech acts, but with idealized or normative speech-act types. That is why Austin or Searle could afford to posit a sentence-grammar as the basis of their studies of speech activity. The study of real discourse, however, must perforce be based on a textual grammar, and is bound to yield somewhat less clear-cut results. Writing a novel is obviously a kind of speech act, but its specificity has to be captured by a theory of discourse which would take into account the real circumstances and contexts in which novels are written. Writing a novel, or writing fiction, is not a 'statement', though it is a derived act of a kind which has statements as its remote ancestor in a structuralist/genetic conception of speech activity. For practical purposes of analysis, writing a novel is that kind of speech act called 'writing a novel': linguistics at this point shades off into the literary theory of genres. Between the linguistic speech act called 'statement' and the literary speech act called 'novel-writing' several conceptual steps could be distinguished, among them a study of the *fictional statement* as derived from the literal statement and a study of the *narrative* as an extended statement derived from the simple sentence.[54]

Theories of action or fabula

The theory of action is a philosophical discipline, with work ranging from traditional ethical treatises (Aristotle's *Nicomachean Ethics*) to modern approaches in the fields of formal logic (Von Wright), hermeneutics (Ricœur) or cognitive psychology (Goffman).[55] Such theories focus on the study of events, action sequences and schemes, functions, actants, characters, settings and the internal laws of narrated worlds. In the realm of literary narratology we find some influential developments in the Russian formalist school. Vladimir Propp develops a model for the functional classification of events and the description of action sequences at fabula level. He draws a clear distinction between, on the one hand, the text itself, which is the manifest level and, on the other, the abstract level of function sequences and spheres of action of the characters (similar to Greimas' 'actants').[56] Drawing on Veselovski's definition of plot or narrative (*siuzhet*) as a succession of basic unanalysable units, the 'motifs' (a subject plus a standardized action), Tomashevski distinguishes two means of classification.[57] First, he differentiates linked motifs from free motifs. Linked motifs are indispensable for the identity of the fabula; free motifs are not important and can be altered without any significant change in the fabula. Secondly, he opposes static to dynamic motifs. Descriptions, for instance, or unimportant actions, are static, while significant actions are dynamic. Barthes and other structuralists further refined these concepts. While the essay by Barthes included in our selection of texts is interesting in many other respects, it has been especially influential as a model for the analysis of narrative actions. Several formalized models, drawn by analogy with linguistics or formal logic, were devised by structuralist critics such as Bremond, Greimas, Todorov and Prince. We include selections from the work of Bremond and Greimas. Many additional formalist theories approach the analysis of action structures, their generation, variations, and possible classifications.[58] Among recent developments of action theories, the most fruitful contributions are those which bridge the gap between literary narratology and cognitive psychology (e.g. in Goffman, Bordwell, Branigan).[59] The study of action patterns in terms of schemata, scripts or frames allows for the formulations of a common model for all narrative actions (both 'inside' the fabula and 'outside', at the levels of story construction and the process of reading). It also permits links to be established between narratology and artificial intelligence.[60]

Theories of story and narration

Many theorists deal with, and many place their main emphasis on, the intermediary structures of story construction and narration. Such theories constitute the traditional narrow core of narratology. They devise modes of analysis of the time structure of the story (order of events, temporal distortions such as flashbacks or flashforwards, duration and selection of scenes, narrative rhythm, etc). The study of point of view (focalization, dramatic irony, suspense, omniscience) and of presentational mode (showing/telling) also fall within the scope of theories of story structure, as does the analysis of characters' discourse (free indirect style, dialogue presentation) and narrative voice. The most influential approaches to story construction and narrative voice were developed by formalist critics (Russian formalists, students of stylistics, New Critics, structuralists). Although they are too numerous for a fair selection, we may refer the reader to key concepts coined or developed by Henry James (reflectors, restricted point of view), Lubbock (scenic or panoramic presentation, showing/telling), Bally (free indirect style), Booth (reliable and unreliable narrators, moral or intellectual distance), Genette (focalization, narrative levels, anachronies, homodiegetic and heterodiegetic narrators, the narratee), Bal (the focalizer, levels of focalization), Bakhtin (dialogism, poliphony, heteroglossia), Dujardin, Humphrey or Cohn (stream of consciousness), Fowler (mind-style).[61] As these studies make up the main body of our selection, we refer the reader to the texts in question, where many of the central narratological concepts are analysed in detail. We have included extracts from works by Culler, Sternberg, Bal and Ricœur which analyse the relationship between the represented sequence of events and the representational structures of the story from the point of view of causality, temporality and perspectival presentation. The two extracts in our brief section on film, by Branigan and Deleyto, also focus on such representational structures. The selections grouped under 'Text', on the other hand, focus on the linguistic surface of narrative and the communicative activity of the narrative subjects (author, reader, narrator, characters). In this section we include key contributions from Booth, Gibson, Stanzel, Genette, Prince and Hutcheon.

Theories of reception

Narrative is, among other things, a communicative speech act, a message transacted between a sender and a receiver. Post-structuralist critical schools have developed the analysis of the reader's role in literary communication, stressing the active and creative nature of reading and, generally speaking, of understanding. Early narratological theories usually took the reader's role for granted, but successive elaborations have approached the reader's role from different perspectives, and reader-figures have proliferated. Walker Gibson speaks of the 'mock reader', a reader-image which is inscribed in the text by means of presupposition and ideological assumptions.[62] Nowadays the term 'implied reader' is more commonly used. The text may also feature a fictionalized version of the reader, a 'narratee'.[63] Narratees may range from fictional characters to less obtrusive fictional addressees to the 'mock' or implied reader.

A different line of inquiry consists in analysing the text from the reader's viewpoint. The static structure of meanings becomes suddenly animated: form becomes a sequential process of construction, a series of provisional hypotheses in the mind of the reader. Total form is not the final 'figure in the carpet' the reader makes up once the book is finished, but rather the progressive formulation and discarding of structural hypotheses during the reading process.[64]

The creative aspect of reading becomes more and more prominent as we move from theories that deal with the construction of action and story structures to theories which try to analyse the ideology or the significance of the text considered as a literary statement. Contemporary theories of reading (deconstruction, hermeneutics, reader-response criticism, reception theory) have systematically questioned the possibility of an objective, formalized analysis of this ideological level. Their contention is that the ideology or significance of a text is not a structure, but a process, the result of the interaction of text and reader. Brooks's text in our selection relates the reader's construction of the plot to the play of desire and basic psychical drives as defined by Freudian psychoanalysis. Some of these enquiries lead towards social, political and cultural studies. Marxist and feminist post-structuralism tries to show how reading is a political act involving the acceptance or questioning of pre-existing representations, ideologically charged models of interpretation and presuppositions. De Lauretis' text in our selection is a re-reading of some previous formalist models in this light, as well as a good instance of the convergence of psychoanalysis, narratology and feminist ideological criticism. Other schools lay more emphasis on the phenomenology of understanding. They analyse the significance of texts as it relates to the figural nature of language (deconstruction), to the experience of otherness and tradition (hermeneutics) or to contemporary developments in psychology, artificial intelligence, linguistics and cognitive science.[65]

Theories of self-referentiality and intertextuality

Theories of literary reflexivity can be traced back to the German romantics,[66] and have become increasingly important in the second half of the twentieth century. Much structuralist and post-structuralist criticism is concerned with experimental fiction, the analysis of reflexive fiction or metafiction perhaps being the most closely related to narratological concerns.[67] By metafiction we mean fiction which experiments with its own form as a way of creating meaning. We usually associate the novel with realism, just as we usually associate art with representation. But realism, the mimetic pull, is always counterbalanced by the fictionality of the novel, establishing a characteristic tension between the strategies of fiction and the drive towards realism. The tension between reality and mimetic representation is perhaps the best starting-point for a discussion of metafiction. Instead of taking reality or realism for granted, the reflexive novel explores the epistemological foundations of both, lays them bare, opening the way either for a more self-conscious realism[68] or for something else. Metafiction, then, can be defined as a way of writing, or more precisely as a way of consciously manipulating fictional structures, of playing games with fiction. Metafiction as writing would constitute a specific sub-genre in which the reflexive element is the dominant one. Robert Alter sees a difference between self-conscious novels and novels which contain self-conscious moments.[69] The self-conscious or reflexive novel must be informed by a consistent effort: self-consciousness must be central to its structure and purpose. The term 'reflexive' calls our attention both to mirror structures (doublings, analogies, frames, *mise en abyme*)[70] and to thought, consciousness, reflection, awareness accompanying action. Indeed, metafiction is reflexive fiction in the sense not only that mirror images are found in it, but also that these mirrorings and reflexive structures are used as a meditation on the nature of fiction. Alter defines the self-conscious novel as 'a novel which systematically flaunts its own condition of artifice and by so doing probes into the problematic relationship between real-seeming artifice and reality'.[71]

But this definition of metafiction is a text-centred one: it leaves out many reflexive phenomena in the literary process. Metafiction may also be defined as a way of reading. The 'reflexive reading' of texts is a critical paradigm which provides a new way of exploring meaning in literary works, unearthing structures of meaning which may be automatic, not deliberately planned by the writer but rather reached by the reader through the spontaneous play of meaning or the interplay between writing and reading.

Metafiction challenges a common critical assumption: that the work is silent about itself and waits for the critic to interpret it. A metafictional work will often be outspoken enough about its aims and technique. It criticizes previous literary conventions (to some extent all literature does this), but also its own conventions. All modern art shares this self-conscious attitude to the past, this anxiety deriving from its belatedness. Josipovici argues that 'There is no better way of defining the achievement of Picasso, Stravinski or Eliot than to say that it is an exploration both of the medium in which they are working and of the traditional exploration of that medium.'[72] The artist's exploration of the possibilities of art is perhaps the main characteristic of the twentieth century: it is not surprising that these explorers transgressed many borders and reached many dead ends. Hutcheon's typology of reflexive devices, included in this reader, is a good instance of the structuralist approach to reflexivity.

The structuralist concern with reflexive texts is both questioned and developed by the deconstructive school. Generally speaking, a deconstructive reading of a text (any text) will trace its staging of its own metaphysics only to undermine this by showing how it leads to contradiction, paradox and aporia – that is, how the text effects its 'self-deconstruction'. Hillis Miller's contention in 'Line' (pp. 286–95 below) is somewhat more ambitious, as it attempts to trace the aporia underlying any use of narratological terminology.

Metafiction often amounts to an act of criticism of previous traditions, because of its links with parody and self-consciousness. A discussion of reflexivity therefore cannot be isolated from intertextuality, the theory of which asserts that no text exists as an autonomous and self-sufficient whole: the writer's and the reader's experience of other texts conditions its form and interpretation. Classical accounts of narrative (Aristotle, Horace) usually assume that the poet as a plot-maker will use traditional stories, rather than invent the action of the work. Plot construction was traditionally discussed within the context of intertextual transformations, so that intertextual studies are anything but new. The term itself, however, was coined by Julia Kristeva, who derived it from Mikhail Bakhtin's work on social linguistics.[73] Bakhtin defined the self and society as being in a dialogical relationship. Individual and social languages define each other: any individual discourse is traversed by social discourses (a state of affairs Bakhtin calls 'heteroglossia'). Some modes of discourse, such as the novel, are especially open to this play of competing ideological voices, hence the 'polyphonic' nature of the novel for Bakhtin. Intertextual analysis leads, therefore, both to the analysis of genre conventions and to ideological and cultural studies.

In sum, we can distinguish several types of intertextual relationship, according to the reader's perception of the relations existing between a given text and:

1   Other literary texts. This approach goes back to the traditional (historicist) study of comparative literature, source and influence studies, which can be integrated within a more general model of intertextual relationships.[74]
2   Generic conventions, patterns of motifs and plots, archetypes. A work such as Northrop Frye's *Anatomy of Criticism* may now be read as a monumental study of intertextual generic conventions.[75]

3   Other social discourses and discursive conventions. This approach,
    which owes much to Bakhtin, has been especially developed by
    contemporary post-structuralism, above all by the new Marxist
    and feminist schools. It has become especially significant of late, in
    view of the present-day tendency to integrate literary and cultural
    studies.
4   The critical commentary of the text (which frequently incorporates
    types 1, 2 and 3). The most sophisticated analyses of this type of
    intertextuality have been carried out by contemporary theorists
    of interpretation (deconstructivists, reader-response theorists,
    etc), who have systematically problematized the relationship
    between a text and its subsequent readings.

Applied narratology

Under this heading we cover theories that formulate relations
between narrative, society, history and ideology. While narratology
has usually been considered an 'intrinsic' approach to literature, it is
possible, in a wider perspective, to see a relationship between the
study of narrative structure and extrinsic approaches to literature
which assess its relations to history, social structures, institutions
and cultural phenomena in general. There are many different schools
of cultural criticism: Weberian, Marxist, Foucauldian, gender studies,
multicultural studies. All of them in one way or another use the
concept of ideology as a critical tool. Ideology is a problematic term,
since its definition depends in part on the ideology of the person
defining it. The original Marxist definition understood 'ideology' as
false consciousness – a set of superstructural representations of society
and culture which tried to perpetuate the status quo. Ideology was
therefore a concept opposed to the scientific social description
provided by Marxism. Later approaches (starting within Marxism
itself in the work of Bakhtin) conceptualize ideology as a necessary
network of semiotic representations: we cannot have access to reality
in an ideology-free way. A corollary of this view is that ideology is
not a substance of some kind we find in a text, but rather a relational
function between the text and the reader.

In *The Rise of the Novel* (1957) Ian Watt explains the appearance of
the novel on the basis of ideological changes brought about by
bourgeois hegemony in the eighteenth century. He relates social
change to such structural elements as increasing accuracy in the
depiction of individual character, and concrete social settings and plot
circumstances which build up realism as a mode of representation.

Marxist critics have studied the ideological function of narrative
genres in the self-representation of social classes and as an

ideological manifestation of social conflicts. We might single out
Fredric Jameson's work on narrative.[76] Jameson incorporates and
reinterprets structuralist narratology in order to study narrative as a
'socially symbolic act', as an imaginative (and ideologically
motivated) response to class struggle. For him, narrative is the main
structuring principle in the articulation of desire as well as of
political and cultural representations.

The question of narrative and desire is also central to
psychoanalytic approaches. Freud himself inaugurated the
psychoanalytic study of narrative functions. In 'Creative Writers and
Daydreaming' Freud analyses the function of the hero and of point
of view as fantasies of power and desire. He also analysed individual
works.[77] But perhaps his most fundamental contribution to the analysis
of narrative is an indirect one: he conceives the whole process of the
development of the self, as well as the process of psychoanalytic
therapy, as narratively structured. Innumerable critics have built on
Freud's insights in ways which are relevant to narratological
analysis. Peter Brooks's *Reading for the Plot* (1984), an extract from
which is reprinted here, is an example of the present-day
convergence of post-structuralist reader-response criticism and
psychoanalysis.

Another extrinsic approach to narrative is gender studies. Among
these, feminist criticism has undoubtedly been the most influential.
There is an immense variety of feminist approaches to literature, and
most of them have made significant contributions to the analysis of
narrative. Feminist analysis of the constructedness of gender has had
far-reaching effects on the study of authorship, character representation
and plot structures. Some key works in this context include Kate
Millett's *Sexual Politics* (1969), Ellen Moers' *Literary Women* (1976)
and Sandra M. Gilbert and Susan Gubar's *The Madwoman in the Attic*
(1979).[78] Feminist critics have also pointed out that narrative
verisimilitude and coherence are gender-conditioned categories,[79] and
have denounced the patriarchal ideology inherent in plot patterns,
implied authorial attitudes and implied readers, calling for a feminist
'resisting reader' (Fetterley). Teresa de Lauretis' *Alice Doesn't* (1984)
develops many of these tenets from the perspective of post-
structuralist psychoanalysis and applies them to the study of filmic
narrative. An excerpt from this work has been included in our reader.

There are countless other significant extensions or applications of
narratology to a number of disciplines. A philosophical variety
of narratology is to be found in the work of Paul Ricœur.[80] A writer
in the tradition of philosophical hermeneutics inaugurated by
Heidegger's *Sein und Zeit*, Ricœur develops his thought as a critique
of modern rationalist approaches such as phenomenology and

structuralism. He insists that myth is an essentially temporal phenomenon, and cannot be reduced to a semantic matrix as Lévi-Strauss contends. He considers narrative ordering as a fundamental human experience, a way of structuring human existence in time and of opening up the possibility of meaningful action. Ricœur's work is a good example of narratology applied to philosophical and religious (Christian) hermeneutics.

The theory of history has always had to account for issues of representation, with the question of narrative as a central problem. The realization that modernist history leaves out of its account many facts that remain ungraspable or untranslatable informs the postmodernist concept of history, which thus becomes 'the problem of the past as unrepresentable burden'.[81] Consistently with this, the contemporary theory of history sets out to question the cognoscibility of the past and the ideological function of history writing in the selection of past events erased or recorded. According to the modernist interpretation, history is not a text at all but rather an idea which becomes accessible in textual form. By contrast, post-structuralist theorists of history such as Hayden White or Dominick LaCapra have questioned the validity of the modernist approach.[82] From their postmodernist perspective, historical meaning is the result of the inextricable unity of idea and textual envelope, of content and form, so that the study of the real can only be the analysis of the textual form reality takes when apprehended by subjects. In *Metahistory* (1973), for example, Hayden White studies the techniques of historical writing as versions of literary or mythical plots. His essay in our selection is also a good instance of the application of structural analysis of narrative to historical writing.

Conclusion

Much might be said about the possible developments of a science of narrative, because, as we have tried to show, narrative is a complex phenomenon whose analysis allows infinite perspectives. Many critics would argue that narratology should be understood as exclusively referring to formalist and structuralist analysis. Other critics envision narratology as an umbrella term, the meeting-place of multiple approaches to narrative, from the standpoint of a variety of disciplines: history, anthropology, psychology, cognitive science, hermeneutic philosophy, ideological criticism, and so on. In this introduction we have attempted to sketch an ample theoretical and historical conception of narrative theory. In our selection of texts, however, we have deliberately followed more restrictive criteria. First, we have only included texts from 1950 onwards. Secondly, the bulk of our selection is based on structuralist narratology, although we have also included a few examples of the most influential alternative theoretical approaches to narratology in the wider sense of the word. We are aware, however, that the differing narratives on narratology which we propose in the introduction and contents of this reader are just two of the countless possible plots in a garden of forking paths.

Notes

1. Gérard Genette, *Narrative Discourse* (1972) trans. Jane E. Lewin (Ithaca, NY: Cornell University Press, 1980); Mieke Bal, *Narratologie: Essais sur la signification narrative dans quartre romans modernes* (Paris: Klincksieck, 1977) and *Narratology: Introduction to the Theory of Narrative* (1978) trans. Christine van Boheemen (Toronto: University of Toronto Press, 1985); Gerald Prince, *Narratology: The Form and Functioning of Narrative* (Berlin: Mouton, 1982).

2. Aristotle, *The Poetics*, trans. W. Hamilton Fyfe. In *Aristotle: The Poetics. 'Longinus': On the Sublime. Demetrius: On Style* (Cambridge, Mass.: Harvard University Press, 1927).

3. Roland Barthes, *S/Z* (1970) trans. Richard Miller (New York: Hill and Wang, 1974).

4. Bal, *Narratology*; Boris Tomashevski, 'Thematics' (1925) in *Russian Formalist Criticism: Four Essays*, ed. and trans. Lee T. Lemon and Marion J. Reis (Lexington: University of Nebraska Press, 1965), pp. 61–98.

5. '1. Un texte est un ensemble fini et structuré de signes linguistiques. 1.1. Un texte *narratif* est un texte dans lequel une instance *raconte* un *récit* ... 2. Un récit est le signifié d'un texte narratif. Un *récit* signifie à son tour une *histoire*.' (Bal, *Narratologie*, p. 4. Our translation.)

6. A simplified version of the one in *Narratologie*, p. 33.

7. See, for instance, Frank Kermode, *The Sense of an Ending* (Oxford: Oxford University Press, 1967), and Peter Brooks, *Reading for the Plot: Design and Intention in Narrative* (Oxford: Clarendon Press, 1984).

8. See Boris Eikhenbaum, 'Theory of the "Formal Method" ' (1926) in Lemon and Reis (eds and trans), *Russian Formalist Criticism*, pp. 99–140; Wolfgang Kayser, *Die Vortragsreise* (Berne: Francke, 1958).

9. Walker Gibson, 'Authors, Speakers, Readers, and Mock Readers' (1950) in *Reader-Response Criticism*, ed. Jane P. Tompkins (Baltimore: Johns Hopkins University Press, 1980), pp. 1–6.

10. Wayne C. Booth, *The Rhetoric of Fiction* (1961), rev. edn (Harmondsworth: Penguin, 1987), pp. 75, 138.

11. Genette, *Narrative Discourse*; Prince, 'Introduction to the Study of the Narratee' (1973), in Tompkins (ed.), *Reader-Response Criticism*, pp. 7–25.

12. Cf. Bal's more limited scheme (*Narratologie*, p. 32).

13. Plato, *The Republic* (trans. Benjamin Jowett), select. in *Critical Theory since Plato*, ed. Hazard Adams (San Diego: Harcourt, 1971), pp. 19–46.

14. EARL MINER, 'Narrative', in *Comparative Poetics: An Intercultural Essay on Theories of Literature* (Princeton: Princeton University Press, 1990, pp. 135–212.

15. For instance, by JOHN DRYDEN, 'An Account of the Ensuing Poem [*Annus Mirabilis*] in a Letter to the Honourable Sir Robert Howard' (1667), in *John Dryden: Selected Criticism*, ed. James Kinsley and George Parfitt (Oxford: Oxford University Press, 1970), pp. 7–15.

16. GEOFFREY OF VINSAUF, *Poetria Nova* (*c.* 1200), trans. Margaret F. Nims (Toronto: Pontifical Institute of Medieval Studies, 1967).

17. F. ROBORTELLO, *In librvm Aristotelis De arte poetica explicationes/Paraphrasis in Librvm Horatii, Qvi Vvlgo De Arte Poetica Ad Pisones Inscribitvr* (1548); LUDOVICO CASTELVETRO, *Poetica d'Aristotele vulgarizzata e sposta* (1576) in *Castelvetro on the Art of Poetry: An Abridged Translation of Ludovico Castelvetro's Poetica d'Aristotele vulgarizzata e sposta*, ed. A. Bongiorno (Binghampton, NY: Medieval and Renaissance Texts and Studies, 1984); JULIUS CAESAR SCALIGER, *Poetices libri septem* (1561) in *Select translations from Scaliger's* Poetics, ed. and trans, F. M. Padelford (New York, 1905).

18. G. E. LESSING, *Laocoon: An Essay on the Limits of Painting and Poetry* (1766) trans. Edward A. McCormick (Baltimore: Johns Hopkins University Press, 1984).

19. HENRY FIELDING, *The History of Tom Jones, a Foundling* (Ware: Wordsworth, 1992), vol. 1, p. 38.

20. FIELDING, preface to *The History of Joseph Andrews* (London: Hutchinson, 1904), p. 8.

21. SAMUEL RICHARDSON, excerpt from *Novelists on the Novel*, ed. Miriam Allott (London: Routledge and Kegan Paul, 1959), p. 258.

22. FRIEDRICH SCHLEGEL, *Schriften und Fragmente* (Stuttgart: Kröner, 1956); G. W. F. HEGEL, *Esthetics* (1835) trans. T. M. Knox (Oxford: Clarendon, 1975); GEORG LUKÁCS, *The Theory of the Novel* (1916) trans. Anna Bostock (Cambridge, Mass.: MIT Press, 1971).

23. GEORGE ELIOT, 'Silly Novels by Lady Novelists' (1856), rpt. in *Victorian Criticism of the Novel*, ed. Edwin M. Eigner and George J. Worth (Cambridge: Cambridge University Press, 1985), pp. 159–80; GEORGE HENRY LEWES, 'Criticism in Relation to Novels' (1865), rpt. in ibid., pp. 181–92.

24. EDWARD BULWER LYTTON, 'On Art in Fiction (II)' (1838), rpt. in ibid., pp. 22–38.

25. EDGAR ALLAN POE, 'Nathaniel Hawthorne', in *Poems and Essays* (London: Dent, 1927), pp. 177–94.

26. POE, 'The Philosophy of Composition' (1846), in ibid., p. 164.

27. EDMOND SCHERER, *Zur Technik der modernen Erzählung* (1879); FRIEDRICH SPIELHAGEN, *Beiträge zur Theorie und Technik des Romans* (Leipzig: Staackmann, 1883).

28. HENRY JAMES, 'The Art of Fiction' (1884, rev. edn 1888), in Adams (ed.), *Critical Theory since Plato*, pp. 660–70.

29. JAMES's essays and prefaces are collected in *The Art of Criticism: Henry James on the Theory and the Practice of Fiction*, ed. William Veeder and Susan M. Griffin (Chicago: University of Chicago Press, 1986).

30. R. L. STEVENSON, 'A Humble Remonstrance' (1884), in *Victorian Criticism of the Novel*, ed. Eigner and Worth, pp. 213–22.

31. PERCY LUBBOCK, *The Craft of Fiction* (London: Cape, 1921; 1926 edn); JOSEPH

WARREN BEACH, *The Method of Henry James* (1918; rev. ed., Philadelphia: Albert Sciler, 1954.)

32. LUBBOCK, *Craft of Fiction*, p. 62.

33. JOSÉ ORTEGA Y GASSET, *The Dehumanization of Art and Other Essays on Art, Culture, and Literature* (1925, etc.) trans. Helene Weyl (Princeton: Princeton University Press, 1948).

34. E. M. FORSTER, *Aspects of the Novel* (London: Arnold, 1927); EDWIN MUIR, *The Structure of the Novel* (London: Hogarth Press, 1928).

35. CLEANTH BROOKS and ROBERT PENN WARREN, *Understanding Fiction* (1943; Englewood Cliffs, NJ: Prentice Hall, 1959).

36. F. R. LEAVIS, 'The Novel as Dramatic Poem: *Hard Times*', *Scrutiny* 14 (1946–7): 185–204; rev. version in *The Great Tradition* (London: Chatto, 1948).

37. VIRGINIA WOOLF, 'Modern Fiction' (1919), in *The Common Reader* [1st series] 1925 (London: Hogarth, 1929), pp. 184–95.

38. ERICH KAHLER, *The Inward Turn of Narrative* (1970) trans. Richard Winston and Clara Winston (Princeton: Princeton University Press, 1973).

39. CHARLES BALLY, 'Le style indirect libre en français moderne', *Germanisch-Romanische Monatschrift* 4 (1912): 549–56, 597–606; MARGUERITE LIPS, *Le style indirect libre* (Paris: Payot, 1926); L. E. BOWLING, 'What Is the Stream of Consciousness Technique?' *PMLA* 65 (1950): 333–45; MELVIN J. FRIEDMAN, *Stream of Consciousness: A Study of Literary Method* (New Haven: Yale University Press, 1955); NORMAN FRIEDMAN, 'Point-of-View in Fiction: The Development of a Critical Concept', *PMLA* 70 (1955): 1160–84.

40. For instance: VERNON LEE, *The Handling of Words and Other Essays in Literary Psychology* (1923; Lincoln: University of Nebraska Press, 1968); BLISS PERRY, *A Study of Prose Fiction* (1902; Boston: Houghton Mifflin, 1920); JOSEPH WARREN BEACH, *The Twentieth-Century Novel: Studies in Technique* (New York: Appleton, 1932).

41. KÄTE FRIEDEMANN, *Die Rolle des Erzählers in der Epik* (1910; Darmstadt: Wissenschaftliche Buchgesellschaft, 1965).

42. See the selections from essays by VIKTOR SHKLOVSKI and BORIS TOMASHEVSKI in Lemon and Reis (eds and trans.), *Russian Formalist Criticism*, and VLADIMIR PROPP's *Morphology of the Folktale* (1928) trans. Laurence Scott. 2nd edn, rev. and ed. Louis A. Wagner (Austin: University of Texas Press, 1968).

43. ROMAN INGARDEN, *The Literary Work of Art: An Investigation on the Borderlines of Ontology, Logic, and Theory of Literature* (1931; 3rd edn 1965; Evanston, Ill.: Northwestern University Press, 1973).

44. INGARDEN, *The Cognition of the Literary Work of Art* (1968; Evanston, Ill.: Northwestern University Press, 1973).

45. WOLFGANG ISER, *The Implied Reader: Patterns of Communication in Prose Fiction from Bunyan to Beckett* (1972; Baltimore: Johns Hopkins University Press, 1974).

46. JAMES G. FRAZER, *The Golden Bough* (abridged edn 1922: Macmillan, 1956); JOSEPH CAMPBELL, *The Hero with a Thousand Faces* (1949; Princeton: Princeton University Press, 1968); CARL G. JUNG, *Collected Works* (19 vols), ed. Herbert Read, Michael Fordham and Gerard Adler (London: Routledge, 1981).

47. NORTHROP FRYE, *Anatomy of Criticism: Four Essays* (Princeton: Princeton University Press, 1957).

48. See, for instance, 'Der Dichter und Phantasieren' (1907), or 'Das Unheimliche' (1919). *The Standard Edition of the Complete Psychological Works of Sigmund Freud* (24 vols), trans. James Strachey (London: Hogarth Press/Institute of Psychology, 1953–66).

49. See for instance CHRISTOPHER NASH (ed.), *Narrative in Culture: The Use of Storytelling in the Sciences, Philosophy, and Literature* (London: Routledge, 1989).

50. DAVID MASSON, *British Novelists and Their Styles* (London: Macmillan, 1859); Sir WALTER RALEIGH, *The English Novel* (1894); Lord DAVID CECIL, *Early Victorian Novelists* (London: Constable, 1934).

51. GEORGE SAINTSBURY, *The Flourishing of Romance and the Rise of Allegory* (Edinburgh: Blackwood, 1897); W. P. KER, *Epic and Romance* (1896); GUSTAVE LANSON, *Histoire de la littérature française* (1894), rev. edn Paul Tuffrau (Paris: Hachette, 1951); E. A. BAKER, *History of the English Novel* (9 vols; London: Witherby, 1924–38).

52. HIPPOLYTE TAINE, *History of English Literature* (1863–4) trans. H. Van Laun (New York: Ungar, 1965); FERDINAND BRUNETIÈRE, *L'Évolution des genres dans l'histoire de la littérature* (1890; Paris: Hachette, 1980); T. S. ELIOT, 'Tradition and the Individual Talent' (1919), in *Selected Essays* (London: Faber and Faber, 1951); LUKÁCS, *Theory of the Novel* and *The Historical Novel* (1937) trans. Hannah Mitchell and Stanley Mitchell (Lincoln: University of Nebraska Press, 1983); ROBERT WEIMANN, 'Erzählerstandpunkt und *Point of View*. Zur Geschichte und Aesthetik der Perspektive im englischen Roman', *Zeitschrift für Anglistik und Amerikanistik* 10 (1962): 369–416; IAN WATT, *The Rise of the Novel* (1957; Harmondsworth: Penguin, 1983); HAYDEN WHITE, *Metahistory: The Historical Imagination in Nineteenth-Century Europe* (Baltimore: Johns Hopkins University Press, 1973).

53. ÉMILE BENVENISTE, *Problems in General Linguistics* (1966) trans. Mary Elizabeth Meck (Coral Gables, Fla.: University of Miami Press, 1977); J. L. AUSTIN, *How to Do Things with Words* (1962; Oxford: Oxford University Press, 1980); M. M. BAKHTIN, *The Dialogic Imagination* (1938, pub. 1970) trans. Caryl Emerson and Michael Holquist (Austin: University of Texas Press, 1981).

54. Some relevant works in literary pragmatics: TEUN A. VAN DIJK (ed.), *Discourse and Literature: New Approaches to the Analysis of Literary Genre* (Amsterdam: Benjamins, 1985); MARY LOUISE PRATT, *Toward a Speech Act Theory of Literary Discourse* (Bloomington: Indiana University Press, 1977); JOHN R. SEARLE, *Expression and Meaning: Studies in the Theory of Speech Acts* (Cambridge: Cambridge University Press, 1979); ROGER D. SELL (ed.), *Literary Pragmatics* (London: Routledge, 1990).

55. GEORGE HENRIK VON WRIGHT, *An Essay in Deontic Logic and the General Theory of Action* (Amsterdam: North Holland, 1968); PAUL RICŒUR, *Du texte à l'action* (Paris: Seuil, 1986); ERVING GOFFMAN, *Frame Analysis: An Essay on the Organization of Experience* (Cambridge, Mass.: Harvard University Press, 1974).

56. PROPP, *Folktale*; A.-J. GREIMAS, *Structural Semantics: An Attempt at a Method* (1966) trans. Daniele McDowell, Ronald Schleifer and Alan Velie, introd. Ronald Schleifer (Lincoln: University of Nebraska Press, 1983).

57. A. N. VESELOVSKI, *Poetika siuzhetov*, in *Sobranie Sochinenii*, 2/1 (Petersburg, 1913), pp. 1–133; TOMASHEVSKI, 'Thematics' (select. and trans. of *Teorija literatury*, 1925) in Lemon and Reis (eds and trans.), *Russian Formalist Criticism*, pp. 61–98.

58. As a sample of three possible directions chosen among innumerable works: KENNETH BURKE, *A Grammar of Motives and A Rhetoric of Motives* (Cleveland:

World, 1962); R. S. Crane, 'The Concept of Plot and the Plot of *Tom Jones'*, in *Critics and Criticism*, ed. R. S. Crane (1952; abridged edn Chicago: University of Chicago Press, 1957), pp. 62–93; William O. Hendricks, *Essays on Semiolinguistics and Verbal Art* (The Hague: Mouton, 1973).

59. Goffman, *Frame Analysis*; David Bordwell, *Narration in the Fiction Film* (Madison: University of Wisconsin Press, 1985); Edward Branigan (see pp. 234–48, below).

60. For instance, in Marvin Minski, 'A Framework for Representing Knowledge', in *The Psychology of Computer Vision*, ed. P. H. Winston (New York: McGraw-Hill, 1975); Daniel G. Bobrow, R. Kaplan et al., 'GUS: A Frame-Driven Dialog System', *Artificial Intelligence* 8 (1977): 155–73; James Meehan, 'Tale-Spin', in *Inside Computer Understanding: Five Programs Plus Miniatures*, ed. Roger C. Schank and Christopher K. Riesbeck (Hillsdale, NJ: Erlbaum, 1981), pp. 197–226; Gregory G. Colomb and Mark Turner, 'Computers, Literary Theory, and Theory of Meaning', in *The Future of Literary Theory*, ed. Ralph Cohen (New York: Routlege, 1989), pp. 386–410.

61. James, 'Art of Fiction'; Lubbock, *Craft of Fiction*; Charles Bally, 'Le style indirect libre en français moderne', *Germanisch-Romanische Monatschrift* 4 (1912): 549–56, 597–606; Booth, *Rhetoric of Fiction*; Genette, *Narrative Discourse* and *Narrative Discourse Revisited* (1983) trans. Jane E. Lewin (Ithaca, NY: Cornell University Press, 1988); Bal, *Narratology*; Bakhtin, *Dialogic Imagination*; Édouard Dujardin, *Le Monologue intérieur* (Paris: Messein, 1931); Robert Humphrey, *Stream of Consciousness in the Modern Novel* (Berkeley: University of California Press, 1954); Dorrit Cohn, *Transparent Minds: Narrative Modes for Presenting Consciousness in Fiction* (Princeton: Princeton University Press, 1978); Roger Fowler, *Linguistics and the Novel* (1977; London: Methuen, 1985).

62. Walker Gibson, 'Authors, Speakers, Readers, and Mock Readers', *College English* 11 (1980): 265–9.

63. Genette, *Narrative Discourse*; Prince, 'Introduction to the Study of the Narratee'.

64. Barthes, *S/Z*; Stanley Fish, *Is There a Text in This Class? The Authority of Interpretive Communities* (Cambridge, Mass.: Harvard University Press 1980); Iser, *The Implied Reader* and *The Act of Reading: A Theory of Aesthetic Response* (1976; Baltimore: Johns Hopkins University Press, 1980); Horst Ruthrof, *The Reader's Construction of Narrative* (London: Routledge, 1981).

65. Peter J. Rabinovitz, *Before Reading: Narrative Conventions and the Politics of Interpretation* (Ithaca, NY: Cornell University Press, 1987); 'Narrative Analysis: An Interdisciplinary Dialogue', special issue of *Poetics* 15 (April 1986); 'Narratology Revisited', special issues of *Poetics Today* 11, 12 (Summer and Winter 1990, all 1991); Nash (ed.), *Narrative in Culture*.

66. Schlegel, *Das Athenäum* (1798–1800) in *Kritische Schriften*, ed. Wolfdietrich Rasch (Munich, 1958); Hegel, *Esthetics*.

67. Alain Robbe-Grillet, *For a New Novel: Essays on Fiction* (1963) trans. Richard Howard (New York: Grove, 1965); Jean Ricardou, *Nouveaux problèmes du roman* (Paris: Seuil, 1978); Michael Boyd, *The Reflexive Novel: Fiction as Critique* (Lewisburg: Bucknell University Press, 1983); Patricia Waugh, *Metafiction: The Theory and Practice of Self-Conscious Fiction* (London: Routledge, 1984); Brian McHale, *Postmodernist Fiction* (London: Methuen, 1987); Linda Hutcheon, *A Poetics of Postmodernism: History, Theory, Fiction* (London: Routledge and Kegan Paul, 1988).

68. DAVID LODGE, 'The Novelist at the Crossroads' (1969) in *The Novel Today: Contemporary Writers on Modern Fiction*, ed. Malcolm Bradbury (1977; new edn London: Fontana, 1990), pp. 87–116.

69. ROBERT ALTER, *Partial Magic: The Novel as a Self-Conscious Genre* (Berkeley: University of California Press, 1975).

70. See LUCIEN DÄLLENBACH, *The Mirror in the Text* (1977) trans. Jeremy Whiteley and Emma Hughes (Oxford: Polity Press, 1989).

71. ALTER, *Partial Magic*, p. x.

72. GABRIEL JOSIPOVICI, *The World and the Book: A Study of Modern Fiction* (Stanford: Stanford University Press, 1971), p. xiv.

73. BAKHTIN, *Dialogic Imagination*; JULIA KRISTEVA, 'Bakhtin, le mot, le dialogue et le roman', *Critique* 239 (1967): 438–65.

74. GENETTE, *Introduction à l'architexte* (Paris: Editions du Seuil, 1979).

75. FRYE, *Anatomy of Criticism*.

76. FREDRIC JAMESON, *The Political Unconscious: Narrative as a Socially Symbolic Act* (Ithaca, NY: Cornell University Press, 1981).

77. FREUD, 'Creative Writers and Daydreaming' (1908) in Adams (ed.), *Critical Theory since Plato*, pp. 749–53, and *Der Wahn und die Träume in W. Jensens Gradiva* (Leipzig: Hellen, 1907).

78. KATE MILLETT, *Sexual Politics* (1969; London: Virago, 1977); ELLEN MOERS, *Literary Women: The Great Writers* (Garden City, NY: Doubleday, 1976); SANDRA M. GILBERT and SUSAN GUBAR, *The Madwoman in the Attic: The Woman Writer and the Nineteenth-Century Literary Imagination* (New Haven: Yale University Press, 1979).

79. See, for instance, JUDITH FETTERLEY, *The Resisting Reader: A Feminist Approach to American Fiction* (Bloomington: Indiana University Press, 1978); NANCY K. MILLER, *Subject to Change: Reading Feminist Writing* (New York: Columbia University Press, 1988).

80. PAUL RICŒUR, *Time and Narrative*, vol. 1 (1983) trans. Kathleen McLaughlin and David Pellauer; vol. 2 (1984) trans. Kathleen McLaughlin and David Pellauer; vol. 3 (1985) trans. Kathleen Blamey and David Pellauer (Chicago: University of Chicago Press, 1984, 1986, 1988).

81. DIANE ELAM, *Romancing the Postmodern* (London: Routledge, 1992), p. 68.

82. WHITE, *Metahistory* and *The Content of the Form: Narrative Discourse and Historical Representation* (Baltimore: Johns Hopkins University Press, 1987): DOMINICK LaCAPRA, *History and Criticism* (Ithaca, NY: Cornell University Press, 1985) and *History, Politics, and the Novel* (Ithaca, NY: Cornell University Press, 1987).

Part One

Narrative structure: fabula

1 Introduction to the Structural Analysis of Narratives*

ROLAND BARTHES

The article reprinted here was originally published as the introduction to no. 8 of *Communications*, perhaps the most memorable issue of the pathbreaking French journal and one generally considered to be a manifesto of the French structuralist school. This issue, wholly devoted to the structural analysis of narrative, included seminal essays by A.-J. Greimas, Claude Bremond, Christian Metz, Tzvetan Todorov and Gérard Genette. In their semiological work, these critics were indebted to a variety of sources: structural linguistics, the Prague School, Russian formalism, structural anthropology and so on. But their most direct influences were Vladimir Propp's *Morphology of the Folktale* (1928) and Lévi-Strauss' *Structural Anthropology* (1958, trans. 1963).

In his introductory essay, Roland Barthes proposed his own deductive model for the structural analysis of narrative at discourse level, closely following the example of generative linguistics. Rejecting all kinds of thematic approach, he aims at the construction of a 'functional syntax' theoretically capable of accounting for every conceivable type of narrative. He bases his model on Propp's concept of 'function' as the structural unit governing the logic of narrative possibilities, the unfolding of the actions performed by the characters and the relations among them. Barthes' model improves on Propp's in that it offers the notions of 'levels of description' and the logic of vertical ('hierarchical') integration of narrative instances, which prefigure those of Genette and Bal. Barthes also contends that traditional classifications of character types are unsatisfactory because they rely excessively on the privileging of one particular kind of character: the subject. In line with Todorov and Greimas, he proposes to void the notion of 'character' of its humanistic connotations in favour of the functional notion of agent or 'actant'. Anticipating the importance given

*ROLAND BARTHES, *Image, Music, Text*. Ed. and trans. Stephen Heath (New York: Hill & Wang, 1977), pp. 79–117. First publ. as 'Introduction à l'analyse structurale du récit' *Communications* 8 (1966): 1–27.

by reader-response criticism to the narratee, Barthes defines narrative communication as an exchange between narrator and listener. He stresses the peculiarities of literary enunciation and insists on the differentiation between narrator (who speaks in the narrative), implied author (who writes), and real author (who is). Barthes' later phase is generally considered to veer towards a post-structuralist concern with desire, the pleasure of the text, the critique of cultural stereotypes and a looser, more contextualized and particularized approach, for instance, in his reading of a short story by Balzac in *S/Z*.

The narratives of the world are numberless. [...] Able to be carried by articulated language, spoken or written, fixed or moving images, gestures, and the ordered mixture of all these substances; narrative is present in myth, legend, fable, tale, novella, epic, history, tragedy, drama, comedy, mime, painting (think of Carpaccio's *Saint Ursula*), stained glass windows, cinema, comics, news item, conversation. Moreover, under this almost infinite diversity of forms, narrative is present in every age, in every place, in every society. [...] Caring nothing for the division between good and bad literature, narrative is international, transhistorical, transcultural: it is simply there, like life itself.

[...]

Faced with the infinity of narratives, the multiplicity of standpoints – historical, psychological, sociological, ethnological, aesthetic, etc. – from which they can be studied, [...] the Russian Formalists, Propp and Lévi-Strauss, have taught us to recognize the following dilemma: either a narrative is merely a rambling collection of events, in which case nothing can be said about it other than by referring back to the storyteller's (the author's) art, talent or genius – all mythical forms of chance – or else it shares with other narratives a common structure which is open to analysis, no matter how much patience its formulation requires. There is a world of difference between the most complex randomness and the most elementary combinatory scheme, and it is impossible to combine (to produce) a narrative without reference to an implicit system of units and rules.

Where then are we to look for the structures of narrative? Doubtless, in narratives themselves.

[...]

Thus, in order to describe and classify the infinite number of narratives, a 'theory' [...] is needed and the immediate task is that of finding it, of starting to define it. Its development can be greatly facilitated if one begins from a model able to provide it with its initial terms and principles. In the current state of research, it seems reasonable[1] that the structural analysis of narrative be given linguistics itself as founding model.

1. The Language of Narrative

1. Beyond the sentence

As we know, linguistics stops at the sentence, the last unit which it considers to fall within its scope.
[...]
And yet it is evident that discourse itself (as a set of sentences) is organized and that, through this organization, it can be seen as the message of another language, one operating at a higher level than the language of the linguists.[2] Discourse has its units, its rules, its 'grammar': beyond the sentence, and though consisting solely of sentences, it must naturally form the object of a second linguistics. For a long time indeed, such a linguistics of discourse bore a glorious name, that of Rhetoric. As a result of a complex historical movement, however, in which Rhetoric went over to belles-lettres and the latter was divorced from the study of language, it has recently become necessary to take up the problem afresh. The new linguistics of discourse has still to be developed, but at least it is being postulated, and by the linguists themselves.[3] This last fact is not without significance, for, although constituting an autonomous object, discourse must be studied from the basis of linguistics.
[...]
Structurally, narrative shares the characteristics of the sentence without ever being reducible to the simple sum of its sentences: a narrative is a long sentence, just as every constative sentence is in a way the rough outline of a short narrative. Although there provided with different signifiers (often extremely complex), one does find in narrative, expanded and transformed proportionately, the principal verbal categories: tenses, aspects, moods, persons. Moreover the 'subjects' themselves, as opposed to the verbal predicates, readily yield to the sentence model. [...] Language never ceases to accompany discourse, holding up to it the mirror of its own structure – does not literature, particularly today, make a language of the very conditions of language?

2. Levels of meaning

From the outset, linguistics furnishes the structural analysis of narrative with a concept which is decisive in that, making explicit immediately what is essential in every system of meaning, namely its organization, it allows us both to show how a narrative is not a simple sum of propositions and to classify the enormous mass of elements which go to make up a narrative. This concept is that of *level of description*.

A sentence can be described, linguistically, on several levels (phonetic, phonological, grammatical, contextual) and these levels are in a hierarchical relationship with one another, for, while all have their own units and correlations (whence the necessity for a separate description of each of them), no level on its own can produce meaning. A unit belonging to a particular level only takes on meaning if it can be integrated in a higher level; a phoneme, though perfectly describable, means nothing in itself: it participates in meaning only when integrated in a word, and the word itself must in turn be integrated in a sentence.[4] The theory of levels (as set out by Benveniste) gives two types of relations: distributional (if the relations are situated on the same level) and integrational (if they are grasped from one level to the next); consequently, distributional relations alone are not sufficient to account for meaning. In order to conduct a structural analysis, it is thus first of all necessary to distinguish several levels or instances of description and to place these instances within a hierarchical (integrationary) perspective.

The levels are operations.[5] It is therefore normal that, as it progresses, linguistics should tend to multiply them. Discourse analysis, however, is as yet only able to work on rudimentary levels. In its own way, rhetoric had assigned at least two planes of description to discourse: *dispositio* and *elocutio*.[6] Today, in his analysis of the structure of myth, Lévi-Strauss has already indicated that the constituent units of mythical discourse (mythemes) acquire meaning only because they are grouped in bundles and because these bundles themselves combine together.[7] As too, Tzvetan Todorov, reviving the distinction made by the Russian Formalists, proposes working on two major levels, themselves subdivided: *story* (the argument), comprising a logic of actions and a 'syntax' of characters, and *discourse*, comprising the tenses, aspects and modes of the narrative.[8] But however many levels are proposed and whatever definition they are given, there can be no doubt that narrative is a hierarchy of instances. To understand a narrative is not merely to follow the unfolding of the story, it is also to recognize its construction in 'storeys', to project the horizontal concatenations of the narrative 'thread' on to an implicitly vertical axis; to read (to listen to) a narrative is not merely to move from one word to the next, it is also to move from one level to the next.

[...]

It is proposed to distinguish three levels of description in the
narrative work: the level of *'functions'* (in the sense this word has in
Propp and Bremond), the level of *'actions'* (in the sense this word has
in Greimas when he talks of characters as actants) and the level of
'narration' (which is roughly the level of 'discourse' in Todorov). These
three levels are bound together according to a mode of progressive
integration: a function only has meaning insofar as it occupies a place
in the general action of an actant, and this action in turn receives its
final meaning from the fact that it is narrated, entrusted to a discourse
which possesses its own code.

II. Functions

1. The determination of the units

Any system being the combinations of units of known classes, the
first task is to divide up narrative and determine the segments of
narrative discourse that can be distributed into a limited number
of classes. In a word, we have to define the smallest narrative units.

Given the integrational perspective described above, the analysis
cannot rest satisfied with a purely distributional definition of the
units. From the start, meaning must be the criterion of the unit: it is
the functional nature of certain segments of the story that makes them
units – hence the name 'functions' immediately attributed to these
first units. Since the Russian Formalists,[9] a unit has been taken as
any segment of the story which can be seen as the term of a
correlation. The essence of a function is, so to speak, the seed that
it sows in the narrative, planting an element that will come to fruition
later – either on the same level or elsewhere, on another level.
[...]

Is everything in a narrative functional? Does everything, down to
the slightest detail, have a meaning? Can narrative be divided up
entirely into functional units? [...] A narrative is never made up of
anything other than functions: in differing degrees, everything in it
signifies. This is not a matter of art (on the part of the narrator), but
of structure; in the realm of discourse, what is noted is by definition
notable. [...] To put it another way, one could say that art is without
noise (as that term is employed in information theory).[10] [...]

From the linguistic point of view, the function is clearly a unit of
content: it is 'what it says' that makes of a statement a functional
unit, not the manner in which it is said. This constitutive signified
may have a number of different signifiers, often very intricate. If I am
told (in *Goldfinger*) that *Bond saw a man of about fifty*, the piece of

49

information holds simultaneously two functions of unequal pressure: on the one hand, the character's age fits into a certain description of the man (the 'usefulness' of which for the rest of the story is not nil, but diffuse, delayed); while on the other, the immediate signified of the statement is that Bond is unacquainted with his future interlocutor, the unit thus implying a very strong correlation (initiation of a threat and the need to establish the man's identity).

[...]

Functions will be represented sometimes by units higher than the sentence (groups of sentences of varying lengths, up to the work in its entirety) and sometimes by lower ones (syntagm, word and even, within the word, certain literary elements only). When we are told that – the telephone ringing during night duty at Secret Service headquarters – *Bond picked up one of the four receivers*, the moneme *four* in itself constitutes a functional unit, referring as it does to a concept necessary to the story (that of a highly developed bureaucratic technology). In fact, the narrative unit in this case is not the linguistic unit (the word) but only its connoted value (linguistically, the word /four/ never means 'four'); which explains how certain functional units can be shorter than the sentence without ceasing to belong to the order of discourse: such units then extend not beyond the sentence, than which they remain materially shorter, but beyond the level of denotation which, like the sentence, is the province of linguistics properly speaking.

2. Classes of units

The functional units must be distributed into a small number of classes. If these classes are to be determined without recourse to the substance of content (psychological substance for example), it is again necessary to consider the different levels of meaning: some units have as correlates units on the same level, while the saturation of others requires a change of levels; hence, straightaway, two major classes of functions, distributional and integrational. The former correspond to what Propp and subsequently Bremond (in particular) take as functions but they will be treated here in a much more detailed way than is the case in their work. The term *'functions'* will be reserved for these units (though the other units are also functional), the model of description for which has become classic since Tomachevski's analysis: the purchase of a revolver has for correlate the moment when it will be used (and if not used, the notation is reversed into a sign of indecision, etc.) [...] As for the latter, the integrational units, these comprise all the *'indices'* (in the very broad sense of the word),[11] the unit now referring not to a complementary and consequential act but to a more or less diffuse concept which is nevertheless necessary to the meaning of the story: psychological indices concerning the characters, data regarding their identity, notations of 'atmosphere', and so on. The relation between the unit and its correlate is now no longer distributional (often several indices refer to the same signified and the order of their occurrence in the discourse is not necessarily pertinent) but integrational. In order to understand what an indicial notation 'is for', one must move to a higher level (characters' actions or narration), for only there is the indice clarified: the power of the administrative machine behind Bond, indexed by the number of telephones, has no bearing on the sequence of actions in which Bond is involved by answering the call; it finds its meaning only on the level of a general typology of the actants (Bond is on the side of order). [...] *Functions* and *indices* thus overlay another classic distinction: functions involve metonymic relata, indices metaphoric relata; the former correspond to a functionality of doing, the latter to a functionality of being.[12]

These two main classes of units, functions and indices, should already allow a certain classification of narratives. Some narratives are heavily functional (such as folktales), while others on the contrary are heavily indicial (such as 'psychological' novels); between these two poles lies a whole series of intermediary forms, dependent on history, society, genre. But we can go further. Within each of the two main classes it is immediately possible to determine two sub-classes of narrative units. Returning to the class of functions, its units are not all of the same 'importance': some constitute real hinge-points of the narrative (or of a fragment of the narrative); others merely 'fill in' the narrative space separating the hinge functions. Let us call the former *cardinal functions* (or *nuclei*) and the latter, having regard to their complementary nature, *catalysers*. For a function to be cardinal, it is enough that the action to which it refers open (or continue, or close) an alternative that is of direct consequence for the subsequent development of the story, in short that it inaugurate or conclude an uncertainty. [...] Between two cardinal functions, however, it is always possible to set out subsidiary notations which cluster around one or other nucleus without modifying its alternative nature: the space separating *the telephone rang* from *Bond answered* can be saturated with a host of trivial incidents or descriptions – *Bond moved towards the desk, picked up one of the receivers, put down his cigarette,* etc. These catalysers are still functional, insofar as they enter into correlation with a nucleus, but their functionality is attenuated, unilateral, parasitic; it is a question of a purely chronological functionality (what is described is what separates two moments of the story), whereas the tie between two cardinal functions is invested with a double functionality, at once chronological and logical. Catalysers are only consecutive units, cardinal functions are both consecutive and consequential.

[...]

Were a catalyser purely redundant (in relation to its nucleus), it would nonetheless participate in the economy of the message. [...] Since what is noted always appears as being notable, the catalyser ceaselessly revives the semantic tension of the discourse, says ceaselessly that there has been, that there is going to be, meaning. Thus, in the final analysis, the catalyser has a constant function which is, to use Jakobson's term, a phatic one: it maintains the contact between narrator and addressee. A nucleus cannot be deleted without altering the story, but neither can a catalyst without altering the discourse.

As for the other main class of units, the indices, an integrational class, its units have in common that they can only be saturated (completed) on the level of characters or on the level of narration. They are thus part of a *parametrical* relation[13] whose second – implicit – term is continuous, extended over an episode, a character or the whole work. A distinction can be made, however, between *indices* proper, referring to the character of a narrative agent, a feeling, an atmosphere (for example suspicion) or a philosophy, and *informants*, serving to identify, to locate in time and space. [...] Indices involve an activity of deciphering, the reader is to learn to know a character or an atmosphere; informants bring ready-made knowledge, their functionality, like that of catalysers, is thus weak without being nil. Whatever its 'flatness' in relation to the rest of the story, the informant (for example, the exact age of a character) always serves to authenticate the reality of the referent, to embed fiction in the real world. [...]

Nuclei and catalysers, indices and informants (again, the names are of little importance), these, it seems, are the initial classes into which the functional level units can be divided. This classification must be completed by two remarks. Firstly, a unit can at the same time belong to two different classes: to drink a whisky (in an airport lounge) is an action which can act as a catalyser to the (cardinal) notation of *waiting*, but it is also, and simultaneously, the indice of a certain atmosphere (modernity, relaxation, reminiscence, etc.). [...] Secondly, it should be noted [...] that the four classes just described can be distributed in a different way which is moreover closer to the linguistic model. Catalysers, indices and informants have a common characteristic: in relation to nuclei, they are *expansions*. Nuclei (as will be seen in a moment) form finite sets grouping a small number of terms, are governed by a logic, are at once necessary and sufficient. Once the framework they provide is given, the other units fill it out according to a mode of proliferation in principle infinite. [. . .]

3. *Functional syntax*

How, according to what 'grammar', are the different units strung together along the narrative syntagm? What are the rules of the functional combinatory system? Informants and indices can combine freely together: as for example in the portrait which readily juxtaposes data concerning civil status and traits of character. Catalysers and nuclei are linked by a simple relation of implication: a catalyser necessarily implies the existence of a cardinal function to which it can connect, but not vice-versa. As for cardinal functions, they are bound together by a relation of solidarity: a function of this type calls for another function of the same type and reciprocally. [. . .]

The functional covering of the narrative necessitates an organization of relays the basic unit of which can only be a small group of functions, hereafter referred to (following Bremond) as a *sequence*.

A sequence is a logical succession of nuclei bound together by a relation of solidarity:[14] the sequence opens when one of its terms has no solidary antecedent and closes when another of its terms has no consequent. [. . .] The sequence indeed is always nameable. Determining the major functions of the folktale, Propp and subsequently Bremond have been led to name them (*Fraud, Betrayal, Struggle, Contract, Seduction*, etc.). [. . .] Yet at the same time they can be imagined as forming part of an inner meta-language for the reader (or listener) who can grasp every logical succession of actions as a nominal whole. [....]

However minimal its importance, a sequence, since it is made up of a small number of nuclei (that is to say, in fact, of 'dispatchers'), always involves moments of risk and it is this which justifies analysing it. It might seem futile to constitute into a sequence the logical succession of trifling acts which go to make up the offer of a cigarette (*offering, accepting, lighting, smoking*), but precisely, at every one of these points, an alternative – and hence a freedom of meaning – is possible. Du Pont, Bond's future partner, offers him a light from his lighter but Bond refuses; the meaning of this bifurcation is that Bond instinctively fears a booby-trapped gadget.[15] A sequence is thus, one can say, a *threatened logical unit*, this being its justification *a minimo*. It is also founded *a maximo*: enclosed on its function, subsumed under a name, the sequence itself constitutes a new unit, ready to function as a simple term in another, more extensive sequence. [. . .] What is in question here, of course, is a hierarchy that remains within the functional level: it is only when it has been possible to widen the narrative out step by step, from Du Pont's cigarette to Bond's battle against Goldfinger, that functional analysis is over – the pyramid of functions then touches the next level (that of the Actions). There is both a syntax within the sequences and a (subrogating) syntax between the sequences together. The first episode of *Goldfinger* thus takes on a 'stemmatic' aspect:

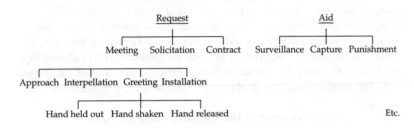

Obviously this representation is analytical; the reader perceives a linear succession of terms. What needs to be noted, however, is that the terms from several sequences can easily be imbricated in one another: a sequence is not yet completed when already, cutting in, the first term of a new sequence may appear. Sequences move in counterpoint;[16] functionally, the structure of narrative is fugued: thus it is this that narrative at once 'holds' and 'pulls on'. Within the single work, the imbrication of sequences can indeed only be allowed to come to a halt with a radical break if the sealed-off blocks which then compose it are in some sort recuperated at the higher level of the Actions (of the characters). *Goldfinger* is composed of three functionally independent episodes, their functional stemmas twice ceasing to intercommunicate: there is no sequential relation between the swimming-pool episode and the Fort Knox episode; but there remains an actantial relation, for the characters (and consequently the structure of their relations) are the same. [. . .] The level of functions (which provides the major part of the narrative syntagm) must thus be capped by a higher level from which, step by step, the first level units draw their meaning, the level of actions.

III. Actions

1. Towards a structural status of characters

[...]
Structural analysis, much concerned not to define characters in terms
of psychological essences, has so far striven, using various
hypotheses, to define a character not as a 'being' but as a 'participant'.
For Bremond, every character (even secondary) can be the agent of
sequences of actions which belong to him (*Fraud, Seduction*); when a
single sequence involves two characters (as is usual), it comprises
two perspectives, two names (what is *Fraud* for the one is *Gullibility*
for the other); in short, every character (even secondary) is the hero
of his own sequence. Todorov, analysing a 'psychological' novel (*Les
Liaisons dangereuses*), starts not from the character-persons but from
the three major relationships in which they can engage and which he
calls base predicates (love, communication, help). The analysis
brings these relationships under two sorts of rules: rules of *derivation*,
when it is a question of accounting for other relationships, and rules
of *action*, when it is a question of describing the transformation of the
major relationships in the course of the story. There are many
characters in *Les Liaisons dangereuses* but 'what is said of them' (their
predicates) can be classified. Finally, Greimas has proposed to
describe and classify the characters of narrative not according to what
they are but according to what they do (whence the name *actants*),
inasmuch as they participate in three main semantic axes (also to be
found in the sentence: subject, object, indirect object, adjunct) which
are communication, desire (or quest) and ordeal.[17] Since this
participation is ordered in couples, the infinite world of characters
is, it too, bound by a paradigmatic structure (*Subject/Object, Donor/
Receiver, Helper/Opponent*) which is projected along the narrative; and
since an actant defines a class, it can be filled by different actors,
mobilized according to rules of multiplication, substitution or
replacement.

These three conceptions have many points in common. The most
important, it must be stressed again, is the definition of the character
according to participation in a sphere of actions, these spheres being
few in number, typical and classifiable; which is why this second
level of description, despite its being that of the characters, has here
been called the level of Actions: the word *actions* is not to be
understood in the sense of the trifling acts which form the tissue of
the first level but in that of the major articulations of *praxis* (desire,
communication, struggle).

2. *The problem of the subject*

[...]

The real difficulty posed by the classification of characters is the place
(and hence the existence) of the *subject* in any actantial matrix,
whatever its formulation. *Who* is the subject (the hero) of a narrative?
Is there – or not – a privileged class of actors? The novel has
accustomed us to emphasize in one way or another – sometimes in a
devious (negative) way – one character in particular. But such
privileging is far from extending over the whole of narrative literature.
Many narratives, for example, set two adversaries in conflict over
some stake; the subject is then truly double, not reducible further by
substitution. [...] If therefore a privileged class of actors is retained
(the subject of the quest, of the desire, of the action), it needs at least
to be made more flexible by bringing that actant under the very
categories of the grammatical (and not psychological) person. [...]
It will – perhaps – be the grammatical categories of the person
(accessible in our pronouns) which will provide the key to the actional
level; but since these categories can only be defined in relation to
the instance of discourse, not to that of reality,[18] characters, as units
of the actional level, find their meaning (their intelligibility) only if
integrated in the third level of description, here called the level of
Narration (as opposed to Functions and Actions).

IV. Narration

1. *Narrative communication*

[...] In linguistic communication, *je* and *tu* (*I* and *you*) are absolutely
presupposed by one another; similarly, there can be no narrative
without a narrator and a listener (or reader). Banal perhaps, but still
little developed. Certainly the role of the sender has been abundantly
enlarged upon (much study of the 'author' of a novel, though without
any consideration of whether he really is the 'narrator'); when it
comes to the reader, however, literary theory is much more modest.
In fact, the problem is not to introspect the motives of the narrator
or the effects the narration produces on the reader, it is to describe
the code by which narrator and reader are signified throughout the
narrative itself. [...]

Who is the donor of the narrative? So far, three conceptions seem
to have been formulated. The first holds that a narrative emanates
from a person (in the fully psychological sense of the term). This
person has a name, the author, [...] the narrative (notably the

novel) then being simply the expression of an *I* external to it. The second conception regards the narrator as a sort of omniscient, apparently impersonal, consciousness that tells the story from a superior point of view, that of God: the narrator is at once inside his characters (since he knows everything that goes on in them) and outside them (since he never identifies with any one more than another). The third and most recent conception (Henry James, Sartre) decrees that the narrator must limit his narrative to what the characters can observe or know, everything proceeding as if each of the characters in turn were the sender of the narrative. All three conceptions are equally difficult in that they seem to consider narrator and characters as real – 'living' – people (the unfailing power of this literary myth is well known), as though a narrative were originally determined as its referential level (it is a matter of equally 'realist' conceptions). Narrator and characters, however, at least from our perspective, are essentially 'paper beings'; the (material) author of a narrative is in no way to be confused with the narrator of that narrative.[19] The signs of the narrator are immanent to the narrative and hence readily accessible to a semiological analysis; but in order to conclude that the author himself (whether declared, hidden or withdrawn) has 'signs' at his disposal which he sprinkles through his work, it is necessary to assume the existence between this 'person' and his language of a straight descriptive relation which makes the author a full subject and the narrative the instrumental expression of that fullness. Structural analysis is unwilling to accept such an assumption: *who speaks* (in the narrative) is not *who writes* (in real life) and *who writes* is not *who is*.[20]

In fact, narration strictly speaking (the code of the narrator), like language, knows only two systems of signs: personal and apersonal. These two narrational systems do not necessarily present the linguistic marks attached to person (*I*) and non-person (*he*): there are narratives or at least narrative episodes, for example, which though written in the third person nevertheless have as their true instance the first person. How can we tell? It suffices to rewrite the narrative (or the passage) from *he* to *I*: so long as the rewriting entails no alteration of the discourse other than this change of the grammatical pronouns, we can be sure that we are dealing with a personal system.

[. . .]

2. Narrative situation

The narrational level is thus occupied by the signs of narrativity, the set of operators which reintegrate functions and actions in the narrative communication articulated on its donor and its addressee.

Some of these signs have already received study; we are familiar in oral literatures with certain codes of recitation (metrical formulae, conventional presentation protocols) and we know that here the 'author' is not the person who invents the finest stories but the person who best masters the code which is practised equally by his listeners: in such literatures the narrational level is so clearly defined, its rules so binding, that it is difficult to conceive of a 'tale' devoid of the coded signs of narrative (*'once upon a time'*, etc.). In our written literatures, the 'forms of discourse' (which are in fact signs of narrativity) were early identified: classification of the modes of authorial intervention (outlined by Plato and developed by Diomedes),[21] coding of the beginnings and endings of narratives, definition of the different styles of representation (*oratio directa, oratio indirecta* with its *inquit, oratio tecta*),[22] study of 'points of view' and so on. All these elements form part of the narrational level, to which must obviously be added the writing as a whole, its role being not to 'transmit' the narrative but to display it.

It is indeed precisely in a display of the narrative that the units of the lower levels find integration: the ultimate form of the narrative, as narrative, transcends its contents and its strictly narrative forms (functions and actions). This explains why the narrational code should be the final level attainable by our analysis, other than by going outside of the narrative-object, other, that is, than by transgressing the rule of immanence on which the analysis is based. Narration can only receive its meaning from the world which makes use of it: beyond the narrational level begins the world, other systems (social, economic, ideological) whose terms are no longer simply narratives but elements of a different substance (historical facts, determinations, behaviours, etc.). Just as linguistics stops at the sentence, so narrative analysis stops at discourse – from there it is necessary to shift to another semiotics. Linguistics is acquainted with such boundaries which it has already postulated – if not explored – under the name of *situations*. Halliday defines the 'situation' (in relation to a sentence) as 'the associated non-linguistic factors',[23] Prieto as 'the set of facts known by the receiver at the moment of the semic act and independently of this act'.[24] In the same way, one can say that every narrative is dependent on a 'narrative situation', the set of protocols according to which the narrative is 'consumed'. In so-called 'archaic' societies, the narrative situation is heavily coded;[25] nowadays, avant-garde literature alone still dreams of reading protocols – spectacular in the case of Mallarmé who wanted the book to be recited in public according to a precise combinatory scheme, typographical in that of Butor who tries to provide the book with its own specific signs. Generally, however, our society takes the greatest pains to conjure away the coding of the narrative situation: [...] epistolary novels, supposedly rediscovered manuscripts, author who met the narrator, films which begin the story before the credits. The reluctance to declare its codes characterizes bourgeois society and the mass culture issuing from it: both demand signs which do not look like signs. Yet this is only, so to speak, a structural epiphenomenon: however familiar, however casual may today be the act of opening a novel or a newspaper or of turning on the television, nothing can prevent that humble act from installing in us, all at once and in its entirety, the narrative code we are going to need. Hence the narrational level has an ambiguous role: contiguous to the narrative situation (and sometimes even including it), it gives on to the world in which the narrative is undone (consumed), while at the same time, capping the preceding levels, it closes the narrative, constitutes it definitively as utterance of a language [*langue*] which provides for and bears along its own metalanguage.

[...]

Notes

1. But not imperative: see CLAUDE BREMOND, 'La logique des possibles narratifs', *Communications* 8 (1966).

2. It goes without saying, as Jakobson has noted, that between the sentence and what lies beyond the sentence there are transitions; co-ordination, for instance, can work over the limit of the sentence.

3. See especially: ÉMILE BENVENISTE, *Problèmes de linguistique générale* (Paris: 1966) [*Problems of General Linguistics* (Coral Gables, Fla.: 1971)], Chapter 10; Z. S. HARRIS, 'Discourse Analysis', *Language* 28 (1952): 18–23, 474–94; N. RUWET, 'Analyse structurale d'un poème français', *Linguistics* 3 (1964): 62–83.

4. The levels of integration were postulated by the Prague School (vid. J. VACHEK, *A Prague School Reader in Linguistics* (Bloomington, Ind.: 1964), p. 468) and have been adopted since by many linguists. It is Benveniste who, in my opinion, has given the most illuminating analysis in this respect; *Problèmes*, Chapter 10.

5. 'In somewhat vague terms, a level may be considered as a system of symbols, rules, and so on, to be used for representing utterances', E. BACH, *An Introduction to Transformational Grammars* (New York: 1964), p. 57.

6. The third part of rhetoric, *inventio*, did not concern language – it had to do with *res*, not with *verba*.

7. CLAUDE LÉVI-STRAUSS, *Anthropologie structurale* (Paris: 1958), p. 233 [*Structural Anthropology* (New York and London: 1963), p. 211].

8. See T. TODOROV, 'Les catégories du récit littéraire', *Communications* 8 (1966). [Todorov's work on narrative is now most easily accessible in two books, *Littérature et Signification* (Paris: 1967); *Poétique de la prose* (Paris: 1972). For a short account in English, see 'Structural analysis of narrative', *Novel* I/3 (1969): 70–6.]

9. See especially B. Tomachevski, 'Thématique' (1925), in *Théorie de la littérature*, ed. T. Todorov (Paris: 1965), pp. 263–307. A little later, Propp defined the function as 'an act of a character, defined from the point of view of its significance for the course of the action', *Morphology of the Folktale* (Austin, Tex. and London: 1968), p. 21.

10. This is what separates art from 'life', the latter knowing only 'fuzzy' or 'blurred' communications. 'Fuzziness' (that beyond which it is impossible to see) can exist in art, but it does so as a coded element (in Watteau for example). Even then, such 'fuzziness' is unknown to the written code: writing is inescapably distinct.

11. These designations, like those that follow, may all be provisional.

12. Functions cannot be reduced to actions (verbs), nor indices to qualities (adjectives), for there are actions that are indicial, being 'signs' of a character, an atmosphere, etc.

13. N. Ruwet calls 'parametrical' an element which remains constant for the whole duration of a piece of music (for instance, the tempo in a Bach allegro or the monodic character of a solo).

14. In the Hjelmslevian sense of double implication: two terms presuppose one another.

15. It is quite possible to identify even at this infinitesimal level an opposition of paradigmatic type, if not between two terms, at least between two poles of the sequence: the sequence *Offer of a cigarette* spreads out, by suspending it, the paradigm *Danger/Safety* (demonstrated by Cheglov in his analysis of the Sherlock Holmes cycle), *Suspicion/Protection, Aggressiveness/Friendliness*.

16. This counterpoint was recognized by the Russian Formalists who outlined its typology; it is not without recalling the principal 'intricate' structures of the sentence.

17. A. J. Greimas, *Sémantique structurale* (Paris: 1966), pp. 129f.

18. See the analyses of person given by Benveniste in *Problèmes*.

19. A distinction all the more necessary, given the scale at which we are working, in that historically a large mass of narratives are without authors (oral narratives, folktales, epics entrusted to bards, reciters, etc.).

20. J. Lacan: 'Is the subject I speak of when I speak the same as the subject who speaks?'

21. *Genus activum vel imitativum* (no intervention of the narrator in the discourse: as for example theatre); *genus ennarativum* (the poet alone speaks: sententiae, didactic poems); *genus commune* (mixture of the two kinds: epic poems).

22. H. Sörensen in *Language and Society* (Studies presented to Jansen), (Copenhagen: 1961), p. 150.

23. M. A. K. Halliday, 'General linguistics and its application to language teaching', *Patterns of Language* (London: 1966), p. 4.

24. L. J. Prieto, *Principes de noologie* (Paris and The Hague: 1964), p. 36.

25. A tale, as Lucien Sebag stressed, can be told anywhere anytime, but not a mythical narrative.

2 The Logic of Narrative Possibilities*

CLAUDE BREMOND

This essay, like Barthes' 'Introduction to the Structural Analysis of Narrative', was also published in no. 8 of *Communications*. Barthes situated the work of the contributors to the journal in a line with the Russian formalists in general and Vladimir Propp and Claude Lévi-Strauss in particular. These writers, Barthes explained, had drawn attention to the fact that, for all the infinite variety of narratives, they share a basic structure which can be isolated and analysed. In his contribution, Claude Bremond sets out to elaborate a comprehensive typology of the structural elements underlying all kinds of fabulas (which he still calls narratives), not just one particular kind, as Propp had done in his *Morphology of the Folktale* (1928). Bremond accepts Propp's fundamental notions of 'function', the basic narrative unit, made up of events and actions; and 'sequence', or basic groupings of functions. The most elementary sequence is made up of three functions: the first opens the possibility of carrying out an action or event; the second achieves the virtuality opened in the first; and the third is the result that closes the process. The range of combinatory possibilities is doubled if the virtuality opened in the first function is not fulfilled. Bremond builds his elementary sequence accordingly: Virtuality – Actualization // Absence of Actualization – Goal attained // Goal not attained. As he explains, this basic triadic scheme can be further subdivided into more complex triadic combinations, according to the most recurrent kinds of events and actions and to the perspective from which they are analysed, for the same event may be described, for example, as 'evil performed' (from the perspective of the victim) and as 'deed to be avenged' (from that of the avenger). Bremond's scheme provided a simple typology of actions and events and helped define the different roles of the characters in the fabula according to their function (the seducer, the seduced, the

---

*Reprinted from *New Literary History* 11 (1980): 387–411. Trans. Elaine D. Cancalon. First publ. as 'La logique des possibles narratifs', *Communications* 8 (1966): 60–76.

avenger, the victim, etc.), thus foregrounding their structural roles as 'actants' (a term coined by Greimas) rather than as characters.

The essay reprinted below included a 'Postface' written by Bremond for the English version in 1988 in which he corrected an important point in his earlier basic scheme. To the notion of 'modification' of the initial situation (which might start a process of 'amelioration' or 'degradation' of a given character), he added the complementary notion of 'blockage of modification' (resulting in 'frustration' or 'protection'). The intersection of these four fundamental processes provides the axis around which all fabulas are structured. Bremond's triadic typology, like the typologies devised by other French structuralists such as Tzvetan Todorov (in *Grammaire du Décaméron*, 1969) and A.-J. Greimas and J. Courtés (in *Sémiotique: Dictionnaire raisonné de la théorie du langage*, 1979) was influenced by generative linguistics in that its overall aim was to establish the 'grammar' of narrative: that is the overall system of rules in the deep structure underlying each and every textual manifestation – whether existent or conceivable – at surface level.

I

Semiological study of narrative can be divided into two parts: on the one hand, an analysis of the techniques of narrative; on the other, a search for the laws which govern the narrated matter. These laws themselves depend upon two levels of organization: they reflect the logical constraint that any series of events, organized as narrative, must respect in order to be intelligible; and they add to these constraints, valid for all narrative, the conventions of their particular universe which is characteristic of a culture, a period, a literary genre, a narrator's style, even of the narration itself.

After examining the method used by Vladimir Propp to discover the specific characteristics of one of these particular domains, that of the Russian folktale, I became convinced of the need to draw a map of the logical possibilities of narrative as a preliminary to any description of a specific literary genre. Once this is accomplished, it will be feasible to attempt a classification of narrative based on structural characteristics as precise as those which help botanists and biologists to define the aims of their studies. But this widening perspective entails the need for a less rigorous method. Let us recall and spell out the modifications which seem indispensable:

First, the basic unit, the narrative atom, is still the *function*, applied as in Propp, to actions and events which, when grouped in sequences, generate the narrative.

Second, a first grouping of three functions creates the *elementary sequence*. This triad corresponds to the three obligatory phases of any process: a function which opens the process in the form of an act to be carried out or of an event which is foreseen; a function which achieves this virtuality in the form of an actual act or event; and a function which closes the process in the form of an attained result.

Third, the foregoing differ from Propp's method in that none of these functions lead necessarily to the following function in the sequence. On the contrary, when the function which opens the sequence is proposed, the narrator always has the choice of having it followed by the act or of maintaining it in a state of virtuality: when an act is presented as having to be realized, or if an event is foreseen, the actualization of the act or of the event can just as well take place as not. If the narrator chooses to actualize the act or the event, he still has the choice of allowing the process to continue on to its conclusion, or he can stop it on the way: the act can attain or fail to attain its goal; the event can follow or not follow its course up to the end which was foreseen. The network of possibilities opened in this way by the elementary sequence follows this pattern:

Virtuality → (e.g., goal to be obtained)

- Actualization → (e.g., act necessary to attain goal)
  - Goal attained (e.g., act successful)
  - Goal not attained (e.g., act fails)
- Absence of actualization (e.g., inertia, impediment to action)

[...]

II. The narrative cycle

All narrative consists of a discourse which integrates a sequence of events of human interest into the unity of a single plot. Without succession there is no narrative, but rather description (if the objects of the discourse are associated through spatial contiguity), deduction (if these objects imply one another), lyrical effusion (if they evoke one another through metaphor or metonymy). Neither does narrative exist without integration into the unity of a plot, but only chronology, an enunciation of a succession of uncoordinated facts. Finally, where there is no implied human interest (narrated events neither being produced by agents nor experienced by anthropomorphic beings), there can be no narrative, for it is only in relation to a plan conceived by man that events gain meaning and can be organized into a structured temporal sequence.

According to whether they favor or oppose this plan, the events of a given narrative can be classed under two basic types which develop according to the following sequences:

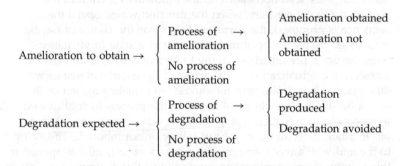

Each elementary sequence which we will eventually isolate is a specification of one or the other of these two categories, which thus establishes the first principle of dichotomous classification. Before examining the various sequences, let us specify the modalities according to which amelioration and degradation combine in a narrative:

(1) By end-to-end succession. It can immediately be seen that narration can alternate phases of amelioration and degradation according to a continuous cycle:

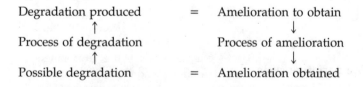

However, and this is not quite so obvious, this alteration is not only possible but necessary. Let us consider the beginning of a story which presents a deficiency affecting an individual or a group (in the form of poverty, illness, stupidity, lack of a male heir, chronic plague, desire for knowledge, love, etc.). For this beginning to develop, the situation must evolve; something must happen which will bring a modification. In what direction? One might suppose either toward amelioration or degradation. Rightfully, however, only an amelioration is possible. Misfortune may, of course, grow worse. There are narratives in which misfortunes follow one after the other so that each degradation brings on another. But in this case the deficiency which marks the end of the first degradation is not the real point of departure of the second. This intermediary interruption – this *reprieve* – is functionally equivalent to a period of amelioration, or at least to a phase which represents the preservation of what can still be saved. The departure point of the new phase of degradation is not the degraded condition, which can only be improved, but the still relatively satisfying state which can only be degraded. Likewise, two amelioration processes cannot follow one another, inasmuch as the improvement brought about by the first still leaves something to be desired. By implying this lack, the narrator introduces the equivalent of a phase of degradation. The still relatively deficient condition which results acts as a point of departure for the new amelioration phase.

(2) By enclave. The failure of a process of amelioration or degradation in progress may result from the insertion of a reverse process which prevents it from reaching its normal conclusion. In this case we have the following schemata:

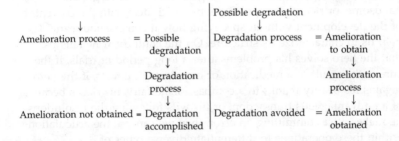

(3) By coupling. The same sequence of events cannot at the same time and in relation to the same agent be characterized both as amelioration and degradation. On the contrary, this simultaneity becomes possible when the event affects at one and the same time two agents moved by opposing interests: the degradation of the fate of the one coincides with the amelioration of the fate of the other. This produces the following schema:

Amelioration to obtain	vs.	Possible degradation
↓		↓
Amelioration process	vs.	Degradation process
↓		↓
Amelioration obtained	vs.	Degradation achieved.

The fact that it is possible and indeed necessary to change viewpoints from the perspective of one agent to that of another is capital for the remainder of our study. It implies the rejection, at our level of analysis, of the notions of Hero, Villain, etc., conceived as labels and attached once and for all to the characters. Each agent is his own hero. His partners are defined from his point of view as allies, adversaries, etc. These definitions are reversed when passing from one perspective to another. Rather than outline the narrative structure in relation to a privileged point of view – the hero's or the narrator's – the patterns that are herein developed will integrate the many perspectives belonging to diverse agents into the unity of a single schema.

III. Amelioration process

The narrator can limit himself to indicating an amelioration process without explicitly outlining its phases. If he simply says that the hero solves his problems or that he gets well, becomes good, handsome, or rich, these specifications which deal with the contents of the development without specifying how it comes about cannot help us to characterize its structure. On the contrary, if he tells us that the hero solves his problems after a long period of trials, if the cure is the result of a medication or of a doctor's efforts, if the hero regains his beauty thanks to a compassionate fairy, his riches because of an advantageous transaction, or his wits following the resolutions he makes after committing an error, then we can use the articulations within these operations to differentiate diverse types of amelioration: the more detail the narrative provides, the further this differentiation can be carried out.

Let us first consider things from the perspective of the beneficiary of the amelioration. (It should be understood that the beneficiary is not necessarily aware of the process engaged in his favor. His perspective can remain in a potential state, like that of Sleeping Beauty while she waits for her Prince Charming.) His initial state of deficiency implies the presence of an *obstacle* which prevents the realization of a more satisfying state. The elimination of the obstacle implies intervening factors which act as means taken against the obstacle and in favor of the beneficiary. So that if the narrator chooses to develop this episode, his narrative will follow the schema:

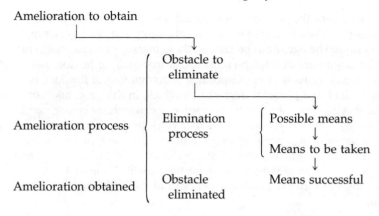

At this stage we may be dealing with a single dramatis persona, the beneficiary of the amelioration, who benefits passively from a fortunate combination of circumstances. In this case neither he nor anyone else bears the responsibility for having brought together and activated the means which overturned the obstacle. Things 'turned out well' without anyone's having seen to them.

There is no such solitude when the amelioration, rather than being ascribed to chance, is attributed to the intervention of an agent endowed with initiative who assumes it as a *task to accomplish*. The amelioration process is then organized into behavior, which implies that it takes on the structure of a network of ends and means which can be analyzed ad infinitum. In addition, this transformation introduces two new roles: on the one hand, the agent who assumes the task for the benefit of a passive beneficiary acts, in relation to that beneficiary, no longer as an inert means, but as one endowed with initiative and with his own interests: he is an *ally*. On the other hand, the obstacle confronted by the agent can also be represented by an agent, also endowed with initiative and his own interests: this agent is an *adversary*. In order to take these new dimensions into account we must examine: the structure of the completion of the task and its possible developments, the full details of the alliance relationship brought about by the intervention of an ally, and the modalities and the consequences of the action undertaken against an adversary.

IV. Completion of the task

The narrator can limit himself to mentioning the performance of the task. If he chooses to develop this episode, he must make clear first the nature of the obstacle encountered, then the structure of the measures taken to eliminate it – intentionally, and not by chance this time. The agent can be lacking these means, perhaps intellectually if he is ignorant of what he must do, or materially if he does not have the necessary tools at his disposal. The recognition of this lack is equivalent to a phase of degradation which, in this case, takes on the specific form of a problem to solve and which, as before, can be dealt with in two ways: things either work out by themselves (heaven may unexpectedly provide the sought-for solution) or an agent may assume the task of arranging them. In this case, this new agent acts as an ally intervening for the benefit of the first who becomes in turn the passive beneficiary of the assistance thus given him.

V. Intervention of the ally

It is possible that the ally's intervention, in the form of an agent who takes charge of the amelioration process, not be given a motive by the narrator, or that it be explained by motives having no link with the beneficiary (if the aid is involuntary). In this case one cannot really speak of the intervention of an ally: deriving from fortuitous encounter between two tales, the amelioration is the product of chance.

Things are quite different when the intervention is motivated, from the ally's point of view, by the merits of the beneficiary. In that case the aid is a sacrifice consented to within the framework of an exchange of services. This exchange itself can assume three forms: either (1) the aid is received by the beneficiary in exchange for assistance which he himself offers his ally in an exchange of simultaneous services: the two paramenters are in this case jointly responsible for the accomplishment of a task of mutual interest; or (2) the aid is offered in gratitude for a past service: in this case the ally acts as the beneficiary's *debtor*; or (3) the aid is offered in the hope of future compensation: in this case the ally acts as the beneficiary's *creditor*.

Three types of allies and three narrative structures are thus determined by the chronological ordering of the services exchanged. If two associates are jointly interested in the completion of a single task, the perspective of the beneficiary and that of the ally come so close together as to coincide: each one is the beneficiary of his own efforts united with those of his ally. In a final stage there could be a single character split into two roles: when an unhappy hero decides to right his fate by 'helping himself,' he splits into two dramatis personae and becomes his own ally. The completion of the task represents a voluntary degradation, a sacrifice (a fact which is supported by the expressions 'to do something with great pain,' 'to toil,' etc.) whose purpose is to pay the price of an amelioration. Whether it is a question of a single character who divides in two, or of two interdependent characters, the role configuration remains identical: the amelioration is obtained through the sacrifice of an ally whose interests are the same as those of the beneficiary.

Rather than coincide, the perspectives oppose one another when the beneficiary and his ally form the couple creditor/debtor. Their roles then take on the following form: for example, *A* and *B* must each obtain an amelioration distinct from that of the other. If *A* receives *B*'s aid in order to achieve amelioration *a*, *A* becomes *B*'s debtor and will be obliged in turn to help *B* achieve amelioration *b*. The narrative will follow the schema:

Perspective of *A* (beneficiary of aid)		Perspective of *B* (obliging ally)		Perspective of *A* (obligated ally)		Perspective of *B* (beneficiary of aid)
Aid to be received	vs.	Possible service				
↓		↓				
Receiving of aid	vs.	Serviceable action				
↓		↓				
Aid received	vs.	Service accomplished	vs.	Debt to be discharged	vs.	Aid to be received
				↓		
				Discharging of debt	vs.	Receiving of aid
				↓		↓
				Debt discharged	vs.	Aid received

The three types of allies that we have just distinguished – the interdependent associate, the creditor, the debtor – act according to a pact which regulates the exchange of services and guarantees the repayment of services rendered. Sometimes this pact remains implicit (it is understood that hard work is worthy of payment, that a son must obey the father who gave him life, that a slave obey the master who saved his life, etc.); sometimes the pact is the result of a particular negotiation, spelled out in the narrative more or less specifically. Just as it was necessary to search for means before implementing them when their lack constituted an obstacle to the completion of the task, so aid must be negotiated when an ally does not cooperate spontaneously. Within the framework of this preliminary task, the abstention of a future ally makes of him an adversary who has to be convinced. This negotiation, soon to be discussed, constitutes the peaceful way of eliminating an adversary.

VI. Elimination of the adversary

Among the obstacles which prevent the completion of a task, some, as we have seen, present only an inert force; others take on the form of adversaries, agents endowed with initiative who can react through chosen acts to the procedures undertaken against them. The result is that the procedure for eliminating the adversary must be organized according to more or less complex strategies in order to take this resistance and its diverse forms into account.

We need not consider the case in which the adversary disappears without the agent's bearing the responsibility for his elimination (if he dies of natural causes, falls under the blows of another enemy, becomes more accommodating with age, etc.): in that case there is only a fortuitous amelioration. Taking into account only cases where the elimination of the adversary is attributable to the initiative of an agent, we will distinguish two forms: (1) peaceful – the agent tries to influence the adversary so that he cease opposition to the agent's plans. This is *negotiation* which transforms the adversary into an ally; (2) hostile – the agent attempts to inflict damage upon the adversary which will incapacitate him and therefore prevent him from any longer opposing the agent's endeavors. This is aggression, which aims to suppress the adversary.

VII. Negotiation

The negotiation consists for the agent in defining, in agreement with the ex-adversary and future ally, the modalities of exchange of services which constitute the goal of their alliance. But it is still necessary that the principle of such an exchange be accepted by both parties. The agent who takes such an initiative must act so as to create a corresponding desire in his partner. In order to obtain this result he can use either *seduction* or *intimidation*. If he chooses seduction he will try to create the need for a service that he will offer in exchange for the one he needs; if he chooses intimidation he tries to create fear of the harm he can cause, but spare just as well, and which can act as a payment for the service he wants to obtain. If this operation succeeds the two partners are equal. *A* desires a service from *B* as *B* does of *A*. The conditions which make the search for an agreement possible are established. There remains to negotiate the modalities of the exchange and to guarantee that all engagements will be faithfully carried out. The following is a simplified schema of negotiation by seduction:

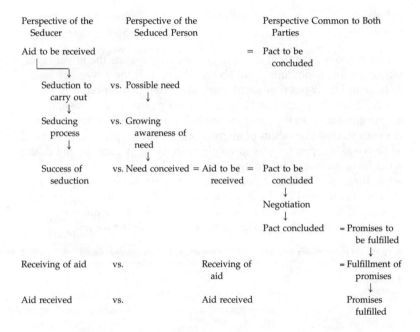

Perspective of the Seducer	Perspective of the Seduced Person		Perspective Common to Both Parties
Aid to be received		=	Pact to be concluded
↓ Seduction to carry out ↓	vs. Possible need ↓		
Seducing process ↓	vs. Growing awareness of need ↓		
Success of seduction	vs. Need conceived	= Aid to be received =	Pact to be concluded ↓ Negotiation ↓
			Pact concluded = Promises to be fulfilled ↓
Receiving of aid	vs.	Receiving of aid	= Fulfillment of promises ↓
Aid received	vs.	Aid received	Promises fulfilled

VIII. Aggression

When he opted for negotiation, the agent chose to eliminate his adversary by an exchange of services which transformed him into an ally; when opting for aggression, he chooses to inflict an injury which will do away with the adversary (at least insofar as he is an obstacle). From the perspective of the victim of aggression, the beginning of this process constitutes a danger which, if it is to be avoided, will normally require an act of self-protection. If this act fails the following occurs:

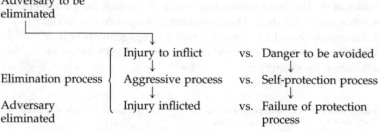

Perspective of the Aggressor			Perspective of the Victim of Aggression
Adversary to be eliminated			
Elimination process	Injury to inflict ↓	vs.	Danger to be avoided ↓
	Aggressive process ↓	vs.	Self-protection process ↓
Adversary eliminated	Injury inflicted	vs.	Failure of protection process

In the above schema it is the aggressor who retains the advantage. However, this is obviously not always the case. If the adversary seems to have at his disposal efficient methods of self-protection, it is desirable for the aggressor to catch him off guard. In that case, the aggression takes on the more complex form of a trap. To use a trap is to act so that the victim of aggression, instead of protecting himself as he could, cooperates unknowingly with the aggressor (by not doing what he ought to, or by doing what he ought not to). The trap is set in three stages: first, a deception; then, if the deception succeeds, an error committed by the dupe; finally, if the error-inducing process is brought to its conclusion, the deceiver exploits his acquired advantage, which places a disarmed adversary at his mercy:

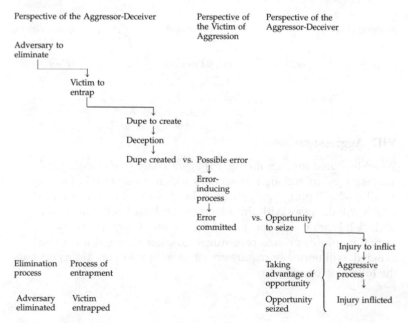

Perspective of the Aggressor-Deceiver

Perspective of the Victim of Aggression

Perspective of the Aggressor-Deceiver

Adversary to eliminate

Victim to entrap

Dupe to create
↓
Deception
↓
Dupe created vs. Possible error
↓
Error-inducing process
↓
Error committed vs. Opportunity to seize

Injury to inflict
↓
Aggressive process
↓
Injury inflicted

Elimination process — Process of entrapment — Taking advantage of opportunity

Adversary eliminated — Victim entrapped — Opportunity seized

The deception, first of the three phases of the trap, is in itself a complex operation. Deception consists of several actions carried on simultaneously: the dissimulation of what is, the simulation of what is not, and the substitution of what is not for what is in order to create a semblance of truth to which the dupe reacts as if it were real. In any deception two combined operations can thus be distinguished, a *dissimulation* and a *simulation*. Dissimulation itself is not sufficient to constitute the deception (except insofar as it simulates the absence of dissimulation); neither does simulation by itself suffice, for an open simulation (that of an actor, for example) is not a deception. In order to go after the bait, the dupe must think it real and be unaware of the hook. The following diagram outlines the deception mechanism:

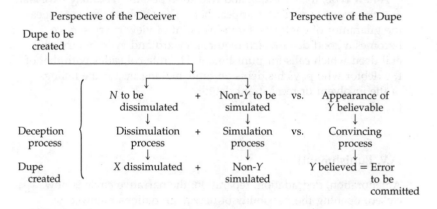

Perspective of the Deceiver			Perspective of the Dupe
Dupe to be created			
	N to be dissimulated	+ Non-Y to be simulated	vs. Appearance of Y believable
	↓	↓	↓
Deception process	Dissimulation process	+ Simulation process	vs. Convincing process
	↓	↓	↓
Dupe created	X dissimulated	+ Non-Y simulated	Y believed = Error to be committed

When the classification is further developed, several types of deception can be distinguished. Differences are created by the type of simulation used by the deceiver to disguise the aggression being planned: (1) the deceiver can simulate a situation implying the absence of any relationship between him and the future victim: he pretends not to be there, literally (if he hides) or figuratively (if he pretends to be asleep, to look away, to lose his mind, etc.); (2) the deceiver can simulate peaceful intentions: he proposes an alliance, tries to seduce or intimidate his victim, while he secretly prepares to break off the negotiations or to betray the pact; (3) the deceiver simulates aggressive intentions so that the dupe, busy defending himself against an imaginary assault, leaves himself open and defenseless against the real attack.

IX. Retributions: recompense and vengeance

The injury inflicted by the aggressor on his victim can be considered as a service in reverse, no longer consented to by the creditor but extorted by the debtor and requiring in return the infliction of an injury of similar proportions, comparable to receiving payment for an open debt: the debtor pays, despite himself, the amount of a loan he was forced to incur. Reward for a service rendered and vengeance directed against an incurred wrong are the two faces of retribution. Like payment for services, payment for wrongs is the consequence of a pact which is at times implicit (all evil acts deserve punishment, an eye for an eye, etc.), at times explicit, spelled out in the terms of a specific alliance which outlines a threat against breaking a contract.

A new type, the *retributor*, and two subtypes, the *rewarding retributor* and the *avenging retributor*, appear here. The retributor is, so to speak, the guarantor of contracts. From his point of view every service becomes a good deed which requires reward and every injury an evil deed which calls for punishment. His role coincides with that of the debtor who pays his debts on time, making up for the failings of the insolvent or recalcitrant debtor.

[...]

[XV. Punishment]

Amelioration, degradation, reparation: the narrative circle is now closed, opening the possibility of new degradations followed by new reparations according to a cycle which can repeat itself indefinitely. Each of the phases can itself be developed ad infinitum. But in the course of its development it will become specified, through a series of alternative choices, into a hierarchy of enclaved sequences, always the same, which exhaustively determine the field of the narratable. The linking of functions in the elementary sequence, then of elementary sequences in a complex sequence, is both free and controlled at the same time: free (for the narrator must at every moment *choose* the continuation of his story) and controlled (for the narrator's only choice, after each option, is between the two discontinuous and contradictory terms of an alternative). It is therefore possible to draw up a priori the integral network of choices offered; to name and to place in the sequence each type of event brought about by these choices; to link these sequences organically in the unity of a role; to coordinate the complementary roles which define the evolution of a situation; to link evolutions in a narration which is at one and the same time unpredictable (because of the play of available combinations) and codifiable (because of the stable properties and the finite number of combined elements).

At the same time this production of narrative types is a structuring of human behavior patterns acted out or undergone. They furnish the narrator with the model and substance of an organized evolution which is indispensable to him and which he could not find elsewhere. Whether it be desired or feared, their end rules over an arrangement of actions which succeed one another and form hierarchies and dichotomies according to an inviolable order. When man, in real life, maps out a plan, explores in his mind the possible developments of a situation, reflects on the course of action undertaken, remembers the phases of a past event, he forms the first narrations of which we can conceive. Inversely, the narrator who wants to order the chronological succession of the events he is relating, to give them a meaning, has no other recourse but to link them together in the unity of an action directed toward an end.

Thus to the elementary narrative types correspond the most general forms of human behavior. Task, contract, error, trap, etc., are universal categories. The network of their internal articulations and of their mutual relationships defines the field of possible experience a priori. By constructing from the simplest narrative forms, sequences, roles, and series of more and more complex and differentiated situations, we can establish the bases of a classification of the types of narration; moreover, we define a framework of reference for the comparative study of these behavior patterns which, always identical in their basic structure, are diversified ad infinitum according to an inexhaustible play of combinations and options, according to cultures, periods, genres, schools, and personal styles. Although it is a technique of literary analysis, the semiology of narrative draws its very existence and its wealth from its roots in anthropology.

3 Reflections on Actantial Models*

A.-J. GREIMAS

The text reprinted here belongs to Chapter 10 of Greimas' *Structural Semantics*, a comprehensive attempt to adapt linguistic categories to the structural analysis of literature. Drawing on the example of generative grammar, Greimas builds an analogy between the deep structure of language and myth, on the one hand, and surface linguistic manifestations and narrative, on the other. He aims to construct a functional model capable of reproducing the overall deep structure of literature and of accounting for each and every existing or conceivable surface manifestation.

Greimas also offers his own typology of actantial categories for the analysis of narrative, developing Vladimir Propp's pioneer work in *Morphology of the Folktale* and Etienne Souriau's analysis of actantial models in drama. As Greimas explains, these earlier typologies of actantial models are insufficient in that they are limited to the analysis of one particular genre and are too formal and descriptive, failing to take into account the thematic element. His own model is built out of Propp's distinction between 'characters' and 'dramatis personae', which Greimas calls 'actors' – the characters who undertake the action in a particular tale – and 'actants' – the types of 'actor' established from the generic corpus as a whole. Drawing strict syntactical analogies, Greimas further reduces Propp's and Souriau's actantial categories to three basic actantial pairs. The first is 'Subject vs. Object', which provides the indispensable syntactical functions. The second is 'Sender vs. Receiver', a pair that is often hard to fit into the analysis of literary narrative, though it should be kept in mind that Greimas' model refers to mythical narrative or folktales. The third pair is 'Helper vs. Opponent', whose function Greimas equates to the circumstantial function of adverbs in the sentence. The relationships governing

*A.-J. GREIMAS, *Structural Semantics: An Attempt at a Method*. Trans. Daniele McDowell, Ronald Schleifer and Alan Velie (Lincoln: University of Nebraska Press, 1983), pp. 197–213, 303. First publ. as *Sémantique structurale: Recherche de méthode* (1966).

this basic actantial model are centred on the notion of desire, which provides the motivation for action at surface level and the mythical impulse in the deep structure.

Greimas' acceptance of this element as an intrinsic part of his actantial model helps him negotiate a leap from the merely descriptive and formal analysis of narrative to the thematic and ideological, a direction which is pursued in, for example, his work on the semiotics of passion (*Sémiotique des passions*, written in collaboration with Jacques Fontanille, 1991). His proposals for evaluating the models elaborated by psychoanalysis for the analysis of myth – such as Freud's analysis of the Oedipus myth – and for designing psychoanalytical actantial models based on Charles Mauron's psychocritical analysis of the obsessive metaphors underlying the creation of personal myths, remain general and inconclusive and show Greimas trying to reduce the often tentative notions and heterogeneous terminologies of psychoanalysis to an overall and permanent 'scientific' system of functional formulas. The most influential aspect of Greimas' semantic model is the componential analysis of meaning which tries to connect the macrostructural and microstructural levels of text and word. He is the coiner of terms such as 'seme', 'sememe' and 'isotopy', which have been adopted and further refined by other structuralist critics.

[...]

2. The actants in linguistics

We were struck with Tesnière's observation[1] – which he probably only intended to be didactic – comparing the elementary utterance to drama [*spectacle*]. If it is remembered that *functions*, according to traditional syntax, are only roles played by words – the subject is 'somebody who does the action,' the object 'somebody who undergoes the action,' and so forth – a proposition, in such a conception, is indeed only a drama which *homo loquens* produces for himself. The drama has, however, this peculiarity, that it is permanent: the content of the actions is forever changing, the actors vary, but the dramatic utterance [*l'énoncé-spectacle*] stays always the same, for its permanence is guaranteed by the unique distribution of its roles.

The permanence of the distribution of a small number of roles, as we were saying, is not simply fortuitous: we have seen that the number of actants was determined by the a priori conditions of the perception of signification. The nature of the distributed roles seemed more difficult for us to articulate: it seemed at least necessary to correct the lame ternary formulation by substituting two actantial categories in the form of oppositions:

subject   vs.   object
sender   vs.   receiver

Beginning here, we have been able to attempt the following extrapolation: since 'natural' speech can neither augment the number of actants nor widen the syntactic comprehension of signification beyond the sentence, it must be the same inside every microuniverse. Or rather the opposite: the semantic microuniverse can be defined as a universe, that is to say, as a signifying whole [*tout de signification*], only to the extent that it can surge up at any moment before us as a simple drama, as an actantial structure.

Two arrangements of a practical order, then, have been necessary to adjust this actantial model borrowed from syntax to its new semantic status and to the new dimensions of a microuniverse. On one hand it was necessary to propose the reduction of syntactic actants to their semantic status (whether she receives the letter or whether the letter is sent to her, Mary is always the 'receiver'); on the other hand, it was necessary to gather all the functions manifested in a corpus and attributed to a single semantic actant whatever their dispersion may be, so that each manifested actant would possess, behind it, its own semantic investment and so that we could say that the ensemble of the recognized actants, whatever the relationship may be between them, are representative of the whole manifestation in its entirety.

Here, then, the hypothesis of an actantial model is proposed as one of the possible principles of organization of the semantic universe, too vast to be grasped in its totality, in a microuniverse accessible to man. However, it is necessary that concrete descriptions of delimited areas – or at least of observations of a general character which, without depending upon precise analysis, would have a bearing upon vast and diversified signifying ensembles – come to confirm these linguistic extrapolations by simultaneously producing information about the signification and the possible articulations of actantial categories.

3. The actants of the Russian folktale

The first confirmation of this hypothesis was advanced by Vladimir Propp, in his *Morphology of the Folktale*, the American translation of which, relatively recent, has been known in France only for a short time.[2] After defining the folktale as a display on a temporal line of its thirty-one functions, Propp raises the question about the actants, or the dramatis personae, as he calls them. His conception of the actants is functional: the characters are defined, according to him, by the 'spheres of action' in which they participate, these spheres being constituted by the bundles of functions which are attributed to them. The invariance that we can observe by comparing all the tale-occurrences of the corpus is that of the spheres of action that are attributed to the characters (whom we prefer to call *actors*), which vary from one tale to another. By illustrating this point with the help of a simple schema (see below), we see that, if we define the functions, F_1, F_2, and F_3, as constituting the sphere of activity of a particular actant, A_1, the invariance of the sphere of activity from one tale to another allows us to consider the actors, a_1, a_2, and a_3, as occurrential expressions of one and the same actant A_1 defined by the same sphere of activity.

	MESSAGE 1		MESSAGE 2		MESSAGE 3	
TALE 1	F_1	a_1	F_2	a_1	F_3	a_1
TALE 2	F_1	a_2	F_2	a_2	F_3	a_2
TALE 3	F_1	a_3	F_2	a_3	F_3	a_3

The result is that if the actors can be established within a tale-occurrence, the actants, which are classifications of actors, can be established only from the corpus of all the tales: an articulation of actors constitutes a particular *tale*; a structure of actants constitutes a *genre*. The actants therefore possess a metalinguistic status in relation to the actors. They presuppose, by the way, a functional analysis – that is to say, the achieved constitution of the spheres of action.

This double procedure – the establishment of the actors by the description of the functions and the reduction of the classifications of actors to actants of the genre – allows Propp to establish a definitive inventory of the actants, which are:

1. *The villain*
2. *The donor (provider)*
3. *The helper*
4. *The sought-for person (and her father)*
5. *The dispatcher*

6. *The hero*
7. *The false hero*

This inventory authorizes Propp to give an actantial definition of the Russian folktale as a story with seven characters.

4. The actants in the theater

At the very point where Propp stops his analysis, we find another inventory which is rather similar, the catalog of the dramatic 'functions' presented by Étienne Souriau in his work *Les Deux cent mille situations dramatiques*.[3] Souriau's thought, however subjective and relying on no concrete analysis, is not very far from Propp's description; it even extends it in a certain way. It is unlikely that Souriau knew Propp's work. But this question is not even pertinent. The interest in Souriau's thought lies in the fact that he has shown that the actantial interpretation can be applied to a kind of narrative – theatrical works – quite different from the folktale and that his results are comparable to Propp's. We find here, although expressed differently, the same distinction between the events of the story [*l'histoire événementielle*] (which is for him only a collection of 'dramatic subjects') and the level of the semantic description (which is made from the 'situations,' which can be decomposed into the action of actants). Finally, we find here a limited inventory of actants (which he calls, according to traditional syntactic terminology, *functions*). Unfortunately, after hesitating for some time between six and seven dramatic functions, Souriau finally decided to limit their number to six (a number challenged, by the way, by Guy Michaud, in his *Techniques de l'oeuvre*, who would like to re-establish the seventh function, that of the traitor): we would thus obtain parallel definitions of the two different 'genres' – folktale and drama – which separately would have claimed to be narratives with seven characters.

Souriau's inventory is presented in the following manner:

Lion . . . the oriented thematic Force
Sun   . . . the Representative of the wished-for Good, of the orienting Value
Earth . . . virtual Recipient of that Good (that for which the Lion is working)
Mars . . . the Opponent
Libra . . . the Arbiter, attributer of the Good
Moon . . . the Rescue, the doubling of one of the preceding forces

We must not be discouraged by the energetic and astrological character of Souriau's terminology: it does not succeed in concealing reflections that are not without coherence.

5. The actantial category 'subject' vs. 'object'

The definitions of Propp and Souriau confirm our interpretation on an important point: a restricted number of actantial terms is sufficient to account for the organization of a microuniverse. Their insufficiency lies in the character, at the same time excessively and insufficiently formal, that was given to these definitions: to define a genre only by the number of actants, while setting aside all the contents, is to place the definition at too high a formal level; to present the actants under the form of a simple inventory, without questioning the possible relationships between them, it is to renounce analysis too early, by leaving the second part of the definition, its specific features, at an insufficient level of formalization. A categorization of the inventory of the actants therefore appears necessary: we will try to attempt it by comparing, in a first approximation, the three inventories at our disposal, those of Propp and Souriau and one more restricted, since it only has two actantial categories, which we have been able to draw from the considerations of the syntactic functioning of discourse.

A first glance allows us to find and identify in the two inventories of Propp and Souriau the two syntactic actants which constitute the category 'Subject' vs. 'Object.' It is striking, we must note at this time, that the relationship between the subject and object which we had so much trouble defining precisely, and never succeeded in defining completely, appears here with a semantic investment identical in both inventories, that of 'desire.' It seems possible to conceive that the transitivity or the *teleological relationship*, as we suggested calling it, situated in the mythical dimension of the manifestation, appears following the semic combination as a sememe realizing the *effect of meaning* of 'desire.' If this is so, the two microuniverses, the genre 'folktale' and the genre 'drama,' defined by a first actantial category articulated in relation to desire, are capable of producing narrative-occurrences where desire will be manifested under the simultaneously practical and mythical form of 'the quest.' The chart of equivalences of that first category will be as shown.

syntax	Subject		Object
Propp	*hero*	vs.	*sought for person*
Souriau	The oriented thematic Force [*Lion*]	vs.	The Representative of the wished-for Good, of the orienting Value [*Sun*]

6. Actantial category 'sender' vs. 'receiver'

The search for what could correspond, in Propp and Souriau's intentions, to that second actantial category cannot fail to raise some difficulties because of the frequent syncretic manifestations of actants (already encountered at the level of syntax), the often noticed plurality of two actants present under the form of a single actor. For instance, in a narrative that is only a common love story ending in marriage without the parents' intervention, the subject is also the receiver, while the object is at the same time the sender of love:

$$\frac{He}{She} \simeq \frac{\text{Subject} + \text{Receiver}}{\text{Object} + \text{Sender}}$$

Four actants are there, symmetrical and inverted, but syncretized under the form of two actors. But we see also – Michel Legrand's couplet sung in the 'Umbrellas of Cherbourg' makes the point in an impressive synopsis:

a man, a woman,
an apple, a drama

– with what ease the disjunction of the object and the sender can produce a model with three actants.

In a narrative of the type of *The Quest for the Holy Grail*, on the contrary, four actants, quite distinct, are articulated in two categories:

$$\frac{\text{Subject}}{\text{Object}} \simeq \frac{Hero}{Holy\ Grail}$$

$$\frac{\text{Sender}}{\text{Receiver}} \simeq \frac{God}{Mankind}$$

Souriau's description does not pose any difficulties. The category

Sender vs. Receiver

is clearly marked there, as the opposition between

Arbiter, attributer of the Good vs. *virtual Recipient of the Good*

In Propp's analysis, in its turn, the sender seems to be articulated into two actors, the first of which is rather naïvely combined with the object of desire:

(the sought-for person and) her father

while the second one appears, as could be expected, under the name of *dispatcher*. In the occurrences, indeed, it is at times the king, at times the father – combined or not into a single actor – who charges the hero with a mission. Thus, without great turmoil and without the help of psychoanalysis, we can reunite the father of the desired person with the dispatcher, and consider them when they are presented separately as two 'actors' of a single actant.

As for the receiver, it seems that, in the Russian folktale, his field of activity is completely fused with that of the subject-hero. A theoretical question that can be raised about this point, one that we will return to later, is whether fusions can be considered as pertinent criteria for the divisions of a genre into subgenres.

It seems that the two actantial categories appear, so far, to constitute a simple model revolving entirely around the object, which is both the object of desire and the object of communication.

7. The actantial category 'helper' vs. 'opponent'

It is much more difficult to be sure of the categorical articulation of the other actants if only because we lack a syntactic model. Two spheres of activity, however, and, inside those, two distinct kinds of functions are recognized without difficulty.

1. The first kinds bring the help by acting in the direction of the desire or by facilitating communication.

2. The others, on the contrary, create obstacles by opposing either the realization of the desire or the communication of the object.

These two bundles of functions can be attributed to two distinct actants that we will designate under the name of

Helper vs. Opponent

This distinction corresponds rather well to the distinction made by Souriau, from whom we borrow the term *opponent*: we prefer the term of *helper* introduced by Guy Michaud, to Souriau's 'rescue.' In Propp's formulation we find that opponent is pejoratively called *villain* (traitor), while *helper* takes in two characters, the *helper* and the *donor* (*provider*). At first sight, this elasticity of analysis may be surprising.

We must not forget, however, that the actants are established by Propp, not to mention Souriau, from their spheres of action, that is to say, with the help of the reduction of the single functions, and without taking into account an indispensable homologation. We do not intend to criticize Propp here, whose role as a precursor is considerable, but simply to register the progress made during the last thirty years by virtue of the general development of structuralist procedures. We should also consider that it is easier to operate when two comparable inventories are at our disposal, instead of simply one.

We can wonder what corresponds, in the mythical universe whose actantial structure we want to make explicit, to this opposition between the helper and the opponent. At first glance, everything takes place as if, besides the principal parties in question, there would appear now in the drama projected on an axiological screen actants representing in a schematic fashion the benevolent and malevolent forces in the world, incarnations of the guardian angel and the devil of medieval Christian drama. What is also striking is the secondary character of these two actants. In a little play on words, we could say, thinking of the participial form by which we designated them (for example, 'the opposing' [*opposant*: i.e. the 'opponent']), that they are the circumstantial 'participants,' and not the true actants of the drama [*spectacle*]. Participles are in fact only adjectives which modify substantives in the same way that adverbs modify verbs.

When in the course of the procedure of normalization we wanted to grant a formal status to the adverbs, we designated them as aspects constituting a hypotactic subclass of functions. There is in French, inside the rather poorly defined class of adverbs, a very restricted inventory of adverbs of quality, which are presented under the form of two oppositional pairs:

willingly	vs.	*unwillingly*
well	vs.	*badly*

These could be justly considered as aspectual categories, the semantic interpretation of which seems difficult: the first category would indicate, in the process in which we find the function invested, the participation of the will, with or without anticipation of resistance; the second category would constitute the projection, upon the function, of appreciation that the subject conveys of its own process (when the subject is identified with the speaker).

It is already obvious where we wanted to come: to the extent that functions are considered as constitutive of actants, there seems to be no reason why one could not admit that the aspectual categories could be considered as *circumstants*, which would be the hypotactic formulations of the actant-subject. In the mythical manifestation which concerns us, it is well understood that helper and opponent are only projections of the will to act and the imaginary resistance of the subject itself, judged beneficial or harmful in relationship to its desire.

This interpretation has a relative value. It attempts to explain the appearance of circumstants as well as true actants in both inventories and to account for both their syntactic and semantic status.

8. The actantial mythical model

Inferred from inventories which remain, in spite of everything, provisional, constructed by considering the syntactic structure of natural languages, this model seems to possess, because of its simplicity and for the analysis of mythical manifestations only, a certain operational value. Its simplicity lies in the fact that it is entirely centred on the object of desire aimed at by the subject and situated, as object of communication, between the sender and the receiver – the desire of the subject being, in its part, modulated in projections from the helper and opponent:

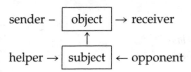

9. The 'thematic' investment

If we wanted to question the possibilities of the use, as a structuring hypothesis, of this model which we consider operational, we should begin with an observation: the desire to compare syntactic categories to Propp's and Souriau's inventories made us consider the relationship between the subject and the object – which first seems to be, in its greater generality, a relationship of teleological character, that is to say, a modality of 'to be able to do,' but which, at the level of the manifestation of functions, would have regained a practical or mythical 'to do' – as a more specialized relationship of 'desire' (having a heavier semic investment) which transforms itself at the level of the manifested functions into 'quest.' Therefore, we would say that the possible particularizations of the model should convey first the relationship between the actants 'subject' vs. 'object' and then be manifested as a class of variables constituted by supplementary investments.

Thus, with great simplification, it could be said that for a learned philosopher of the classical age the relationship of desire would be specified, by a semic investment, as the desire of knowing, and the actants of his drama of knowledge would be distributed more or less in the following manner:

Subject	...	*philosopher*
Object	...	*world*
Sender	...	*God*
Receiver	...	*mankind*
Opponent	...	*matter*
Helper	...	*mind*

In the same way, Marxist ideology as expressed by a militant could be distributed, thanks to its desire to help man, in a parallel fashion:

Subject	...	*man*
Object	...	*classless society*
Sender	...	*history*
Receiver	...	*mankind*
Opponent	...	*bourgeois class*
Helper	...	*working class*

[...]

We see that the proposed actantial model, centered on the relationship of 'desire,' is susceptible to a negative transformation, that the substitutions of the terms inside the category

obsession vs. phobia

should in principle have deep repercussions on the articulation of the ensemble of the terms of the model.
[...]

11. Actants and actors

Even granted, the simple fact that the procedure of thematic investment in the account of the object at each moment risks confusing the description of the actantial model with the qualificative analysis is not sufficient to account for the variation of actantial models and to establish their typology. Nothing is left but to return to the actants themselves, to see in what measure the distributional schemas of the actants, on the one hand, and types of stylistic relationships between the actants and actors, on the other, can serve as criteria for a 'typologizing' particularization of actantial models.

The first typological criterion of this kind can well be the syncretism, often recorded, of the actants. We can thus subdivide the models into genres, according to the nature of the actants which let themselves be syncretized: in the folktale, we have seen, the subject and the receiver constitute an arche-actant. [...] Taken in the nonaxiological domain, the example can be made clearer: thus the queen, in the game of chess, is the syncretic arche-actant of the bishop and the rook.

For the second criterion, the syncretism is distinguished by the analytic division of the actants into hyponymic and hypotactic actors, which corresponds to the complementary distribution of their functions. It is thus that Propp has tried – in an unhappy enough way, it seems to us – to define the receiver as the *sought-for person and her father* (he probably was seeking to preserve the human dignity of the woman-object). The analyses of Lévi-Strauss have shown that mythology, in order to account for complementary distributions of functions, often manifests at the level of the actors a preference for the actantial denominations proper to the structures of kinship. The actants often are grouped in pairs of actors such as husband and wife, father and son, grandmother and grandchild, twins, and so forth. [...] It is here that we can question what exactly corresponds to the models of kinship used by psychoanalysis in the description of individual actantial structures: are they situated at the level of the distribution of the actants into actors, or do they represent, at the end of a generalization which at first sight appears excessive, metaphoric formulations of the actantial categories?

A third typological criterion can possibly be that of the absence of one or more of the actants. Theoretical considerations permit proposing such a possibility only with much skepticism. The examples of absence of actants cited by Souriau are all interpreted as the dramatic effects produced by waiting for the manifestation of an actant, which is not the same thing as absence, but rather its contrary: the absence of Tartuffe during the two first acts of the comedy or the delay of the rescues in the history of Blue Beard only render more acute the presence of the actant not yet manifested in the economy of the actantial structure.

From the operational point of view, and without addressing the problem of the reality of any particular distribution of actants, we can consider the proposed actantial model as a descriptive optimum, reducible to a simpler arche-actantial structure, but also extendible (the limits of which it is difficult, at first sight, to be precise about, but which are certainly not considerable), because of the possible articulation of the actants in simple hypotactic structures.

A whole other question is that of the denomination of actants, which only depends in small part upon the functional analysis from which, in following Propp, we are trying to construct the actantial model. [. . .] While agreeing, in principle with Lévi-Strauss when he says, à propos of Propp's analysis, that the description of the universe of the folktale cannot be complete because of our ignorance of the axiological cultural network which sustains it, we do not think that this constitutes a major obstacle for description, which, while remaining incomplete, can still be pertinent.[4] Thus, to proceed from comparable sequences borrowed from different tale-occurrences, such as:

a tree shows the way . . .
a crane makes a gift of a horse . . .
a bird spies . . .

we can well reduce the predicates to one common function of 'aide' and propose for the three actors a helper-actant which subsumes them: we are incapable of recovering, without the aid of an axiological description, impossible in this case, the explanation of the particularizing denominations of actors.

Nevertheless, the first elements of an actantial stylistic may not be impossible to formulate from only a single functional analysis.
[. . .]

Notes

1. Lucien Tesnière, *Éléments de syntaxe structurale* (Paris: Klincksieck, 1965) p. 109.

2. Vladimir Propp, *Morphology of the Folktale*, trans. Laurence Scott (Austin: University of Texas Press, 1968).

3. Étienne Souriau, *Les Deux cent mille situations dramatiques* (Paris: Flammarion, 1950).

4. Claude Lévi-Strauss, 'Structure and Form: Reflections on a Work by Vladimir Propp', in *Structural Anthropology*, vol. 2, trans. Monique Layton (New York: Basic Books, 1976).

Part Two

Narrative structure: story

4 Fabula and Sjuzhet in the Analysis of Narrative: Some American Discussions*

JONATHAN CULLER

Jonathan Culler is one of the main semioticians in the Anglo-Saxon sphere. He has both adapted and criticized the European structuralist schools in his influential *Structuralist Poetics* (1975) and *The Pursuit of Signs: Semiotics, Literature, Deconstruction* (1983). He is also the author of *On Deconstruction* (1982), probably the most influential overview and assessment of deconstructive theory. Culler argues that the deconstructivist project does not delegitimize structuralist theory, but complements it. In the article reprinted here he attacks the widespread assumption among French narratologists that events at fabula level are arranged according to a true or natural order, later modified and disrupted by the requirements of narrative presentation at discourse level. Drawing on the American theoretical tradition, Culler contends that literary as well as non-literary narratives are organized around a double, contradictory logic, the logic of events, which reinforces the causal efficacy of origins and assumes the primacy of events regardless of their signification, and the order of coherence, which denies their causal efficacy and treats the events as primarily the products of meaning. Culler's thesis is that these opposed logics do not cancel each other, but rather create a tension on which the power of the narration depends, as he forcefully demonstrates in his analysis of several literary and non-literary narratives. Culler's definition of fabula as a tropological construction, the product, rather than the reality reported by discourse, is in line with Mieke Bal's view in *Narratology* (1985) that the fabula is the most abstract of all narrative levels.

Although the idea of narratology and the project of a *grammaire du récit* seem to have arisen and acquired their force within French structuralism and recent work in this expanding field has been dominated or provoked by the problems raised in structuralist

*Reprinted from *Poetics Today* 1.3 (1980): 27–37. First presented at *Synopsis 2* 'Narrative Theory and Poetics of Fiction', an International Symposium held at the Porter Institute for Poetics and Semiotics, Tel Aviv University, and the Van Leer Jerusalem Foundation, 16–22 June 1979.

accounts of narrative, there has been an important American tradition in the study of narrative, whose salient moments are Henry James's Prefaces, Percy Lubbock's *The Craft of Fiction* and Wayne Booth's *The Rhetoric of Fiction*. Inspired by these examples, critics have done much detailed and perceptive work on problems of narrative technique and in particular on narrative point of view. If one were to summarize very crudely the theoretical claims of this critical tradition, they might run somewhat as follows: every narrative has a narrator, whether or not he is explicitly identified. To interpret a narrative one must identify the implied narrator and what in the story belongs to his perspective, distinguishing between the action itself and the narrative perspective on that action, for one of the central thematic issues of every story is the relationship between the implied narrator (with his knowledge, values, etc.) and the story which he narrates.

The effect of recent French work in narratology on this tradition has been to provoke more attempts to systematize and refine the models and concepts which had often been used in an ad hoc way to interpret individual texts. So we have witnessed, for example, Gerald Prince's development of the concept of 'narratee,' as distinguished from 'implied reader' – an important distinction which previous writers had generally overlooked – and Seymour Chatman's important work of synthesis, *Story and Discourse*. Indeed, narratology seems to me at the moment a flourishing area of American criticism, perhaps because it is the area in which it seems most possible to achieve integration, or at least dialogue, between an American critical tradition and various European theoretical developments.

What I am going to discuss is not, however, this tradition – the study of point of view leavened with structuralism and formalism – but rather some recent discussions of narrative which can be aligned with this tradition in that they investigate something which the tradition of point of view studies must, as it were, take for granted. If one is to study point of view and narrative technique, if, more generally, one is to study the relationship between the discourse of a text and the story it tells, then the notion of *fabula*, story, plot, action – call it what you will – becomes the ground of one's endeavor, the *point d'appui* which makes the study of point of view possible. For the study of point of view to make any sense, there must be various contrasting ways of viewing and telling a given story, and this makes 'story' an invariant core, a sequence of actions which can be presented in any of various ways. Action becomes something that exists independently of narrative presentation; in principle it exists prior to any narrative presentation and could be presented in other ways. For example, when Gérard Genette sets out to study the complicated temporal relationships between *récit* and *discours* in his 'Discours du récit,' he must assume that events of the *récit* occurred in some order and that each event occurred either once or more than once (Genette, 1972). Then he can describe the narrative presentation as a transformation of the true or original order of events. Of course, in a particular narrative it may be impossible to tell from the evidence presented whether event A preceded or followed event B, but since it is assumed that at the level of *fabula* there must have been a true order, this impossibility can be taken as a fact about point of view. Without the assumption that there is a true order of events prior to narrative presentation, one could not claim that the lack of order was the result of point of view.

Of course it is not unreasonable to assume that events do occur in some order and that a description of events presupposes the prior existence of those events. But in applying to the text of narrative these perfectly reasonable assumptions about the world, we isolate a level of structure, call it *fabula*, which we treat as something given, a constant, a sequence of events, which the narrative presupposes and which it could describe in various ways. By identifying this sequence of actions as what the text is describing, we make it possible to treat everything else in the text as ways of viewing, presenting, valuing, or ordering this non-textual substratum.

This has generally been a fruitful way of proceeding, but as my description may already have suggested, it involves an operation which can certainly be questioned: the heuristic definition of a 'true sequence of actions' which narrative discourse is then said to present. The analyses of narrative which I propose to discuss bracket the question of point of view and implied narrator and treat the *fabula* itself not as a given but as a tropological construct. If one wished to identify this sort of analysis by its theoretical allegiances, one might cite Nietzsche's tropological deconstruction of causality (De Man, 1974, 1975) or Kenneth Burke's account of narrative as the tropological 'temporalizing of essence' (1969: 430–40) [. . .]

Paul de Man's view of narrative as the expansion or literalization of tropological structures (1977) and J. Hillis Miller's account of the way narratives claim the status of history for their plots and then show history to originate in an act of discursive interpretation (1974) also belong to this general approach to narrative, but I am interested in more restricted analyses which explicitly identify *fabula* not as the reality reported by discourse but as its product.

To illustrate the kind of problems and issues involved, let us start with a familiar example, the story of Oedipus. Traditional narrative analysis would identify the series of events which constitute the action of the story (Oedipus is abandoned on Mt. Cithaeron, rescued by a shepherd, raised in Corinth; he kills Laius at the crossroads, answers the Sphinx's riddle, marries Jocasta, seeks the murderer of Laius, discovers his guilt and blinds himself), and would describe the order and perspective in which these events of the plot are presented in the discourse of the play. It assumes, in other words, that these events constitute the reality of the story and it then asks about the significance of the way in which they are presented. In the case of Oedipus as in many other narratives, of which the detective story is the most common instance, the discourse focuses on the bringing to light of a crucial event, which the story identifies as a reality which determines significance. Someone killed Laius, and the problem is to discover what in fact happened at that fateful moment in the past.

This way of thinking about the play is clearly essential to its power, but one can also argue that this supposed event, Oedipus's slaying of Laius, is not something given as reality but is produced by a tropological operation, the result of narrative requirements. Once we are well into the play, it is clear to us that Oedipus must be guilty, otherwise the tale will not work at all. And this is not simply a matter of the reader responding to a peculiar aesthetic logic. Oedipus too feels the force of this logic. It has been prophesied, after all, that he would kill his father. It was prophesied that Laius would be killed by his son. Oedipus admits to having killed an old man at about the right time and place. So when the shepherd reveals that Oedipus is in fact the son of Laius, Oedipus leaps to the conclusion, and every reader leaps with him, that he did in fact kill Laius. He leaps to this conclusion not on the basis of empirical evidence or eyewitness accounts (the only witness has told a story that is incompatible with Oedipus's guilt: that there were many murderers, whereas Oedipus claims he acted alone), but is compelled rather by *meaning*, by the interweaving of prophesies and the demands of narrative coherence. Instead of saying, therefore, that there are events which took place and which the play reveals in a certain order and with certain detours, we can say that the crucial event itself is a product of the demands of signification. Instead of event determining meaning and meaning being the result or effect of a crucial event, it turns out that meaning is the cause of the event, the cause of its cause, in a tropological operation that can be assimilated to metonymy ('substitution of cause for effect or effect for cause').

Oedipus becomes the murderer of his father not by a violent act that is brought to light but by deeming this act to have taken place, by bowing to the demands of narrative coherence. Readers cannot escape this process either: the text persuades us that this event must have taken place. Although in theory the deed ought to be the cause of Oedipus's guilt, the play makes possible an alternative reading in which cause and effect are reversed and guilt is what produces the deed. And it is essential to the tragic force of the play that Oedipus should take this leap, embrace guilt and deem the act to have taken place rather than, say, resist the logic of signification and deny his guilt until actual proof is obtained. In identifying this alternative logic in which the event is not a cause but an effect of theme, one is helping to account for the force of the narrative.

But it is certainly not the case that in describing the play in this way we have replaced a deluded or incorrect model of narrative by a correct one. On the contrary, it is obvious that much of the power of *Oedipus* depends on the assumption that there is a prior fact which occupies a determinate place in the causal sequence of actions but which the narrative perspective only gradually reveals. It is essential to believe that Oedipus's innocence or guilt is determined by an event in the past which has already taken place but which has not yet been revealed. On the other hand, as we have already suggested, the tragic force of the ending depends on precisely the contrary logic whereby Oedipus posits the act on the basis of a structure of signification and whereby he and the readers are convinced that he did kill his father not by decisive testimony of witnesses (the witness is never even asked the crucial question) but by the demands of signification.

The play requires, then, a double analysis, a reading in two registers, one of which assumes the priority of acts to their narrative representation or presentation, the other which sees plot as a tropological product of narrative requirements. If *Oedipus* seems an unusual case in that it contains a possible uncertainty about a central event in the plot, let us consider an example from a very different period and genre, George Eliot's *Daniel Deronda*, as analysed in a recent article by Cynthia Chase (1978). Deronda, the adopted son of an English nobleman, is a talented, sensitive young man, moving in good society, who has been unable to decide on a profession. He happens to rescue a poor Jewish girl who was trying to drown herself, and in searching for her family later, he meets her brother Mordecai, an ailing scholar with whom he begins to study Hebrew. He develops an intense interest in Jewish culture, falls in love with Mirah, the girl he has saved, and is accepted by Mordecai and others as a kindred spirit.

At this point Deronda receives a summons from his mother who, obeying her father's injunction, reveals to him the secret of his birth: he is a Jew. The novel emphasizes the causal force of this past event: because he was born a Jew, he is a Jew. Origin, cause, and identity are linked in a implicit argument that is common to narrative. With the revelation of Deronda's parentage it is implied that his present character and involvement with things Jewish have been caused by his Jewish origin.

But on the other hand, as Chase notes, the novel's account of Deronda's situation has made it clear to the reader that the progression of his destiny and thus of the story positively requires that he turn out to be Jewish. Suspense is focused on his relationship with Mirah and Mordecai, so that something like this revelation is required for the resolution of the plot; and Mordecai has explicitly stressed his faith that Deronda is Jewish. Thus it seems that Deronda's Jewish parentage is something that can be deduced first from his identity – his qualities and behavior as presented in his relations with Mordecai and Mirah – and second from the patent strategy and direction of the narrative. 'The revelation of Deronda's origins therefore appears as the effect of narrative requirements. The supposed cause of his character and vocation (according to the chapters recounting the disclosure), Deronda's origin presents itself (in the light of the rest of the text) rather as the effect of the account of his vocation: his origin is the effect of its effects' (Chase, 1978: 218).

It is important to stress here that, as in the case of *Oedipus*, there is no question of finding a compromise formulation which would do justice to both presentations of the event by avoiding extremes, for the power of the narrative depends precisely on the alternative use of extremes, the rigorous deployment of two logics, each of which works by excluding the other. It won't do to say, for example, that Deronda's involvement with Judaism is partly but not completely the result of his birth, and that the revelation of his birth is therefore in part an explanation and in part a narrative fulfillment. This sort of formulation is wrong because the power of Eliot's novel depends precisely on the fact that Deronda's commitment to Judaism and idealism, instead of to the frivolous society in which he has been raised, is presented as a free choice. To have exemplary moral value it must be presented as a choice, not as the ineluctable result of the hidden fact of parentage. It also must be presented as wholehearted, not as a dilettantish dabbling which would then be transformed into commitment by revelation of the fact of birth. The novel requires that Deronda's commitment to Judaism be independent of the revelation of his Jewishness – this is thematically and ethically essential – yet its account of Jewishness does not allow for the possibility of conversion and insists on the irreplaceability of origins: to be a Jew is to have been born a Jew. These two logics, one of which insists upon the causal efficacy of origins and the other of which denies their causal efficacy, are in contradiction but they are essential to the way in which the narrative functions. Once logic assumes the primacy of events; the other treats the events as the products of meanings.

One could argue that every narrative operates according to this double logic, presenting its plot as a sequence of events which is prior to and independent of the given perspective on these events, and, at the same time, suggesting by its implicit claims to significance that these events are justified by their appropriateness to a thematic structure. As critics we adopt the first perspective when we debate the significance of a character's actions (taking those actions as given). We adopt the second perspective when we discuss the appropriateness or inappropriateness of an ending (when we debate whether these actions are appropriate expressions of the thematic structure which ought to determine them). Theorists of narrative have always, of course, recognized these two perspectives, but they have perhaps been too ready to assume that they can be held together, synthesized in some way without contradiction. It is precisely this contradiction which will often manifest itself as a moment in the story that seems either superflous or else too neat, which recent work on narrative has brought to the fore, stressing its importance to the rhetorical force of the text.

Though my examples so far have been *Oedipus Rex* and *Daniel Deronda*, this double logic is by no means confined to fictional narratives. In several interesting articles Peter Brooks has discussed narrative in Freud, describing a complex situation (1977, 1979). On the one hand, Freudian theory makes narrative the preferred mode of explanation. Psychoanalysis does not propose scientific laws of the form 'if X, then Y.' Psychoanalytic understanding involves tracing a phenomenon to its origin, seeing how one thing leads to another. Freud's case histories are themselves often narratives of his conduct of the case, but, more important, he explains a neurosis or psychosis by reconstructing a plot, by telling what happened. Like *Oedipus* and *Daniel Deronda*, Freud's narratives lead to the revelation of a decisive event which, when placed in the true sequence of events, can be seen as a the cause of the present situation.

[. . .]

In *Totem and Taboo* Freud tells of a decisive historical event in primitive times: a jealous and tyrannical father, who kept all the women for himself and drove away the sons as they reached maturity, was killed and devoured by the sons who had banded together. This 'memorable and criminal deed' was the beginning of social organization, religion, and moral restrictions, since the guilt led to the creation of taboos. This historical event, Freud claims, remains efficacious to this day. We inherit and repeat the wish if not the actual deed, and the guilt which arises from this wish keeps the consequences of the deed alive in an unbroken narrative.

But clearly if guilt can be created by desires as well as by acts, it is possible that the originary act never took place. Freud admits that the remorse may have been provoked by the sons' fantasy of killing the father (by the imagination of an event). This is a plausible hypothesis, he says, 'and no damage would thus be done to the causal chain stretching from the beginning to the present day' (1950: 16). Choosing between these alternatives is no easy matter; however, he adds, 'it must be confessed that the distinction which may seem fundamental to other people does not in our judgment affect the heart of the matter.' [. . .] Emphasis on event and emphasis on meaning give the same narrative. But once again, one cannot fail to wish to choose, and Freud does: primitive men were uninhibited; for them thought passed directly into action. 'With them it is rather the deed that is the substitute for thought. And this is why, without laying claim to any finality of judgment, I think that in the case before us it may be assumed that "in the beginning was the Deed" ' (1950: 161).

A safe assumption, perhaps, but safe because it is so equivocal. Freud here starts with the fantasy and asserts that for primitive men the deed was a substitute for the fantasy. The deed truly took place, he claims, but his formulation prevents one from taking the deed as a given since it is itself but a substitute for the fantasy, a product of this primal fantasy. And in claiming that in the beginning was the Deed, Freud refers us not to an event but to a signifying structure, another text, Goethe's *Faust* in which 'deed' is but a substitute for 'word'. Quoting Goethe in asserting an originary deed, Freud cannot but refer us to an originary word: the word that was in the beginning and the original authoritative word of Scripture. The two perspectives, in the beginning was the Deed and in the beginning was the Word, are certainly in conflict, and ethical concerns demand a choice, but as Freud's text shows, even when one tries to choose one does not escape the alternative one tried to reject.

I have been offering examples of an approach to narrative which, unlike studies of point of view that have dominated American narrative theory in the past, does not assume the primacy of event so as to focus on means of presentation but rather explores the complex interaction of two modes of determination which both seem necessary to narrative but which do not give rise to a harmonious synthesis. The examples I have used have been literary and theoretical narratives and I would like to conclude with a brief discussion of another species, what William Labov calls 'natural narrative.'

In his studies of the black English vernacular, Labov became

interested in the narrative skills displayed by adolescents and pre-
adolescents in responding to questions like 'Were you ever in a fight
with somebody bigger than you?' followed by 'What happened?' if
they answered 'Yes.' Labov's formal analysis of the elements of these
stories (1967, 1972) begins by assuming the primacy of events,
defining a narrative as a way of recapitulating past experience by
matching a series of clauses to a sequence of events (1972: 360–1).
However, what Labov discovers as a result of this orientation is that
'there is one important aspect of narrative which has not been
discussed – perhaps the most important element in addition to the
basic narrative clause. That is what we term the *evaluation* of the
narrative: the means used by the narrator to indicate the point of
the narrative, its raison d'être' (1972: 366). Indeed, it becomes clear
that for Labov the narrator's primary concern is not to report a
sequence of events but to tell a story that will not be seen as
pointless. 'Pointless stories are met (in English) with the withering
rejoinder, "So what?" Every good narrator is continually warding off
this question; when his narrative is over it should be unthinkable for
a bystander to say, "So what?" ' (1972: 366).

Labov's narrators prove skilled at warding off this question, at
constructing their narratives in such a way that the demands of
significance are met and the story is perceived as narratable, as
'reportable.' The question of whether any given story is being told
primarily in order to report a sequence of events or in order to tell a
tellable story is of course difficult to decide, but the ethical and
referential lure of stories makes listeners want to decide (is that the
way it really happened or is he just trying to impress us?). Labov
avoids this question, either because he thinks it makes no difference
to his analysis or because he thinks that the two projects can and
should coincide, evaluative clauses being added to narrative clauses
to produce a good story. As long as narrative clauses can be
distinguished from evaluative clauses it is possible to maintain the
view that a narrative is a sequence of clauses reporting events (which
may be true or false) with clauses added which evaluate the event
(and which are neither true nor false), but when Labov comes to
describe the evaluative devices, he notes that some of the most
powerful evaluative elements are not comments external to the
action but embedded in the action itself. One can emphasize the
reportability of a story, for example, by narrating as an event an
evaluative comment: 'And when we got down there her brother
turned to me and whispered, "I think she's dead, John!" ' (1967: 39).
Indeed, the evaluation 'may itself be a narrative clause' (1967: 37) as
in 'I never prayed to God so fast and so hard in all my life!'

Labov's claim is certainly correct, that many clauses reporting action are in fact determined by the evaluative function, i.e., the attempt to make the story a truly tellable story and avoid the question 'So what?' But given this possibility, we find ourselves in an awkward situation. For any report of an action there is always the possibility that it should be thought of as evaluative, as determined by requirements of significance, rather than as a representation of a given event. Whichever option we choose, we have the same narrative, of course, and in this sense it may not matter, but if we are concerned with the force of the story, and tellers and listeners of natural narrative are especially concerned with the force of narrative, then we are invited to choose and cannot take for granted the harmonious reconciliation of these two functions or logics.

So even here, in these most unliterary of narratives, we find the same problematic relationship between the determinations of *fabula* and the discourse of *sjuzhet*. [. . .]

References

BOOTH, W., 1961. *Rhetoric of Fiction* (Chicago: Chicago University Press).

BROOKS, PETER, 1977. 'Freud's Masterplot: Questions of Narrative,' *Yale French Studies* 55/6: 280–300.

—— 1979 'Fictions of the Wolfman,' *Diacritics* 9.1: 72–83.

BURKE, KENNETH, 1969. *A Grammar of Motives* (Berkeley: California University Press).

CHASE, CYNTHIA, 1978. 'The Decomposition of the Elephants: Double-Reading *Daniel Deronda*.' *PMLA* 93: 215–27.

—— 1979 'Oedipal Textuality: Reading Freud's Reading of *Oedipus*,' *Diacritics* 9.1: 54–71.

CHATMAN, S., 1978. *Story and Discourse: Narrative Structure in Fiction and Film* (Ithaca, NY: Cornell University Press).

DE MAN, PAUL, 1974. 'Nietzsche's Theory of Rhetoric,' *Symposium*: 33–45.

—— 1975 'Action and Identity in Nietzsche,' *Yale French Studies* 52: 16–30.

—— 1977 'The Purloined Ribbon,' *Glyph* 1: 28–49.

FREUD, SIGMUND, 1950. *Totem and Taboo* (New York: Norton).

GENETTE, GÉRARD, 1972. 'Discours du récit,' *Figures III* (Paris: Seuil).

LABOV, WILLIAM, 1967. 'Narrative Analysis: Oral Versions of Personal Experience,' *Essays on the Verbal and Visual Arts: Proc. of the Annual Spring Meeting of the American Ethnological Society* (Seattle: Washington University Press), pp. 12–44.

—— 1972 *Language in the Inner City* (University Park: University of Pennsylvania Press).

LUBBOCK, P., 1957, *Craft of Fiction* (New York: Viking).

MILLER, J. HILLIS, 1974. 'Narrative and History,' *ELH* 41: 455–73.

5   What is Exposition? An Essay in Temporal Delimitation*

MEIR STERNBERG

In line with Wolfgang Iser, Umberto Eco and Horst Ruthrof, Meir Sternberg offers a reader-response approach to narrative. He defines narrative as a system of 'gap filling' and hypothesis testing and contends that the textual structure must be studied as it is dynamically constructed by the reader. The endurance of first impressions is a law of human perception. First impressions condition further perceptions. Sternberg therefore proposes the elaboration of a scale of rhetorical effects according to 'the rise and fall of first impressions' and a classification of retardatory structures in the presentation of narrative information. He likewise contends that literary texts are the result of the selection and combination of motifs and that the temporal distortion of the chronological order of events is an indication of artistic purpose.

In this excerpt from chapter 1 of his book *Expositional Modes and Temporal Ordering in Fiction*, Sternberg attempts to define exposition functionally and transgenerically. He contends that the Russian formalist distinction between *fabula* and *siuzhet* is not equivalent but complementary to E. M. Forster's notions of 'story' and 'plot'. He defines exposition as the beginning of the fabula; that is, as the first part of the chronologically ordered sequence of motifs as reconstructed by the reader, which may or may not coincide with the beginning of the *siuzhet*. Sternberg further differentiates between represented time and representational time (Genette's story time and narrative time). He argues that every work establishes its own time-norm and that there is a logical correlation between the amount of time devoted to an element and the degree of its aesthetic relevance or centrality. For Sternberg, the closer the two times become, the more aesthetically relevant is the scene.

As the whole of anything is never told, the writer of fiction is necessarily confined to presenting his characters in action within the

---

* MEIR STERNBERG, *Expositional Modes and Temporal Ordering in Fiction* (Baltimore: Johns Hopkins University Press, 1978), pp. 1–23, 307–9.

limits of a certain fictive period of time. It is thus unavoidable that he should intersect the lives of his dramatis personae at a given hour. His problem is only to decide which hour it shall be and in what situation they shall be discovered. [. . .]

It is the function of the exposition to introduce the reader into an unfamiliar world, the fictive world of the story, by providing him with the general and specific antecedents indispensable to the understanding of what happens in it. There are some pieces of information, varying in number and nature from one work to another, that the reader cannot do without. He must usually be informed of the time and place of the action; of the nature of the fictive world peculiar to the work or, in other words, of the canons of probability operating in it; of the history, appearance, traits and habitual behavior of the dramatis personae; and of the relations between them.

In some instances it may indeed seem (though I shall argue this is not the case) that a certain amount of prior information – about the characters and the fictive world – that is not fully contained in the work itself may be assumed beforehand. In Greek drama, for example, the dramatists, restricted to a well-defined field of material, told and retold myths with which their audience was familiar. Whenever the narrative materials are derived from history, it may likewise seem that the communication of at least part of the expositional information may be dispensed with on the assumption that the author takes for granted his reader's possession of a certain amount of common knowledge. [. . .]

Even a number of modern writers may seem to share the expositional privileges or exemptions of their ancient predecessors. I am referring especially to novelists celebrated for their progressive creation of some private, full-fledged fictive world – Trollope's Barchester, Balzac's nineteenth-century France, or Faulkner's Yoknapatawpha County – repeatedly carrying over not only settings but whole casts of characters and clusters of incidents from one work to another of the same cycle. But the same may be true of any series of works, notably detective stories, in which at least one central character recurs (e.g., Agatha Christie's Hercule Poirot), even though the setting of the fictive world varies.

Many critics work on the implicit (and sometimes even explicit) assumption that in all these cases at least part of the expositional antecedents may indeed be taken as known or obtained by the reader outside the limits of the single work, particularly with reference to different stories of the same cycle, which they regard as a single unit. A close examination of the literary evidence, however, indicates that this assumption is untenable. In their contempt for the fatal futility of Fact, writers usually have no scruples about supplementing, modifying, or even distorting historical evidence or tradition to suit their artistic purposes. Shakespeare is notorious for the free use he made of his sources. In *Julius Caesar*, he drastically both simplifies and complicates the history of the two years between Caesar's triumphant return to Rome and the decisive battle at Philippi.[1] [...] Still more audaciously, a popular historical tradition may be initially embodied in the work only to be demolished or reversed at a later stage, as is the case with the gruesome figure of Richard III in Josephine Tey's *The Daughter of Time*.

When a character or a situation is carried over from one work to another, the writer feels no less free to introduce in them any changes dictated by the distinctive artistic conception of the new work. [...] As Malcolm Cowley himself admits, 'as one book leads into another, Faulkner sometimes falls into inconsistencies of detail. . . . Henry Armstid is a likable figure in *As I Lay Dying* and *Light in August*; in *The Hamlet* he is mean and half-demented'; and so on.[2] [...] Whether we are to shrug such changes off as 'inconsequential errors,'[3] as Cowley does, or, as can easily be established, take them to be deliberate and revealing deviations from previous thematic and structural conceptions, it is evident that they constitute or call for new expositional material. [...]

Moreover, notwithstanding general *ex cathedra* declarations to the contrary, writers as a rule take the necessary precautions to render each of their works as expositionally autonomous as possible, even when the carrying over of characters and fictive world involves no divergence from previous conceptions. In the second chapter of Trollope's *Barchester Towers*, for instance, the narrator informs the reader that 'it is hardly necessary that [he] should here give to the public any lengthened biography of Mr. Harding up to the period of the commencement of this tale.' [...] Although Trollope ostensibly professes to assume that Mr. Harding's ordeal, formerly narrated in *The Warden*, must by now be a matter of common knowledge, he in fact cunningly recapitulates the occurrences expositionally relevant to *Barchester Towers*. What was there the core of the action proper is here telescoped into a few passages; and some additional sentences then bring the account up to date and effect the necessary transition to 'the commencement of this tale.' [...]

In conclusion, [...] the limits of a literary unit cannot be fixed *a priori* but are dynamic in that they vary according to the kind of questions the critic poses. [...] Exposition, therefore, can never be dispensed with with impunity; and the peculiar problems it raises must be confronted and solved by every writer, in every work afresh.

The location of exposition

So far I have discussed the distinctive function of the exposition. The question arises, however, whether, bearing in mind this function, we can point to any specific part or parts of a narrative work (or any literary text subsuming a narrative sequence) that can be called 'the exposition.' What is the location of the expositional sections or elements? Is it fixed or variable? And finally, how are the expositional sections or elements to be distinguished from the nonexpositional?

The most detailed and widely accepted theory of exposition is the time-honored view first proposed by Gustav Freytag, whose scheme of dramatic structure includes exposition as an integral part: 'The drama possesses . . . a pyramidal structure. It arises from the *introduction* with the entrance of the exciting forces to the *climax*, and falls from there to the *catastrophe*. Between these three parts lie (the parts of) the *rise* and the *fall*.'[4] An important dramatic effect called the exciting moment or force 'stands between the introduction and the rise': 'the beginning of the excited action (or complication) occurs at a point where, in the soul of the hero, there arises a feeling or volition which becomes the occasion of what follows; or where the counterplay resolves to use its lever to set the hero in motion. . . . In *Julius Caesar* this impelling force is the thought of killing Caesar, which, by the conversation with Cassius, gradually becomes fixed in the soul of Brutus' (pp. 115, 121). [. . .]

Freytag's conception of exposition, however, plausible and tidy-looking as it is, seems to me untenable. Its fatal weakness consists not so much in its limited range of applicability as in its internal inconsistency and its failure to stand up to the facts even when tested against works that are constructed 'pyramidally.' If the function of the exposition is, in Freytag's own words, 'to explain the place and time of the action, the nationality and life relations of the hero' (pp. 117–18), it is hardly possible to prescribe or to determine *a priori* that all authors must invariably choose to locate the expositional information within the first act or before the 'rising action.' And indeed, writers seldom impose on themselves any limitations of this kind. In Ibsen's *Ghosts*, for instance, the exposition is distributed throughout, and new vital facts concerning the past of the agents keep cropping up as late as the last act. But the fallacy can be demonstrated even with reference to the plays. Freytag himself cites

in illustration of his theory. In *Julius Caesar*, he maintains, the exciting force 'is the thought of killing Caesar, which, by the conversation with Cassius [act 1, scene 2], gradually becomes fixed in the soul of Brutus' (p. 121). In fact, the exposition is not concentrated within the limits of the first act, and only a small part of it precedes the impelling moment. Most of the expositional material is widely distributed: one important aspect of Brutus's expositional 'life relations,' his relations with his wife Portia, is 'explained' only in act 2, scene 1, after Brutus has already assumed the leadership of the conspiracy; Caesar's 'life relations' with Calpurnia are dramatically conveyed even later, in act 2, scene 2; while the full disclosure of Antony's relations with Caesar is delayed until his famous soliloquy in act 3, scene 1. These various antecedents ('life relations'), all of them indisputably expositional according to Freytag's definition of the *function* of exposition, turn out to be as indisputably nonexpositional according to his description of its location; and as Freytag's definition of the function of exposition is basically sound, we must conclude that his prescriptive view of its location must be wrong.
[. . .]

The weakness of Freytag's theory of exposition stems, in fact, from a major flaw in his general model of structure. Freytag purports to describe the structure of the action as a movement in time, in a definite direction and through definite stages – in the temporal order in which the reader or audience learns of the developments of the action. But what he really describes is not the movement of the action but the structure of the conflict. He divorces this from the actual temporal movement of the action, presenting a structure that is viewed by the reader only when he retrospectively looks back on the action and rearranges or reassembles it chronologically in his mind. What Freytag and his followers fail to take into account is that the chronological order in which events happen need not necessarily coincide with the order in which they are imparted to the reader. Consequently, the 'absolute,' chronological order of occurrence (in which exposition is indeed preliminary in point of time) does not necessarily correspond with the actual temporal movement or order of presentation of the same events in an actual work, in which expositional information may even be deferred to the last scene or chapter, as it is in Gogol's *Dead Souls* or in the detective story.

In short, as innumerable literary works where the exposition or part of it is either delayed or distributed cannot be fitted into Freytag's Procrustean scheme, his claims about the fixed and static location of exposition must be rejected. The only acceptable theory of exposition will be one flexible enough to hold good equally for all kinds of structure and to cut across the boundaries of genre.

Exposition, fabula and sujet, story and plot

It seems to me possible to define exposition satisfactorily only in terms of fabula, sujet, and scenic norm. The important distinction between fabula and sujet, first proposed by the Russian Formalists,[5] is still amenable to further discrimination and development. A narrative work is composed of myriads of motifs, that is, basic and contextually irreducible narrative units.[6] Examples of such motifs in *The Ambassadors* would be 'Strether reached the hotel at Chester,' 'He found himself facing a lady in the hall,' or 'Waymarsh made a sudden dash into a shop.' The *fabula* of the work is the chronological or chronological-causal sequence into which the reader, progressively and retrospectively, reassembles these motifs; it may thus be viewed as the second-degree 'raw material' (postselected and straightforwardly combined narrative) that the artist compositionally 'deforms' and thus re-contextualizes in constructing his work (mainly by way of temporal displacements, manifold linkage, and perspectival manipulations). The *sujet*, in contrast, is the actual disposition and articulation of these narrative motifs in the particular finished product, as their order and interrelation, shaping and coloring, was finally decided on by the author. To put it as simply as possible, the *fabula* involves what happens in the work as (re)arranged in the 'objective' order of occurrence, while the *sujet* involves what happens in the order, angle, and patterns of presentation actually encountered by the reader.

[...]

Apart from this – to repair a pronounced bias of the Formalists' – one must also take into account that the fabula is equally amenable to manipulations of point of view, a form of artistic deformation and re-contextualization that frequently coincides with and sometimes even accounts for temporal displacements. The author can postulate an omniscient narrator, or compose an epistolary story, or employ any of the characters as the narrator, or record the action as it passes through the consciousness of any or all of them; in each case the temporal order of the motifs, their combination, significance, weight, and coloring will vary. Henry James used to say that there are five million ways of telling a story. He meant, of course, that out of a given, basically similar fabula, five million sujets can be molded, each with its own temporal structure and narrative strategy and consequently with its own peculiar effect on the reader.

[...]

It is accordingly in terms of the distinction between fabula and sujet that I can now redefine my main objection to Freytag's theory – its failure to differentiate the absolute dynamics of the causally propelled action from the variable dynamics of the reading-process. To assert that the first act of any play (or the first few chapters of a novel) contains the exposition is to confuse the beginning of the sujet and that of the fabula. The exposition always constitutes the beginning of the fabula, the first part of the chronologically ordered sequence of motifs as reconstructed by the reader; but it is not necessarily located at the beginning of the sujet. The two beginnings coincide and overlap only when the author presents his tale in a straight chronological sequence (as happens, more or less, in the Book of Job, or in the *Laxdaela Saga*, or in James's *Washington Square*). The author, however, may as legitimately choose to plunge *in medias res* or to distribute the expositional material throughout the work; and in these cases, though the exposition is still located at the beginning of the fabula, its position in the order actually devised to present the motifs to the reader radically varies.

Represented time and representational time: the quantitative indicator

So far I have defined exposition as the 'beginning' or 'first part' of the fabula. This definition, however, though it firmly establishes the expositional *terminus a quo* and though it flexibly covers the innumerable possibilities of combining and ordering a given number of motifs, may still be regarded as seriously incomplete unless we can determine exactly up to what point in the fabula the motifs are expositional. To discover this elusive line of demarcation, we must first consider more of the time values of fiction (time as a dimension, object and indicator of artistic selection as well as of combination and ordering) and the important role they play in guiding the reader's interpretation of the work.

Narrative presents characters in action during a certain fictive period of time. As a rule, however, one finds that the author has not treated the whole of the fictive period in the life of the characters with the same degree of attention. This period falls naturally or is artificially divided into different subperiods, stages, or time-sections. Some of these are rendered at great length, some galloped through or rapidly summarized, some dismissed with a perfunctory sentence or two, while others are even passed over unmentioned. Even within the framework of a single work, therefore, we generally discover different ratios of *represented time* (i.e., the duration of a projected period in the life of the characters) to *representational time* (i.e., the time that it takes the reader, by the clock, to peruse that part of the text projecting this fictive period).

[...]

The differentiation between what I call representational and represented time dates back, in fact, to the Renaissance and the Neo-Classical age, during which it was exclusively employed as a normative tool for checking the adherence of dramatists to the so-called Aristotelian unity of time. Castelvetro, for example, distinguishes 'perceptible time' from 'intellectual time', and Dryden denounces the practice of 'mak[ing] too great a disproportion betwixt the imaginary time of the play, and the real time of its representation.' The concern with time-ratios has, moreover, been revived in modern criticism. Various German scholars distinguish *'erzählte Zeit'* from *'erzählzeit'*; and A. A. Mendilow elaborates a similar distinction between 'the chronological duration of the novel' and 'the chronological duration of the reading.' I believe, however, that these various pairs of terms have not been sufficiently exploited. They have traditionally been used mainly to indicate the ratio between the representational and the represented time of the work *as a whole* – 'the time it takes to read a novel' as against 'the length of the time covered by the content of the novel' – and also the disparities between different works in this regard, but less often to investigate the variations in time-ratios within a single work. And even when such variations have been pointed out, this has usually been done in order to discuss their implications for the work's tempo or its narrative rhythm. I certainly agree that a comparison of the time-ratios in different works may yield highly significant results, some of which will be referred to below. [...] It is, however, at least equally important to trace the variations in time-ratio within the limits of a single work as well; for these variations not only lead the reader to various 'formal' conclusions (as to tempo) but at the same time play a central role in the interpretation of the text.

The reader is always confronted and frequently baffled by such questions as, Who is the protagonist or center of interest in the work? What is the relative importance of the various characters, incidents and themes? And how do they combine with the center? He is obliged to pose and answer dozens of questions of this sort if he is to construct, or reconstruct, the work's structure and hierarchy of meaning and to compose a fully integrated picture of its art. However, these questions are never settled explicitly and satisfactorily by the text itself, even when overt rhetoric is employed – not even when the author refers to one of the characters as 'my hero' or openly calls the reader's attention to the role played by a certain incident or agent. The reader is therefore forced to follow the multifarious implications of the text (its dramatized rhetoric) as to its peculiar principles of selection and combination in order to work

out adequate answers. The *quantitative indicator*, revealing the
principles of selection operating in the text, forms one of the reader's
indispensable guides in the process of interpretation in that it helps
him to determine the text's general tendency ('intention') and its
particular structure of meaning. For owing to the selectivity of art,
there is a logical correlation between the amount of space devoted
to an element
and the degree of its aesthetic relevance or centrality, so that there
is a good prima facie case for inferring the latter from the
former.

As the variations in time-ratios form one manifestation of the
quantitative indicator, it can be determined that, *mutatis mutandis*,
the time-ratio of a narrative time-span or event generally stands in
direct proportion to its contextual relevance: one whose
representational time approximates its represented time is implied to
be more central to the work in question than another in which these
two time factors are incommensurate.
[. . .]

It is quite understandable that different writers, each with his own
conception of life and poetics of art, should differ as to what fields of
material merit (thorough) treatment. But the reader finds himself in
an altogether different situation. Qua reader, he has no private
artistic axe to grind. His only business is to endeavor to grasp the
nature and functions of the compositional principles operating in
the text, so that he may comprehend as fully as possible its structure
of meaning. Having this in view, he cannot apply to the work any
scale of intrinsic interest (including his own), because there is not a
single one that is universally valid. He must, therefore, measure the
value of narrative elements in terms of contextual significance, largely
suggested by the quantitative indicator.[7] [. . .] Laurence Sterne, for
example, demonstrates his acute awareness of the functionality of his
seemingly bizarre selective procedure when he claims that 'the
happiness of the Cervantic humour arises from this very thing – of
describing silly and trifling Events, with the Circumstantial Pomp
of great Ones.'

Fielding himself was, in fact, well aware of the value-determining
aspect of the temporal variations, though in his polemical impetus
against what seemed to him Richardson's petty psychological
preoccupations he at times tended to overstate his plea to the contrary.
Regardless of the overt motivation of his selective decisions, they are
actually based not on the ostensible criterion of intrinsic interest
versus dullness but on that of artistic relevance versus irrelevance, as
he himself is driven to admit openly immediately after the muff
incident in *Tom Jones*:

Though this incident will probably appear of little consequence to many of our readers, yet trifling as it was, it had so violent an effect on poor Jones that we thought it our duty to relate it. In reality, there are many little circumstances too often omitted by injudicious historians, from which events of the utmost importance arise. [. . .]

(5.4)

Quantitative indicator, scenic norm, and fictive present

The quantitative indicator is also an indispensable factor in the delimitation of the exposition, especially in determining the precise temporal point in the fabula which marks the end of the exposition.

As argued above, the literary artist exploits the possibilities of varying the time-ratios in order to throw the contextual centrality of certain fictive periods into high relief against the background of other periods belonging to the total span of the sujet. It is thus the approximation of representational to represented time that draws the reader's attention to some subperiods constituting 'discriminated occasions' in the [Jamesian] sense of the word. And vice versa: the very disparity between the different time-ratios (and the greater it is the more conspicuously significant it becomes) suggests that the cursorily treated time-sections are non-discriminated because they are meant to occupy but a relatively minor position in the particular structure of meaning established by the work.

Moreover, in most fictional (and dramatic) works we find not only variations but also a basic similarity between the time-ratios of the various scenes or discriminated occasions. Every narrative establishes a certain scenic time-norm of its own. This norm may, of course, vary from one writer, and even from one work, to another. And even within a single work certain scenes may turn out to deviate from the basic time-norm established by the majority of the discriminated occasions. But such deviations (say, a ratio of 2:3 or even 1:5 where the norm is 1:2), which may indeed appear considerable when examined in isolation, generally prove insignificant when considered, as they must be, in the context of the whole work – in the light of the nonscenic as well as the scenic time-ratios. [. . .]

Since every work does establish a scenic norm and since the scenic treatment accorded to a fictive time-section underscores its high aesthetic importance, the first scene in every work naturally assumes a special conspicuousness and significance. The author's finding it to be the first time-section that is 'of consequence enough' to deserve full scenic treatment turns it, implicitly but clearly, into a conspicuous signpost, signifying that this is precisely the point in time that the author has decided, for whatever reason, to make the reader regard as the beginning of the action proper. That is, the text suggests, why this 'occasion' is the first to have been so 'discriminated.' [...] If, therefore, the first discriminated occasion is the beginning of what Trollope happily calls 'the real kernel of [the] story,'[8] it follows that any motif that antedates it in time (i.e., precedes it in the fabula) is expositional – irrespective of its position in the sujet.

The expositional material, always antedating the first scene, may correspondingly precede it in point of its actual position in the sujet. In this case, the large disparity between the time-ratio of the expositional part and that of the opening scene (a disparity concomitant with several other indicators, to be discussed) lays bare the preparatory nature of whatever precedes the temporal signpost. The communication of the expositional material, however, may also be delayed, so that it will succeed the first discriminated occasion in its actual ordering. In this case, the expositional information will retrospectively throw light on it, that is, enrich, modify or even drastically change the reader's understanding of it; for, within the sharply circumscribed, enclosed world of the literary text, almost every motif or occurrence antedating another tends to illuminate it in some way, no matter what their order of presentation in the sujet. The point marking the end of the exposition in the fabula thus coincides with that point in time which marks the beginning of the *fictive present* in the sujet – the beginning of the first time-section that the work considers important enough to be worthy of such full treatment as will involve, according to the contextual scenic norm, a close approximation or correspondence between its representational time and the clock-marked time we employ in everyday life.

It will be noticed that I dissociate my use of the term *fictive present* from any dependence on dramatic or fictive illusion, with which it is usually thought to be interchangeable.

[...]

If we grasp 'fictive present' as a descriptive metaphor denoting an indisputably objective ratio between representational time and represented time, a ratio that involves an approximation of the two times; and if this approximation is interpreted as aiming to achieve (to adopt Mendilow's own phrase in another context) a 'closer correspondence between the pace of living ... and [the] depiction of it',[9] then we shall be able to account for the possibility that a

113

temporal transfer takes place at such a point by referring to the objective compositional elements that may produce it.
[. . .]

Notes

1. See ERNEST SCHANZER, *The Problem Plays of Shakespeare* (London, 1966), chap. 2.

2. MALCOLM COWLEY, ed., *The Portable Faulkner* (New York, 1954), pp. 7–8.

3. Ibid., p. 8. Cowley, significantly enough, adds in the same sentence that these inconsistencies are 'afterthoughts rather than oversights.'

4. GUSTAV FREYTAG, *Technique of the Drama*, trans. Elias J. MacEwan (Chicago, 1908; first published 1863), pp. 114–15.

5. See especially BORIS TOMASHEVSKI's 'Thématique,' in *Théorie de la littérature*, ed. Tzvetan Todorov (Paris, 1965), pp. 240–2; part of this essay has been reprinted in *Russian Formalist Criticism: Four Essays*, ed. Lee T. Lemon and Marion J. Reis (Lincoln, Nebr., 1965). Strangely enough, Tomashevsky himself gives but an indifferent account of exposition, neither fully exploiting the terms he himself suggests nor taking into account the complex of time-problems involved (e.g., the fictive present).
    Historically, as I have argued elsewhere, the distinction between *fabula* and *sujet* is already implicit in the Aristotelian view of 'whole' as against 'mythos' ('Elements of Tragedy and the Concept of Plot in Tragedy: On the Methodology of Constituting a Generic Whole,' *Hasifrut* 4 [1973]: 23–69); and it was later formulated in the prevalent Renaissance and Neo-classical opposition of the 'natural order' (employed by historians) and the 'artificial order' (distinctive of literary art). There is no doubt that in the hands of the Russian Formalists some of the practical implications of this fundamental distinction were brought out more impressively than ever before; and that is why I am using *fabula* and *sujet* here rather than the more ancient terminology or, as is the fashion nowadays, some new terminology of my own. But I should perhaps warn the reader that in view of various theoretical and methodological weaknesses from which I believe the Formalist position(s) on this issue suffer, my account of these terms significantly diverges from theirs at a number of points. I should be held responsible only for the distinctions as explicitly defined in this chapter and further developed and demonstrated throughout the argument.

6. This conception of 'motif' must be sharply distinguished from that of many folklorists and literary critics, who refer by this term to a recurrent, and sometimes migratory, thematic unit, often reducible to smaller units (e.g., the victory of the Cinderella or the son's quest for his father). As used here, *motif* primarily designates an irreducible narrative unit, which may or may not recur. Cf. Tomashevski, 'Thématique,' pp. 268–9.

7. The reader may of course find this contextually determined scale false or stereotyped or trivial – that is, not compatible with what he or any other reader holds intrinsically significant in life or art or both. But this is already a question of evaluation, which should not affect the interpretative procedure leading him to the normative conclusion.

8. ANTHONY TROLLOPE, *Is He Poperjoy?*, chap. 1.

9. A. A. MENDILOW, *Time and the Novel* (London, 1952), p. 73.

6 Focalization*

Mieke Bal

The fragment reprinted below is part of the subsection on 'Focalization' in chapter 7 of *Narratology*, devoted to the analysis of the story level (Genette's 'narrative'). Genette, in his *Narrative Discourse*, corrected preceding theories of narrative point of view, like those of Norman Friedman and Wayne Booth, separating the functions of focalizer – who sees – and narrator – who tells. Bal refines Genette's theory of focalization, developing, for example, the difference between the subject and the object of focalization and assigning an autonomous role to the focalizer. This is perhaps the most controversial aspect of her theory. Her insistence that focalization is the most subtle means of manipulating the information presented to the reader and the most difficult to spot gives preeminence to a function that had consistently been overlooked by the critics until Genette (1972), thus opening up a whole range of possibilities for microscopic analysis of all kinds of narrative, including film, where focalization is carried out by the camera and the actors' gaze.

Narratology became the most accessible introduction to narratology in English soon after its publication in 1985. It is an attempt at formulating an overall theory of narrative, integrating previous work by structuralist critics in the areas of action sequences, the trait analysis of characters and setting, temporal structures, point of view, narrative voice, the addressee, and so on. There are other books in the same line, such as Mieke Bal's own *Narratologie*, published in French in 1977, Gerald Prince's *Narratology* and Steven Cohan and Linda Shires's *Telling Stories*.

Difficulties

Whenever events are presented, they are always presented from within a certain 'vision.' A point of view is chosen, a certain way of

---

*Mieke Bal, *Narratology: Introduction to the Theory of Narrative*. Trans. Christine van Boheemen (Toronto: University of Toronto Press, 1985), pp. 100–14. First publ. as *De Theorie van vertellen en verhalen* (1980).

seeing things, a certain angle, whether 'real' historical facts are concerned or fictitious events. It is possible to try and give an 'objective' picture of the facts. But what does that involve? An attempt to present only what is seen or is perceived in some other way. All comment is shunned and implicit interpretation is also avoided. Perception, however, is a psychological process, strongly dependent on the position of the perceiving body; a small child sees things in a totally different way from an adult, if only as far as measurements are concerned. The degree to which one is familiar with what one sees also influences perception. When the Central American Indians first saw horsemen, they did not see the same things we do when we see people riding. They *saw* gigantic monsters, with human heads and four legs. These had to be gods. Perception depends on so many factors that striving for objectivity is pointless. To mention only a few factors, one's position with respect to the perceived object, the fall of the light, the distance, previous knowledge, psychological attitude towards the object; all this and more affects the picture one forms and passes on to others. In a story, elements of the fabula are presented in a certain way. We are confronted with a vision of the fabula. What is this vision like and where does it come from? These are the questions that will be discussed in these subsections. I shall refer to the relations between the elements presented and the vision through which they are presented with the term *focalization*. Focalization is, then, the relation between the vision and that which is 'seen', perceived. By using this term I wish to dissociate myself from a number of current terms in this area, for reasons which I shall now explain.

The theory of narration, as it has been developed in the course of this century, offers various labels for the concept here referred to. The most current one is *point of view* or *narrative perspective*. Narrative situation, narrative viewpoint, narrative manner are also employed. [. . .] All these typologies have proved more or less useful. They are all, however, unclear on one point. They do not make an explicit distinction between, on the one hand, the vision through which the elements are presented and, on the other, the identity of the voice that is verbalizing that vision. To put it more simply: they do not make a distinction between *those who see* and *those who speak*. Nevertheless, it is possible, both in fiction and in reality, for one person to express the vision of another. This happens all the time [. . .]

The existing typologies have achieved solid respectability in current literary criticism. There must be an explanation for this: their evident usefulness. All offer interesting possibilities, despite the objection just mentioned. I am of the opinion, however, that their distinctions should be adapted to the insight that the agent that sees must be given a status other than that of the agent that narrates.

If we examine the current terms from this point of view, only the term *perspective* seems clear enough. This label covers both the physical and the psychological points of perception. It does not cover the agent that is performing the action of narration, and it should not do so. Nevertheless, my own preference lies with the term *focalization* for two reasons. [...] The first reason concerns tradition. Although the word 'perspective' reflects precisely what is meant here, it has come to indicate in the tradition of narrative theory both the narrator and the vision. [...]

There is yet another, more practical, objection to this term. No substantive can be derived from 'perspective' that could indicate the subject of the action. [...] *Focalization* offers a number of extra, minor advantages as well. It is a term that looks technical. It is derived from photography and film; its technical nature is thus emphasized. [...]

The Focalizor

In Southern India, at Mahaballipuram, is what is said to be the largest *bas-relief* of the world, the seventh-century *Arjuna's penance*. At the upper left, the wise man Arjuna is depicted in a yoga position. At the bottom right stands a cat [in the same position]. Around the cat are a number of mice. The mice are laughing. It is a strange image. Unless the spectator interprets the signs. The interpretation runs as follows. Arjuna is in a yoga position and is meditating to win Lord Siva's favour. The cat, impressed by the beauty of absolute calm, imitates Arjuna. Now the mice realize they are safe. They laugh. Without this interpretation, there is no relation between the parts of the relief. Within this interpretation the parts form a coherent narrative.

The picture is a comical one, in addition to being a real comic. The comical effect is evoked by the narrativity of the picture. The spectator sees the relief as a whole. Its contents include a succession in time. First, Arjuna assumes the yoga position. Then, the cat imitates him. After that, the mice start laughing. These three successive events are logically related in a causal chain. According to every definition I know, that means this is a fabula.

But there is more. Not only are the events chronologically in succession and logically in a causal relation. They can only occur through the semiotic activity of the actors. And the comical effect can only be explained when this particular mediation is analysed. We laugh because we can identify with the mice. Seeing what they see, we realize with them that a meditating cat is a contradiction; cats hunt, and only wise men meditate. Following the chain of events in reverse, we also arrive at the next one by perceptual identification. The cat has brought about the event for which he is responsible because he has seen Arjuna do something. This chain of perceptions also runs in time. The wise man sees nothing since he is totally absorbed in his meditation; the cat has seen Arjuna and now sees nothing more of this world; the mice see the cat *and* Arjuna. That is why they know they are safe. (Another interpretation is that the cat is simulating; this doesn't weaken my statements but only adds an element of suspense to the fabula.) The mice are laughing because of that very fact, finding the imitation a ridiculous enterprise. The spectator sees more. S/he sees the mice, the cat and the wise man. S/he laughs at the cat, and s/he laughs sympathetically with the mice, whose pleasure is comparable to that felt by a successful scoundrel.

This example, paradoxical because it is not linguistic, illustrates quite clearly the theory of focalization. We can view the picture of the relief as a (visual) sign. The elements of this sign, the standing Arjuna, the standing cat, the laughing mice, only have spatial relations to one another. The elements of the fabula – Arjuna assumes a yoga position, the cat assumes a yoga position, the mice laugh – do not form a coherent significance as such. The relation between the sign (the relief) and its contents (the fabula) can only be established by mediation of an interjacent layer, the view of the events. The cat sees Arjuna. The mice see the cat. The spectator sees the mice who see the cat who has seen Arjuna. And the spectator sees that the mice are right. Every verb of perception (*to see*) in this report indicates an activity of focalization. Every verb of action indicates an event.

Focalization is the relationship between the 'vision,' the agent that sees, and that which is seen. This relationship is a component of the story part, of the content of the narrative text: A says that B sees what C is doing. Sometimes that difference is void, e.g. when the reader is presented with a vision as directly as possible. The different agents then cannot be isolated, they coincide. That is a form of 'stream of consciousness.' Consequently, focalization belongs in the story, the layer in between the linguistic text and the fabula. Because the definition of focalization refers to a relationship, each pole of that relationship, the subject and the object of focalization, must be studied separately. The subject of focalization, the *focalizor*, is the point from which the elements are viewed. That point can lie with a character (i.e. an element of the fabula), or outside it. If the focalizor coincides with the character, that character will have a technical advantage over the other characters. The reader watches with the character's eyes and will, in principle, be inclined to accept the vision presented by that character. In Mulisch's *Massuro*, we see with the eyes of the character who later also draws up a report of the events. The first symptoms of Massuro's strange disease are the phenomena which the other perceives. These phenomena communicate Massuro's *condition* to us, they tell us nothing about the way he feels about it. Such a character-bound focalizor, which we could label, for convenience's sake, CF, brings about *bias* and *limitation*. In Henry James's *What Maisie Knew* the focalization lies almost entirely with Maisie, a little girl who does not understand much about the problematic relations going on around her. Consequently, the reader is shown the events through the limited vision of the girl, and only gradually realizes what is actually going on. But the reader is not a little girl. S/he does more with the information s/he receives than Maisie does, s/he interprets it differently. Where Maisie sees only a strange gesture, the reader knows that s/he is dealing with an erotic one. The difference between the childish vision of the events and the interpretation that the adult reader gives to them determines the novel's special effect.

Character-bound focalization (CF) can vary, can shift from one character to another. In such cases, we may be given a good picture of the origins of a conflict. We are shown how differently the various characters view the same facts. This technique can result in neutrality towards all the characters. Nevertheless, there usually is never a doubt in our minds which character should receive most attention and sympathy. On the grounds of distribution, for instance the fact that a character focalizes the first and/or the last chapter, we label it the hero(ine) of the book.

When focalization lies with one character which participates in the fabula as an actor, we could refer to *internal* focalization. We can then indicate by means of the term *external* focalization that an anonymous agent, situated outside the fabula, is functioning as focalizor. Such an external, non-character-bound focalizor is abbreviated EF. In the following fragment from the opening of Doris Lessing's *The Summer before the Dark* we see the focalization move from EF to CF.

a   A woman stood on her back step, arms folded, waiting.
     Thinking? She would not have said so. She was trying to catch hold of something, or to lay it bare so that she could look and define; for some time now she had been 'trying on' ideas like so many dresses off a rack. She was letting words and phrases as worn as nursery rhymes slide around her tongue:

> for towards the crucial experiences custom allots certain attitudes, and they are pretty stereotyped. A yes, first love! . . . Growing up is bound to be painful! . . . My first child, you know. . . . But I was in love! . . . Marriage is a compromise. . . . I am not as young as I once was.

From sentence two onwards the contents of what the character experiences are given. A switch thus occurs from an external focalizor (EF) to an internal one (CF). An alternation between external focalizors, between EF and CF, is visible in a good many stories. In *The Evenings*, Frits is the only character that functions as focalizor. Therefore, the two different focalizors are EF and CF-Frits. A number of characters can also alternate as CF focalizor; in that case, it can be useful to indicate the various characters in the analysis by their initials, so that one can retain a clear overview of the division of focalization: in Frits' case, this would mean the notation CF (Fr). An example of a story in which a great many different characters act as focalizor is *Of Old People*. However, the characters do not carry an equal load; some focalize often, others only a little, some do not focalize at all. It is also possible for the entire story to be focalized by EF. The narrative can then appear objective, because the events are not presented from the point of view of the characters. The focalizor's bias is, then, not absent, since there is no such thing as 'objectivity,' but it is unclear.

The Focalized Object

In *Of Old People* Harold is usually the focalizor when the events in the Indies are being focalized; Lot often focalizes his mother, mama Ottilie, and it is mainly because of this that we receive a fairly likeable image of her despite her unfriendly behaviour. Evidently, it is important to ascertain which character focalizes which object. The combination of a focalizor and a focalized object can be constant to a large degree (Harold-Indies; Lot-mama Ottilie), or it can vary greatly. Research into such fixed or loose combinations is of importance because the image we receive of the object is determined by the focalizor. Conversely, the image a focalizor presents of an object says something about the focalizor itself. Where focalization is concerned, the following questions are relevant.

1 *What* does the character focalize: what is it aimed at?
2 *How* does it do this; with what attitude does it view things?

3   *Who* focalizes it: whose focalized object is it?

What is focalized by a character F? It need not be a character. Objects, landscapes, events, in short all the elements are focalized, either by an EF or by a CF. Because of this fact alone, we are presented with a certain, far from innocent, interpretation of the elements. The degree to which a presentation includes an *opinion* can, of course, vary: the degree to which the focalizor points out its interpretative activities and makes them explicit also varies. Compare, for instance, the following descriptions of place:

b   Behind the round and spiny forms around us in the depth
    endless coconut plantations stretch far into the hazy blue distance
    where mountain ranges ascended ghostlike. Closer, at my side,
    a ridged and ribbed violet grey mountainside stretches upward
    with a saw-tooth silhouette combing the white cloudy sky. Dark
    shadows of the clouds lie at random on the slopes as if
    capricious dark-grey pieces of cloth have been dropped on them.
    Close by, in a temple niche, Buddha sits meditating in an
    arched window of shadow. A dressing-jacket of white exudation
    of bird-droppings on his shoulders. Sunshine on his hands
    which lie together perfectly at rest.
                                                (Jan Wolkers, *The Kiss*)

c   Then we must first describe heaven, of course. Then the
    hundreds of rows of angels are clad in glorious shiny white
    garments. Everyone of them has long, slightly curly fair hair
    and blue eyes. There are no men here. 'How strange that all
    angels should be women.' There are no dirty angels with
    seductive panties, garterbelts and stockings, not to mention bras.
    I always pictured an angel as a woman who presents her breasts
    as if on saucers, with heavily made up eyes, and a bright red
    mouth, full of desire, eager to please, in short, everything a
    woman should be. (Formerly, when I was still a student, I
    wanted to transform Eve into a real whore. I bought her
    everything necessary, but she did not want to wear the stuff.)
                    (J. M. A. Biesheuvel, *The Way to the Light*, 'Faust')

In both cases, a CF is clearly involved; both focalizors may be localized in the character 'I'. In *b*, the spatial position of the CF ('I') is especially striking. It is obviously situated on a high elevation, considering the wide prospect it has. The words 'around us,' combined with 'in the depths,' stress that high position. The proximity of the niche with the Buddha statue makes clear that CF ('I') is situated in an eastern temple (the Burubudur in fact), so that 'the round and spiny form' (must) refer to the temple roof. The presentation of the whole, temple roof and landscape, seems fairly impersonal. If the CF ('I') had not been identified itself by the use of the first-person personal pronoun in 'at my side' and 'around us,' this would have seemed, on the face of it, an 'objective' description, perhaps taken from a pamphlet or a geography book.

On closer analysis, this proves not to be the case. Whether the CF ('I') is explicitly named or not, the 'internal' position of the focalizor is, in fact, already established by expressions such as 'close by,' 'closer,' and 'at my side,' which underline the vicinity between the place and the perceiver. 'Behind' and 'far into' indicate a specification of the spatial perspective (in the pictorial sense). But more happens here. Without appearing to do so, this presentation *interprets*. This is clear from the use of metaphors, which points to the facts that the CF ('I') attempts to reduce the objects it sees, which impress it a great deal, to human, everyday proportions. In this way, the CF ('I') is undoubtedly trying to fit the object into its own realm of experience. Images like 'sawtooth' and 'combing,' capricious dark-grey pieces of cloth,' and clichés like 'mountain ranges' bear this out. The 'dressing-jacket of white exudation of bird-droppings' is the clearest example. Actually, the image is also interesting because of the association mechanism it exhibits. With the word 'dressing-jacket,' the Buddha's statue becomes human, and as soon as it is human, the white layer on its head could easily be dandruff, a possibility suggested by the word 'exudation.' The realistic nature of the presentation – CF ('I') does 'really' *see* the landscape – is restored immediately afterwards by the information about the real nature of the white layer: bird-droppings. Thus, what we see here is the presentation of a landscape which is realistic, reflecting what is actually perceived, and at the same time interpreting the view in a specific way, so that it can be assimilated by the character.

Example *c* exhibits to a certain extent the same characteristics. Here, too, an impressive space is humanized However, the CF ('I') observes the object less and interprets it more. It concerns a fantasy object with which the CF ('I') is sketchily familiar from religious literature and painting, but which it can adapt as much as it wishes, to its own taste. This is what it does, and its taste is clear. Here, too, an association mechanism is visible. From the traditional image of angels, implied in the second or third sentence, the CF ('I') moves to the assumption that angels are women. In this, the vision already deviates from the traditional vision, in which angels are asexual or male.

Against the image thus created of asexual male angels, the CF ('I') sets up, in contrast, its own female image, which by now has moved very far away from the image that we have of angels.

And even before the reader realizes that in doing so a link is made with another tradition, that of the opposition angel-whore, in which 'angel' is used in a figurative sense, the word 'whore' itself appears in the text. In this, the interpretive mode of the description manifests itself clearly. The solemn 'we' of the beginning contrasts sharply with the personal turn which the description takes. The humour is here based on the contrast between the solemn-impersonal and the personal-everyday. The interpretive focalization is emphasized in several ways. The sentence in quotation marks is presented as a reaction to the sentence preceding it. Here, the interpreting focalizor makes an explicit entrance. Later this is stressed again: 'not to mention' is a colloquial expression, and points at a personal subject, expressing an opinion: 'I always pictured an angel as . . .' accentuates even more strongly that a personal opinion is involved.

The way in which a subject is presented gives information about that object itself and about the focalizor. These two descriptions give even more information about the CFs ('I') than about the object; more about the way they experience nature (*b*) or women (*c*), respectively, than about the Burubudur temple and heaven. In principle, it doesn't matter whether the object 'really exists' in actuality, or is part of a fictitious fabula, or whether it is a fantasy created by the character and so a doubly fictitious object. The comparison with the object referred to served in the above analysis only to motivate the interpretation by the CF ('I') in both fragments. The internal structure of the descriptions provides in itself sufficient clues about the degree to which one CF ('I') showed similarity to and differed from the other.

These two examples indicate yet another distinction. In *c* the object of the focalization was perceptible. The CF ('I') 'really' sees something that is outside itself. This is not always the case. An object can also be visible only inside the head of the CF. And only those who have access to it can perceive anything. This cannot be another character, at least not according to the classical rules of the narrative genre, but it might possibly be an EF. Such a 'non-perceptible' object occurs in cases where, for instance, the contents of a character's dream are presented. Concerning the heaven in *c*, we can only decide whether that object is perceptible or not perceptible when we know how the fragment fits into its context. If the 'I', together with another person – a devil, for instance – is on an excursion to heaven, we will have to accept the first part of the description, until the sentence in quotation marks, as 'perceptible.' Thus, our criterion is that within the fabula there must be another character present that can also perceive the object; if they are the dreams, fantasies, thoughts, or feelings of a character, then these objects can be part of the category 'non-perceptible' objects. This distinction can be indicated by adding to the notation of the focalizor a 'p' or an 'np.' For *a* we end up with CF (woman)–np; for *b*, CF ('I')–p, and for *c*, CF ('I')–np. This distinction too is of importance for an insight into the power-structure between the characters. When in a conflict situation one character is allotted both CF–p and CF–np, and the other exclusively CF–p, then the first character has the advantage as a party in the conflict. It can give the reader insight into its feelings and thoughts, while the other character cannot communicate anything. Moreover, the other character will not have the insight which the reader receives, so that it cannot react to the feelings of the other (which it does not know), cannot adapt itself to them or oppose them. Such an inequality in position between characters is obvious in the so-called 'first-person novels,' but in other kinds this inequality is not always as clear to the reader. Yet the latter is manipulated by it in forming an opinion about the various characters. Consequently, the focalization has a strongly manipulative effect. Colette's novel *La Chatte* is a strong case: the reader is manipulated by this device into taking the man's side against his wife.

In this respect, it is important to keep sight of the difference between spoken and unspoken *words* of the characters. Spoken words are audible to others and are thus perceptible when the focalization lies with someone else. Unspoken words – thoughts, internal monologues – no matter how extensive, are not perceptible to other characters. Here, too, lies a possibility for manipulation which is often used. Readers are given elaborate information about the thoughts of a character, which the other characters do not hear. If these thoughts are placed in between the sections of dialogue, readers do not often realize how much less the other character knows than they do. An analysis of the perceptibility of the focalized objects supplies insight into these objects' relationships.

Levels of Focalization

Compare the following sentences:

  d Mary participates in the protest march.
  e I saw that Mary participated in the protest march.
  f Michele saw that Mary participated in the protest march.

In all three sentences it is stated that Mary participated in the protest march. That is a clearly perceptible fact. We assume that there is an agent which is doing the perceiving, and whose perceptions are being presented to the reader. In *e* this is an 'I', in *f* it is Michele. In *d* no party is indicated. Consequently, we assume that there is an external focalizor situated outside the fabula. This could be an EF or a CF ('I'), which remains implicit in this sentence but manifests itself elsewhere. We can thus analyse:

d EF–p
e CF ('I')–p
f CF (Michele)–p

The dash indicates the relation between the subject and the object of focalization. However, the difference between these sentences has not yet been expressed completely. Sentences *e* and *f* are complex sentences. The focalization, too, is complex. The analysis, as it is given here, only applies to the subordinate clause. In *e* it is stated that 'I' saw, and in *f* that Michele saw. Who focalized that section? Either an EF or a CF. We can only conclude that from the rest of the story. For *e* the possibilities are:

1   EF–[np CF ('I')–p]: an external focalizor focalizes CF ('I'), which sees. 'Seeing' is a non-perceptible action, in contrast to 'looking,' so the complex focalized object is np. That object consists itself of a focalizor, CF ('I'), which sees something that is perceptible.
2   CF ('I')–[np CF ('I')–p], a so-called 'first-person narrative,' in which the external focalizor remembers afterwards that at a certain moment in the fabula, it saw Mary participating in a protest march.

The first possibility exists in theory, but will not easily occur, unless the sentence is in direct speech, and the CF ('I') can be identified as one of the persons speaking (temporarily). In *f* only the first formula is possible: EF–[np CF (Michele)–p]. This is easy to see once we realize that a personal focalizor cannot perceive a non-perceptible object, unless it is part of that object, is the same 'person'.

Two conclusions can be drawn from this. Firstly, it appears that various focalization *levels* can be distinguished; secondly, where the *focalization level* is concerned, there is no fundamental difference between a 'first-person narrative' and a 'third-person narrative.' When EF seems to 'yield' focalization to a CF, what is really happening is that the vision of the CF is being given within the all-encompassing vision of the EF. In fact, the latter always keeps the focalization in which the focalization of a CF may be embedded as object. This too is explicable in terms of the general principles of narratology. When we try to reflect someone else's point of view, we can only do so in so far as we know and understand that point of view. That is why there is no difference in focalization between a so-called 'first-person narrative' and a 'third-person narrative'. [. . .] In a so-called 'first-person narrative' too an external focalizor, usually the 'I' grown older, gives its vision of a fabula in which it participated earlier as an actor, from the outside. At some moments it can present the vision of its younger alter ego, so that a CF is focalizing on the second level.

One remark about the notation of these data. If we wish to include the question of levels in the analysis, we can do so in an elaborate manner, as I have done here. That is useful if we wish to know what the relationship between the various focalizors is like: who allows whom to watch whom? If, however, we are only concerned with the relationship between the subject and the object of the focalization – for instance, in *e* between CF ('I') and Mary, or in *f* between CF (Michele) and Mary – then it is easier to remind ourselves of the fact that we are dealing with an embedded focalization, because at any moment the narrative may return to the first level. In that case, it is simple to indicate the level with a number following the F. For *e* this would be: CF2 ('I')–p and for *f* CF2 (Michele)–p.

If we summarize briefly what has preceded, it appears that the three sentences each differ one from another, in various ways. There is always *one* sentence which differs from the other two. Thus *d* differs from *e* and *f* in focalization level. Consequently focalization in *d* is singular and in *e* and *f* it is complex. And *d* and *e* differ from *f* as far as 'person' is concerned. In both cases it can be an EF or a CF ('I'). Finally, *d* and *f* differ from *e* because in *e* an EF cannot simply be assumed without doubt. This is only possible if the sentence is in direct speech.

We assume, therefore, a first level of focalization (F1) at which the focalizor is external. This external focalizor delegates focalization to an internal focalizor, the focalizor on the second level (F2). In principle there are more levels possible. In these sample sentences it is clear *where* the focalization is transferred from the first to the second level. The verb form 'saw' indicates that. Such markers of shifts in level we call *coupling signs*. There are signs which indicate the shift from one level to another. These signs can remain implicit. Sometimes we are forced to deduce them from other, less clear information. In example *b*, the description of the view on *and* from the Burubudur, we needed the preceding passage to find the sign with which the shift was indicated explicitly. In *c* a whole sentence – 'Then we must first describe heaven of course' – is used to indicate that the internal CF is now going to give its own vision of heaven. Verbs like 'see' and 'hear,' in short all verbs that communicate perception, can function as explicit coupling signs.

There is yet another possibility. The external EF can also *watch along with* a person, without leaving focalization entirely to a CF. This happens when an object (which a character can perceive) is focalized, but nothing clearly indicates whether it is actually perceived. This procedure is comparable to free indirect speech, in which the narrating party approximates as closely as possibly the character's own words without letting it speak directly. [...] An example of such a 'free indirect' focalization, or rather, ambiguous focalization, is the beginning of the story 'Lady with Lapdog' by Chekhov.

g 1 The appearance on the front of a new arrival – a lady with a lapdog – became the topic of general conversation. 2 Dmitri Dmitrich Gurov, who had been a fortnight in Yalta and got used to its ways, was also interested in new arrivals. 3 One day, sitting on the terrace of Vernet's restaurant, he saw a young woman walking along the promenade; she was fair, not very tall, and wore a toque; behind her trotted a white pomeranian.

4 Later he came across her in the park and in the square several times a day. 5 She was always alone, always wearing the same toque, followed by the white pomeranian, no one knew who she was, and she became known simply as the lady with the lapdog.

This fragment as a whole is focalized by an external EF. In the third sentence a shift of level takes place, indicated by the verb 'to see.' In sentence 4, level one has been restored. But in sentence 5 it is ambivalent. This sentence follows the one in which it was stated that Dmitri meets the lady regularly. The description of the lady which follows would, according to our expectation, have to be focalized by that character: CF2 (Dmitri)–p, but there is no indication which signals that change of level. In the second part of the sentence focalization clearly rests again with EF1. The first part of sentence 5 may be focalized both by EF1 as by CF2. Such a double focalization, in which EF 'looks over the shoulder' of CF, we may indicate with the double notation EF1/CF2. Such a part of the story might be called *hinge*, a fragment with a double, or at any rate ambiguous, focalization in between two levels. It is also possible to distinguish between *double* focalization, which can be represented as EF1+CF2, and *ambiguous*

127

focalization, in which it is hard to decide who focalizes: EF1/CF2. In *g* this difference cannot be established. In view of the development of the rest of the story EF1+CF2 seems most likely.

[...]

7 The Time of Narrating (Erzählzeit) and Narrated Time (Erzählte Zeit)*

PAUL RICŒUR

Ricœur's work as a whole provides a bridge between narratology, contemporary theology and existential philosophy. He is one of the most important practitioners of the hermeneutic philosophy inaugurated by Heidegger in his *Being and Time*. Like Heidegger, Ricœur considers that the experience of time is constitutive of human reality. In the section from *Time and Narrative* reprinted here, Ricœur takes up Günther Müller's distinction between 'Erzählzeit' and 'erzählte Zeit' and compares it to Gérard Genette's structuralist work on the interpretation of time in fiction. Although Müller's and Genette's approaches are widely different, they coincide in articulating their analyses of fictional time at two levels: the time of the act of narrating and the time that is narrated. In addition to these two kinds of time, Ricœur proposes a third one that is not intrinsically textual: the time of life. In other words, his analysis of the conjunctions/disjunctions of time runs along a threefold axis: utterance – statement – world. Ricœur argues that the analysis of this third category of time, generated by the writer's selection, pacing and distribution of the most meaningful sequences, captures some important experiential aspects of narratives which are left out by formalist approaches.

With this distinction introduced by Günther Müller and taken up again by Gérard Genette, we enter into a problematic that [...] does not seek in the utterance itself an internal principle of differentiation that would be apparent in the distribution of the tenses, but instead looks for a new key for interpreting time in fiction in the distinction *between* utterance and statement.

It is of the utmost importance to state, without further delay, that [...] Müller introduces a distinction that is not confined to within discourse. It opens onto a *time of life* which is not unlike the reference

---

*PAUL RICŒUR, *Time and Narrative* vol. 2. Trans. Kathleen McLaughlin and David Pellauer (Chicago: University of Chicago Press, 1985), pp. 77–88, 178–82. First publ. as *Temps et récit* II (Paris: Seuil, 1984).

to a narrated world in Weinrich. This feature does not carry over in Genette's structural narratology and can only be pursued in a meditation belonging to a hermeneutics of the world of the text. [. . .] For Genette, the distinction between the time of the utterance and the time of the statement is maintained within the bounds of the text, without any kind of mimetic implication.

My aim is to show that Genette is more rigorous than Müller in his distinction between two narrative times, but that Müller, at the cost perhaps of formal coherence, preserves an opening that is left to us to exploit. What we require is a three-tiered scheme: utterance–statement–world of the text, to which correspond a time of narrating, a narrated time, and a fictive experience of time projected by the conjunction/disjunction between the time it takes to narrate and narrated time. Neither of these two authors replies exactly to this need. Müller does not clearly distinguish the second from the third level, and Genette eliminates the third level in the name of the second one.

I am going to attempt to reorder these three levels by means of a critical examination of these two analyses, to which I am indebted for what are, at times, opposite reasons.

The philosophical context in which Müller introduces the distinction between *Erzählzeit* and *erzählte Zeit* is very different from that of French structuralism. This framework is that of a 'morphological poetics,'[1] directly inspired by Goethe's meditations on the morphology of plants and animals.[2] The reference of art to life, which constantly underlies this morphological poetics can only be understood within this context. As a result, the distinction presented by Müller is condemned to oscillate between an overall opposition of narrative to life and a distinction internal to narrative itself. His definition of art allows both these interpretations: 'narrating is presentifying [*vergegenwärtigen*] events that are not perceptible to the listener's senses' (p. 247). It is in this act of presentification that the fact of 'narrating' and the thing 'narrated' are distinguished. This is therefore a phenomenological distinction by reason of which every narrating is narrating something (*erzählen von*), yet something which itself is not a narrative. From this basic distinction follows the possibility of distinguishing two times: the time taken to narrate and narrated time. But what is the correlate of presentification to which narrated time corresponds? Here we find two answers. On the one hand, what is narrated and is not narrative is not itself given in flesh and blood in the narrative but is simply 'rendered or restored' (*Wiedergabe*). On the other hand, what is narrated is essentially the 'temporality of life' (p. 251). However, 'life does not narrate itself, it is lived' (p. 254). Both these interpretations are assumed by the following statement: 'every narrating is narrating something that is not a narrative but a life process' (p. 261). Every narrative since the *Iliad* narrates this flowing (*Fliessen*): 'je mehr Zeitlichkeit des Lebens, desto reinere Epik' – 'the richer life is in temporality, the purer the epic' (p. 250).

Let us keep for later discussion this apparent ambiguity concerning the status of narrated time, and let us turn toward the aspects of the division into the time of narrating and narrated time that result from a morphological poetics.

Everything stems from the observation that narrating is, to use an expression borrowed from Thomas Mann, 'setting aside' (*aussparen*), that is, both choosing and excluding.[3] We should thus be able to submit to scientific investigation the various modes of 'folding' (*Raffung*) by means of which the time of narrating is separated from narrated time. More precisely, comparing the two times truly becomes the object of a science of literature once literature lends itself to measurement. Whence comes the idea of a metric comparison of the two times in question. This idea of a metric comparison of the two times seems to have come from a reflection on Fielding's narrative technique in *Tom Jones*. It is Fielding, the father of the novel that recounts the growth and development of a character, who concretely posed the technical question of *Erzählzeit*. As a master, conscious of playing with time, he devotes each of his eighteen books to temporal segments of varying lengths – from several years to several hours – slowing down or speeding up, as the case may be, omitting one thing or emphasizing another. If Thomas Mann raised the problem of *Aussparung*, Fielding preceded him by consciously modulating the *Zeitraffung*, the unequal distribution of narrated time in the time of narrating.

However, if we measure something, just what are we measuring? And is everything measurable here?

What we are measuring, under the name of *Erzählzeit*, is, as a matter of convention, a chronological time, equivalent to the number of pages and lines in the published work by reason of the prior equivalence posited between the time elapsed and the space covered on the face of a clock. It is by no means, therefore, a question of the time taken to compose the work. To what time is the number of pages and lines equivalent? To a conventional time of reading that is hard to distinguish from the variable time of actual reading. The latter is an interpretation of the time taken to tell the story which is comparable to the interpretation that a particular orchestra conductor gives to the theoretical time of performing a piece of music.[4]

131

Once these conventions are admitted, we may say that narrating requires 'a fixed lapse of physical time' that the clock measures. What is then compared are indeed 'lengths' of time, both with respect to the now measurable *Erzählzeit* as well as to narrated time, which is also measured in terms of years, days, and hours.

Can everything now be measured by means of these 'temporal compressions'? If the comparison of times were limited to the comparative measurement of two chronologies, the inquiry would be most disappointing – although, even reduced to these dimensions, it leads to surprising and frequently neglected conclusions (so great is the attention paid to thematics that the subtleties of this strategy of double chronology have been largely overlooked). These compressions do not consist only in abbreviations along a variable scale. They also consist in skipping over dead time, in precipitating the progress of the narrative by a staccato rhythm in the expression (*Veni, vidi, vici*), in condensing into a single exemplary event iterative or durative features ('every day,' 'unceasingly,' 'for weeks,' 'in the autumn,' and so on). Tempo and rhythm thus enrich, in the course of the same work, the variations of the relative lengths of the time of narration and the time narrated. Taken together, all these notations contribute to outlining the narrative's *Gestalt*. And this notion of a *Gestalt* opens the way for investigations into structural aspects further and further removed from linearity, sequence, and chronology, even if the basis continues to be the relation between measurable time-lapses.

In this respect, the three examples used in Müller's essay 'Erzählzeit and Erzählte Zeit,' namely, Goethe's *Wilhelm Meisters Lehrejahre*, Virginia Woolf's *Mrs. Dalloway*, and Galsworthy's *Forsyte Saga*, are examined with an extraordinary minuteness, which makes these analyses models worthy of imitation.

By the choice of method, this investigation is based in each instance on the most linear aspects of narrativity but is not confined to them. The initial narrative schema is that of sequence, and the art of narrating consists in restoring the succession of events (*die Wiedergabe des Nacheinanders*) (p. 270).[5] The remarks that shatter this linearism are therefore all the more precious. The narrative tempo, in particular, is affected by the way in which the narration stretches out in descriptions of scenes as if they were tableaux or speeds up through a series of strong, quick beats. Like Braudel the historian, we must not speak of time as being simply long or short, but as rapid or slow. The distinction between 'scenes' and 'transitions,' or 'intermediary episodes,' is also not strictly quantitative. The effects of slowness or of rapidity, of briefness or of being long and drawn out are at the borderline of the quantitative and the qualitative. Scenes that are narrated at length and separated by brief transitions or iterative summaries – Müller calls them 'monumental scenes' – carry the narrative process along, in contrast to those narratives in which 'extraordinary events' form the narrative skeleton. In this way, non-quantifiable structural relations add complexity to the *Zusammenspiel* at play between two time-spans. The arrangement of scenes, intermediary episodes, important events, and transitions never ceases to modulate the quantities and extensions. To these features are added anticipations and flashbacks, the interlinkings that enable the memory of vast stretches of time to be included in brief narrative sequences, creating the effect of perspectival depth, while breaking up chronology. We move even further away from a strict comparison between lengths of time when, to flashbacks, are added the time of remembering, the time of dreaming, and the time of the reported dialogue, as in Virginia Woolf. Qualitative tensions are thus added to quantitative measurements.

What is it, then, that inspires in this way the transition from the analysis of the measurement of time-spans to an evaluation of the more qualitative phenomenon of contraction? It is the relation of the time of narration to the time of life through narrated time. Here Goethe's meditation comes to the fore: life in itself does not represent a whole. Nature can produce living things but these are indifferent (*gleichgültig*). Art can produce only dead things, but they are meaningful. Yes, this is the horizon of thinking: drawing narrated time out of indifference by means of the narrative. By saving or sparing and compression, the narrator brings what is foreign to meaning (*sinnfremd*) into the sphere of meaning. Even when the narrative intends to render what is senseless (*sinnlos*), it places this in relation to the sphere of making sense (*Sinndeutung*).

Therefore if we were to eliminate this reference to life, we would fail to understand that the tension between these two times stems from a morphology that at one and the same time resembles the work of formation/transformation (*Bildung-Umbildung*) active in living organisms and differs from it by elevating meaningless life to a meaningful work by the grace of art. It is in this sense that the comparison between organic nature and poetic work constitutes an irreducible component of poetic morphology.

If, following Genette, we may call the relation between the time of narrating and the narrated time in the narrative itself a 'game with time,' this game has as its stakes the temporal experience (*Zeiterlebnis*) intended by the narrative. The task of poetic morphology is to make apparent the way in which the quantitative relations of time agree with the qualities of time belonging to life itself. Conversely, these temporal qualities are brought to light only by the play of derivations and insertions, without any thematic meditation on time having to be grafted onto them, as in Laurence Sterne, Joseph Conrad, Thomas Mann, or Marcel Proust. A fundamental time is implied, without itself being considered as a theme. Nevertheless, this time of life is 'codetermined' by the relation and the tension between the two times of the narrative and by the 'laws of form' that result from them. In this respect, we might be tempted to say that there are as many temporal 'experiences' as poets, even as poems. This is indeed the case, and this is why this 'experience' can only be intended obliquely through the 'temporal armature,' as what this armature is suited to, what it fits. It is clear that a discontinuous structure suits a time of dangers and adventures, that a more continuous, linear structure suits a *Bildungsroman* where the themes of growth and metamorphosis predominate, whereas a jagged chronology, interrupted by jumps, anticipations, and flashbacks, in short, a deliberately multidimensional configuration, is better suited to a view of time that has no possible overview, no overall internal cohesiveness. Contemporary experiments in the area of narrative techniques are thus aimed at shattering the very experience of time. It is true that in these experiments the game itself can become the stakes. But the polarity of temporal experience (*Zeiterlebnis*) and temporal armature (*Zeitgerüst*) seems inescapable.

In every case, an actual temporal creation, a 'poietic time' (p. 311) is uncovered on the horizon of each 'meaningful composition' (p. 308). This temporal creation is what is at stake in the structuration of time at play between the time of narrating and narrated time.

Utterance, Statement, and Object in Genette's Narrative Discourse

Günther Müller's *Morphologische Poetik* has in the end left us with three times: the time of the act of narrating, the time that is narrated, and finally the time of life. The first is a chronological time; it is a time of reading rather than of writing. We can measure only its spatial equivalent, which is counted by the number of pages and lines. Narrated time, for its part, is counted in years, months, and days and may even be dated in the work itself. It is, in turn, the result of the 'compression' of a time 'spared' or 'set aside,' which is not narrative but life. The nomenclature Gérard Genette proposes is also ternary.[6] But it cannot, for all this, be superimposed upon Müller's. It results from the effort of structural narratology to derive all of its categories from features contained in the text itself, which is not the case for Müller with respect to the time of life.

134

Genette's three levels are determined starting from the middle level, the narrative statement. This is the narrative properly speaking. It consists in relating real or imaginary events. In written culture this narrative is identical with the narrative text. The narrative statement, in its turn, stands in a twofold relation. In the first place, the statement is related to the object of the narrative, namely, the events recounted, whether they be fictitious or real. This is what is ordinarily called the 'told' story. (In a similar sense, the universe in which the story takes place can be termed 'diegetic.') Secondly, the statement is related to the act of narrating taken in itself, to the narrative 'utterance.' (For Ulysses, recounting his adventures is just as much an action as is massacring the pretenders.) A narrative, we shall therefore say, tells a story, otherwise it would not be a narrative. And it is proffered by someone, otherwise it would not be discourse. 'As a narrative, it lives by its relationship to the story that it recounts; as discourse, it lives by its relationship to the narrating that utters it' (*Narrative Discourse*, p. 29).[7]

[...]

The relation to Günther Müller is complex. The distinction between *Erzählzeit* and *erzählte Zeit* is retained by Genette but is entirely made over. This reworking results from the difference in status of the levels to which temporal features are ascribed. In Genette's terminology the diegetic and the utterance designate nothing external to the text. The relation between the statement and what is recounted is assimilated to the relation between signifier and signified in Saussurean linguistics. What Müller calls life is therefore set out of bounds. Utterance, for its part, does indeed come out of the self-referential character of discourse and refers to the person who is narrating. Narratology, however, strives to record only the marks of narration found in the text.

A complete redistribution of temporal features results from this reorganization of the levels of analysis. First, the *Zeiterlebnis* is set out-of-bounds. All that remain are the relations internal to the text between utterance, statement, and story (or diegetic universe). It is to these relations that the analyses of a model text are devoted, Proust's *Remembrance of Things Past*.

[...]

What is the time of the narrative, if it is neither that of the utterance nor that of the diegesis? Like Müller, Genette holds it to be the equivalent of and the substitute for the time of reading, that is, the time it takes to cover or traverse the space of the text: 'the narrative text, like every other text, has no other temporality than what it borrows, metonymically, from its own reading' (*Narrative Discourse*, p. 34). We must, therefore, take 'for granted and accept literally the quasi-fiction of the *Erzählzeit*, this false time standing in for a true time and to be treated – with the combination of reservation and approval that this involves – as a *pseudo-time*' (p. 79, his emphasis).[8]

I shall not take up in detail Genette's analysis of the three essential determinations – order, duration, frequency – in terms of which the relations between the time of the story and the pseudo-time of narrative can be studied. In these three registers, what is meaningful are the discordances between the temporal features of the events in the diegesis and the corresponding features in the narrative.

With respect to order, these discordances may be placed under the general heading of anachrony.[9] The epic narrative, since the *Iliad*, is noted in this regard for the way it begins *in medias res* and then moves backward in order to explain events. In Proust, this procedure is used to oppose the future, become present, to the idea one had of it in the past. [. . .] Whether it is a question of completing the narration of an event by bringing it into the light of a preceding event, of filling in an earlier lacuna, or provoking involuntary memory by the repeated recalling of similar events, or of correcting an earlier interpretation by means of a series of reinterpretations – Proustian analepsis is not a gratuitous game. It is governed by the meaning of the work as a whole.[10] This recourse to the opposition between meaningful and unmeaningful opens a perspective on narrative time that goes beyond the literary technique of anachrony.[11]

The uses of prolepsis within a globally retrospective narrative seems to me to illustrate even better than analepsis this relation to overall meaning opened by narrative understanding. Some prolepses take a particular line of action to its logical conclusion, to the point of rejoining the narrator's present. Others are used to authenticate the narrative of the past through testimony to its persistence in current memory ('today, I can still see . . .'). [. . .]

Taking an overall view of the anachronies in Proust's *Recherche*, Genette declares that 'the importance of the "anachronic" narrative in *Recherche du temps perdu* is obviously connected to the retrospectively synthetic character of Proustian narrative, which is totally present in the narrator's mind at every moment. Ever since the day when the narrator in a trance perceived the unifying significance of his story, he never ceases to hold all of its places and all of its moments, to be capable of establishing a multitude of "telescopic" relations amongst them' (p. 78). But must we not then say that what narratology takes as the pseudo-time of a narrative is composed of the set of temporal strategies placed at the service of a conception of time that, first articulated in fiction, can also constitute a paradigm for redescribing lived and lost time?

Genette's study of the distortions of duration leads me to the same reflections. I shall not go back over the impossibility of measuring the duration of the narrative, if by this is meant the time of reading (p. 86). Let us admit with Genette that we can only compare the respective speeds of the narrative and of the story, the speed always being defined by a relation between a temporal measure and a spatial one. In this way, in order to characterize the speeding up or slowing down of the narrative in relation to the events recounted, we end up comparing, just as Müller did, the duration of the text, measured by pages and lines, with the duration of the story measured by clock time. As in Müller, the variations – here called 'anisochronies' – have to do with large narrative articulations and their internal chronology, whether expressly given or inferred. We may then apportion the distortions in speed between the drastic slowing down of 'pauses' and the dramatic acceleration of ellipses by situating the classical notion of a 'scene' or 'description' alongside that of a pause, and that of a 'summary' alongside of that of an ellipsis.[12] A highly detailed typology of the comparative dimensions of the length of the text and the duration of the narrated events can then be sketched out. However, what seems to me to be important is that narratology's mastery of the strategies of acceleration and slowing down serves to enhance our understanding of procedures of emplotment that we have acquired through our familiarity with the procedures of emplotment and the function of such emplotment procedures. For example, Genette notes that in Proust the fullness (and hence the slow pace of the narrative, which establishes a sort of coincidence between the length of the text and the time taken by the hero to be absorbed by a spectacle) is closely related to the 'contemplative halts' (p. 102) in the hero's experience.[13] Likewise, the absence of a summary narrative, the absence of descriptive pauses, the tendency of the narrative to constitute itself as a scene in the narrative sense of this term, the inaugural character of the five major scenes – morning, dinner, evening – which by themselves take up some six hundred pages, the repetition that transforms them into typical scenes; all these structural features of *Remembrance of Things Past* – features that leave intact none of the traditional narrative movements (p. 112), features that can be discerned, analyzed, and classified by an exact narratological science – receive their meaning from the sort of temporal immobility created by the narrative on the level of fiction.

However, the modification that gives the narrative temporality of *Remembrance* 'a completely new cadence – perfectly unprecedented' (ibid.) is certainly the iterative character of the narrative, which narratology places under the third temporal category, that of frequency (recounting once or n times an event that occurs once or n times) and that it sets in opposition to the 'singulative' narrative.[14] How is this 'intoxication with the iterative' (p. 123) to be interpreted? The strong tendency of instants in Proust to merge together and become confused with one another is, Genette grants, 'the very condition for experiencing "involuntary memory" ' (p. 124). And yet in this exercise of narratology, it is never once a question of this experience. Why?

If the memory experience of the narrator-hero is so easily reduced to a mere 'factor in (I should say rather a means of) the emancipation of the narrative with respect to temporality' (p. 156), this is in part because the inquiry concerning time has been until this point artificially contained within the limits of the relation between the stated narrative and the diegesis, at the expense of the temporal aspects of the relationship between statement and utterance, described in terms of the grammatical category of 'voice.'

Postponing any discussion of the time of the narration is not without its drawbacks. For example, we cannot understand the meaning of the reversal by which, at the turning point in Proust's work, the story, with its steady chronology and the predominance of the singulative, takes control over the narrative, with its anachronisms and its iterations, if we do not attribute the distortions of duration, which then take over, to the narrator himself, 'who in his impatience and growing anguish is desirous both of *loading* his final scenes . . . and of jumping to the denouement . . . that will finally give him being and legitimate his discourse' (p. 157, his emphasis). Within the time of the narrative must therefore be integrated 'another temporality, no longer the temporality of the narrative but in the final instance governing it: the temporality of the narrating itself' (ibid.).

What, then, may be said about the relation between utterance and statement? Does it possess no temporal character at all? The basic phenomenon whose textual status can be preserved here is that of the 'voice,' a notion borrowed from grammarians and one that characterizes the implication of the narration itself in the narrative, that is, of the narrative instance (in the sense in which Benveniste speaks of the instance of discourse) with its two protagonists: the narrator and the real or virtual receiver. If a question about time arises at this level of relation, it is insofar as the narrative instance, represented in the text by the voice, itself presents temporal features.

If the time of utterance is examined so briefly and so late in *Narrative Discourse*, this has in part to do with the difficulties involved in establishing the proper order of the relations between utterance, statement, and story, but more importantly, it has to do with the difficulty that, in *Remembrance*, is connected to the relation between the real author and the fictive narrator, who here happens to be the same as the hero, the time of narration displaying the same fictive quality as the role of the narrator-hero's 'I' calls for an analysis that is, precisely, an analysis of voice. Indeed, if the act of narration does not carry within itself any mark of duration, the variations in its distance from the events recounted is important for 'the narrative's significance' (p. 216). In particular, the changes referred to above concerning the temporal dimension of the narrative find a certain justification in these variations. They make us feel the gradual shortening of the very fabric of the narrative discourse, as if, Genette adds, 'the story time tended to dilate and make itself conspicuous while drawing near to its end, *which is also its origin*' (p. 226, his emphasis). The fact that the time of the hero's story approaches its own source, the narrator's present, without being able to catch up with it, is part of the meaning of the narrative, namely that it is ended or at least broken off when the hero becomes a writer.

Its recourse to the notion of the narrative voice allows narratology to make a place for subjectivity, without confusing this with the subjectivity of the real author. If *Remembrance* is not to be read as a disguised autobiography, this is because the 'I' uttered by the narrator-hero is itself fictive. However, for lack of a notion like that of a world of the text (a notion I shall justify in the next chapter), this recourse to the notion of narrative voice is not sufficient to do justice to the fictive experience the narrator-hero has of time in its psychological and metaphysical dimensions.

Without this experience, which is just as fictive as the 'I' who unfolds it and recounts it, and yet which is worthy of being called 'experience' by virtue of its relation to the world projected by the work, it is difficult to give a meaning to the notions of time lost and time regained, which constitute what is at stake in *Remembrance of Things Past.*[15]

[...]

Over and above the discussion of the interpretation of *Remembrance* proposed by Genette, the question remains whether, in order to preserve the *meaning* of the work, it is not necessary to subordinate the narrative technique to the *intention* that carries the text beyond itself, toward an experience, no doubt feigned but nonetheless irreducible to a simple game with time. To pose this question is to ask whether we must not do justice to the dimension that Müller, recalling Goethe, named *Zeiterlebnis*, and that narratology, by decree and as a result of its strict methodology, sets out of bounds. The major difficulty is then to preserve the fictive quality of this *Zeiterlebnis*, while resisting its reduction to narrative technique alone.

[...]

Notes

1. *Morphologische Poetik*, ed. Elena Müller (Tubingen: Niemeyer, 1968) is the title that was adopted by Gunther Müller for a collection of his essays dating from 1964–8.

2. It is worth recalling that Propp was also inspired by Goethe.

3. The term *Aussparung* emphasizes both what is omitted (life itself, as we shall see) and what is retained, chosen, or picked out. The French word *épargne* sometimes has these two meanings: what is spared is what is available to someone and it is also what is not touched, as when we say that a village was spared by (*épargné par*) the bombing. The word 'savings' (*l'épargne*), precisely, includes what is put aside for one to make use of and what is left aside and sheltered.

4. Müller is somewhat ill at ease in speaking of this time of the narrative in itself, which is neither narrated nor read, a sort of disembodied time, measured by the number of pages, in order to distinguish it from the time of reading, to which each reader contributes his own *Lesetempo* (ibid., p. 275).

5. For example, the study of Goethe's *Lehrejahre* begins with a comparison between the 650 pages taken as 'the measure of the physical time required by the narrator to tell his story' (ibid., p. 270) and the eight years covered by the narrated events. It is, however, the incessant variations in relative lengths that create the work's tempo.

6. GÉRARD GENETTE, 'Frontiers of Narrative,' in *Figures of Literary Discourse*, trans. Alan Sheridan (New York: Columbia University Press, 1982), pp. 127–44; *Narrative Discourse: An Essay in Method*, trans. Jane E. Lewin (Ithaca, NY: Cornell University Press, 1980); *Nouveau Discours du récit* (Paris: Seuil, 1983).

7. Narrative theory has never, in fact, stopped oscillating between bipartition and tripartition. The Russian formalists recognize the distinction between *sjužet* and *fabula*, the subject and the tale. For Schklovsky, the tale designates the material used in forming the subject; the subject of *Eugene Onegin*, for example, is the elaboration of the tale, and hence a construction. Cf. *Théorie de la littérature. Textes des formalistes russes*, collected, presented, and translated by Tzvetan Todorov, Preface by Roman Jakobson (Paris: Seuil, 1965), pp. 54–5. Tomashevski adds that the development of the tale may be characterized as 'the passage from one situation to another' (ibid., p. 273). The subject is what the reader perceives as resulting from the techniques of composition (ibid., p. 208). In a similar sense, Todorov himself makes a distinction between discourse and story ('Les catégories du récit littéraire'). Bremond uses the terms 'narrating narrative' and 'narrated narrative' (*Logique de récit*, p. 321, no. 1). Cesare Segre, however, proposes the triad: discourse (signifier), plot (the signified in the order of literary composition), and fabula (the signified in the logical and chronological order of events) (*Structures and Time: Narration, Poetry, Models*, trans. John Meddemmen (Chicago: University of Chicago Press,

1979)). It is thus time, considered as the irreversible order of succession, that serves as the discriminating factor. The time of discourse is that of reading, the time of plot that of the literary composition, and the time of the fabula that of the events recounted. On the whole, the pairs subject/tale (Schklovsky, Tomashevski), discourse/story (Todorov), and narrative/story (Genette) correspond rather well. Their reinterpretation in Saussurean terms constitutes the difference between the Russian and the French formalists. Ought we to say then that the reappearance of a tripartition (in Cesare Segre and Genette himself) marks the return to a Stoic triad: what signifies, what is signified, what occurs?

8. We might wonder in this regard if the time of reading, from which the time of the narrative is borrowed, does not belong for this reason to the plane of utterance, and if the transposition brought about through the metonymy does not conceal this filiation by projecting onto the plane of the statement what rightfully belongs to the plane of utterance. In addition, I would not call this a pseudo-time, but precisely a fictive time, so closely is it tied, for narrative understanding, to the temporal configurations of fiction. I would say that the fictional is transposed into the pseudo when narrative understanding is replaced by the rationalizing simulation that characterizes the epistemological level of narratology, an operation that I reemphasize once again is both legitimate and of a derivative nature. *Nouveau Discours du récit* makes this more precise: 'the time of the (written) narrative is a "pseudo-time" in the sense that it exists empirically for the reader of a text-space that only reading can (re)convert into duration' (ibid., p. 15).

9. The study of anachronies (prolepsis, analepsis, and their combinations) may be superimposed rather easily on Harald Weinrich's study of 'perspective' (anticipation, retrospection, zero degree).

10. I refer the reader here to the lovely page in *Narrative Discourse* where Genette evokes Marcel's general 'play' with the principal episodes of his existence, 'which until then were lost to significance because of their dispersion and are now suddenly reassembled, now made significant by being bound all together. . . . chance, contingency, arbitrariness now suddenly wiped out, his life's portrait is now suddenly "captured" in the web of a structure and the cohesiveness of a meaning' (ibid., pp. 56–67).

11. The reader cannot help comparing this remark by Genette to Müller's use of the notion of *Sinngehalt*, discussed above, as well as the opposition between meaningful and unmeaningful (or indifferent) inherited from Goethe. This opposition, in my opinion, is entirely different from the opposition between signifier and signified coming from Saussure.

12. The notion of *Raffung* in Müller, therefore, finds an equivalent here in that of acceleration.

13. 'The duration of these contemplative halts is generally such that it is in no danger of being exceeded by the duration of the reading (even a very slow reading) of the text that "tells of" them' (ibid., p. 102).

14. In his *Maupassant*, Greimas introduces the same categories of the iterative and the singulative, and, in order to account for them, adopts the grammatical category of 'aspect.' The alternation of iterative and singulative also forms a parallel with Weinrich's category of 'putting into relief.'

15. We ought to be able to say of the metaphysical experience of time in *Remembrance of Things Past* exactly what Genette says of the 'I' of the book's hero, namely, that he is neither entirely Proust nor entirely another. This is by no means a 'return to the self,' a 'presence to the self' that would be

postulated by an experience expressed in the fictional mode, but instead a 'semi-homonymy' between real experience and fictive experience, similar to that which the narratologist discerns between the hero-narrator and the work's signatory (cf. ibid., pp. 251–2).

Part Three

Narrative structure: text

8 Types of Narration*

WAYNE C. BOOTH

Wayne C. Booth devotes chapter 6 of *The Rhetoric of Fiction* to an analysis of the different types of narration theoretically available. As he explains, earlier classifications of point of view, such as Norman Friedman's 'Point of View' (1955), are simplistic in that they are exclusively based on the notions of first/third-person narration and the degree of omniscence of the narrator. Although these notions are important, he contends, further refinements should be made. He proposes a differentiation between real author, implied author, narrator, characters and readers. The implied author is the real author's literary version of him/herself. The narrator is the mediating instance between author and reader, the one who tells. Figuratively placed between implied author and characters in the narrative chain, the narrator may be closer to one or to the others. Impersonal or 'undramatized' narrators, who try to efface themselves from their narration, are often difficult to distinguish from the implied author. 'Dramatized' narrators, that is, narrators with a well-developed personality, are more easily perceptible in their own right. These may choose to participate in the action as characters or 'narrator-agents', or to stand apart as mere 'observers'. Narrators can participate in the action in different ways according to the moral, physical and/or temporal distance separating them from the other characters and/or from the author and reader. Thus, narrator-agents can be further classified as 'reliable' or 'unreliable' – if their opinions and values coincide or clash with those of the others – and they can also be 'isolated' or 'supported' by other narrators in the story. Finally, all kinds of narrators can choose to be omniscient – including free access to the minds of the characters, which is the most interesting kind of omniscience, according to Booth – or to limit their knowledge to what could be learned by natural means or inference, thus producing a realism-enhancing effect.

*WAYNE C. BOOTH, *The Rhetoric of Fiction* (Chicago: University of Chicago Press, 1961), pp. 149–64.

145

Booth's typology constituted a landmark in the analysis of the narrative instance. Although some of his categories are not clearly defined and his terminology is often tentative or misleading (for example, he often forgets his own distinction between real author, implied author and narrator), he nevertheless coined key concepts, like 'implied author', 'unreliable narrator' and 'distance', that would provide the basis for the more systematic typologies of narratologists like Genette, Bal and Stanzel.

We have seen that the author cannot choose to avoid rhetoric; he can choose only the kind of rhetoric he will employ. He cannot choose whether or not to affect his readers' evaluations by his choice of narrative manner; he can only choose whether to do it well or poorly. As dramatists have always known, even the purest of dramas is not purely dramatic in the sense of being entirely presented, entirely shown as taking place in the moment. There are always what Dryden called 'relations' to be taken care of, and try as the author may to ignore the troublesome fact, 'some parts of the action are more fit to be represented, some to be related.'[1] But related by whom? The dramatist must decide, and the novelist's case is different only in that the choices open to him are more numerous.

If we think through the many narrative devices in the fiction we know, we soon come to a sense of the embarrassing inadequacy of our traditional classification of 'point of view' into three or four kinds, variables only of the 'person' and the degree of omniscience. If we name over three or four of the great narrators – say Cervantes' Cide Hamete Benengeli, Tristram Shandy, the 'I' of *Middlemarch*, and Strether, through whose vision most of *The Ambassadors* comes to us, we realize that to describe any of them with terms like 'first-person' and 'omniscient' tells us nothing about how they differ from each other, or why they succeed while others described in the same terms fail. It should be worth our while, then, to attempt a richer tabulation of the forms the author's voice can take. [...]

Person

Perhaps the most overworked distinction is that of person. To say that a story is told in the first or the third person[2] will tell us nothing of importance unless we become more precise and describe how the particular qualities of the narrators relate to specific effects. It is true that choice of the first person is sometimes unduly limiting; if the 'I' has inadequate access to necessary information, the author may be led into improbabilities. And there are other effects that may dictate a choice in some cases. But we can hardly expect to find useful criteria in a distinction that throws all fiction into two, or at most three, heaps. In this pile we see *Henry Esmond*, 'A Cask of Amontillado,' *Gulliver's Travels*, and *Tristram Shandy*. In that, we have *Vanity Fair*, *Tom Jones*, *The Ambassadors*, and *Brave New World*. But in *Vanity Fair* and *Tom Jones* the commentary is in the first person, often resembling more the intimate effect of *Tristram Shandy* than that of many third-person works. And again, the effect of *The Ambassadors* is much closer to that of the great first-person novels, since Strether in large part 'narrates' his own story, even though he is always referred to in the third person.

Further evidence that this distinction is less important than has often been claimed is seen in the fact that all of the following functional distinctions apply to both first- and third-person narration alike.

Dramatized and undramatized narrators

Perhaps the most important differences in narrative effect depend on whether the narrator is dramatized in his own right and on whether his beliefs and characteristics are shared by the author.

The implied author (the author's 'second self'). – Even the novel in which no narrator is dramatized creates an implicit picture of an author who stands behind the scenes, whether as stage manager, as puppeteer, or as an indifferent God, silently paring his fingernails. This implied author is always distinct from the 'real man' – whatever we may take him to be – who creates a superior version of himself, a 'second self', as he creates his work.

In so far as a novel does not refer directly to this author, there will be no distinction between him and the implied, undramatized narrator; in Hemingway's 'The Killers,' for example, there is no narrator other than the implicit second self that Hemingway creates as he writes.

Undramatized narrators. – Stories are usually not so rigorously impersonal as 'The Killers'; most tales are presented as passing through the consciousness of a teller, whether an 'I' or a 'he.' Even in drama much of what we are given is narrated by someone, and we are often as much interested in the effect on the narrator's own mind and heart as we are in learning what *else* the author has to tell us. When Horatio tells of his first encounter with the ghost in *Hamlet*, his own character, though never mentioned, is important to us as we listen. In fiction, as soon as we encounter an 'I,' we are conscious of an experiencing mind whose views of the experience will come between us and the event. When there is no such 'I,' as in

'The Killers,' the inexperienced reader may make the mistake of thinking that the story comes to him unmediated. But no such mistake can be made from the moment that the author explicitly places a narrator into the tale, even if he is given no personal characteristics whatever.

Dramatized narrators. – In a sense even the most reticent narrator has been dramatized as soon as he refers to himself as 'I,' or, like Flaubert, tells us that 'we' were in the classroom when Charles Bovary entered. But many novels dramatize their narrators with great fulness, making them into characters who are as vivid as those they tell us about (*Tristram Shandy, Remembrance of Things Past, Heart of Darkness, Dr. Faustus*). In such works the narrator is often radically different from the implied author who creates him. The range of human types that have been dramatized as narrators is almost as great as the range of other fictional characters – one must say 'almost' because there are some characters who are not fully qualified to narrate or 'reflect' a story (Faulkner can use the idiot for *part* of his novel only because the other three parts exist to set off and clarify the idiot's jumble).*

We should remind ourselves that many dramatized narrators are never explicitly labeled as narrators at all. In a sense, every speech, every gesture, narrates; most works contain disguised narrators who are used to tell the audience what it needs to know, while seeming merely to act out their roles.

Though disguised narrators of this kind are seldom labeled so explicitly as God in Job, they often speak with an authority as sure as God's. Messengers returning to tell what the oracle said, wives trying to convince their husbands that the business deal is unethical, old family retainers expostulating with wayward scions – these often have more effect on us than on their official auditors; the king goes ahead with his obstinate search, the husband carries out his deal, the hell-hound youth goes on toward hell as if nothing had been said, but we know what we know – and as surely as if the author himself of his official narrator had told us. [. . .]

The most important unacknowledged narrators in modern fiction are the third-person 'centers of consciousness' through whom authors have filtered their narratives. Whether such 'reflectors,' as James sometimes called them, are highly polished mirrors reflecting complex mental experience, or the rather turbid, sense-bound 'camera eyes' of much fiction since James, they fill precisely the function of avowed narrators – though they *can* add intensities of their own. [. . .]

---

*Benjy, in *The Sound and the Fury* [editor's note].

Observers and narrator-agents

Among dramatized narrators there are mere observers (the 'I' of *Tom Jones, The Egoist, Troilus and Criseyde*), and there are narrator-agents, who produce some measurable effect on the course of events (ranging from the minor involvement of Nick in *The Great Gatsby*, through the extensive give-and-take of Marlow in *Heart of Darkness*, to the central role of Tristram Shandy, Moll Flanders, Huckleberry Finn, and – in the third person – Paul Morel in *Sons and Lovers*). Clearly, any rules we might discover about observers may not apply to narrator-agents, yet the distinction is seldom made in talk about point of view.

Scene and summary

All narrators and observers, whether first or third person, can relay their tales to us primarily as scene ('The Killers,' *The Awkward Age*, the works of Ivy Compton-Burnett and Henry Green), primarily as summary or what Lubbock called 'picture' (Addison's almost completely non-scenic tales in *The Spectator*), or, most commonly, as a combination of the two.

Like Aristotle's distinction between dramatic and narrative manners, the somewhat different modern distinction between showing and telling does cover the ground. But the trouble is that it pays for broad coverage with gross imprecision. Narrators of all shapes and shades must either report dialogue alone or support it with 'stage directions' and description of setting. But when we think of the radically different effect of a scene reported by Huck Finn and a scene reported by Poe's Montresor, we see that the quality of being 'scenic' suggests very little about literary effect. And compare the delightful summary of twelve years given in two pages of *Tom Jones* (Book III, chap. i) with the tedious showing of even ten minutes of uncurtailed conversation in the hands of a Sartre when he allows his passion for 'durational realism' to dictate a scene when summary is called for. [. . .] The contrast between scene and summary, between showing and telling, is likely to be of little use until we specify the kind of narrator who is providing the scene or the summary.

Commentary

Narrators who allow themselves to tell as well as show vary greatly depending on the amount and kind of commentary allowed in addition to a direct relating of events in scene and summary. Such commentary can, of course, range over any aspect of human experience, and it can be related to the main business in innumerable ways and degrees. To treat it as a single device is to ignore important differences between commentary that is merely ornamental, commentary that serves a rhetorical purpose but is not part of the dramatic structure, and commentary that is integral to the dramatic structure, as in *Tristram Shandy.*

Self-conscious narrators

Cutting across the distinction between observers and narrator-agents of all these kinds is the distinction between *self-conscious narrators* aware of themselves as writers (*Tom Jones, Tristram Shandy, Barchester Towers, The Catcher in the Rye, Remembrance of Things Past, Dr. Faustus*), and narrators or observers who rarely if ever discuss their writing chores (*Huckleberry Finn*) or who seem unaware that they are writing, thinking, speaking, or 'reflecting' a literary work (Camus's *The Stranger,* Lardner's 'Haircut,' Bellow's *The Victim*).

Variations of distance

Whether or not they are involved in the action as agents or as sufferers, narrators and third-person reflectors differ markedly according to the degree and kind of distance that separates them from the author, the reader, and the other characters of the story. In any reading experience there is an implied dialogue among author, narrator, the characters, and the reader. Each of the four can range, in relation to each of the others, from identification to complete opposition, on any axis of value, moral, intellectual, aesthetic, and even physical. (Does the reader who stammers react to the stammering of H. C. Earwicker as I do? Surely not.) [...]

1. The *narrator* may be more or less distant from the *implied author.* The distance may be moral (Jason vs. Faulkner, the barber vs. Larner, the narrator vs. Fielding in *Jonathan Wild*). It may be intellectual (Twain and Huck Finn, Sterne and Tristram Shandy on the influence of noses, Richardson and Clarissa). It may be physical or temporal: most authors are distant even from the most knowing narrator in that they presumably know how 'everything turns out in the end.' And so on.

2. The *narrator* also may be more or less distant from the *characters* in the story he tells. He may differ morally, intellectually, and temporally (the mature narrator and his younger self in *Great Expectations* or *Redburn*); morally and intellectually (Fowler the

narrator and Pyle the American in Greene's *The Quiet American*, both departing radically from the author's norms but in different directions); morally and emotionally (Maupassant's 'The Necklace,' and Huxley's 'Nuns at Luncheon,' in which the narrators affect less emotional involvement than Maupassant and Huxley clearly expect from the reader); and thus on through every possible trait.

3. The *narrator* may be more or less distant from the *reader's* own norms; for example, physically and emotionally (Kafka's *The Metamorphosis*); morally and emotionally (Pinkie in *Brighton Rock*, the miser in Mauriac's *Knot of Vipers*, and the many other moral degenerates that modern fiction has managed to make into convincing human beings).

With the repudiation of omniscient narration, and in the face of inherent limitations in dramatized reliable narrators, it is hardly surprising that modern authors have experimented with unreliable narrators whose characteristics change in the course of the works they narrate. [. . .] The mature Pip, in *Great Expectations*, is presented as a generous man whose heart is where the reader's is supposed to be; he watches his young self move away from the reader, as it were, and then back again. But the third-person reflector can be shown, technically in the past tense but in effect present before our eyes, moving toward or away from values that the reader holds dear. Authors in the twentieth century have proceeded almost as if determined to work out all of the possible plot forms based on such shifts: start far and end near; start near, move far, and end near; start far and move farther; and so on. [. . .]

4. The *implied author* may be more or less distant from the *reader*. The distance may be intellectual (the implied author of *Tristram Shandy*, not of course to be identified with Tristram, more interested in and knowing more about recondite classical lore than any of his readers), moral (the works of Sade), or aesthetic. From the author's viewpoint, a successful reading of his book must eliminate all distance between the essential norms of his implied author and the norms of the postulated reader. [. . .]

5. The *implied author* (carrying the reader with him) may be more or less distant from *other characters*. Again, the distance can be on any axis of value. [. . .]

What we call 'involvement' or 'sympathy' or 'identification,' is usually made up of many reactions to author, narrators, observers, and other characters. And narrators may differ from their authors or readers in various kinds of involvement or detachment, ranging from deep personal concern (Nick in *The Great Gatsby*, MacKellar in *The Master of Ballantrae*, Zeitblom in *Dr. Faustus*) to a bland or mildly amused or merely curious detachment (Waugh's *Decline and Fall*).

For practical criticism probably the most important of these kinds of distance is that between the fallible or unreliable narrator and the implied author who carries the reader with him in judging the narrator. If the reason for discussing point of view is to find how it relates to literary effects, then surely the moral and intellectual qualities of the narrator are more important to our judgment than whether he is referred to as 'I' or 'he,' or whether he is privileged or limited. If he is discovered to be untrustworthy, then the total effect of the work he relays to us is transformed.

Our terminology for this kind of distance in narrators is almost hopelessly inadequate. For lack of better terms, I have called a narrator *reliable* when he speaks for or acts in accordance with the norms of the work (which is to say, the implied author's norms), *unreliable* when he does not. It is true that most of the great reliable narrators indulge in large amounts of incidental irony, and they are thus 'unreliable' in the sense of being potentially deceptive. But difficult irony is not sufficient to make a narrator unreliable. Nor is unreliability ordinarily a matter of lying, although deliberately deceptive narrators have been a major resource of some modern novelists (Camus' *The Fall*, Calder Willingham's *Natural Child*, etc.). It is most often a matter of what James calls *inconscience*; the narrator is mistaken, or he believes himself to have qualities which the author denies him. Or, as in *Huckleberry Finn*, the narrator claims to be naturally wicked while the author silently praises his virtues behind his back.

Unreliable narrators thus differ markedly depending on how far and in what direction they depart from their author's norms; the older term 'tone,' like the currently fashionable terms 'irony' and 'distance,' covers many effects that we should distinguish. Some narrators, like Barry Lyndon, are placed as far 'away' from author and reader as possible, in respect to every virtue except a kind of interesting vitality. Some, like Fleda Vetch, the reflector in James's *The Spoils of Poynton*, come close to representing the author's ideal of taste, judgment, and moral sense. All of them make stronger demands on the reader's powers of inference than do reliable narrators.

Variations in support or correction

Both reliable and unreliable narrators can be unsupported or uncorrected by other narrators (Gully Jimson in *The Horse's Mouth*, Henderson in Bellow's *Henderson the Rain King*) or supported or corrected (*The Master of Ballantrae*, *The Sound and the Fury*). Sometimes it is almost impossible to infer whether or to what degree a narrator is fallible; sometimes explicit corroborating or conflicting testimony makes the inference easy. Support or correction differs radically, it should be noted, depending on whether it is provided from within the action, so that the narrator-agent might benefit from it in sticking to the right line or in changing his own views (Faulkner's *Intruder in the Dust*), or is simply provided externally, to help the reader correct or reinforce his own views as against the narrator's (Graham Greene's *The Power and the Glory*). Obviously, the effects of isolation will be extremely different in the two cases.

Privilege

Observers and narrator-agents, whether self-conscious or not, reliable or not, commenting or silent, isolated or supported, can be either privileged to know what could not be learned by strictly natural means or limited to realistic vision and inference. Complete privilege is what we usually call omniscience. But there are many kinds of privilege, and very few 'omniscient' narrators are allowed to know or show as much as their authors know.
[...]

The most important single privilege is that of obtaining an inside view of another character, because of the rhetorical power that such a privilege conveys upon a narrator. There is a curious ambiguity in the term 'omniscience.' Many modern works that we usually classify as narrated dramatically, with everything relayed to us through the limited views of the characters, postulate fully as much omniscience in the silent author as Fielding claims for himself. Our roving visitation into the minds of sixteen characters in Faulkner's *As I Lay Dying*, seeing nothing but what those minds contain, may seem in one sense not to depend on an omniscient author. But this method is omniscience with teeth in it: the implied author demands our absolute faith in his powers of divination. We must never for a moment doubt that he knows everything about each of these sixteen minds or that he has chosen correctly how much to show of each. In short, impersonal narration is really no escape from omniscience – the true author is as 'unnaturally' all-knowing as he ever was.
[...]

Inside views

Finally, narrators who provide inside views differ in the depth and the axis of their plunge. Boccaccio can give inside views, but they are extremely shallow. Jane Austen goes relatively deep morally, but scarcely skims the surface psychologically. All authors of stream-of-consciousness narration presumably attempt to go deep psychologically, but some of them deliberately remain shallow in the moral dimension. We should remind ourselves that any sustained inside view, of whatever depth, temporarily turns the character whose mind is shown into a narrator; inside views are thus subject to variations in all of the qualities we have described above, and most importantly in the degree of unreliability. Generally speaking, the deeper our plunge, the more unreliability we will accept without loss of sympathy.

Narration is an art, not a science, but this does not mean that we are necessarily doomed to fail when we attempt to formulate principles about it. There are systematic elements in every art, and criticism of fiction can never avoid the responsibility of trying to explain technical successes and failures by reference to general principles. But we must always ask where the general principles are to be found. [...]

In dealing with the types of narration, the critic must always limp behind, referring constantly to the varied practice which alone can correct his temptations to overgeneralize.

[...]

Notes

1. *An Essay of Dramatic Poesy* (1668). Though this quotation comes from Lisideius, in his defense of French drama, and not from Neander, who seems to speak more nearly for Dryden, the position is taken for granted in Neander's reply; the only dispute is over *which* parts are more fit to be represented.

2. Efforts to use the second person have never been very successful, but it is astonishing how little real difference even this choice makes. When I am told, at the beginning of a book, 'You have put your left foot. . . . You slide through the narrow opening. . . . Your eyes are only half open . . . ,' the radical unnaturalness is, it is true, distracting for a time. But in reading Michel Butor's *La Modification* (Paris, 1957), from which this opening comes, it is surprising how quickly one is absorbed into the illusory 'present' of the story, identifying one's vision with the 'vous' almost as fully as with the 'I' and 'he' in other stories.

9 Authors, Speakers, Readers, and Mock Readers*

WALKER GIBSON

In this article Walker Gibson, taking up the New Critical distinction between author and dramatic speaker, differentiates between real reader and 'mock reader'. The mock reader is the narrator's addressee, a fictional figure whose knowledge, taste and personality may often differ from those of the real reader. As Gibson explains, the mock reader is most easily identifiable in such subliterary genres as advertising and propaganda. Although better hidden in more complex and sophisticated literary narratives, it nevertheless constitutes an indispensable element in all kinds of text. The term 'mock reader' has been generally replaced by that of 'implied reader' by analogy with Booth's 'implied author'. According to Gibson, in order for propaganda or advertising to achieve its aim, it must be able to create a mock reader with whom the real reader will be ready to identify. Likewise, in the case of literary narrative, the test of its moral quality can be measured by the moral status attributed to the mock reader. This moral factor, Gibson contends, may be used to differentiate between 'good' and 'bad' literature. The emphasis on rhetoric and the concern with the morality or ideology of the text are similarly found in Chicago School critics such as Wayne Booth in his *Rhetoric of Fiction* (chapter 8 above).

It is now common in the classroom as well as in criticism to distinguish carefully between the *author* of a literary work of art and the fictitious *speaker* within the work of art. [...]

Closely associated with this distinction between author and speaker, there is another and less familiar distinction to be made, respecting the *reader*. For if the 'real author' is to be regarded as to a great degree distracting and mysterious, lost in history, it seems equally true that the 'real reader,' lost in today's history, is no less

*Reprinted from *Reader-Response Criticism: From Formalism to Post-Structuralism*. Ed. JANE P. TOMPKINS (Baltimore: Johns Hopkins University Press, 1980) pp. 1–6. First publ. in *College English* 11 (Feb. 1950): 265–9.

mysterious and sometimes as irrelevant. The fact is that every time we open the pages of another piece of writing, we are embarked on a new adventure in which we become a new person – a person as controlled and definable and as remote from the chaotic self of daily life as the lover in the sonnet. Subject to the degree of our literary sensibility, we are recreated by the language. We assume, for the sake of the experience, that set of attitudes and qualities which the language asks us to assume, and, if we cannot assume them, we throw the book away.

I am arguing, then, that there are two readers distinguishable in every literary experience. First, there is the 'real' individual upon whose crossed knee rests the open volume, and whose personality is as complex and ultimately inexpressible as any dead poet's. Second, there is the fictitious reader – I shall call him the 'mock reader' – whose mask and costume the individual takes on in order to experience the language. The mock reader is an artifact, controlled, simplified, abstracted out of the chaos of day-to-day sensation.

The mock reader can probably be identified most obviously in subliterary genres crudely committed to persuasion, such as advertising and propaganda. We resist the blandishments of the copywriter just in so far as we refuse to become the mock reader his language invites us to become. Recognition of a violent disparity between ourself as mock reader and ourself as real person acting in a real world is the process by which we keep our money in our pockets. 'Does your toupee collect moths?' asked the toupee manufacturer, and we answer, 'Certainly not! My hair's my own. You're not talking to *me*, old boy; I'm wise to you.' Of course we are not always so wise.

Consider the mock reader in a case only slightly less obvious, the following opening paragraph from a book review of Malcolm Cowley's recent collection, *The Portable Hawthorne:*

> Our thin self-lacerating and discontinuous culture automatically produces such uneasy collaborations as this one between Mr. Cowley, the hard-working scribe and oddly impressionable cultural sounding board, and the publishing industry with its concept of the 'Portable.' The Hawthorne who emerges has had such a bad fall between stools, or clichés, that he appears almost as giddy and shattered as we. . . .
>
> [(Partisan Review)]

The assumptions buried rather shallowly in this passage can very easily be brought to light. A nimble and sympathetic conversation is passing back and forth here – as always – between the speaker and the mock reader, a conversation that goes in part something like this:

> You and I, in brave rebellion against the barbarousness of a business culture, can see this book for what of course it is – an 'uneasy collaboration' and a defamation of that fine Hawthorne whom you and I know and love. *We* would not be content, would we, to be mere 'scribes'; how stupid other people are to think that industry alone is sufficient. You and I are quickly able to translate 'oddly impressionable' into what of course more literally describes the situation, though we were too polite to say so – namely, that Cowley is a weak sister. Nothing 'odd' about it – you and I know what's going on all right.

It is interesting to observe how frankly the speaker throws his arm around the mock reader at the end of the passage I have quoted, as the two comrades experience their common giddiness at the appalling quality of this book. Remember that the *real* reader has in all likelihood not even seen the book yet, and, if he takes his own mock-reader-personality seriously enough, he probably never will.
[. . .]
It is evident that imaginative literature too makes similar demands on its readers. There is great variation from book to book in the ease and particularity with which one can describe the mock reader, but he is always present, and sometimes is so clearly and rigorously defined as to suggest serious limitations on the audience. The mock reader of the opening paragraphs of *The Great Gatsby*, for instance, is a person determined within fairly rigid limits of time and space.

> In my younger and more vulnerable years my father gave me some advice that I've been turning over in my mind ever since.
> 'Whenever you feel like criticising any one,' he told me, 'just remember that all the people in this world haven't had the advantages that you've had.'
> He didn't say any more, but we've always been unusually communicative in a reserved way, and I understood that he meant a good deal more than that. In consequence, I'm inclined to reserve all judgments, a habit that has opened up many curious natures to me and also made me the victim of not a few veteran bores. The abnormal mind is quick to detect and attach itself to this quality when it appears in a normal person, and so it came about that in

a college I was unjustly accused of being a politician, because I was privy to the secret griefs of wild, unknown men. Most of the confidences were unsought – frequently I have feigned sleep, preoccupation, or a hostile levity when I realized by some unmistakable sign that an intimate revelation was quivering on the horizon. . . .

Here the mock reader must not only take in stride a series of 'jokes' formed by some odd juxtapositions – vulnerable years, not a few veteran bores, etc. – but must also be quick to share the attitudes and assumed experiences of the speaker. For instance, the speaker by overt statement and the mock reader by inference have both attended a particular kind of college in a particular way; notice how 'in college' appears grammatically as a dependent phrase within a dependent clause, supporting the casual, offhand tone.

Of course we remember, you and I, how it was in college, where as normal persons we certainly had no wish to be confused with campus politicians, yet were even warier of the wild unknown men, those poets, those radicals and misfits. You and I understand with what deliberate and delicate absurdity I make fun of both the wild unknown men and the formal-literary language to which you and I have been exposed in the course of our expensive educations: 'an intimate revelation was quivering on the horizon.'

It is probable that *Gatsby* today enjoys a greater reputation among real-life wild unknown men than it does among the equivalents of Nick Carraway's class. Somehow many people are able to suspend their antagonisms against Nick's brand of normalcy in order to participate in the tone. Yet it is neither necessary nor desirable to suspend all one's judgments against Nick and his society, for in so far as Nick himself is self-critical, of course we can and must join him. And, finally, Nick is not the speaker at all, I think, but a kind of mock speaker, as our mock reader is a more complex and discerning person than Nick himself. There is another speaker somewhere – almost as if this novel were written in the third person – and it is from this other speaker that the mock reader ultimately takes on some important attitudes. They speak right over Nick Carraway's head.

You and I recognize the weaknesses in Nick, do we not: his snobbery and his facile assumptions. But we like him pretty well,

after all – and it's a question whether his shallowness is really his
fault. . . .

The concept of the mock reader need not be 'taught' in so many
words to be useful to the teacher of literature. The question the
teacher might well ask himself is no more than this: Is there among
my students a growing awareness that the literary experience is not
just a relation between themselves and an author, or even between
themselves and a fictitious speaker, but a relation between such a
speaker and a projection, a fictitious modification of themselves? The
realization on the part of a student that he is many people as he
reads many books and responds to their language worlds is the
beginning of literary sophistication in the best sense. One crucial
objective of the teacher, I take it, is simply the enlargement of his
'mock' possibilities. But this is not to imply that one reading
experience is as good as another and that there are not value
discriminations that are appropriate among various mock readers. In
fact, the term may be particularly useful in recognizing just such
discriminations and in providing one way of pointing out what we
mean by a bad book. A bad book, then, is a book in whose mock
reader we discover a person we refuse to become, a mask we refuse
to put on, a role we will not play. If this seems to say little more than
'A bad book is a bad book,' consider an example:

> Alan Foster wanted to go to Zagazig. He wasn't exactly sure why,
> except that he liked the name, and after having spent four months
> in Cairo Alan was ready to go places and do things. Twenty-two
> years old, tall, blond with powerful shoulders and trim waist,
> Alan found no difficulty in making friends. He had had a good
> time in Egypt. Now he wanted to leave Cairo and try out Zagazig.

What is so irritating about this? Many things, but if we isolate the
third sentence and describe its mock reader, we can begin to express
why this is bad writing. For the mock reader of the third sentence is
a person for whom there is a proper and natural relation between
powerful shoulders and making friends. No student in a respectable
English course, I assume, should be willing to accept such a relation
except perhaps as part of an irony. Only by irony could this passage
be saved. ('You and I recognize that he makes friends all right, but
what friends! This parody of a matinee idol is of course an ass.') No
such irony is perceptible, however; the mock reader is expected to
make one simple assumption only, and if the real reader has any

sophistication at all, the passage collapses. It collapses precisely because the real reader finds in the mock reader a fellow of intolerable simplicity.

It is a question of rejecting the toupee ad, of recognizing that one's hair is one's own. However, the possibility must immediately suggest itself that a skillful control of tone could persuade us in an instant to don a fictitious toupee and to feel in all possible vividness the tug of a textile scalp against our own suddenly naked head. It is, finally, a matter of the details of language, and no mock reader can be divorced for long from the specific words that made him.

And the question remains: By what standard does one judge mock readers, how does one arrive at the decision that this one or that one is intolerable? Often it is as easy as in the case above – a case of oversimple assumptions. But obviously the problem is larger than that, and the tremendous importance, as it seems to me, of distinguishing for students between the mock world of the literary experience and the real world of everyday experience must not obscure the fact that in the end our appeals for decisions of value are toward sanctions of society in a very real world indeed. For the student, the problem of what mock reader – or part of a mock reader – it is proper for him to accept, and what to reject, involves the whole overwhelming problem of learning to read and learning the enormously difficult job of becoming the mock reader of *Paradise Lost*, or *Antigone*, or Wallace Stevens. The student's hesitation is no more than a part of a larger question that possibly no teacher can presume to answer for him: Who do I want to be?

10   A New Approach to the Definition of the Narrative Situations*

F. K. STANZEL

F. K. Stanzel is one of the earliest and most outstanding narratologists in German. His *Narrative Situations in the Novel: Tom Jones, Moby Dick, The Ambassadors, Ulysses* (1971) was published in German as early as 1955. However, the impact of his work on the narratological scene was comparatively small outside the German-speaking countries before the belated translation of *A Theory of Narrative*. In *Narrative Situations in the Novel* Stanzel precedes Wayne Booth and the French structuralists in the analysis and further development of basic tenets of Russian Formalism, such as the opposition *'fabula/siuzhet'*. He also foreshadows Genette's differentiation in 'Discours du récit' (1972) between focalizer and narrator, which Stanzel calls 'reflector' and 'narrator'. Other oppositions such as 'scene/summary' and 'telling/showing' are also analysed by Stanzel. In *A Theory of Narrative*, he attempts to devise a comprehensive typology of all the ways in which a novel might be structured. Starting from the Platonic difference between mimesis and diegesis, Stanzel defines the essence of narrative in terms of the generic concept of 'mediacy', the presence of a mediator, a narrator whose voice is audible whenever a piece of news is conveyed, whenever something is reported. Mediacy is 'the generic characteristic which distinguishes narration from other forms of literary art' (p. 4). Stanzel further differentiates three basic narrative situations: 'the first person narrative situation', in which the mediator is a character and belongs within the world of the other characters; 'the authorial narrative situation', in which the narrator is outside the world of the characters, at a different level, and 'the figural narrative situation', in which, instead of the narrator-as-mediator, we find a 'reflector', defined as 'a character in the novel who thinks, feels and perceives, but does not speak to the reader like a narrator' (p. 5). Stanzel's definition of the 'reflector' – a term borrowed from

---

*F. K. STANZEL, *A Theory of Narrative*. Trans. Charlotte Goedsche (Cambridge: Cambridge University Press, 1984), pp. xvi, 46–62. 248–50. First publ. as *Theorie des Erzählens* (1979; rev. 1982).

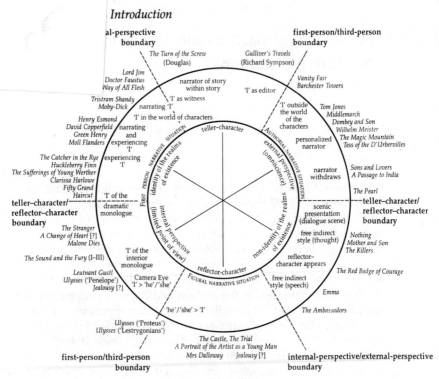

Figure 1
THE TYPOLOGICAL CIRCLE

Henry James – as a narrator 'who does not speak' shows his intuitive need to account for the difference between 'who sees' and 'who tells' and his failure to separate these functions theoretically. The distinction was made later by Genette and Bal, who introduced the concept of focalizer. Another important notion Stanzel proposes is that of narrative levels, which is also found in Roland Barthes (1966) and is further developed by Genette and Bal.

In the excerpt reprinted below, Stanzel proposes a typology of all narrative situations conceivable, based on three constitutive elements – person, perspective and mode – and their corresponding binary oppositions. Stanzel's sixfold typological axis (p. 167), arranged circularly, is intended to account for all possible in-between varieties, concrete examples of which are given in the titles of individual novels in the outer ring of the more complex figure (above). Analysis of a particular novel according to Stanzel's typology should reveal its narrative profile, that is, the dynamics of its narrative process as well as the rhythm derived from the alternation or predominance of particular situations. If carried out transhistorically, Stanzel claims, this analysis should be capable of accounting for the evolution of all narrative forms through history and even of predicting the genre's possible developments in the future.

The constitutive elements of the narrative situations: person, perspective, mode

Mediacy as the generic characteristic of narration is a complex and multi-layered phenomenon. In order to use this generic characteristic as the basis for a typology of the forms of narration, it is necessary to break down this complex into its most important constitutive elements. [. . .]

The first constitutive element is contained in the question 'Who is narrating?' The answer may be: a narrator who appears before the reader as an independent personality or one who withdraws so far behind the narrated events that he becomes practically invisible to the reader. The distinction between these two basic forms of narration is generally accepted in narrative theory. The following pairs of terms are usually applied: 'true' and 'scenic narration' (Otto Ludwig), 'panoramic' and 'scenic presentation' (Lubbock), 'telling' and 'showing' (Friedman), 'reportorial narration' and 'scenic presentation' (Stanzel).[1] While the concepts proposed for the narrative mode of a personalized narrator are relatively unambiguous, the terms designating scenic presentation conflate two techniques which often occur in conjunction but which must be distinguished in theory. One of these is the dramatized scene consisting of pure dialogue, dialogue with brief stage directions, or dialogue with very condensed narratorial report. This procedure is well illustrated by Hemingway's short story 'The Killers.' The other technique is the reflection of the fictional events through the consciousness of a character in the novel without narratorial comment. I call such a character a reflector to distinguish him from the narrator as the other narrative agent. Stephen in Joyce's *A Portrait of the Artist as a Young Man* has this function. Because of this ambiguity I should like to introduce another distinction. Narration can be considered to be effected by two kinds of narrative agents, narrators (in a personalized or unpersonalized role) and reflectors. Together these two comprise the first constitutive element of the narrative situation, the *mode* of narration. By mode I mean the sum of all possible variations of the narrative forms between the two poles narrator and reflector: *narration* in the true sense of mediacy, that is, the reader has the impression that he is confronted by a personalized narrator, as opposed to direct or immediate *presentation*, that is, the reflection of the fictional reality in the consciousness of a character.

While the first constitutive element, mode, is a product of the various relations and reciprocal effects between the narrator or reflector and the reader, the second constitutive element is based on the relations between the narrator and the fictional characters. Again, the multiplicity of possibilities is delimited by two polar positions. Either the narrator exists as a character within the world of the fictional events of the novel or else he exists outside this fictional reality. In referring to this situation I shall also speak of the identity or non-identity of the realms of existence of the narrator and the fictional characters. If the narrator exists in the same world as the characters, he is a first-person narrator according to traditional terminology. If the narrator is existentially outside the world of the characters, we are dealing with third-person narration in the traditional sense. The time-honored terms first-person and third-person narration have already caused much confusion, because the criterion of their distinction, the personal pronoun, refers in the former to the narrator, but in the latter to a character in the narrative who is *not* the narrator. In a third-person narrative, for example in *Tom Jones* or in *The Magic Mountain*, there is also a narratorial 'I.' It is not the occurrence of the first person of the personal pronoun in a narrative outside the dialogue which is decisive, but rather the location of the designated person within or outside the fictional world of the characters of a novel or a story. The term *person* will be retained nevertheless, as the distinguishing attribute of this second constitutive element because of its succinctness. The essential criterion of the second constitutive element, however – and this cannot be overemphasized – is not the relative frequency of occurrence of one of the two personal pronouns 'I' or 'he'/'she,' but the question of the identity or non-identity of the realms of existence to which the narrator and the characters belong. The narrator of *David Copperfield* is a first-person narrator because he exists in the same world as the other characters of the novel, Steerforth, Peggotty, the Murdstones and the Micawbers; the narrator of *Tom Jones* is a third-person narrator or an authorial narrator because he exists outside the fictional world in which Tom Jones, Sophia Western, Partridge and Lady Bellaston live. The identity and non-identity of the realms of the narrator and the characters are fundamentally different prerequisites for the narrative process and its motivation.

While mode focuses the reader's attention primarily on his relation to the process of narration or presentation, the third constitutive element, *perspective*, directs the reader's attention to the way in which he perceives the fictional reality. The manner of this perception depends essentially on whether the point of view according to which the narration is oriented is located *in* the story, in the protagonist or in the centre of action, or else *outside* the story or its centre of action, in a narrator who does not belong to the world of the characters or who is merely a subordinate figure, perhaps a first-person narrator in the role of observer or a contemporary of the hero. In this way an internal and an external perspective can be differentiated.

The opposition internal perspective–external perspective embraces an additional aspect of the mediacy of narration different from the other constitutive elements, person and mode, namely, that of the orientation of the reader's imagination within the time and especially the space of the narrative, or, in other words, that of the regulation of the spatio-temporal arrangement with respect to the centre or the focus of the narrated events. If the story is presented from within, as it were, then the perceptive situation of the reader is different from when the events are seen or reported from outside. Accordingly, there are differences in the ways in which the spatial relations of the characters and things in the represented reality are treated (perspectivism–aperspectivism), as well as in the restrictions placed on the knowledge and experience of the narrator or reflector ('omniscience'–'limited point of view').[2]

Narrative theory in the past has dealt with the state of affairs described by the opposition internal perspective–external perspective in diverse ways. Eduard Spranger, a psychologist, essentially anticipated my opposition more than half a century ago with his distinction between 'reportorial perspective' and 'inside view perspective.'[3] Later, Erwin Leibfried termed perspective the most important factor in the differentiation of narrative texts.[4] On the other hand, in the work of Pouillon, Todorov, and Genette,[5] what I call perspective is subordinated to other components, specifically to those which coincide largely with my concepts of mode and person. [...] The triadic basis proposed here as a basis for the three narrative situations has proven itself in practice, as is evidenced by its application in numerous studies of narrative theory over the last twenty years.[6] It will thus be retained in spite of the fact that most of the recent typologies of narrative theory are designed either as monadic (Hamburger) or, more frequently, as dyadic (Brooks and Warren, Anderegg, Doležel, Genette).[7]

Dorrit Cohn has proposed the elimination of the constitutive element perspective from my typology, suggesting that it coincides essentially in its content with the constitutive element mode.[8] I cannot agree to this suggestion for several reasons, one of them being that this elimination could also remove one very important advantage which my system has over dyadic or monadic ones. This advantage lies above all in the fact that the triadic arrangement brings out very clearly the character of the system as a continuum of forms, while the dualistic character of the monadic and dyadic system always leads to more abrupt differentiation by confronting one form group with another directly.[9] [. . .]

The narrative situations are thus constituted by the triad mode, person and perspective. Each of these constitutive elements permits of a great number of actualizations which can be represented as continua of forms between the two extreme possibilities. [. . .] Thus each of the formal continua corresponding to the three constitutive elements can be comprehended as a binary opposition of two discrete concepts. For my three constitutive elements and their corresponding formal continua, the binary oppositions are as follows:

Formal continuum mode:	Opposition narrator–non-narrator (reflector)
Formal continuum person:	Opposition identity–non-identity (of the realms of existence of the narrator and the characters)
Formal continuum perspective:	Opposition internal perspective–external perspective (perspectivism–aperspectivism)

[. . .]

My theory of narration based on the narrative situations distinguishes itself from [other] theories principally by the fact that it projects a triadic system in which all three constitutive elements are taken into account *in the same way*. In each of the three narrative situations another constitutive element or pole of the binary opposition associated with it attains dominance over the other constitutive elements and their oppositions:

Authorial narrative situation	Dominance of external perspective (aperspectivism)
First-person narrative situation	Dominance of the identity of the realms of existence of the narrator and the characters
Figural narrative situation	Dominance of the reflector mode

If the narrative situations are systematically arranged in a circle according to the correspondences existing among them so that the opposition axes belonging to the narrative situations intersect this circle at equal intervals, the resulting diagram will clearly illustrate the coordination of the narrative situations and their relations to the poles of the opposition axes. [Figure 2] shows the dominance of one oppositional element but also the participation of the contiguous oppositional elements, which exercise a secondary effect on the narrative situation. Thus, for example, the figural narrative situation is distinguished primarily by the dominance of a reflector-character and secondarily by the internal perspective, on the one hand, and by the non-identity of the realms of existence, that is, third-person reference (to the reflector-character), on the other.[10]

[...]

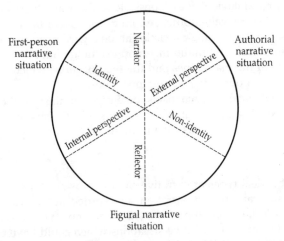

Figure 2

The typological circle

[...] As I have already stated, the points corresponding to the ideal types of the three narrative situations are located at one of the poles of each of the three axes of the typological circle which represent the three oppositions. (See diagram of typological circle, p. 162, and [Figure 2].)

Compared with simple dyadic or simple monadic systems, a number of advantages result from the triadic arrangement of a system such as this:

Each narrative situation is defined by three constitutive elements

167

(person, perspective, mode). The concept is thus determined more comprehensively according to generic theory than are the types of a monadic system based on a single opposition.

The triadic structure of the typology permits the arrangement of the types in a circle. The circular form reveals the closed nature or inclusiveness of the system, on the one hand, and its essentially dialectic character, on the other. The secondary constitutive elements of each narrative situation involve the suspension and in this sense the resolution of the oppositions which define the other two narrative situations. In the first-person narrative situation, for example, the contrasts in mode and perspective between the authorial and the figural narrative situations are suspended.

The arrangement of the narrative situations on the diagram of the typological circle makes it possible to illustrate the systematic locus of all conceivable forms and modifications of the main types. In this sense the typological circle can be regarded as an inclusive continuum. This continuum incorporates the unlimited number of variations of the main types and the modifications which approach each of the two contiguous types.

The typological circle connects ideal types or ahistorical constants – the three narrative situations – with historical forms of narration, which can be described as modifications of the ideal types.

[...]

Between the ideal types of narrative situations as ahistorical constants and the historical forms of narration, as recorded in the history of the novel and the short story, there exists one more very revealing connection. Of the six narrative situations which could have been established at the six poles of the three oppositions, only three were actually realized. These three types are those which have been developed most frequently in the history of the novel. This approach is advantageous in that the vast majority of the works can be readily classified in terms of one of the three types of narrative situations. Consequently there remain only relatively few novels which are situated near the unrealized but theoretically possible positions. This decision in favour of the majority of those typical forms which have developed historically can be revised at any time, should the future development of the novel demand it. [...]

The diagram of the typological circle thus reveals a close relation between the system of narrative situations and the history of the novel and the short story. For example, if one entered all novels recorded in the history of the novel in the appropriate places on the typological circle in chronological order, one would find that until shortly after the turn of the century only certain portions of the typological circle were 'colonized,' specifically the sectors in which the positions of the first-person narrative situation and the authorial narrative situation are located. The sector representing the figural narrative situation, on the other hand, does not begin to fill until after the turn of the century, slowly at first, but then – after Joyce – more quickly. As I have already mentioned, this tendency continues in the most recent development illustrated by Beckett's works, by those of the *nouveau roman* and by the Americans Barth, Pynchon, Vonnegut, among others. Seen in this light the diagram of the typological circle looks like a program for the structure of the novel which is being gradually realized, as it seems, by historical developments of the novel. Without the cognitive device of the typology and the system of interrelationships among individual narrative forms which the typology reveals, this correspondence between the general system and the particular historical form would scarcely be so evident.

Finally, the diagram of the typological circle also offers an approach to the modification of the theory of norms and deviation. Because of the arrangement of the forms of transmission of a story on the typological circle, a deviation from one type is always concurrently an approach toward the type of another narrative situation. The operations which Jacques Dubois and his collaborators perform on the norm of narration illustrate this point. Insofar as such operations as detraction, adjection, immutation, transmutation[11] relate to elements of the narrative transmission of a story, they amount to shifting the locus of a narrative on the typological circle away from one narrative situation and toward another. The model norm–deviation is thus replaced by a new one, namely the concept of a closed continuum of transformationally generated forms, in which, strictly speaking, there can no longer exist a norm and a deviation from this norm, but only a continuous motion from form to form in either direction along the typological circle. What appears as deviation according to the norm model turns out, on the basis of my model, to be a historically consistent step in the further realization of the structural potentialities of this genre.

[. . .]

Notes

1. See OTTO LUDWIG, 'Formen der Erzählung,' in his *Epische Studien: Gesammelte Schriften*, ed. A. Stern (Leipzig, 1891), Vol. 6, pp. 202–6; PERCY LUBBOCK, *The Craft of Fiction* (New York, 1947), p. 67; N. FRIEDMAN, 'Point of View in Fiction:

The Development of a Critical Concept,' *PMLA* 70 (1955): 1161ff.
STANZEL, *Narrative Situations in the Novel: Tom Jones, Moby Dick, The Ambassadors, Ulysses*, trans. James P. Pusac (Bloomington: Indiana University Press, 1971), p. 22.

2. See N. FRIEDMAN, 'Point of View,' 1169–78.

3. See EDUARD SPRANGER, 'Der psychologische Perspektivismus im Roman' rpt. in VOLKER KLOTZ (ed.), *Zur Poetik des Romans* (Darmstadt, 1965), pp. 217–38.

4. ERWIN LEIBFRIED, *Kritische Wissenschaft vom Text: Manipulation, Reflexion, Transparente Poetologie*, 2nd edn (Stuttgart, 1972), p. 244. The new approach to the definition of the narrative situations on the basis of person, perspective and mode has, I hope, made it clear that the term narrative situation does not merely mean perspective, as Leibfried implies.

5. See JEAN POUILLON, *Temps et roman* (Paris, 1946), pp. 74–114; TODOROV, 'Les Catégories du Récit Littéraire', *Communications* 8 (1966): 125–59; GÉRARD GENETTE, *Narrative Discourse* (Ithaca, NY, 1980), pp. 185–98, where perspective and focalization are subordinated to the aspect of mood.

6. A partial list of such works is given in STANZEL, 'Zur Konstituierung der typischen Erzählsituationen,' in *Zur Struktur des Romans*, ed. BRUNE HILLEBRAND (Darmstadt, 1978), pp. 568ff.

7. See KÄTE HAMBURGER, *The Logic of Literature*, trans. Marilynn J. Rose (Bloomington: Indiana University Press), 1973, pp. 3ff. and 311ff.; JOHANNES ANDEREGG, *Fiktion und Kommunikation: Ein Beitrag Zur Theorie der Prosa* (Göttingen, 1977), pp. 43ff.; ERWIN LEIBFRIED, *Kritische Wissenschaft vom Text: Manipulation, Reflexion, Transparente Poetologie* (Stuttgart, 1972), pp. 244–5; CLEANTH BROOKS and ROBERT PENN WARREN, *Understanding Fiction* (New York, 1943), pp. 659ff.; GENETTE, *Narrative Discourse*, pp. 30–2; LUBOMIR DOLEŽEL, 'The Typology of the Narrator: Point of View in Fiction,' in *To Honor Roman Jakobson* (The Hague: Mouton, 1967), pp. 541–52. Doležel further develops his typology in the introduction to his *Narrative Modes in Czech Literature* (Toronto, 1973).

8. See COHN, 'The Encirclement of Narrative. On Franz Stanzel's *Theorie des Erzählens*,' *Poetics Today* 2 (Winter 1981), 174ff. and 179–80.

9. Note how the forms in the dyadic system suggested by Cohn are located in clearly differentiated sectors or quadrants, while the individual forms in my typological circle with a triadic basis can always be located on one of the continua linking two narrative situations. See COHN, 'Encirclement,' 163, Chart II, and 179, Figure 2.

10. The principal objections to my typology on a triadic basis can be divided into four groups. One group demands a reduction of the three constitutive elements to the third-/first-person opposition (Hamburger), to which the teller/reflector opposition is then subordinated (Lockemann, Staffhorst). The other group demands the reduction of the three constitutive elements to the teller-reflector opposition, to which the third-/first-person opposition is then subordinated (Anderegg, Herbert Kraft, and others). A third group wants to subordinate person and mode to perspective (Leibfried, Füger). The fourth group suggests abandoning the constitutive element perspective (Cohn, Lockemann, Staffhorst and others). Considering the incompatibility of the objections and the suggestions for change, it seems to me that it remains to be a real advantage of my approach that it embodies all three constitutive elements without postulating an order of rank for them. See ALBRECHT STAFFHORST, *Die Subjekt–Objekt-Struktur: Ein Beitrag zur Erzähltheorie*

(Stuttgart, 1979), pp. 17–22, and Herbert Kraft, *Um Schiller betrogen* (Pfullingen, 1978), pp. 48–58.

11. Jacques Dubois *et al.*, *Rhétorique générale* (Paris, 1971), pp. 187ff.

11 Voice*

GÉRARD GENETTE

In chapter 5 of his *Narrative Discourse*, under the general heading of 'Voice', Gérard Genette offers a systematic analysis of the role of the 'narrating instance' (the one who narrates) as distinct from that of the 'writing instance' (the one who writes) and that of the characters (the agents of the action). Genette's use of the word 'instance' is meant to erase the ideological associations of subjectivity that accompany traditional concepts of narrator and author, and to underline the functionality of their roles, in the same way Greimas uses the term 'actant' (instead of character) to describe the functional role of the agents of the action, whether human or otherwise, at fabula level. Genette's contribution to the definition of the narrative instance involves the coining of key concepts like that of the 'time of the narrating' (that is, of the narrative's temporal position with respect to the time of the story narrated), and the notion of narrative levels, which he conceives as intangible and yet impenetrable boundaries separating the worlds of the characters and events narrated; of the narrator and his addressee, the narratee; and of the author and his addressee, the reader. The theoretical separation of these levels permits analysis of the effects produced in a narrative when the boundaries are transgressed or blurred (although Genette's scheme makes insufficient distinction between the narrative levels and other semiotic levels which may likewise involve a difference in fictional status). Finally, developing Wayne Booth's objections in *The Rhetoric of Fiction*, Genette refines the traditional concepts of first- or third-person narrative, adding to them the more functional notions of 'homodiegetic' and 'heterodiegetic' narrations, which allow for the theoretical distinction between a narrator who participates in the action as character and a narrator who does not.

Narrative Discourse is a seminal work, presenting a systematic

---

*GÉRARD GENETTE, *Narrative Discourse: An Essay in Method*. Trans. Jane E. Lewin (Ithaca, NY: Cornell University Press, 1980), pp. 212–60. First publ. in *Figures III* (Paris: Editions du Seuil, 1972), pp. 65–282.

theoretical framework for the analysis of what Genette calls the 'constant literary forms' existing or conceivable in all kinds of narrative. He undertakes the analysis of narrative tense, studying such temporal aspects as 'order', 'duration' and 'frequency'. Another key concept introduced for the first time is 'focalization', a term which helps clarify the difference between 'perspective' (who sees) and 'point of view' (who narrates). (Incidentally, in *Narrative Discourse Revisited* (1983, trans. 1988), Genette rejected Mieke Bal's reinterpretation of his concept reprinted as chapter 6 above.) Also innovative is the parallel Genette draws between 'showing' and 'telling' in the different areas of 'narration of words' and 'narration of events'. The impact of the book, when it first appeared as 'Discours du récit' in Genette's collection *Figures III* (1972), was enormous, and marked a turning-point in the consolidation of French narratology.

The Narrating Instance

'For a long time I used to go to bed early': obviously, such a statement – unlike, let us say, 'Water boils at one-hundred degrees Celsius' or 'The sum of the angles of a triangle is equal to two right angles' – can be interpreted only with respect to the person who utters it and the situation in which he utters it. *I* is identifiable only with reference to that person, and the completed past of the 'action' told is completed only in relation to the moment of utterance. [...] Even historical narrative of the type 'Napoleon died at Saint Helena' implies in its preterite that the story precedes the narrating, and I am not certain that the present tense in 'Water boils at one-hundred degrees' (iterative narrative) is as atemporal as it seems. Nevertheless, the importance or the relevance of these implications is essentially variable, and this variability can justify or impose distinctions and contrasts that have at least an operative value. When I read *Gambara* or *Le Chef-d'oeuvre inconnu*, I am interested in a story, and care little to know who tells it, where, and when; if I read *Facino Cane*, at no time can I overlook the presence of the narrator in the story he tells. [...]

This kind of effect is what we are going to look at under the category of *voice*: 'the mode of action,' says Vendryès, 'of the verb considered for its relations to the subject' – the subject here being not only the person who carries out or submits to the action, but also the person (the same one or another) who reports it, and, if need be, all those people who participate, even though passively, in this narrating activity. [...] On the one hand critics restrict questions of narrative enunciating to questions of 'point of view'; on the other hand they identify the narrating instance with the instance of 'writing,' the narrator with the author, and the recipient of the narrative with the reader of the work:[1] a confusion that is perhaps legitimate in the case of a historical narrative or a real autobiography, but not when we are dealing with a narrative of fiction, where the role of narrator is itself fictive, even if assumed directly by the author, and where the supposed narrating situation can be very different from the act of writing (or of dictating) which refers to it. [. . .] The references in *Tristram Shandy* to the situation of writing speak to the (fictive) act of Tristram and not the (real) one of Sterne; but in a more subtle and also more radical way, the narrator of *Père Goriot* 'is' not Balzac, even if here and there he expresses Balzac's opinions, for this author-narrator is someone who 'knows' the Vauquer boarding-house, its landlady and its lodgers, whereas all Balzac himself does is imagine them; and in this sense, of course, the narrating situation of a fictional account is *never* reduced to its situation of writing.

So it is this narrating instance that we have still to look at, according to the traces it has left – the traces it is considered to have left – in the narrative discourse it is considered to have produced. But it goes without saying that the instance does not necessarily remain identical and invariable in the course of a single narrative work. Most of *Manon Lescaut* is told by Des Grieux, but some pages revert to M. de Renoncourt; inversely, most of the *Odyssey* is told by 'Homer,' but Books IX-XII revert to Ulysses; and the baroque novel, *The Thousand and One Nights*, and *Lord Jim* have accustomed us to much more complex situations.[2]

[. . .]

A narrating situation is, like any other, a complex whole within which analysis, or simply description, cannot *differentiate* except by ripping apart a tight web of connections among the narrating act, its protagonists, its spatio-temporal determinations, its relationship to the other narrating situations involved in the same narrative, etc. [. . .] Therefore, we will look successively at elements of definition whose actual functioning is simultaneous: we will attach these elements, for the most part, to the categories of *time of the narrating, narrative level,* and *'person'* (that is, relations between the narrator – plus, should the occasion arise, his or their narratee[s][3] – and the story he tells).

Time of the Narrating

By a dissymmetry whose underlying reasons escape us but which is inscribed in the very structures of language (or at the very least of the main 'languages of civilization' of Western culture), I can very well tell a story without specifying the place where it happens, and whether this place is more or less distant from the place where I am telling it; nevertheless, it is almost impossible for me not to locate the story in time with respect to my narrating act, since I must necessarily tell the story in a present, past, or future tense.[4] This is perhaps why the temporal determinations of the narrating instance are manifestly more important than its spatial determinations. With the exception of second-degree narratings, whose setting is generally indicated by the diegetic context (Ulysses with the Phaeacians, the landlady of *Jacques le fataliste* in her inn), the narrating place is very rarely specified, and is almost never relevant. [. . .]

The chief temporal determination of the narrating instance is obviously its position relative to the story. It seems evident that the narrating can only be subsequent to what it tells, but this obviousness has been belied for many centuries by the existence of 'predictive' narrative[5] in its various forms (prophetic, apocalyptic, oracular, astrological, chiromantic, cartomantic, oneiromantic, etc.), whose origin is lost in the darkness of time – and has been belied also, at least since *Les Lauriers sont coupés,* by the use of narrative in the present tense. We must consider, further, that a past-tense narrating can to some extent be split up and inserted between the various moments of the story, much like a 'live' running commentary[6] – a common practice with correspondence and private diary, and therefore with the 'novel by letters' or the narrative in the form of a journal (*Wuthering Heights, Journal d'un curé de campagne*). It is therefore necessary, merely from the point of view of temporal position, to differentiate four types of narrating: *subsequent* (the classical position of the past-tense narrative, undoubtedly far and away the most frequent); *prior* (predictive narrative, generally in the future tense, but not prohibited from being conjugated in the present, like Jocabel's dream in *Moyse sauvé*); *simultaneous* (narrative in the present contemporaneous with the action); and *interpolated* (between the moments of the action).

The last type is a priori the most complex, since it involves a narrating with several instances, and since the story and the narrating can become entangled in such a way that the latter has an effect on the former. This is what happens particularly in the epistolary novel with several correspondents where, as we know, the letter is at the same time both a medium of the narrative and an element in the plot. This type of narrating can also be the most delicate, indeed, the one most refractory to analysis, as for example when the journal form loosens up to result in a sort of monologue after the event, with an indefinite, even incoherent, temporal position:

attentive readers of *L'Etranger* have not missed these uncertainties, which are one of the audacities – perhaps unintentional – of that narrative. Finally, the extreme closeness of story to narrating produces here, most often, a very subtle effect of friction (if I may call it that) between the slight temporal displacement of the narrative of events ('Here is what happened to me today') and the complete simultaneousness in the report of thoughts and feelings ('Here is what I think about it this evening'). The journal and the epistolary confidence constantly combine what in broadcasting language is called the live and the prerecorded account, the quasi-interior monologue and the account after the event. Here, the narrator is at one and the same time still the hero and already someone else: the events of the day are already in the past, and the 'point of view' may have been modified since then; the feelings of the evening or the next day are fully of the present, and here focalization through the narrator is at the same time focalization through the hero. [...] We know how the eighteenth-century novel, from *Pamela* to *Obermann*, exploited that narrative situation propitious to the most subtle and the most 'irritating' counterpoints: the situation of the tiniest temporal interval.

The third type (simultaneous narrating), by contrast, is in principle the simplest, since the rigorous simultaneousness of story and narrating eliminates any sort of interference or temporal game. We must observe, however, that the blending of the instances can function here in two opposite directions, according to whether the emphasis is put on the story or on the narrative discourse. A present-tense narrative which is 'behaviorist' in type and strictly of the moment can seem like the height of objectivity, since the last trace of enunciating that still subsisted in the Hemingway-style narrative (the mark of temporal interval between story and narrating, which the use of the preterite unavoidably comprises) now disappears in a total transparency of the narrative, which finally fades away in favor of the story. That is how the works that come under the heading of the French 'new novel,' and especially Robbe-Grillet's early novels,[7] have generally been received: 'objective literature,' 'school of the look' – these designations express well the sense of the narrating's absolute transitivity which a generalized use of the present tense promotes. But inversely, if the emphasis rests on the narrating itself, as in narratives of 'interior monologue,' the simultaneousness operates in favor of the discourse; and then it is the action that seems reduced to the condition of simple pretext, and ultimately abolished. This effect was already noticeable in Dujardin, and became more marked in a Beckett, a Claude Simon, a Roger Laporte. So it is as if use of the present tense, bringing the instances together, had the effect of unbalancing their equilibrium and allowing the whole of the narrative to tip, according to the slightest shifting of emphasis, either onto the side of the story or onto the side of the narrating, that is, the discourse. And the facility with which the French novel in recent years has passed from one extreme to the other perhaps illustrates this ambivalence and reversibility.

The second type (prior narrating) has until now enjoyed a much smaller literary investment than the others, and certainly even novels of anticipation, from Wells to Bradbury – which nevertheless belong fully to the prophetic genre – almost always postdate their narrating instances, making them implicitly subsequent to their stories (which indeed illustrates the autonomy of this fictive instance with respect to the moment of actual writing). Predictive narrative hardly appears at all in the literary corpus except on the second level. [. . .] The common characteristic of these second narratives is obviously that they are predictive in relation to the immediate narrating instance (Aaron, Jocabel's dream) but not in relation to the final instance (the implied author of *Moyse sauvé*, who explicitly identifies himself with Saint-Amant): clear examples of prediction after the event.

Subsequent narrating (the first type) is what presides over the immense majority of the narratives produced to this day. The use of a past tense is enough to make a narrative subsequent, although without indicating the temporal interval which separates the moment of the narrating from the moment of the story. In classical 'third-person' narrative, this interval appears generally indeterminate, and the question irrelevant, the preterite marking a sort of ageless past: the story can be dated, as it often is in Balzac, without the narrating being so. It sometimes happens, however, that a relative contemporaneity of story time and narrating time is disclosed by the use of the present tense, either at the beginning, as in *Tom Jones* or *Le Père Goriot*, or at the end, as in *Eugénie Grandet* or *Madame Bovary*. These effects of final convergence (the most striking of the two types) play on the fact that the very length of the story gradually lessens the interval separating it from the moment of the narrating. But the power of these final convergences results from their unexpected disclosure of a temporal isotopy (which, being temporal, is also to a certain extent diegetic) between the story and its narrator, an isotopy which until then was hidden (or, in the case of *Bovary*, long forgotten). In 'first-person' narrative, on the other hand, this isotopy is evident from the beginning, where the narrator is presented right away as a character in the story, and where the final convergence is the rule,[8] in accordance with a mode that the last paragraph of *Robinson Crusoe* can furnish us with a paradigm of: 'And here, resolving to harrass my self no more, I am preparing for a longer Journey than all these, having liv'd 72 Years, a Life of infinite Variety, and learn'd sufficiently to know the Value of Retirement, and the Blessing of ending our Days in Peace.'[9] No dramatic effect here, unless the final situation should itself be a violent denouement, as in *Double Indemnity*, in which the hero writes the last line of his confession-narrative before slipping with his accomplice into the ocean where a shark awaits them: 'I didn't hear the stateroom door open, but she's beside me now while I'm writing. I can feel her./The moon.'[10]

In order for the story to overtake the narrating in this way, the duration of the latter must of course not exceed the duration of the former. Take Tristram's comic aporia: in one year of writing having succeeded in telling only the first day of his life, he observes that he has gotten 364 days behind, that he has therefore moved backward rather than forward, and that, living 364 times faster than he writes, it follows that the more he writes the more there remains for him to write; that, in short, his undertaking is hopeless.[11] Faultless reasoning, whose premises are not at all absurd. Telling takes time (Scheherazade's life hangs by that one thread), and when a novelist puts on his stage an oral narrating in the second degree, he rarely fails to take that into account. [. . .] Flaubert needed almost five years to write *Madame Bovary*. Nevertheless – and this is finally very odd – the fictive narrating of that narrative, as with almost all the novels in the world except *Tristram Shandy*, is considered to have no duration; or, more exactly, everything takes place as if the question of its duration had no relevance. One of the fictions of literary narrating – perhaps the most powerful one, because it passes unnoticed, so to speak – is that the narrating involves an instantaneous action, without a temporal dimension. Sometimes it is dated, but it is never measured. [. . .] Contrary to simultaneous or interpolated narrating, which exist through their duration and the relations between that duration and the story's, subsequent narrating exists through this paradox: it possesses at the same time a temporal situation (with respect to the past story) and an atemporal essence (since it has no duration proper).[12] [. . .]

The narrating instance of the *Recherche* obviously corresponds to this last type. We know that Proust spent more than ten years writing his novel, but Marcel's act of narrating bears no mark of duration, or of division: it is instantaneous. The narrator's present, which on almost every page we find mingled with the hero's various pasts, is a single moment without progression. [. . .]

Narrative Levels

When Des Grieux, having reached the end of his narrative, states that he has just sailed from New Orleans to Havre-de-Grâce, then from Havre to Calais to meet his brother who is waiting for him several miles away, the temporal (and spatial) interval that until then separated the reported action from the narrating act becomes gradually smaller until it is finally reduced to zero: the narrative has reached the *here* and the *now*, the story has overtaken the narrating. Yet a distance still exists between the final episodes of the Chevalier's loves and the room in the 'Lion d'or' with its occupants, including the Chevalier himself and his host, where after supper he recounts these episodes to the Marquis de Renoncourt: the distance between episodes and inn lies neither in time nor in space, but in the difference between the relations which both the episodes and the inn maintain at that point with Des Grieux's narrative. We will distinguish those relations in a rough and necessarily inadequate way by saying that the episodes of the Chevalier's loves are inside (meaning inside the narrative) and the inn with its occupants is outside. What separates them is less a distance than a sort of threshold represented by the narrating itself, a difference of *level*. The 'Lion d'or,' the Marquis, the Chevalier in his function as narrator are for us inside a particular narrative, not Des Grieux's but the Marquis's, the *Mémoires d'un homme de qualité*; the return from Louisiana, the trip from Havre to Calais, the Chevalier in his function as hero are inside another narrative, this one Des Grieux's, which is *contained* within the first one, not only in the sense that the first frames it with a preamble and a conclusion (although the latter is missing here), but also in the sense that the narrator of the second narrative is already a character in the first one, and that the act of narrating which produces the second narrative is an event recounted in the first one.

We will define this difference in level by saying that *any event a narrative recounts is at a diegetic level immediately higher than the level at which the narrating act producing this narrative is placed.* M. de Renoncourt's writing of his fictive *Mémoires* is a (literary) act carried out at a first level, which we will call *extradiegetic*; the events told in those *Mémoires* (including Des Grieux's narrating act) are inside this first narrative, so we will describe them as *diegetic*, or *intradiegetic*; the events told in Des Grieux's narrative, a narrative in the second degree, we will call *metadiegetic*.[13] In the same way, M. de Renoncourt as 'author' of the *Mémoires* is extradiegetic: although fictive, he addresses the actual public, just like Rousseau or Michelet; the same Marquis as hero of the same *Mémoires* is diegetic, or intradiegetic, and

179

so also is Des Grieux the narrator at the 'Lion d'or,' as well as the Manon noticed by the Marquis at the first meeting in Pacy; but Des Grieux the hero of his own narrative, and Manon the heroine, and his brother, and the minor characters, are metadiegetic. These terms (metadiegetic, etc.) designate, not individuals, but relative situations and functions.[14]

The narrating instance of a first narrative is therefore extradiegetic by definition, as the narrating instance of a second (metadiegetic) narrative is diegetic by definition, etc. Let us emphasize the fact that the possibly fictive nature of the first instance does not modify this state of affairs any more than the possibly 'real' nature of the subsequent instances does: M. de Renoncourt is not a 'character' in a narrative taken charge of by the Abbé Prévost; he is the *fictive author* of *Mémoires*, whose real author, of course, is Prévost, just as Robinson Crusoe is the fictive author of the novel by Defoe that bears his name; subsequently, each of them (the Marquis and Crusoe) becomes a character in his own narrative. Neither Prévost nor Defoe enters the space of our inquiry, which, let us recall, bears on the narrating instance, not on the literary instance. M. de Renoncourt and Crusoe are author-narrators, and as such they are at the same narrative level as their public – that is, as you and me. This is not the case with Des Grieux, who never addresses himself to us, but only to the patient Marquis; and inversely, even if this fictive Marquis had met a real person at Calais (say, Sterne on a journey), this person would nonetheless be diegetic, even though real – just like Richelieu in Dumas, Napoleon in Balzac, or the Princesse Mathilde in Proust. In short, we shall not confound extradiegetic with real historical existence nor diegetic (or even metadiegetic) status with fiction. [. . .]

But not every extradiegetic narrating is necessarily taken up as a literary work with its protagonist an author-narrator in a position to address himself, like the Marquis de Renoncourt, to a public termed such.[15] A novel in the form of a diary (like the *Journal d'un curé de campagne* or the *Symphonie pastorale*) does not in principle aim at any public or any reader, and it is the same with an epistolary novel, whether it include a single letter writer (like *Pamela, Werther,* or *Obermann,* often described as journals disguised as correspondence)[16] or several (like *La Nouvelle Héloïse* or *Les Liaisons dangereuses*). Bernanos, Gide, Richardson, Goethe, Senancour, Rousseau, and Laclos present themselves here simply as 'editors,' but the fictive authors of these diaries or 'letters collected and published by . . .' – as distinct from Renoncourt, or Crusoe, or Gil Blas – obviously did not look on themselves as 'authors.' What is more, extradiegetic narrating is not even necessarily handled as written narrating: nothing claims that Meursault or The Unnamable wrote the texts we read as their interior monologues, and it goes without saying that the text of the *Lauriers sont coupés* cannot be anything but a 'stream of consciousness' – not written, or even spoken – mysteriously caught and transcribed by Dujardin. It is the nature of immediate speech to preclude any formal determination of the narrating instance which it constitutes.

Inversely, every intradiegetic narrating does not necessarily produce, like Des Grieux's, an oral narrative. It can consist of a written text, like the memoir with no recipient written by Adolphe, or even a fictive literary text, a work within a work, like the 'story' of the Curious Impertinent discovered in a cloak bag by the curate in *Don Quixote*. [. . .] But the second narrative can also be neither oral nor written, and can present itself, openly or not, as an inward narrative (for instance, Jocabel's dream in *Moyse sauvé*) or (more frequently and less supernaturally) as any kind of recollection that a character has (in a dream or not). [. . .] Finally, the second narrative can be handled as a nonverbal representation (most often visual), a sort of iconographic document, which the narrator converts into a narrative by describing it himself (the print representing the desertion of Ariadne, in *The Nuptial Song of Peleus and Thetis*, or the tapestry of the flood in *Moyse sauvé*), or, more rarely, by having another character describe it (like the tableaux of Joseph's life commented on by Amram, also in *Moyse sauvé*).

Metadiegetic Narrative

Second-degree narrative is a form that goes back to the very origins of epic narrating, since Books IX-XII of the *Odyssey*, as we know, are devoted to the narrative Ulysses makes to the assembled Phaeacians. [. . .] The formal and historical study of this technique would go well beyond our intention, but for the sake of what follows it is necessary here at least to differentiate the main types of relationships that can connect the metadiegetic narrative to the first narrative, into which it is inserted.

The first type of relationship is direct causality between the events of the metadiegesis and those of the diegesis, conferring on the second narrative an *explanatory* function. It is the Balzacian 'this is why,' but taken on here by a character, whether the story he tells is someone else's or, more often, his own. All these narratives answer, explicitly or not, a question of the type 'What events have led to the present situation?' Most often, the curiosity of the intradiegetic listener is only a pretext for replying to the curiosity of the reader. [. . .]

The second type consists of a purely *thematic* relationship, therefore implying no spatio-temporal continuity between metadiegesis and diegesis: a relationship of contrast (the deserted Ariadne's unhappiness, in the midst of Thetis' joyous wedding) or of analogy (as when Jocabel, in *Moyse sauvé*, hesitates to execute the divine command and Amram tells her the story of Abraham's sacrifice). The famous *structure en abyme*, not long ago so prized by the 'new novel' of the 1960s, is obviously an extreme form of this relationship of analogy, pushed to the limits of identity. Thematic relationship can, moreover, when it is perceived by the audience, exert an influence on the diegetic situation: Amram's narrative has as its immediate effect (and, moreover, as its aim) to convince Jocabel; it is an *exemplum* with a function of persuading. We know that regular genres, like the parable or the apologue (the fable), are based on that monitory effect of analogy. [. . .]

The third type involves no explicit relationship between the two story levels: it is the act of narrating itself that fulfills a function in the diegesis, independently of the metadiegetic content – a function of distraction, for example, and/or of obstruction. Surely the most illustrious example is found in the *Thousand and One Nights*, where Scheherazade holds off death with renewed narratives, whatever they might be (provided they interest the sultan). We notice that, from the first type to the third, the importance of the narrating instance only grows.

[. . .]

Metalepses

The transition from one narrative level to another can in principle be achieved only by the narrating, the act that consists precisely of introducing into one situation, by means of a discourse, the knowledge of another situation. Any other form of transit is, if not always impossible, at any rate always transgressive. Cortázar tells the story of a man assassinated by one of the characters in the novel he is reading;[17] this is an inverse (and extreme) form of the narrative figure the classics called *author's metalepsis*, which consists of pretending that the poet 'himself brings about the effects he celebrates,'[18] as when we say that Virgil 'has Dido die' in Book IV of the *Aeneid*, or when Diderot, more equivocally, writes in *Jacques le fataliste*: 'What would prevent me from *getting the Master married* and *making him a cuckold*?' or even, addressing the reader, 'If it gives you pleasure, *let us set* the peasant girl back in the saddle behind her escort, *let us let* them go and *let us come back* to our two travelers.'[19]

Sterne pushed the thing so far as to entreat the intervention of the reader, whom he beseeched to close the door or help Mr. Shandy get back to his bed, but the principle is the same: any intrusion by the extradiegetic narrator or narratee into the diegetic universe (or by diegetic characters into a metadiegetic universe, etc.), or the inverse (as in Cortázar), produces an effect of strangeness that is either comical (when, as in Sterne or Diderot, it is presented in a joking tone) or fantastic.

We will extend the term *narrative metalepsis*[20] to all these transgressions. Some of them, as ordinary and innocent as those of classical rhetoric, play on the double temporality of the story and the narrating. Here, for example, is Balzac, in a passage from *Illusions perdues*: 'While the venerable churchman climbs the ramps of Angoulême, it is not useless to explain . . . ,' as if the narrating were contemporaneous with the story and had to fill up the latter's dead spaces. [. . .] Sterne's temporal games, of course, are a bit bolder, a bit more *literal*, in other words, as when the digressions of Tristram the (extradiegetic) narrator require his father (in the diegesis) to prolong his nap by more than an hour,[21] but here, too, the principle is the same. In a certain way, the Pirandello manner of *Six Characters in Search of an Author* or *Tonight We Improvise*, where the same actors are in turn characters and players, is nothing but a vast expansion of metalepsis. [. . .] All these games, by the intensity of their effects, demonstrate the importance of the boundary they tax their ingenuity to overstep, in defiance of verisimilitude – a boundary *that is precisely the narrating (or the performance) itself*: a shifting but sacred frontier between two worlds, the world in which one tells, the world of which one tells. Whence the uneasiness Borges so well put his finger on: 'Such inversions suggest that if the characters in a story can be readers or spectators, then we, their readers or spectators, can be fictitious.'[22] The most troubling thing about metalepsis indeed lies in this unacceptable and insistent hypothesis, that the extradiegetic is perhaps always diegetic, and that the narrator and his narratees – you and I – perhaps belong to some narrative.

[. . .]

Person

Readers may have noticed that until now we have used the terms 'first-person – or third-person – narrative' only when paired with quotation marks of protest. Indeed, these common locutions seem to me inadequate, in that they stress variation in the element of the narrative situation that is in fact invariant – to wit, the presence (explicit or implicit) of the 'person' of the narrator. This presence is invariant because the narrator can be in his narrative (like every subject of an enunciating in his enunciated statement) *only* in the 'first person' – except for an enallage of convention as in Caesar's *Commentaries*; and stressing 'person' leads one to think that the choice the narrator has to make – a purely grammatical and rhetorical choice – is always of the same order as Caesar's in deciding to write his Memoirs 'in' one or another person. In fact, of course, this is not the issue. The novelist's choice, unlike the narrator's, is not between two grammatical forms, but between two narrative postures (whose grammatical forms are simply an automatic consequence): to have the story told by one of its 'characters,'[23] or to have it told by a narrator outside of the story. The presence of first-person verbs in a narrative text can therefore refer to two very different situations which grammar renders identical but which narrative analysis must distinguish: the narrator's own designation of himself as such, as when Virgil writes '*I* sing of arms and the man . . . ,' or else the identity of person between the narrator and one of the characters in the story, as when Crusoe writes '*I* was born in the year 1632, in the city of York . . .' The term 'first-person narrative' refers, quite obviously, only to the second of these situations, and this dissymmetry confirms its unfitness. Insofar as the narrator can at any instant intervene *as such* in the narrative, every narrating is, by definition, to all intents and purposes presented in the first person (even if in the editorial plural, as when Stendhal writes, '*We* will confess that . . . *we* have begun the story of *our* hero . . .'). The real question is whether or not the narrator can use the first person to designate *one of his characters*. We will therefore distinguish here two types *of narrative*: one with the narrator absent from the story he tells (example: Homer in the *Iliad*, or Flaubert in *L'Education sentimentale*), the other with the narrator present as a character in the story he tells (example: *Gil Blas*, or *Wuthering Heights*). I call the first type, for obvious reasons, *heterodiegetic*, and the second type *homodiegetic*.

But from the examples selected no doubt a dissymmetry in the status of these two types already emerges. Homer and Flaubert are both totally, and therefore *equally*, absent from the two narratives in question; on the other hand, we cannot say that Gil Blas and Lockwood are equally present in their respective narratives: Gil Blas is incontestably the hero of the story he tells, Lockwood is incontestably not (and we could easily find examples of even weaker 'presence'; I will come back to this momentarily). Absence is absolute, but presence has degrees. So we will have to differentiate within the homodiegetic type at least two varieties: one where the narrator is the hero of his narrative (*Gil Blas*) and one where he plays only a secondary role, which almost always turns out to be a role as observer and witness: Lockwood, the anonymous narrator of *Louis Lambert*, Ishmael in *Moby Dick*, Marlow in *Lord Jim*, Carraway in *The Great Gatsby*, Zeitblom in *Doctor Faustus* – not to mention the most illustrious and most representative one of all, the transparent (but inquisitive) Dr. Watson of Conan Doyle.[24] It is as if the narrator cannot be an ordinary walk-on in his narrative: he can be only the star, or else a mere bystander. For the first variety (which to some extent represents the strong degree of the homodiegetic) we will reserve the unavoidable term *autodiegetic*.

Defined this way, the narrator's relationship to the story is in principle invariable: even when Gil Blas and Watson momentarily disappear as characters, we know that they belong to the diegetic universe of their narrative and that they will reappear sooner or later. So the reader unfailingly takes the transition from one status to the other – when he perceives it – as an infraction of an implicit norm: for instance the (discreet) disappearance of the initial witness-narrator of the *Rouge* or *Bovary*, or the (noisier) one of the narrator of *Lamiel*, who openly leaves the diegesis 'in order to become a man of letters. Thus, O benevolent reader, farewell; you will hear nothing more of me.'[25] An even more glaring violation is the shift in grammatical person to designate the same character: for instance, in *Autre étude de femme*, Bianchon moves all of a sudden from 'I' to 'he',[26] as if he were unexpectedly abandoning the role of narrator; for instance, in *Jean Santeuil*, the hero moves inversely from 'he' to 'I.'[27] In the field of the classical novel, and still in Proust, such effects obviously result from a sort of narrative pathology, explicable by last-minute reshufflings and states of textual incompleteness. But we know that the contemporary novel has passed that limit, as it has so many others, and does not hesitate to establish between narrator and character(s) a variable or floating relationship, a pronominal vertigo in tune with a freer logic and a more complex conception of 'personality.' The most advanced forms of this emancipation[28] are perhaps not the most perceptible ones, because the classical attributes of 'character' – proper name, physical and moral 'nature' – have disappeared and along with them the signs that direct grammatical (pronominal) traffic.

[. . .]

If in every narrative we define the narrator's status both by its narrative level (extra- or intradiegetic) and by its relationship to the story (hetero- or homodiegetic), we can represent the four basic types of narrator's status as follows: (1) *extradiegetic-heterodiegetic* – paradigm: Homer, a narrator in the first degree who tells a story he is absent from; (2) *extradiegetic-homodiegetic* – paradigm: Gil Blas, a narrator in the first degree who tells his own story; (3) *intradiegetic-heterodiegetic* – paradigm: Scheherazade, a narrator in the second degree who tells stories she is on the whole absent from; (4) *intradiegetic-homodiegetic* – paradigm: Ulysses in Books IX–XII, a narrator in the second degree who tells his own story. [. . .]

LEVEL: RELATIONSHIP:	*Extradiegetic*	*Intradiegetic*
Heterodiegetic	Homer	Scheherazade
Homodiegetic	Gil Blas	Ulysses

[. . .]

The Narratee

[. . .]

Like the narrator, the narratee is one of the elements in the narrating situation, and he is necessarily located at the same diegetic level; that is, he does not merge a priori with the reader (even an implied reader) any more than the narrator necessarily merges with the author.

To an intradiegetic narrator corresponds an intradiegetic narratee. [. . .] We, the readers, cannot identify ourselves with those fictive narratees anymore than those intradiegetic narrators can address themselves to us, or even assume our existence.[29] [. . .]

The extradiegetic narrator, on the other hand, can aim only at an extradiegetic narratee, who merges with the implied reader and with whom each real reader can identify. This implied reader is in principle undefined, although Balzac does turn particularly sometimes toward a reader from the provinces, sometimes toward a Parisian reader, and Sterne sometimes calls him Madam or Sir Critick. The extradiegetic narrator can also pretend, like Meursault, to address no one, but this posture – fairly widespread in the contemporary novel – obviously cannot change the fact that a narrative, like every discourse, is necessarily addressed to someone and always contains below the surface an appeal to the receiver. And if the existence of an intradiegetic narratee has the effect of keeping us at a distance, since he is always interposed between the narrator and us [. . .] it is also true that the more transparent the receiving

instance and the more silent its evocation in the narrative, so undoubtedly the easier, or rather the more irresistible, each real reader's identification with or substitution for that implied instance will be.
[. . .]

Notes

1. For example, TODOROV, 'Les Catégories du Récit Littéraire,' *Communications* 8 (1966): 146–7.

2. On the *Thousand and One Nights*, see TODOROV, 'Narrative-Men,' in *The Poetics of Prose*, trans. Richard Howard (Ithaca, NY: Cornell University Press; Oxford: Blackwell, 1977): 'The record [for embedding] seems to be held by the narrative which offers us the story of the bloody chest. Here

    > Scheherazade tells that
    >   Jaafer tells that
    >   the tailor tells that
    >   the barber tells that
    >   his brother (and he has six brothers) tells that . . .

    The last story is a story to the fifth degree' (p. 71). But the term 'embedding' does not do justice to the fact precisely that each of these stories is at a higher 'degree' than the preceding one, since its narrator is a character in the preceding one; for stories can also be 'embedded' at the same level, simply by digression, without any shift in the narrating instance: see Jacques's parentheses in the *Fataliste*.

3. This is what I will call the receiver of the narrative, patterned after the contrast between *sender* and *receiver* proposed by A. J. GREIMAS (*Sémantique structurale* (Paris, 1966), p. 177).

4. Certain uses of the present tense do indeed connote temporal indefiniteness (and not simultaneousness between story and narrating), but curiously they seem reserved for very particular forms of narrative (joke, riddle, scientific problem or experiment, plot summary) and literature does not have much investment in them. The case of the 'narrative present' with preterite value is also different.

5. I borrow the term 'predictive' from TODOROV, *Grammaire du Décaméron* (The Hague, 1969), p. 48, to designate any kind of narrative where the narrating precedes the story.

6. Radio or television reporting is obviously the most perfectly live form of this kind of narrative, where the narrating follows so closely on the action that it can be considered practically simultaneous, whence the use of the present tense. We find a curious literary use of simultaneous narrative in chapter 29 of *Ivanhoe*, where Rebecca is telling the wounded Ivanhoe all about the battle taking place at the foot of the castle, a battle she is following from the window.

7. All written in the present tense except *Le Voyeur*, whose temporal system, as we know, is more complex.

8. The Spanish picaresque seems to form a notable exception to this 'rule,' at any rate *Lazarillo*, which ends in suspense ('It was the time of my prosperity, and I

was at the height of all good fortune'). *Guzmán* and *Buscón* also, but while promising a continuation and end, which will not come.

9. *Robinson Crusoe* (Oxford: Blackwell, 1928), III, 220.

10. JAMES M. CAIN, *Double Indemnity*, in *Cain X3* (New York: Knopf, 1969), p. 465.

11. LAURENCE STERNE, *Tristram Shandy*, IV, chap. 13.

12. Temporal indications of the kind 'we have *already* said' and 'we will see *later,*' etc., do not in fact refer to the temporality of the narrating, but to the space of the text (= *we have said above, we will see further on . . .*) and to the temporality of reading.

13. These terms have already been put forth in my *Figures II* (Paris: Seuil, 1969), p. 202. The prefix *meta-* obviously connotes here, as in 'metalanguage,' the transition to the second degree: the *metanarrative* is a narrative within the narrative, the *metadiegesis* is the universe of this second narrative, as the *diegesis* (according to a now widespread usage) designates the universe of the first narrative. We must admit, however, that this term functions in a way opposite to that of its model in logic and linguistics: metalanguage is a language in which one speaks of another language, so metanarrative should be the first narrative, within which one would tell a second narrative. But it seemed to me that it was better to keep the simplest and most common designation of the first degree, and thus to reverse the direction of interlocking. Naturally, the eventual third degree will be a meta-metanarrative, with its meta-metadiegesis, etc.

14. The same character can, moreover, assume two identical (parallel) narrative functions at different levels: for example, in *Sarrasine*, the extradiegetic narrator himself becomes intradiegetic narrator when he tells his companion the story of Zambinella. Thus he tells us that he tells this story – a story of which he is not the hero: this situation is the exact opposite of the (much more common) one of *Manon*, where the first narrator becomes on the second level the listener of another character who tells his own story. The situation of a *double narrator* occurs only, to my knowledge, in *Sarrasine*.

15. See the 'Notes by the Author' published at the head of *Manon Lescaut*.

16. There remains, however, an appreciable difference between these 'epistolary monodies,' as Rousset calls them, and a diary: the difference is the existence of a receiver (even a mute one), and his traces in the text.

17. JULIO CORTÁZAR, 'Continuidad de los Parques,' in *Final del Juego* (Madrid: Alfuguara, 1956).

18. PIERRE FONTANIER, *Commentaire raisonné sur 'Les Tropes' de Dumarsais*, vol. 2 of Dumarsais' *Les Tropes* (1818; repr. Geneva: Slatkine Reprints, 1967), p. 116.

19. DENIS DIDEROT, *Jacques le fataliste et son maître* (Paris: Garnier), pp. 495 and 497.

20. *Metalepsis* here forms a system with *prolepsis, analepsis, syllepsis,* and *paralepsis,* with this specific sense: 'taking hold of (telling) by changing level.'

21. STERNE, *Tristram Shandy*, III, chap. 38, and IV, chap. 2.

22. JORGE LUIS BORGES, *Other Inquisitions, 1937–1952*, trans. R. Simms (Austin, Tex., 1964), p. 46.

23. This term [*personnages*] is used here for lack of a more neutral or more extensive term which would not unduly connote, as this one does, the 'humanness' of the narrative agent, even though in fiction nothing prevents us from entrusting

that role to an animal (*Mémoires d'un âne* [*Memoirs of a Donkey*]) or indeed to an 'inanimate' object (I don't know whether we should put into this category the successive narrators of the *Bijoux indiscrets* [*Indiscreet Jewels*]).

24. A variant of this type is the narrative with a collective witness as narrator: the crew of *The Nigger of the 'Narcissus,'* the inhabitants of the small town in 'A Rose for Emily.' We remember that the opening pages of *Bovary* are written in this mode.

25. STENDHAL, *Lamiel* (Paris: Divan, 1948), p. 43. The inverse case, the sudden appearance of an autodiegetic 'I' in a heterodiegetic narrative, seems more rare. The Stendhalian 'I believe' (*Leuwen*, p. 117, *Chartreuse*, p. 76) can belong to the narrator as such.

26. HONORÉ DE BALZAC, *Autre étude de femme* (Geneva: Skira), pp. 75–7.

27. *Jean Santeuil, Les Plaisirs et les jours*, ed. PIERRE CLARAC and YVES SANDRE (Bibliothèque de la Pléiade) (Paris: Gallimard, 1971), p. 319, trans. Hopkins, pp. 118–19.

28. See for example J. L. BAUDRY, *Personnes* (Paris: Seuil, 1967).

29. A special case is the metadiegetic literary work, of the *Curious Impertinent* or *Jean Santeuil* kind, which can possibly aim at a reader, but a reader who in principle is himself fictive.

12 Introduction to the Study of the Narratee*

GERALD PRINCE

In this seminal article, Gerald Prince, following Genette, draws
attention to the figure of the narratee, the narrator's addressee,
which, he contends, is a strangely neglected although essential
element of all types of narrative. The narratee as defined by Genette
and Prince should not be confused with either the actual or the
implied reader, since neither of these need be the immediate
addressee of the narrator. Prince's proposal is threefold. First, to
elaborate a typology of narratees, according to the kind of 'signals'
portraying the narratee that appear in the text. This typology is
generated by a comparison with the ideal notion of 'zero-degree
narratee'. Secondly, to classify narratees according to their narrative
situation, that is, according to their position with reference to the
narrator, the characters and the narration. Thirdly, to define and
enumerate the narratee's functions, from the most obvious one as
mediator between narrator and reader to such others as contributing to the definition of the personality and reliability of the narrator, of the moral or ideological position of the work, and so on.

Gerald Prince's other contributions to narratology are mainly
concerned with devising formalized models for the representation
of action, for instance in *A Grammar of Stories: An Introduction* (1973)
and *Narratology: The Form and Functioning of Narrative* (1982).

All narration, whether it is oral or written, whether it recounts real
or mythical events, whether it tells a story or relates a simple
sequence of actions in time, presupposes not only (at least) one
narrator but also (at least) one narratee, the narratee being someone
whom the narrator addresses. In a fiction-narration – a tale, an epic,
a novel – the narrator is a fictive creation as is his narratee. Jean-
Baptiste Clamence, Holden Caulfield, and the narrator of *Madame
Bovary* are novelistic constructs as are the individuals to whom they

---

*Reprinted from *Reader-Response Criticism: From Formalism to Post-Structuralism*, ed.
JANE P. TOMPKINS, (Baltimore: Johns Hopkins University Press, 1980), pp. 7–25.
First published in *Poetics* 14 (1973): 177–96. Trans. Francis Mariner.

write. From Henry James and Norman Friedman to Wayne C. Booth and Tzvetan Todorov, numerous critics have examined the diverse manifestations of the narrator in fictive prose and verse, his multiple roles and his importance.[1] By contrast, few critics have dealt with the narratee and none to date has undertaken an in-depth study;[2] this neglect persists despite the lively interest raised by Benveniste's fine articles on discourse (*le discours*), Jakobson's work on linguistic functions, and the evergrowing prestige of poetics and semiology.

Nowadays, any student minimally versed in the narrative genre differentiates the narrator of a novel from its author and from the novelistic *alter ego* of the author and knows the difference between Marcel and Proust, Rieux and Camus, Tristram Shandy, Sterne the novelist, and Sterne the man. Most critics, however, are scarcely concerned with the notion of the narratee and often confuse it with the more or less adjacent notions of receptor (*récepteur*), reader, and arch-reader (*archilecteur*).

[...]

The zero-degree narratee

In the very first pages of *Le Père Goriot*, the narrator exclaims: 'That's what you will do, you who hold this book with a white hand, you who settle back in a well-padded armchair saying to yourself: perhaps this is going to be amusing. After reading about old Goriot's secret misfortunes, you'll dine with a good appetite attributing your insensitivity to the author whom you'll accuse of exaggeration and poetic affectation.' This 'you' with white hands, accused by the narrator of being egotistical and callous, is the narratee. It's obvious that the latter does not resemble most readers of *Le Père Goriot* and that consequently the narratee of a novel cannot be automatically identified with the reader: the reader's hands might be black or red and not white; he might read the novel in bed instead of in an armchair; he might lose his appetite upon learning of the old merchant's unhappiness. The reader of a fiction, be it in prose or in verse, should not be mistaken for the narratee. The one is real, the other fictive. If it should occur that the reader bears an astonishing resemblance to the narratee, this is an exception and not the rule.

Neither should the narratee be confused with the virtual reader. Every author, provided he is writing for someone other than himself, develops his narrative as a function of a certain type of reader whom he bestows with certain qualities, faculties, and inclinations according to his opinion of men in general (or in particular) and according to the obligations he feels should be respected. This virtual reader is different from the real reader: writers frequently have a public they don't deserve. He is also distinct from the narratee. In *La Chute*, Clamence's narratee is not identical to the reader envisioned by Camus: after all, he's a lawyer visiting Amsterdam. It goes without saying that a virtual reader and a narratee can be alike, but once again it would be an exception.

Finally, we should not confuse the narratee with the ideal reader, although a remarkable likeness can exist between the two. For a writer, an ideal reader would be one who would understand perfectly and would approve entirely the least of his words, the most subtle of his intentions. For a critic, an ideal reader would perhaps be one capable of interpreting the infinity of texts that, according to certain critics, can be found in one specific text. On the one hand, the narratees for whom the narrator multiplies his explanations and justifies the particularities of his narrative are numerous and cannot be thought of as constituting the ideal readers dreamed up by a novelist. We need only think of the narratees of *Le Père Goriot* and *Vanity Fair*. On the other hand, these narratees are too inept to be capable of interpreting even a rather restricted group of texts with the text.

If narratees are distinct from real, virtual, or ideal readers,[3] they very often differ from each other as well. Nonetheless, it should be possible to describe each one of them as a function of the same categories and according to the same models. It is necessary to identify at least some of these characteristics as well as some of the ways in which they vary and combine with each other. These characteristics must be situated with reference to a sort of 'zero-degree' narratee, a concept which it is now time to define.

In the first place, the zero-degree narratee knows the tongue (*langue*) and the language(s) (*langage[s]*) of the narrator. In his case, to know a tongue is to know the meanings (*dénotations*) – the signifieds as such and, if applicable, the referents – of all the signs that constitute it; this does not include knowledge of the connotations (the subjective values that have been attached to them). It also involves a perfect mastery of grammar but not of the (infinite) paragrammatical possibilities. It is the ability to note semantic and/or syntactic ambiguities and to be able to resolve these difficulties from the context. It is the capacity to recognize the grammatical incorrectness or oddness of any sentence or syntagm – by reference to the linguistic system being used.[4]

Beyond this knowledge of language, the zero-degree narratee has certain faculties of reasoning that are often only the corollaries of this knowledge. Given a sentence or a series of sentences, he is able to grasp the presuppositions and the consequences.[5] The zero-degree narratee knows narrative grammar, the rules by which any story is elaborated.[6] He knows, for example, that a minimal complete narrative sequence consists in the passage from a given situation to the inverse situation. He knows that the narrative possesses a temporal dimension and that it necessitates relations of causality. Finally, the zero-degree narratee possesses a sure memory, at least in regard to the events of the narrative about which he has been informed and the consequences that can be drawn from them.

Thus, he does not lack positive characteristics. But he also does not want negative traits. He can thus only follow a narrative in a well-defined and concrete way and is obliged to acquaint himself with the events by reading from the first page to the last, from the initial word to the final word. In addition, he is without any personality or social characteristics. He is neither good nor bad, pessimistic nor optimistic, revolutionary nor bourgeois, and his character, his position in society, never colors his perception of the events described to him. Moreover, he knows absolutely nothing about the events or characters mentioned and he is not acquainted with the conventions prevailing in that world or in any other world. Just as he doesn't understand the connotations of a certain turn of phrase, he doesn't realize what can be evoked by this or that situation, this or that novelistic action. The consequences of this are very important. Without the assistance of the narrator, without his explanations and the information supplied by him, the narratee is able neither to interpret the value of an action nor to grasp its repercussions. He is incapable of determining the morality or immorality of a character, the realism or extravagance of a description, the merits of a rejoinder, the satirical intention of a tirade. And how would he be able to do so? By virtue of what experience, what knowledge, or what system of values?

More particularly, a notion as fundamental as verisimilitude only counts very slightly for him. Indeed, verisimilitude is always defined in relation to another text, whether this text be public opinion, the rules of a literary genre, or 'reality.' The zero-degree narratee, however, is acquainted with no texts and in the absence of commentary, the adventures of Don Quixote would seem as ordinary to him as those of Passemurailles (an individual capable of walking through walls) or of the protagonists of *Une Belle Journée*.[7] The same would hold true for relations of implicit causality. [...] The narratee with no experience and no common sense does not perceive relations of implicit causality and does not fall victim to this confusion. Finally, the zero-degree narratee does not organize the narrative as a function of the major codes of reading studied by Roland Barthes in *S/Z*. He doesn't know how to unscramble the different voices that shape the

narration. After all, as Barthes has said: 'The code is a convergence
of quotations, a structural mirage ... the resulting units ... made up
of fragments of this something which always has *already* been read,
seen, done, lived: the code is the groove of this *already*. Referring
back to what has been written, that is, to the Book (of culture, of life,
of life as culture), the code makes the text a prospectus of this Book.'[8]
For the zero-degree narratee, there is no *already*, there is no Book.

The signals of the narratee

Every narratee possesses the characteristics that we have enumerated
except when an indication to the contrary is supplied in the narration
intended for him: he knows, for example, the language employed by
the narrator, he is gifted with an excellent memory, he is unfamiliar
with everything concerning the characters who are presented to him.
It is not rare that a narrative might deny or contradict these
characteristics: a certain passage might underline the language-related
difficulties of the narratee, another passage might disclose that he
suffers from amnesia, yet another passage might emphasize his
knowledge of the problems being discussed. It is on the basis of these
deviations from the characteristics of the zero-degree narratee that
the portrait of a specific narratee is gradually constituted.

Certain indications supplied by the text concerning a narratee are
sometimes found in a section of the narrative that is not addressed to
him. [...] At the beginning of *L'Immoraliste*, for example, we learn
that Michel has not seen his narratees for three years and the story
he tells them quickly confirms this fact. Nonetheless, sometimes these
indications contradict the narrative and emphasize certain
differences between the narratee as conceived by the narrator and as
revealed by another voice. The few words spoken by Doctor
Spielvogel at the end of *Portnoy's Complaint* reveal that he is not what
the narrative has led us to believe.[9]

Nevertheless, the portrait of a narratee emerges above all from the
narrative addressed to him. If we consider that any narration is
composed of a series of signals directed to the narratee, two major
categories of signals can be distinguished. On the one hand there are
those signals that contain no reference to the narratee or, more
precisely, no reference differentiating him from the zero-degree
narratee. On the other hand, there are those signals that, on the
contrary, define him as a specific narratee and make him deviate
from the established norms. In *Un Coeur simple* a sentence such as
[...] 'His entire person produced in her that confusion into which
we are all thrown by the spectacle of extraordinary men' not only

records the reactions of the heroine in the presence of M. Bourais, but also informs us that the narratee has experienced the same feelings in the presence of extraordinary individuals.

[...]

The signals capable of portraying the narratee are quite varied and one can easily distinguish several types that are worth discussing. In the first place, we should mention all passages of a narrative in which the narrator refers directly to the narratee. We retain in this category statements in which the narrator designates the narratee by such words as 'reader' or 'listener' and by such expressions as 'my dear' or 'my friend.' In the event that the narration may have identified a specific characteristic of the narratee, for example, his profession or nationality, passages mentioning this characteristic should also be considered in this first category. Thus, if the narrator is a lawyer, all information concerning lawyers in general is pertinent. Finally, we should retain all passages in which the addressee is designated by second-person pronouns and verb forms.

Besides those passages referring quite explicitly to the narratee, there are passages that, although not written in the second person, imply a narratee and describe him. When Marcel in *A la recherche du temps perdu* [...] declares: 'Undoubtedly, in these coincidences which are so perfect, when reality withdraws and applies itself to what we have dreamt about for so long a time, it hides it from us entirely,' the 'we' includes the narratee.[10] [...]

Then again, there are often numerous passages in a narrative that, though they contain apparently no reference – even an ambiguous one – to a narratee, describe him in greater or lesser detail. Accordingly, certain parts of a narrative may be presented in the form of questions or pseudo-questions. Sometimes these questions originate neither with a character nor with the narrator who merely repeats them. These questions must then be attributed to the narratee and we should note what excites his curiosity, the kinds of problems he would like to resolve. In *Le Père Goriot*, for example, it is the narratee who makes inquiries about the career of M. Poiret: 'What had he been? But perhaps he had been employed at the Ministry of Justice . . .' Sometimes, however, the narrator addresses questions to the narratee himself, some of whose knowledge and defenses are thus revealed in the process. Marcel will address a pseudo-question to his narratee asking him to explain the slightly vulgar, and for that reason surprising, behavior of Swann: 'But who has not seen unaffected royal princesses . . . spontaneously adopt the language of old bores? . . .'

Other passages are presented in the form of negations. [...] The narrator of *Les Faux-Monnayeurs* vigorously rejects the theory advanced by the narratee to explain Vincent Molinier's nocturnal departures: 'No, it was not to his mistress that Vincent Molinier went each evening.' Sometimes a partial negation can be revelatory. In *A la recherche du temps perdu*, the narrator, while believing that the narratee's conjectures about the extraordinary suffering of Swann are well-founded, at the same time finds them insufficient. [. . .]

There are also passages that include a term with demonstrative significance that instead of referring to an anterior or ulterior element of the narrative, refers to another text, to extra-textual experience (*hors-texte*) known to the narrator and his narratee. [. . .]

Comparisons or analogies found in a narration also furnish us with information more or less valuable. [. . .]

But perhaps the most revelatory signals and at times the most difficult to grasp and describe in a satisfactory way are those we shall call – for lack of a more appropriate term – *over-justifications* (*surjustifications*). Any narrator more or less explains the world inhabited by his characters, motivates their acts, and justifies their thoughts. If it occurs that these explanations and motivations are situated at the level of meta-language, meta-commentary, or meta-narration, they are over-justifications. When the narrator of *La Chartreuse de Parme* [. . .] asks to be excused for a poorly phrased sentence, when he excuses himself for having to inter-rupt his narrative, when he confesses himself incapable of describing well a certain feeling, these are over-justifications that he employs. Over-justifications always provide us with interesting details about the narratee's personality, even though they often do so in an indirect way; in overcoming the narratee's defenses, in prevailing over his prejudices, in allaying his apprehensions, they reveal them.

The narratee's signals – those that describe him as well as those that only provide him with information – can pose many problems for the reader who would wish to classify them in order to arrive at a portrait of the narratee or a certain reading of the text. It's not simply a question of their being sometimes difficult to notice, to grasp, or to explain, but in certain narratives, one can find contradictory signals. Sometimes they originate with a narrator who wishes to amuse himself at the expense of the narratee or underscore the arbitrariness of the text; often the world presented is a world in which the principles of contradiction known to us don't exist or are not applicable; finally, the contradictions – the entirely obvious ones – often result from the different points of view that the narrator strives to reproduce faithfully. Nonetheless it occurs that not all contradictory data can be entirely explained in this fashion. In these cases, they should be attributed to the author's ineptness – or temperament. [. . .] Coherence is certainly not an imperative for the pornographic genre in which a wild variation is the rule rather than the exception. It nonetheless remains that in these cases, it is difficult – if not impossible – to interpret the semantic material presented to the narratee.

Sometimes it is the signals describing the narratee that form a strangely disparate collection. Indeed, every signal relating to a narratee need not continue or confirm a preceding signal or announce a signal to follow. There are narratees who change much as narrators do or who have a rich enough personality to embrace various tendencies and feelings. But the contradictory nature of certain narratees does not always result from a complex personality or a subtle evolution. [...]

Despite the questions posed, the difficulties raised, the errors committed, it is evident that the kinds of signals used, their respective numbers, and their distribution determine to a certain extent the different types of narrative.[11] [...]

Classification of narratees

Thanks to the signals describing the narratee, we are able to characterize any narration according to the type of narratee to whom it is addressed. It would be useless, because too long, too complicated, and too imprecise, to distinguish different categories of narratees according to their temperament, their civil status, or their beliefs. On the other hand, it would be comparatively easy to classify narratees according to their narrative situation, to their position in reference to the narrator, the characters, and the narration.

Many narrations appear to be addressed to no one in particular: no character is regarded as playing the role of narratee and no narratee is mentioned by the narrator either directly ('Without a doubt, dear reader, you have never been confined in a glass bottle') or indirectly ('We could hardly do otherwise than pluck one of its flowers and present it to the reader'). [...]

In many other narrations, if the narratee is not represented by a character, he is at least mentioned explicitly by the narrator. The latter refers to him more or less frequently and his references can be quite direct (*Eugene Onegin, The Gold Pot, Tom Jones*) or quite indirect (*The Scarlet Letter, The Old Curiosity Shop, Les Faux-Monnayeurs*). These narratees are nameless and their role in the narrative is not always very important. Yet because of the passages that designate them in an explicit manner, it is easy to draw their portrait and to know what their narrator thinks of them. [...]

Often instead of addressing – explicitly or implicitly – a narratee

197

who is not a character, the narrator recounts his story to someone who is (*Heart of Darkness, Portnoy's Complaint, Les Infortunes de la vertu*). [. . .]

The narratee-character might play no other role in the narrative than that of narratee (*Heart of Darkness*). But he might also play other roles. It is not rare, for example, for him to be at the same time a narrator. [. . .] In *La Nausée*, for example, as in most novels written in the form of a diary, Roquentin counts on being the only reader of his journal.

Then again, the narratee-character can be more or less affected, more or less influenced by the narrative addressed to him. In *Heart of Darkness*, the companions of Marlowe are not transformed by the story that he recounts to them. In *L'Immoraliste*, the three narratees, if they are not really different from what they were before Michel's account, are nonetheless 'overcome by a strange feeling of malaise.' And in *La Nausée*, as in many other works in which the narrator constitutes his own narratee, the latter is gradually and profoundly changed by the events he recounts for himself.

Finally, the narratee-character can represent for the narration someone more or less essential, more or less irreplaceable as a narratee. In *Heart of Darkness*, it's not necessary for Marlowe to have his comrades on the *Nellie* as narratees. He would be able to recount his story to any other group; perhaps he would be able to refrain from telling it at all. On the other hand, in *L'Immoraliste*, Michel wished to address his friends and for that reason gathered them around him. [. . .] And in *A Thousand and One Nights*, to have the caliph as narratee is the difference between life and death for Scheherazade. If he refuses to listen to her, she will be killed. He is thus the only narratee whom she can have.

[. . .]

We could probably think of other distinctions or establish other categories, but in any case, we can see how much more precise and more refined the typology of narrative would be if it were based not only upon narrators but also upon narratees.

[. . .]

The narratee's functions

The type of narratee that we find in a given narrative, the relations that tie him to narrators, characters, and other narratees, the distances that separate him from ideal, virtual, or real readers partially determine the nature of this narrative. But the narratee exercises other functions that are more or less numerous and important and are more or less specific to him. It will be worth the effort to enumerate these functions and to study them in some detail.

The most obvious role of the narratee, a role that he always plays in a certain sense, is that of relay between the narrator and the reader(s), or rather between the author and the reader(s). Should certain values have to be defended or certain ambiguities clarified, this can easily be done by means of asides addressed to the narratee. Should the importance of a series of events be emphasized, should one reassure or make uneasy, justify certain actions or underscore their arbitrariness, this can always be done by addressing signals to the narratee. [...] There exist other conceivable relays than direct and explicit asides addressed to the narratee, other possibilities of mediation between authors and readers. Dialogues, metaphors, symbolic situations, allusions to a particular system of thought or to a certain work of art are some of the ways of manipulating the reader, guiding his judgments, and controlling his reactions. Moreover, those are the methods preferred by many modern novelists, if not the majority of them; perhaps because they accord or seem to accord more freedom to the reader, perhaps because they oblige him to participate more actively in the development of the narrative, or perhaps simply because they satisfy a certain concern for realism. [...]

Besides the function of mediation, the narratee exercises in any narration a function of characterization. [...] The relations that a narrator-character establishes with his narratee reveal as much – if not more – about his character than any other element in the narrative. In *La Religieuse*, Sister Suzanne, because of her conception of the narratee and her asides addressed to him, emerges as much less naïve and much more calculating and coquettish than she would like to appear.

[...]

Moreover, the relations between the narrator and the narratee in a text may underscore one theme, illustrate another, or contradict yet another. Often the theme refers directly to the narrative situation and it is the narration as theme that these relations reveal. In *A Thousand and One Nights*, for instance, the theme of narration as life is emphasized by the attitude of Scheherazade toward the caliph and vice-versa: the heroine will die if her narratee decides not to listen to her any more, just as other characters in the narrative die because he will not listen to them: ultimately, any narrative is impossible without a narratee. But often, themes that do not concern the narrative situation – or perhaps concern it only indirectly – reveal the positions of the narrator and the narratee in relation to each other. In *Le Père Goriot*, the narrator maintains relations of power with his narratee.

From the very beginning, the narrator tries to anticipate his narratee's objections, to dominate him, and to convince him. [...] This sort of war, this desire for power, can be found at the level of the characters. On the level of the events as well as on the level of narration, the same struggle takes place.

If the narratee contributes to the thematic of a narrative, he is also always part of the narrative framework, often of a particularly concrete framework in which the narrator(s) and narratee(s) are all characters (*Heart of Darkness, L'Immoraliste, The Decameron*). The effect is to make the narrative seem more natural. The narratee like the narrator plays an undeniable *verisimilating (vraisemblabilisant)* role. Sometimes this concrete framework provides the model by which a work or narration develops. In *The Decameron* or in *L'Heptameron*, it is expected that each of the narratees will in turn become a narrator. More than a mere sign of realism or an index of verisimilitude, the narratee represents in these circumstances an indispensable element for the development of the narrative.

... Finally it sometimes happens that we must study the narratee in order to discover a narrative's fundamental thrust. In *La Chute*, for example, it is only by studying the reactions of Clamence's narratee that we can know whether the protagonist's arguments are so powerful that they cannot be resisted, or whether, on the contrary, they constitute a skillful but unconvincing appeal. To be sure, the narratee doesn't say a single word throughout the entire novel and we don't even know if Clamence addresses himself or someone else: [...] whatever the identity of the narratee may be, the only thing that counts is the extent of his agreement with the theses of the hero. The latter's discourse shows evidence of a more and more intense resistance on the part of his interlocutor. Clamence's tone becomes more insistent and his sentences more embarrassed as his narrative progresses and his narratee escapes him. Several times in the last part of the novel he even appears seriously shaken. If at the end of *La Chute* Clamence is not defeated, he certainly has not been triumphant. [...]

The narratee can, thus, exercise an entire series of functions in a narrative: he constitutes a relay between the narrator and the reader, he helps establish the narrative framework, he serves to characterize the narrator, he emphasizes certain themes, he contributes to the development of the plot, he becomes the spokesman for the moral of the work. Obviously, depending upon whether the narrator is skillful or inept, depending upon whether or not problems of narrative technique interest him, and depending upon whether or not his narrative requires it, the narratee will be more or less important, will play a greater or lesser number of roles, will be used in a way more or less subtle and original. Just as we study the narrator to evaluate the economy, the intentions, and the success of a narrative, so too we should examine the narratee in order to understand further and/or differently its mechanisms and significance.

[. . .] In the final analysis, the study of the narratee can lead us to a better understanding not only of the narrative genre but of all acts of communication.

Notes

1. See, for example, HENRY JAMES, *The Art of Fiction and Other Essays*, ed. Morris Roberts (New York: Oxford University Press, 1948); NORMAN FRIEDMAN, 'Point of View in Fiction: The Development of a Critical Concept,' *PMLA* 70 (December 1955): 1160–84; WAYNE C. BOOTH, *The Rhetoric of Fiction* (Chicago: University of Chicago Press, 1961); TZVETAN TODOROV, 'Poétique' in Oswald Ducrot *et al.*, *Qu'est-ce que le structuralisme?* (Paris: Seuil, 1968), pp. 97–166; and GÉRARD GENETTE, *Figures III* (Paris: Seuil, 1972).

2. See, among others, WALKER GIBSON, 'Authors, Speakers, Readers, and Mock Readers,' *College English* 11 (February 1950): 265–9 (chap. 9 in this volume); ROLAND BARTHES, 'Introduction à l'analyse structurale des récits,' *Communications* 8 (1966): 18–19; TODOROV, 'Les Catégories du Récit Littéraire,' *Communications* 8 (1966): 146–7; GERALD PRINCE, 'Notes Towards a Characterisation of Fictional "Narratees," ' *Genre* 4 (March 1971): 100–5; and GENETTE, *Figures III*, pp. 265–7.

3. For convenience's sake, we speak (and will speak often) of readers. It is obvious that a narratee should not be mistaken for a listener – real, virtual, or ideal.

4. This description of the linguistic capabilities of the zero-degree narratee nonetheless raises many problems. Thus, it is not always easy to determine the meaning(s) (*dénotation[s]*) of a given term and it becomes necessary to fix in time the language (*langue*) known to the narratee, a task that is sometimes difficult when working from the text itself. In addition, the narrator can manipulate a language in a personal way. Confronted by certain idiosyncrasies that are not easy to situate in relation to the text, do we say that the narratee experiences them as exaggerations, as errors, or on the contrary do they seem perfectly normal to him? Because of these difficulties and many others as well, the description of the narratee and his language cannot always be exact. It is, nevertheless, to a large extent reproducible.

5. We use these terms as they are used in modern logic.

6. See in this regard, PRINCE, *A Grammar of Stories: An Introduction* (The Hague: Mouton, 1973). A formal description of the rules followed by all narratives can be found in this work.

7. On verisimilitude, see the excellent issue 11 of *Communications* (1968).

8. BARTHES, *S/Z* (Paris: Seuil, 1970), pp. 27–8.

9. We should undoubtedly distinguish the 'virtual' narratee from the 'real' narratee in a more systematic manner. But this distinction would perhaps not be very helpful.

10. Note that even an 'I' can designate a 'you.'

11. See, in this regard, GENETTE, 'Vraisemblance et motivation,' in his *Figures II* (Paris: Seuil, 1969).

13 Modes and Forms of Narrative Narcissism: Introduction of a Typology*

LINDA HUTCHEON

The text reprinted here belongs to chapter 1 of *Narcissistic Narrative* (1980). In it, Linda Hutcheon underlines the intrinsic fictionality and artificiality of all kinds of narrative, from the classic realist novel to the *nouveau nouveau roman*, and sets out to define what she calls 'narcissistic narrative' as the kind that transforms the process of its own making into part of the shared pleasure of reading. Hutcheon's narcissistic narrative is more or less equivalent to such terms as Robert Scholes's 'fabulation', William H. Gass's 'metafiction', Raymond Federman's 'surfiction' and Ronald Binn's 'anti-novel', all of which were coined to account for the widespread tendency to introversion and self-referentiality of much postmodernist fiction. Hutcheon's contention is that narcissistic or metafictional narrative is as mimetic as any other narrative genre, including classic realism. Central to her definition of the new genre is a rejection of the traditional definition of parody as a necessary movement away from mimesis and towards mockery, ridicule or mere destruction. Following the formalist theorists, she defines parody as the result of a conflict between realistic motivation and an aesthetic motivation which has become weak and obvious, resulting in the unmasking and defamiliarization of the system. Deconstruction of the old conventions does not, however, involve destruction of the genre, but rather (as John Barth contended in 'The Literature of Exhaustion' and 'The Literature of Replenishment: Postmodernist Fiction') brings about a revitalization of the old 'exhausted' forms, their transformation into a new literature of 'replenishment'.

Hutcheon also undertakes to refine Jean Ricardou's typology of metaficational modes. She proposes a typology based on a fourfold axis: overt and covert narcissism; linguistic and diegetic narcissism. Analysis of these basic theoretical modes or metaphoric patterns is complemented by an awareness of the central role of the reader,

---

*Reprinted from HUTCHEON, *Narcissistic Narrative: The Metafictional Paradox* (1980; New York: Methuen, 1984), pp. 17–35.

who is forced to control, organize and interpret the self-reflective text actively and effortfully. Hutcheon's taxonomy, like all such structuralist models, inevitably becomes problematic in many practical cases of analysis, but it remains useful as a measuring grid for metafictional structures.

[...]

If self-awareness is a sign of the genre's disintegration, then the novel began its decline at birth.

[...]

What narcissistic narrative does do in flaunting, in baring its fictional and linguistic systems to the reader's view, is to transform the process of making, of *poiesis*, into part of the shared pleasure of reading. [...]

Despite both the hostile accusations of 'preening narcissism' of many reviews, and the increasing number of self-reflective novels that appear, very little systematic study has been devoted thus far to determining the types, much less the causes of such literary introversion. [...]

Jean Ricardou conveniently provides us with a horizontal and vertical auto-representational cross[1] on which to crucify – systematically – metafictional modes. [...] Ricardou presents a system which is structured on two types of self-reflectiveness, or, to use his term, auto-representation – vertical and horizontal. The vertical variety is *inter*dimensional, operating between the 'fiction' (what is said) and the 'narration' (how it is said). Horizontal auto-representation is *intra*dimensional. There are two sub-groups within these types, yielding four separate modes; (1) 'auto-représentation verticale, descendante, expressive': here the 'fiction' is in control of the 'narration,' as it is traditionally in realistic texts in which the referential dimension dominates; (2) 'auto-représentation verticale, ascendante, productrice': this is in operation when it is the 'narration' that controls, or at least influences, the 'fiction.' This is what Ricardou earlier[2] had labelled as a 'littérature du faire' or 'scripturalisme,' for the text points to itself allegorically or metaphorically as a written text, as an active production of writer and reader; (3) 'auto-représentation horizontale, référentielle, productrice' operates on the level of the 'fiction' only, in the form of structural event repetition, *mise en abyme*, or perhaps microcosmic sabotages of chronology and suspense; (4) 'auto-représentation horizontale, littérale, productrice' functions on the 'narration' level alone and indeed the 'narration' becomes the 'fiction.'

There are at least three potential problems with Ricardou's structure here. In the first place, it is hard to see how his initial category qualifies as any kind of *auto*-representation except in his example of alliteration, a not particularly important technique in narrative. He does separate it from the others by its pejorative label of 'expressive' (as opposed to the modern 'productrice'), but one must still question its usefulness as a category of *auto*-representation. The second limitation of this system lies in Ricardou's lack of distinction between texts which are self-conscious about their *diegetic* or narrative processes and those which are *linguistically* self-reflective. This causes distinct problems in Ricardou's own analyses of, for example, Raymond Roussel, in which he confuses and combines the author's generative linguistic *procédé* with the different but equally self-reflective structural narrative mirrorings, a confusion he senses but does not clarify in his more recent writing on Roussel.[3] Both language and narrative structures are included in his category of 'narration,' but some texts – such as John Barth's *Chimera* – reveal their own diegetic operations, while others – Ricardou's own fiction – concentrate on their own linguistic functioning. It is true that, in the latter case, language often works to order diegetic modes, but as this is not necessarily so in the reverse instance (that narrative structures determine language), there would seem to be a need for a distinction between the two.

The third difficulty with Ricardou's cross of horizontal and vertical auto-representative categories lies in its very neatness, its *a priori* deductive nature. It has already been suggested that its fearful symmetry is rather questionable in allowing (or rather, requiring) the presence of what he calls the 'auto-représentation verticale, descendante, expressive.' However, one would still be left with a pleasantly structured triangle of types, were it not for the fact that there seem to be *more* kinds of metafictional self-consciousness than it can account for. There are texts which are, as has been mentioned, diegetically self-aware, that is, conscious of their own narrative processes. Others are linguistically self-reflective, demonstrating their awareness of both the limits and the powers of their own language. In the first case, the text presents itself as diegesis, as narrative; in the second, it is unobfuscated text, language.

A further distinction must be made, however, within these two modes, for each can be present in at least two forms, what one might term an overt and a covert one. Overt forms of narcissism are present in texts in which the self-consciousness and self-reflection are clearly evident, usually explicitly thematized or even allegorized within the 'fiction.' In its covert form, however, this process would be structuralized, internalized, actualized. Such a text would, in fact, be self-reflective, but not necessarily self-conscious. One is left again with a four-part system, this time of overt diegetic and linguistic types of literary narcissism, and their covert counterparts, both diegetic and linguistic. In order to clarify and expand this system and to see its diachronic as well as synchronic implications, it is necessary to deal with each mode and form in turn.

In its most overt form the self-consciousness of a text often takes the shape of an explicit thematization – through plot allegory, narrative metaphor, or even narrational commentary. This latter possibility opens up again the entire question of the modernity and origins of recent metafiction. It has already been suggested that these new manifestations are rooted in a tradition of literary self-awareness that dates back, through Romantic inner mirroring to the eighteenth-century garrulous, guiding narrator to *Don Quixote's* Cide Hamete Benengeli. That is to say, that there would appear to be a developing tradition of narcissism, rather than a definite rupture out of which sprang metafiction. [. . .] Perhaps each novel has always had within itself the seeds of a 'narcissistic' reading, of an interpretation which would make it an allegorical or metaphorical exploration of the process of articulating a literary world.

This admittedly appears more convincing a speculation if one does accept *Don Quixote* (rather than *Pamela*, the voyage tale, the *fabliaux*, etc.) as the first novel, since its parodic intent is essential to its formal identity. The Russian formalist concept of parody as an autonomous art, based on the discovery of 'process' would therefore be of interest to the study of the novel's dialectic growth. Parody, according to the formalist theoreticians, is the result of a conflict between realistic motivation and an aesthetic motivation which has become weak and been made obvious. The consequence is the unmasking of the system or of the creative process whose function has given way to mechanical convention. It is as if a dialectic were established, as if this parodied material were backgrounded to the new forms and thus a formal synthesis effected. If a new parodic form does not develop when an old one becomes insufficiently motivated, the old form tends to degenerate into pure convention; witness the popular traditional novel, the best-seller.

Another operation is at work in metafictional parody, however, and this the formalists called 'defamiliarization.' The laying bare of literary devices in metafiction brings to the reader's attention those formal elements of which, through over-familiarization, he has become unaware. Through his recognition of the backgrounded material, new demands for attention and active involvement are brought to bear on the act of reading. [. . .]

[Thus,] one finds John Fowles's narrator in *The French Lieutenant's Woman* parodying the conventions of the Victorian novel – but doing so as a means to a new and relevant, modern synthetic form. Yet this play could well be seen as the very essence of the novel genre: Quixote imitates *Amadis of Gaul*, Cervantes pretends to be Don Quixote. [...]

Indeed, the techniques of the 'littérature citationnelle' can be seen as both parodic and generative. Quotations from one text, when inserted in the context of another, are the same and yet new and different, a microcosmic version of T. S. Eliot's concept of 'tradition' in literature. The parodic creation of new fiction through the rewriting of old is itself the narcissistic subject of metafictional parody in Borges' tale of Pierre Menard, author of the *Quixote*.

Parody is, therefore, an exploration of difference and similarity; in metafiction it invites a more literary reading, a recognition of literary codes. But it is wrong to see the end of this process as mockery, ridicule, or mere destruction.[4] Metafiction parodies and imitates as a way to a new form which is just as serious and valid, as a synthesis, as the form it dialectically attempts to surpass. It does not necessarily involve a movement away from *mimesis*, however, unless by that term is meant only a rigid object-imitation or behaviouristic-realistic motivation.

A text may self-consciously present its own creative processes, perhaps as a model of man's exercise of language and meaning production. And, it may do so, as Jonathan Culler suggests in *Structuralist Poetics*, with an eye to disarming attacks on its *vraisemblance* by admitting its artificiality. However, it might also be done in order to make a specific demand upon the reader, a demand for recognition of a new code, for a more open reading that entails a parodic synthesis of back- and fore-grounded elements.

There is yet another reason, of course, why modern self-informing fiction is not *anti*-mimetic. The 'psychological realism' of early twentieth-century fiction, made possible by Romantic self-consciousness, expanded (again through a kind of dialectic movement) the meaning of novelistic mimesis to include process as well as product. For many social or philosophical reasons, Joyce, Proust, Virginia Woolf, Pirandello, Svevo, Gide, and many others began to question the increasingly narrow view of fictional realism that had grown out of the naturalism of the preceding century. [...]

Their new 'subjective realism' had two major effects on the reified novelistic tradition of the preceding century that are significant here, especially for overt forms of narcissism. The once important detailed presentation of external reality became somewhat atrophied or, at least, stylized as the focus of attention shifted to the character's inner *processes* – imaginative and psychological. Secondly, the role of the reader began to change. Reading was no longer easy, no longer a comfortable controlled experience; the reader was now forced to control, to organize, to interpret. [. . .]

What, then, is the difference between this type of auto-representation and what has here been named *modern* metafiction? It is not a matter of date, for William Saroyan's self-consciousness is in the service of traditional realism in stories such as 'Seventy Thousand Assyrians' or 'Myself Upon the Earth,' and it is not quite what has here been called overt narcissism. [. . .] One difference seems to lie in the role allotted to the reader. In its concern about writers and about novels, the 'expressionistic' novel focuses on its own idea;[5] the main interest is in the *writing* process and its product. In both the covert and overt forms of metafictional narcissism, this focus does not *shift*, so much as *broaden*, to include a parallel process of equal importance to the text's actualization – that of *reading*. The reader is explicitly or implicitly forced to face his responsibility toward the text, that is, toward the novelistic world he is creating through the accumulated fictive referents of literary language. As the novelist actualizes the world of his imagination through words, so the reader – from those same words – manufactures in reverse a literary universe that is as much his creation as it is the novelist's. This near equation of the acts of reading and writing is one of the concerns that sets modern metafiction apart from previous novelistic self-consciousness.

It is certainly true that from its origins the novel has displayed an interest in *moulding* its reader, but few earlier texts will grant or demand of the reader, his *freedom*. Tristram Shandy constantly worries about his reader's qualifications and needs. In *Tom Jones*, it is almost as if the reader's primary relationship were meant to be with the guiding narrator-writer, rather than with the characters. Rovani and Manzoni chide their female readers; Diderot is quite amusingly rude to his presumed impatient readers. The epistolary novel form, in general, explicitly places the reader as letter reader within the structure of the novel, a convention neatly parodied by Gide in *Les Faux-monnayeurs*: everyone in that novel reads the letters and journals of others, forestalling and defamiliarizing many possible reader responses *en route*.

This earlier kind of thematizing and structuralizing of the reading role is close to that of overt narcissism, but without the necessary mirroring (the reflecting, as of mirrors, in reverse) of the reading process in that of writing. For instance, in *Uno, nessuno, e centomila*, Pirandello's narrator addresses the reader as if in a soliloquy, bringing him almost onto the stage, as if to invite (but fail at) dialogue. The crisis in human relations that is dramatized in the novel through the *characters*, is also presented, through the *reader*, in the form and structure, but the parallelism of the acts of writing and reading is not suggested by Pirandello. [. . .] Metafiction, however, seems aware of the fact that it (like all fiction, of course) actually has *no* existence apart from that constituted by the inward act of reading which counterpoints the externalized act of writing.

In the overt form of narcissism, several techniques are employed which are compatible with Ricardou's 'auto-représentation horizontale, référentielle, productrice' and also with the 'auto-représentation verticale, ascendante, productrice' – that is to say, the use of *mise en abyme*, allegory, metaphor, microcosm to shift the focus from the 'fiction' to the 'narration' by either making the 'narration' into the very substance of the novel's content, or by undermining the traditional coherence of the 'fiction' itself, in the latter case.

The distinction between the two modes of narcissism within this overt form is necessary at this stage. In the diegetic mode, the reader is made aware of the fact that he too, in reading, is actively creating a fictional universe. Often a parodied, backgrounded narrative code will guide his awareness of this fact. In *The French Lieutenant's Woman*, for instance, Fowles's freedom-granting core plot involving Sarah and Charles is an allegory of the freedom granted the reader, the thematized reader, by another character, the narrator. [. . .]

Other overtly diegetic narcissistic texts, such as Coover's 'The Magic Poker,' are also explicitly aware of their status as literary artifacts, of their narrative and world-creating processes, and of the necessary presence of the reader: 'perhaps tomorrow I will invent Chicago and Jesus Christ and the history of the moon. Just as I have invented you, dear reader, while lying here in the afternoon sun.'[6] However, the second mode within this form, the linguistic, operates self-consciously at a somewhat more basic stage. In diegetic narcissism, the text displays itself as narrative, as the gradual building of a fictive universe complete with character and action. In the linguistic mode, however, the text would actually show its building blocks – the very language whose referents serve to construct that imaginative world. That these referents are fictive and not real is assured by the generic code instituted by the word 'novel' on the cover. Mailer's *Armies of the Night* is deliberately schizoid for this reason: it is subtitled both 'the novel as history' and 'history as a novel.' Some linguistic referents in the text will be functional in building up plot and character; others may seem gratuitous but will actually operate towards the creation of what Barthes has called an 'effet de réel.'[7]
[. . .]

In order to comprehend the language of fiction, the reader must share with the writer certain recognizable codes – social, literary, linguistic, etc. Many texts thematize, through the characters and plot, the inadequacy of language in conveying feeling, in communicating thought, or even fact. Often this theme is introduced as an allegory of the frustration of the writer when faced with the need to present, only through language, a world of his making that must be actualized through the act of reading: Hilary Burd is not the only 'word child' of Iris Murdoch's novel of that name. Other texts, on the other hand, thematize the overwhelming power and potency of words, their ability to create a world more real than the empirical one of our experience. Paolo Volponi's *La macchina mondiale* is only one instance of this quite common variety of overt linguistic narcissism.

In both the linguistic and diegetic modes the focus is as much on the creative processes of the reader as it is on those of the writer: 'Reader ... we have roles to play, thou and I: you are the doctor (washing your hands between hours), and I, I am, I think, the nervous dreary patient. I am free associating, brilliantly, brilliantly, to put you into the problem. Or for fear of boring you: which?'[8] Overtly narcissistic novels place fictionality, structure, or language at their content's core. They play with different ways of ordering, and allow (or force) the reader to learn how he makes sense of this literary world (if not his own real one). Such texts are not outside the mimetic code. Twentieth-century realism allows for a mimesis of dynamic process, as well as static product, or object. And it is not the rise of structuralism that has brought this about, as some feel,[9] but rather metafiction or fiction itself. [...]

What has *always* been a truism of fiction, though rarely made conscious, is brought to the fore in modern texts: the making of fictive worlds and the constructive, creative functioning of language itself are now self-consciously shared by author and reader. The latter is no longer asked merely to recognize that fictional objects are 'like life'; he is asked to participate in the creation of worlds and of meaning, through language. He cannot avoid this call to action for he is caught in that paradoxical position of being forced by the text to acknowledge the fictionality of the world he too is creating, yet his very participation involves him intellectually, creatively, and perhaps even affectively in a human act that is very real, that is, in fact, a kind of metaphor of his daily efforts to 'make sense' of experience.

[...] The reader and writer are engaged in acts which are parallel, if reversed in direction, for both make fictive worlds in and through the actual functioning of language. This is the responsibility, the almost existentialist freedom in responsibility, that metafiction offers and requires of the reader.

[...]

Just as overt narcissism forces a consideration of the origin and 'newness' of metafictional technique, so any discussion of this covert form of literary introversion raises the other important question, that of the outer limits of the novel as a narrative mimetic genre. How far can auto-representation go before it becomes non- or anti-representation? In order to answer this the two different modes of covert narcissism must be examined.

On this covert level, the self-reflection is implicit; that is to say, it is structuralized, internalized within the text. As a result, it is not necessarily self-conscious. This alters the form it takes and the form of the analysis. Since Ricardou does not separate the diegetic and the linguistic modes, he would probably have to group both of these under his category of 'auto-représentation horizontale, littérale, productrice,' for they both operate on the level of his 'narration.' Since the reader is not usually addressed directly here as he might be in the overt form, it is more difficult to generalize concerning the various shapes these two covert modes might adopt. However, one possible approach would be to take note of recurring structural models found internalized in this kind of metafiction.

On the diegetic level there are many models, or what might be termed paradigms, that are discernible. Among these are the following: 1) *The detective story* (the written plot and the plot to kill).[10] Based on the general pattern of the puzzle or the enigma, this literary form is itself a very self-conscious one: in fact, the reader of a murder mystery comes to *expect* the presence of a detective-story writer within the story itself. [...] The murder mystery plot also has extremely strong and obvious structural conventions. There is a crime; it will be solved because of both the characters' psychological consistency and the detective's slightly superior powers. The incriminating evidence is within the text; some details might seem in the end irrelevant to the plot, but they are all functional, even if only in leading the reader astray. However, the cerebral intellectual triumphs of a Sherlock Holmes or a Nero Wolfe, who logically interpret the clues and discover the solution to the enigmas, are in effect the reader's triumphs. [...] The hermeneutic gaps of such fiction are explicitly made textually functional. [...] 2) *Fantasy.* Covert narcissistic texts share with all fantasy literature the ability to force the reader (not overtly *ask* him) to create a fictive imaginative world separate from the empirical one in which he lives. [...] Whereas in overt narcissism the reader is explicitly told that what he is reading is imaginary, that the referents of the text's language are fictive, in fantasy (and the covert forms of narcissism for which it acts as model) the fictiveness of the referents is axiomatic. [...] 3) *Game Structure.* At the Cerisy conference of 1971, Robbe-Grillet claimed that all his work was an attempt to bring to light the structures of 'jeu' and the ideology that its gratuity entails.[11] The *nouveaux romanciers* have certainly been the most outspoken in their use of the game model. In their fiction, the concepts of codes, or of rules, known and followed in the acts of writing and reading (and which become ends unto themselves) can be found. The following of these rules, which places the emphasis on the process being enacted and not the product finally attained, can also be seen, however, as a demand made on the reader by the narcissistic use of the actualized game model in general. This is true in texts which differ radically in effect: from the baseball game structure of Robert Coover's *The Universal Baseball Association, Inc. J. Henry Waugh, Prop.* to Sollers' chess board in *Drame* to Sanguineti's more explicit dice shooting by the reader in order to arrange the 111 parts of *Il giuoco dell'oca*. [. . .] 4) *The Erotic*. All fictional texts attempt to tantalize, to seduce the reader. As Roland Barthes has suggested in both *S/Z* and the more recent *Le Plaisir du texte*, they also seek to escape the desired possession. The essentially erotic relationship of text and reader or of writer and reader is one of the overtly thematized subjects of John Barth's *Chimera*. But the erotic model can be actualized covertly as well. The act of reading becomes both literally sensual and metaphorically sexual in its process of uniting 'all the polarities' in Leonard Cohen's *Beautiful Losers*. [. . .] In *Willie Masters' Lonesome Wife*, William Gass compares the loneliness of writing to that of sexual encounter. His 'heroine' also invents worlds (and parodies existing literary ones) during intercourse; she sees herself in Beckettian terms as 'imagination imagining itself imagine.' [. . .]

These four diegetic models are not intended as exclusive and complete, but only as four already observed models or metaphoric patterns that are structurally internalized in self-reflective texts. [. . .]

The only type of narcissistic text left to be considered is the covertly linguistic variety. Here part of Ricardou's intradimensional (at the level of 'narration') auto-representation category ('horizontale, littérale, productrice') comes into play. The models here are less easily discussed in generalized non-textual terms. One, however, would be the riddle or joke, a form which directs the reader's attention to language itself, to its potential for semantic duplicity. Language can both convey and conceal meaning. Other generative models are the pun and the anagram. Saussure felt that anagrammatic lay existed in early Latin and Greek texts. [. . .] Such linguistic play can be found too in Hugo ('Gal, amant de la reine, alla, tout magnanime' yielding 'Galamment de l'arène à la Tour Magne, à Nîmes') and in Jules Verne's *La Jangada* or *Bourses de voyage* ('Rosam angelum letorum' yields 'Rose a mangé l'omelette au rhum'). But rarely before the 'textes de jeunesse' of Raymond Roussel did

anagrammatic play function as the sole forming model of the 'fiction.'
[. . .]

Joyce's foregrounding of language in *Finnegans Wake* is perhaps the
real forbear of the *nouveau nouveau romancier*'s creation of 'fiction'
in the space between words. In the early Roussel, language begets
language which begets a verisimilar narrative 'fiction.' In Joyce, as in
Ricardou, language begets language which *is* the 'fiction.' The
difficulty in reading these texts bears witness to the increased
demands made on the reader. The creative dynamism and the delight
in infinite interpretative possibilities that once were the property of
the writer are now shared by the reader in the process of
concretizing the text he is reading. In overt narcissism this new role
is taught; it is thematized. In the covert form, it is actualized.

This mirroring in reverse of the creative process again raised the
important issue regarding the limits of the novel genre. At what
stage does auto-representation become anti-representation?
[. . .]

The decentralizing of the traditional realistic interest of fiction,
away from the story told to the story telling, to the functioning of
language and of larger diegetic structures, is important to the *nouveau
nouveau roman*. Language becomes material with which to work, the
object of certain transforming operations which give it meaning. There
is a self-conscious recognition of the multiple contextual
significances yielded by textual selection and organization. As such,
this 'new new novel' can remain within the novel genre, since these
are the very operations or processes that form the link between
reading and writing – that is, between life and art, reality and fiction
– that seems to be a minimal requirement for a mimetic genre.
[. . .]

Notes

1. 'La Population des miroirs,' *Poétique* 22 (1975): 212.

2. *Problèmes du nouveau roman* (Paris: Seuil, 1967), pp. 12, 54; and *Pour une théorie du nouveau roman* (Paris: Seuil, 1971), pp. 105, 107, 156. See also 'Penser la littérature aujourd'hui,' *Marche Romane* 21 nos. 1–2 (1971): 7–17.

3. 'Disparition élocutoire' in Leonardo Sciascia, *Actes relatifs à la mort de Raymond Roussel* (Paris: L'Herne, 1972), pp. 7–30.

4. Cf. JONATHAN CULLER, *Structuralist Poetics* (London: Routledge and Kegan Paul, 1975), p. 153, and ROBERT SCHOLES re romance modes in 'Metafiction,' *Iowa Review* 1 (Fall 1970): 103. See the author's 'Parody Without Ridicule: Observations on Modern Literary Parody,' *Canadian Review of Comparative Literature* 5 no. 2 (Spring 1978): 201–11.

5. MURRAY BAUMGARTEN, 'From Realism to Expressionism: Toward a History of the Novel,' *New Literary History* 6 (Winter 1975): 418.

6. *Pricksongs and Descants* (New York: New American Library, 1969), p. 40.

7. 'L'Effet de réel,' *Communications* 11 (1968): 84–9.

8. DONALD BARTHELME, 'Florence Green Is 81,' in *Come Back, Dr. Caligari* (1961: reprinted, Boston: Little, Brown and Col., 1964), p. 4.

9. CULLER, *Structuralist Poetics*, p. 238.

10. In Thomas Pynchon's *V.*, one of the characters, Herbert Stencil, has the function of plot-building, linking, connecting. But here, the plot-making instinct reveals itself as *paranoia*, perhaps another structural metaphor for diegetic narcissism.

11. *Nouveau Roman: hier, aujourd'hui* 1 (Paris: Union Générale d'Éditions, 10/18, 1972): 127.

Part Four

Narratology and film

14 Focalisation in Film Narrative*

CELESTINO DELEYTO

Deleyto's article is a pathbreaking attempt to adapt Genette's and Bal's concept of 'focalization' to the specific analysis of film narrative. Drawing on the distinction between narrator (who speaks) and focalizer (who sees), Deleyto rejects the traditional view that the 'camera narrates'. Following Bordwell (1985), he contests the position of 'invisible observer' theories according to which analysis of film narration should be exclusively based on the position of the camera. He accepts Bal's distinction between internal and external focalization, and concludes, disagreeing with Bordwell, that the external focalizer occupies the position of the camera. While Bal sharply separates focalization in the novel (which she ascribes to the story level) from narration (situated at text level), Deleyto argues that, in film, focalization has to be studied simultaneously with narration. Deleyto's most suggestive contention is that, whereas in the novel the two kinds of focalization alternate, in film several internal and external focalizers can appear simultaneously at different points inside or outside the frame, all contributing to the development of the narrative and to the creation of a permanent tension between subjectivity and objectivity. His analysis of classical film shows the general tendency of film narrative to combine internal with external focalization and to return to the objective presentation of external narration to make the internal gazes in the text understandable. Finally, Deleyto proposes an analysis of the relationship between internal focalizer and focalized through the use of four main techniques: editing, framing, movement of the camera and *mise-en-scène*.

[...]

Narratology is the study of narrative texts in general, not only novels. There are other ways of presenting a story, from the narrative poem

---

*CELESTINO DELEYTO, 'Focalisation in Film Narrative', *Atlantis* 13.1/2 (Nov. 1991): 159–77.

to the cartoon strip. Some of them do not use the written or spoken word as their only means of expression. Indeed, in some cases, spoken or written language is not used at all, as is the case in some paintings which clearly convey a narrative, or in certain silent films. It is through cinema, television and video, and not through novels that most stories are 'told' nowadays. For a narrative theory to be consistent and complete, it must work when applied to languages other than that of the novel. Most importantly in our culture, it must work when applied to the study of a film narrative. On the other hand, narratology has proved an efficient method of analysis when consistently applied to film texts.[1] Mieke Bal (1985: 5) bases her analysis of a narrative text on a three-layer distinction. Two of these three layers, the *fabula* – 'a series of logically and chronologically related events that are caused or experienced by actors' – and the *story* – 'a fabula that is presented in a certain manner' – can be shared by several narrative texts expressed through different media. It is only at the last level, that of the *text*, that the analysis would vary depending on the language signs of which it is composed. The implication here is that the analysis of focalisation, which belongs to the story layer, could be applied, as it stands in her theory, to a film text, together with time manipulation, character and space. Both fabula and story are abstract instances, analytical constructs of the critic, which do not appear explicitly in the narrative text. Only the linguistic or visual signs, which form the text, are there to be seen. Focalisation is, therefore, like character or space, narrated in the text.

It is mainly in this distinction between story and text (which does not exist in Genette or in Chatman) that the application of Mieke Bal's theory to film narrative becomes most problematic. Is focalisation, as Bal defines it, not textual in a film? Is the focaliser not a narrating agent like the narrator? In more general terms, who is the narrator in a film text? In films like *Rebecca* (1940), *Duel in the Sun* (1946) or *Double Indemnity* (1944), there are clearly voice-over narrators, who may be character-bound (*Rebecca*, *Double Indemnity*) or external (*Duel in the Sun*). In the case of many silent films or some sound films, like *Gone with the Wind* (1939) or *Arsenic and Old Lace* (1944), the intertitles fulfil the function of the narrator. But the activity of the narrator in all of these examples does not appear throughout the text, but only intermittently, sometimes hardly at all. In all of the narrative theories discussed above, the existence of a narrative presupposes the existence of a narrator, who performs the activity of narration. No narrator, no narrative. Does this mean that films are only narratives in those cases in which the activity of narration can be clearly ascribed to a narrator's voice or printed words? What about those silent films in which there are no intertitles or sound films with no voice-over narrators or printed words? Are these not narrative films at all?

The answer to all these questions is that a film narrative does not need the existence of an explicit narrator, as this agent is defined by theories of the novel, for the activity of narration to take place. As Branigan (1984: 40) says: 'In film, the narrator is not necessarily a biological person, not even a somehow identifiable agent like in the novel, but a symbolic activity: *the activity of narration*'. This symbolic activity, which has been sometimes called *narrative instance* ('instance narratrice'), does not solve the problem of how a film narrative works, since it seems to place the activity of narration outside the text, in a position which seems dangerously close, once again, to that of the implied author. The existence of some abstract or explicit instance, superior to the narrator, and which controls its activity, seems to be denied here, by equating the two figures. As if to corroborate this impression, Branigan redefines narration towards the end of his work: 'A set of frames within larger frames leading to a frame which cannot itself be framed within the boundary of the text – an unavoidable and implicit omniscience which may now be called "effaced" ' (1984: 71). This is certainly far from Mieke Bal's concept of narrator and narration, and it does seem to associate the narrator (or that symbolic activity of narration which Branigan substitutes for it) with that persona of the real author which has been referred to with Wayne Booth's term 'implied author'. Notice how the adjectives 'implied' and 'effaced' have a very similar sense here. This 'narrator' does not utter any signs at all, visual or otherwise, at least not in the same sense as the narrator of words does, and cannot even be immediately identified with the explicit voice-over or onscreen narrator, when such an agent appears in the film.

There is another term which Branigan uses and which, in spite of the abstract, symbolic slant it is given in his theory, seems closer to the role of the narrator. That is the concept of *camera*, which he defines as a 'construct of the spectator' and a 'hypothesis about space' (1984: 54). The camera has often been used as the equivalent of the narrator in film, notably by such classical theorists as V. S. Pudovkin, Karel Reisz and Gavin Millar.[2] The camera would define the position of that invisible observer that could be identified with the narrator, a more identifiable agent which would indeed seem to be the origin of narration in a film. We could even extend the concept of camera to account for editing devices. This invisible but identifiable narrator would be able not only to present, in various ways, the space contained in the frame, but would change from one shot to another when it is necessary for the development of the narrative. However, there is at

219

least one textual code which could not be accounted for by any definition of camera. Apart from editing devices and the position of the camera, there is in a film text a group of elements which come under the general term of *mise-en-scene*, that is, the *staging* of the events in front of the camera. To say that these elements are not textual but correspond only to the level of the fabula would be the same as to say that a dramatic text does not exist. As far as the mise-en-scene is concerned, a film narrative works in a similar way to a play. According to theorists of drama, there is no narration in a play but *representation*.[3] There is a story and, therefore, a fabula; but that story is not narrated but represented by means of actors and a dramatic space, with a certain relationship with the audience.

A film is, therefore, at a textual level, a mixture of narration and representation. Narration, performed by a voice-over or onscreen explicit narrator or as a metaphoric activity whose origin is the camera, does not cover all the textual activities that appear in a film. The mise-en-scene of a film, a term which can only metaphorically be applied to the novel, falls outside narration. Because there is no way of including the mise-en-scene code within the concept of film narration, there is no point any more in identifying the camera with the narrator. Since we have to accept that some textual elements in a film are not produced by the narrator (however wide we make this concept to be), it is preferable to keep the term *narrator* for those cases in which there is an explicit narrator (voice-over, onscreen or intertitles), with a similar status to that of the narrator in prose fiction. For the rest, we cannot accept the phrase 'the camera narrates', since its activity is so clearly different from that of the narrator, even though it is obviously textual, in the sense that it produces visual signs.[4] We are, therefore, still in need of a term which describes the textual activity that takes place in a film outside narration and representation.[5] The term *camera* is not satisfactory for three reasons:

a) Its connotations are too physical (the profilmic machine that records the images).

b) There is no verb to describe its activity or noun to indicate the agent that performs the action.[6]

c) Finally, as I shall try to prove in the next chapter, there are elements belonging to this code that we are seeking to define that have very little to do with that vantage position which is occupied by the camera.

I have rejected the phrase 'the camera narrates'. If we are to leave metaphors aside, what the camera does is *look* at something which it then defines in terms of what is inside the *frame*. [...] Words like the English 'gaze', the French 'regard' or the Spanish 'mirada' seem much closer to how a story is presented in a filmic text than 'narration'. Just as the activity of reading a novel implies a narrator at textual level, the spectator of a film, apart from reading and listening, *looks* and, therefore, his activity requires a textual agent that produces the signs he is looking at. This brings us back to focalisation.

It will have been noticed how close this concept comes to what I have been trying to describe here. 'Focalisation', says Bal in a more elaborate account, 'is the relationship between the "vision", the agent that sees and that which is seen' (1985: 104). Focalisation, a purely narratological term, with no profilmic connotations like camera, and more precise and unambiguous than perspective or point of view, covers precisely the textual area that had been left empty by the restriction of the role of the narrator. To return to the questions on pp. 218–19, the answer to the first one, 'is focalisation textual in a film?', has just been given and is affirmative. Whether the 'focaliser narrates' or not is a question of terminology, but there is no reason to accept the sentence if we had previously rejected 'camera narrates'. If we admit that focalisation is textual, then there is nothing to prevent us from saying that the focaliser focalises in a film text. In answer to the last question, 'who is the narrator in a film text?', we would have to say that the role which is performed by the narrator in a novel is, in a film text, carried out by both the narrator and the focaliser. Finally we must remember that narration and focalisation are not the only activities that take place in a film text. The code of mise-en-scene includes elements which fall outside the realm of either of them.[7] We would say, therefore, that where there is narration in a novel, there is narration, focalisation and representation in film (and probably also the activity performed by nondiegetic music).

Focalisation and narration, therefore, exist at the same level, and simultaneously in film. It is not my aim to prove the inadequacy of Mieke Bal's theory for the analysis of film, but it remains to be seen whether the differentiation between story and text would still hold after my discussion. This basic difference between novel and film exposes, in any case, Bal's theory as a theory of the novel. The very example used by her to illustrate the importance of focalisation is from a visual text, the *basrelief Arjuna's penance*, in Southern India. The gaze of the mice and the supposed gaze of the cat in this text are not narrated but 'narrative'. They are elements of the text (1985: 102). It is no coincidence, however, that the example was chosen from the visual arts, because it is in them, with no mediation between the vision and its representation, where the crucial importance of focalisation can best be evaluated. This modification of narratological theory in its adaptation to film narratives is not without problems. Jost (1983) is aware of it when he distinguishes between focalisation and ocularisation. It seems to me, however that its use in film is unnecessary since both terms designate much the same thing. What Jost does realise is the fact that not all focalisation is textual in a film. When the narrator or the characters speak, at least, the contents of what they say is focalised, but much in the same way as in prose fiction. The perceptual selection operated in such cases is then narrated textually. This, however, does not mean that we are faced with two different activities but only that, in film, they can be textualised in, at least, two different ways, through narration or through focalisation. In a way, therefore, the story/text differentiation still holds, but, as far as our analysis is concerned, focalisation (and probably other aspects too, like character and space) must be studied simultaneously with narration.

Summing up what has been said so far, we are now in a position to point at two general differences between novel and film from a narrative point of view. In both genres, focalisation and narration are key concepts in the analysis of the narrative. In the novel focalisation is not explicit in the text, but must be elicited by the critic from the information given by the narrator. We read what the narrator says but only metaphorically do we perceive what the focaliser perceives. In film, focalisation may be explicit in the text, in general through external or internal 'gazes' and works simultaneously and independently from narration. Both activities, focalisation and narration, are textual. More specifically, the almost permanent existence of an external focaliser in a film narrative accounts for the general tendency of the medium towards narrative objectivity. Regardless of the various subjectivities that may appear in the text, the almost permanent external presence of the camera ensures a vantage point for the spectator, which continually tends to dissociate itself from and supersede that of the various characters involved in the action; in the novel, on the other hand, both narration and focalisation can be exclusively subjective and are so on many occasions. Even in the inappropriately called 'third-person narratives', internal focalisation, through the perception of one character, subjectivises the narrative in a way which has hardly been achieved in film.

In studies of the novel before Bal, subjectivity has usually been associated with narration.[8] In film, narration as I understand it here has generally been overlooked in studies of subjectivity, and the emphasis has been on visual aspects.[9] Mitry (1965), Kawin (1978) and Branigan (1984), among others, suggest different taxonomies of subjective images. [. . .] There are, however, problems in all of these categorisations. Mitry only thinks in terms of the shot, although film theory has for a long time rejected the idea that the shot was the equivalent unit of the word in human language. He has, therefore, no use for eyeline matches, shots/reverse shots, etc. Kawin seems to mix different levels of generalisation: subjective camera seems much more specific, for example, than self-consciousness, which could include the other three. Branigan firmly bases his system on the position of the camera and largely ignores such important aspects as mise-en-scene, movements of the camera, etc. The very special relationships between objectivity and subjectivity in film – their simultaneity, the unmarked transitions from one to the other, and the distance between apparent and real subjectivity in the classical film – fall outside the scope of any of these studies. The study of visual subjectivity in film can, on the other hand, be approached from a more abstract, less taxonomical standpoint; that is, once again, through the analysis of focalisation.

Focalisation in film can be external or internal. In a novel, external and internal focalisation can appear simultaneously in what Mieke Bal calls double focalisation (1985: 113–14); or it may not be clear whether a character or an external agent are focalisers (ambiguous focalisation). In either case, the origin of focalisation is the same (the external focaliser associating itself perceptually with the character, or not) and the focalised object identical. In film, on the other hand, there can appear, simultaneously, several focalisers, external and internal, on different points of the frame (or outside). It is through the study of the relationship between all these different agents, their possible positions on the frame, and the relationship between them, that the study of focalisation can contribute to the analysis of subjectivity in film.

At a textual level, the focaliser always occupies the position of the camera.[10] A movement of the camera or an editing device (cut, dissolve, fade, wipe, etc.) imply a change in the position of the focaliser. One striking exception would be the split screen, in which the external focaliser would occupy several positions at the same time. Such is the case in films like *Napoléon* (1927), or, more recently, *Twilight's Last Gleaming* (1977). A superimposition would also imply, in theory, the same multiplicity of vantage points for the external focaliser, although, generally, superimpositions are used to express the mind of the character, and would therefore denote an internal focaliser. Superimposition and the balloon technique are used, for example, in *The Crowd* (1928) with this particular function. Similarly, gradual transitions from shot to shot, like wipes or dissolves, would momentarily imply this characteristic omnipresent power of the focaliser. There is a spectacular use of wipes and split screen in *Dr Jekyll and Mr Hyde* (1932). A characteristic description of New York through several dissolves happens again in *The Crowd*. In *North by Northwest* (1959), the omniscience provided by the dissolve is put to a more original narrative use in a quick double dissolve from the United Nations building to the Capitol in Washington and the CIA office, as is explained by James Monaco (1981: 190).

As a general rule, we could say that the external focaliser yields focalisation to a character less readily in film than in the novel. Subjectivity is often expressed in a film without the complete disappearance of the external focaliser as a distinct agent from the character whose vision or mind we are made to share. There are, however, several cases in which the external focaliser totally disappears. In the usually called point of view (POV) shot or subjective shot, we have a shot of a character looking offscreen and a cut to what s/he is looking at, from the exact position s/he is looking. Although there is external focalisation in the first shot – the character looking is being focalised from the position of the camera – after the cut, this same position becomes internal as it expresses the exact origin of the character's gaze.

The eyeline match is not absolutely necessary in order to express total identification between camera position and character gaze. Other clues to subjectivity may be given in the dialogue, voice-over narration, movement of the camera or, most characteristically, when another character looks straight at the camera (and straight at the spectator) as he addresses the character whose vision we are supposed to share. An interesting example of consistent use of subjective camera is *La mort en direct* (1979), in which a character has a device installed in his eyes in order to record visually everything that he sees. In this case, not only does the camera place itself in the position of his gaze, but his gaze imitates, within the world of the fabula, the profilmic activity of the camera. The best known examples of a sustained use of subjective camera are *The Lady in the Lake* (1946) and the first section of *Dark Passage* (1947). Unlike *La mort en direct*, in these two cases, we never get to see the character whose vision we are made to share. He is always focaliser and never focalised. The lack of effectiveness of these two films seems to imply that film, unlike the novel, needs the alternation or simultaneity of external and internal textual focalisation in order to express subjectivity efficiently.

External focalisation may also disappear in the case of dreams, fantasies and flashbacks. In the famous dream sequence from *Spellbound* (1945), it is the mind of the character that is visualising the contents of the frame. Focalisation is here only internal (and supported intermittently by internal narration). Flashbacks, a very common narrative aspect in classical film, are frequently supposed to express the memory of a character who would then become focaliser. In theory, external focalisation would disappear throughout flashback. This is actually not so in most films. In *Rebecca*, we have two flashbacks. The film starts with a dream which the character played by Joan Fontaine has the night previous to the film's present. Internal focalisation is adhered to during this first flashback, as we see Manderley, the house where most of the subsequent action takes place, through her 'mind's eye'. There are several cues to the strictly internal nature of textual focalisation in this scene: for example, the dream-like tracking shot and the connection with the narration (also internal) as when she crosses the gate or when she sees the house. The rest of the film is formed by the second flashback, in which we are shown the events that led to her arrival at Manderley and its eventual destruction by the fire. This section is cued as a memory of the character by voice-over narration at the beginning, but from then on, all textual signs in this direction disappear and they do not even reappear at the end of the film. Although internal focalisation falls more heavily on the main character, this is not the same internal focaliser as the one who is supposed to be telling us the story from the present, but the character from the past. Although there has been no explicit sign that signifies that what we are looking at is not her memory any more, the spectator forgets that he is supposed to be witnessing a memory of a character of the fabula, and interprets the focalisation that does not correspond to any of the characters of this second level of the fabula as external.

[. . .] Even in films in which flashbacks have a much greater load of subjectivity, like *Out of the Past* (1947) or *Double Indemnity*, the tendency towards interpreting focalisation as external, when there are no recurrent explicit cues, is still strong. Again the mixture of external and internal focalisation seems to be a crucial fact in film narrative. *A Letter to Three Wives* (1948) is formed in its story structure by a present time and three flashbacks which occupy the central part of the film and consist of memories of the three female protagonists. The beginning of each flashback is marked by more or less complex transitions which cue the contents of what follows as subjective (although narration corresponds to a fourth agent, Addie Ross, whom we never see but whose presence is constantly felt). The first shots of the second and third flashbacks, so conspicuously marked as subjective, show two rooms (two kitchens): in both cases, the person to whom the memory corresponds enters the room a few seconds after. They are not in the room when the flashback starts and focalisation must therefore be external, although this contradicts, at a superficial level, the subjective character of the flashback. It is as if film narratives required a constant return to objective presentation for a better understanding of the internal gazes that occur in the text.

One reason for this is the difficulty that film has to present the mind of a character outside narration. In a novel, in a passage in internal focalisation, the mind of the character can be shown without a change in focalisation. The character can be focaliser and focalised at the same time, while keeping perceptual control over other characters or objects. In film, although, as we have seen, dreams, hallucinations, memories, etc., can be shown, it is problematic to express the characteristics of the vision while showing its object, hence the resource to shots in external focalisation, in which the focaliser becomes focalised and in which we can analyse better how what he perceives affects him. The completely subjective shot, on the other hand, because of its relatively rare occurrence, and because of the total disappearance in it of external focalisation, may become an effective tool to express some particular mental state in the character whose origin it is, whether it is curiosity, surprise, puzzlement, or a mind at work. This special state is sometimes intensified through what Branigan calls *perception shot*, which he defines as a shot that shows the heightened attention of a character (1984: 81). The typical example is the blurred shot that presents the vision of a drunkard. In *The Stranger* (1946), a character sees the image of her brother blurred before she faints. [. . .] In *Vertigo* (1958), towards the end of the film, we get two subjective shots that express the vertigo that the main character suffers from as he ascends the staircase to a church tower, through a mixture of tracking and zoom shots. Branigan finds another perception shot in *The Birds* (1963). In this case, a woman sees a dead man, and the eyeline match shows two quick cuts into a dead man's face (1984: 81). This, according to Branigan, expresses the horror of the internal focaliser at the sight of her lifeless neighbour. I, however, would interpret the shot after the second cut as an intervention of an external focaliser that places itself closer to the focalised so that the spectator can 'enjoy' a better view of it. Here, once more, we come across the apparent smoothness with which internal focalisation is replaced or accompanied by the external agent in the expression of subjectivity. It is a clear case of Bal's *ambiguous focalisation*, 'in which it is hard to decide who focalises' (1985: 114).

Subjectivity in film is, however, not restricted to instances in which a character focaliser seems to completely take over the external focaliser. Most times, the perception of one or several characters of the fabula is emphasised by the text while the external focaliser still keeps its enveloping position. In these cases in which two or several focalisers coexist, all the gazes present contribute to the development of the narrative. The degree of subjectivity of the scene will depend on our awareness of its internal gazes. Typical cases of external focalisation prevailing would be the long and extreme long shot. The influence on our reception of the impressions provided by the text of the gazes of each one of the characters included in such shots is usually minimal. However, there are no fixed rules and an internal gaze can be of crucial importance in a long shot. In *The Man Who Knew Too Much* (1956), an overhead long shot shows the character played by Doris Day watching a church from the street, whereas at the other side of the wall that separates the back entrance to the church from the street, the villains lead her son into a car and escape. The fact that she cannot see this action because of the wall in spite of her watchfulness, is the main narrative function of this shot. Film language is so flexible that any set of rules or classifications of textual elements is always risky and becomes invariably incomplete. The most we can do is observe and point out recurrent elements in classical texts, which are more highly codified. In this restricted sense, and without any attempt at covering the whole spectrum, there seem to be four textual codes that are frequently used to establish relevant internal focalisation, without making the external focaliser disappear. These are editing, movements of the camera, framing and mise-en-scene.

To start with editing, two of the most important techniques in continuity editing, the *eyeline match* and the *shot/reverse shot*, reinforce internal focalisation.[11] Like the subjective shot, the eyeline match, one of the basic rules of classical film narration, relates two shots by means of the gaze of one or several characters. As in the former case, shot A focalises externally on a character looking offscreen. Shot B shows what the character is looking at, but, unlike the subjective shot, from a position which is not the one occupied by the character (the order could be reversed). The external focaliser remains present throughout and its position typically ensures for the spectator a better vantage point than those of any of the characters concerned. Sometimes it is difficult to decide whether an eyeline match is a proper subjective shot or not. However, for the difference to be relevant, some more marks of subjectivity are necessary, apart from the complete coincidence between character and camera in the origin of the vision. A very usual mark is camera movement, which, in the truly subjective shot, imitates the movement of the character. Such instances are common in Hitchcock's films, usually at moments in which the character discovers some relevant visual information. [. . .]

The second editing element that emphasises subjectivity is the shot/reverse shot, used frequently, although not exclusively, in dialogues. In *Rear Window* (1954) there is a long dialogue between Jeff and Lisa (played by James Stewart and Grace Kelly) filmed in shot/reverse shot, with the two characters sitting at opposite ends of a sofa in his apartment. The external focaliser shifts alternately from one end to the other of the imaginary line that joins both characters together, depending on where the higher point of interest in conversation lies. As one of the characters is focalised, the position of the other one is very close to that of the external focaliser. Our position with respect to the frame is, therefore, very close to that of the character, and internal focalisation is thus activated. Again, character perception becomes crucial in the narrative. In this example, the external focaliser stays close to Jeff for much longer periods than at the other end of the line and therefore, the narrative depends for its development more on his internal focalisation than on hers. This is only right in a film which plays with our position as viewers by having as its main protagonist a person who performs diegetically a very similar activity to ours. As the scene comes to an end, the shot/reverse shot strategy becomes a set of reciprocal eyeline matches between the two characters. In this brief set of shots only one character appears on the frame. The difference between the two sequences of shots in the scene emphasises the increasing separation that exists between the two characters, which is emphasised here by focalisation.

The shot/reverse shot directs our attention to one or another part of the film space, which is organised along the *axis line*, and makes, consequently, for some of the most striking changes in textual focalisation in film narrative. In *Grapes of Wrath* (1940), a character narrates in several flashbacks the takeover by the banks of the house and land where he and his family lived. In one shot, the external focaliser is placed next to the car where the representative of the bank sits, and the emphasis is here on the precarious conditions of the laborers who are focalised. Later on, as the tractors arrive to demolish their house, the tractor is seen from a position close to that of the labourers in what is a virtual shot/reverse shot structure, although some film action has intervened between the two. Here, the opposite vantage point selected by the focaliser underlines the growing awareness of the peasants with respect to the previous shot. Also, the effect of the tractor destroying the arable land is much intenser if we are placed in the approximate position of those who are being most affected by its action within the diegesis.

Although in the shot/reverse shot strategy a character might be directing his/her gaze to an object or character onscreen (this is the case in the example used from *Rear Window*), we have been dealing so far with units of two shots – shot A that establishes the origin of internal focalisation and shot B that shows (internally or externally) the focalised. But in a film both internal focaliser and focalised may appear simultaneously onscreen, while the external focaliser occupies a specific position, different from theirs, in the film space. In these cases, the relationship between the camera and the filmic space, or, to be more precise, the *composition of the frame* is usually crucial for the establishment or intensification of subjectivity. As a general rule, the most active internal focalisation would correspond to the character that is framed closest to the camera. This is the case of the individual shots in the shot/reverse shot sequences studied above. It is also the case of shots in which foreground and background are clearly separated. The most usual device of this kind has the camera placed somewhere behind a character who is looking while the object of the gaze is also included in the frame. This is what Mitry calls a 'semi-subjective shot' or a way of 'subjectivising the objective' (1965: 75).[12] Two elements are at least necessary for this kind of internal focalisation to be active: the framing and the gaze. In *The Burmese Harp* (1956) and in most of Orson Welles's films the constant appearance of characters in an extreme foreground position and the use of wide-angle lens, which keeps both foreground and background in focus, do not usually activate internal focalisation because their perception of the rest of the frame is not underlined. In these films, the object of this near identification of character and external focaliser is mainly used in order to create onscreen a much larger film space than in other films. We must remember that focalisation is not only a textual element. It originates at the level of the story, an analytical layer in which the very existence of a camera and a frame are immaterial. The camera and the frame are some of the vehicles through which perception may be textualised but not the only ones. The textual element that comes into play here is again mise-en-scene. In a film, perception can be intensified independently of the camera. A character's gaze may be crucial for our understanding of the narrative regardless of the position of the external focaliser. What matters sometimes is simply the relationship between the figures in the film space and the importance of the gaze of one or several of them. In *The Thief of Bagdad* (1924), the main character goes into a mosque, in which some people are at prayer, through a window in a wall opposite the position of the camera. His amazed perception of what is going on inside is one of the basic narrative elements of the scene and yet he is nowhere near the camera. In *Chimes at Midnight* (1966), Hal and Poins eavesdrop on Falstaff and Doll Tearsheet from the top of the bed in which the other two are lying. The important factor in these two examples is the fact that the three internal focalisers are looking (or listening) without being seen or heard. Focalisation, consequently, can originate in the fabula, become active in the story and be textualised by the mise-en-scene.

Summing up what has been said so far, the relationship between internal focaliser and focalised can be established through editing (eyeline match, shot/reverse shot, subjective shot), framing or mise-en-scene. Another textual device which is often used is camera movement. We have seen how a camera movement, as a part of a subjective shot, can contribute to express internal focalisation. The classic example here would be the shot at the end of *Vertigo*, already referred to, when Scottie climbs the staircase to the church tower. There a mixture of an ascending tracking shot and a descending zoom shot transmits the impression of vertigo that the character is feeling and that has been so central to the development of the story. In this case, however, the tracking shot expresses the subjectivity of the character but keeps him offscreen. Sometimes, however, the movement of the camera can relate both object and subject onscreen, like the other devices that I have revised here. We would say, in general terms, that internal focalisation, as a relationship between a subject A and an object B in the diegetic space of the film, can be presented textually by cutting from A to B, by including both in the frame and, if necessary, emphasising A's gaze, or by tracking, panning and tilting from A to B. As a general rule, the eyeline match is preferred to camera movement in classical film because the latter calls the viewer's attention to the heterodiegetic position of the camera. The eyeline match is a much more unobtrusive choice (like all the other strategies of the system of continuity editing) and, therefore, much preferred by a system that finds the best way of manipulation through character subjectivity in giving the impression that the film narrates itself. Some modern films, however, are less concerned with transparence. [...]

Camera movement can be combined with framing to present as subjective a shot which was apparently objective. In *Jubal* (1955), a man on horseback is following a woman through a wood without being seen. His gaze is intensified by framing as the camera is placed somewhere behind him and the focalised is left in the background. After two cuts, the focaliser becomes focalised when a quick tracking shot discloses the presence of another character, who had been following the first one, and had been left offscreen occupying a hypothetical position behind the external focaliser up to that moment. The framing after the tracking shot underlines the new subjectivity in a similar way to the former one.

Another possibility is illustrated by two similar shots from *North by Northwest*. At the beginning of the film, several characters are talking in the bar of a hotel. Roger Thornhill calls the bellboy to ask him for a telephone, and, simultaneously, the boy calls out the name George Kaplan. At this precise moment the camera tracks left and forward to disclose the presence of two strangers who had been standing just outside the lobby, overlooking the scene. The simultaneity of the two events leads them to believe that Roger Thornhill is George Kaplan, a misunderstanding which changes Thornhill's life and sets the narrative mechanism of the film in motion. The movement of the camera, with the unexpected presence of the two internal focalisers that it reveals, underlines the coincidental nature of the beginning of the protagonist's misfortunes. Later on, the auction scene starts with a close-up of Philip Vandamm's hand lying on the back of Eve Kendall's neck. Then the camera tracks back and laterally to what is apparently an establishing shot of the new film space (the auction room), but finally discloses Thornhill standing at the back of the room, looking towards the position occupied by Eve and Vandamm. In the first scene, the most relevant information was the mistaken perception of the two men. In the second one, the discovery that Thornhill makes of the relationship between the other two. In both cases, an apparently objective presentation is abruptly shown to be internally focalised by a movement of the camera from object to subject. In neither of them does framing contribute to the establishment of internal focalisation at the end of the tracking shot, as the two subjects in the first scene and the one in the second one are ostensibly focalised externally. In both, the need for the viewer's concentration on the relevant gaze asks for this *décalage* between external and internal focalisation in the same shot. Mise-en-scene, therefore, replaces framing once again in the expression of subjectivity.

I have discussed here only a few elements that contribute to the textualisation of internal focalisation in a film text. Many others could have been referred to: lighting, colour, camera distance, internal sound, etc. [. . .] In most cases, the different codes work simultaneously and inseparably, in such a way that the function of each particular one cannot be fully understood without the contribution of the others. I prefer, therefore, to keep them all in sight and observe how they work in each individual scene. Focalisation is, at any rate, an essential code in film narratives. As opposed to the novel, it is also textual and, therefore, explicit, working at the same level as narration and the rest of the codes. More specifically, it is the permanent tension between internal and external focalisation that has been revealed as most relevant for our study. This tension could, in general terms, be described as the tension between the cinema's natural tendency towards objectivity and the centrality of the gaze in film narration. The apparent inconsistency inherent in the eyeline match or the classical flashback is in fact an element of richness and complexity, which provides film texts with the unique possibility of combining simultaneous internal and external gazes in such a way that, most times, the coexistence of both is taken for granted by the viewer, thus constituting a permanent source for subtle fabula manipulation and irony.

Notes

1. BORDWELL (1985) is the most complete specifically narratological approach to the study of film texts to date.

2. For a discussion of the main theories in this line, see 'The Invisible Observer', in BORDWELL (1985: 9–12).

3. The *chorus* of a classical tragedy or similar devices in modern drama would have a similar function to that of the narrator, but it would be always second-level narration. Narration, if it exists at all in a play, is always framed by representation. The same happens in a film when an onscreen character tells a story. The story is always framed by the outer level of the mise-en-scene.

4. In spite of several attempts to bring both concepts together, as for example, by ALEXANDRE ASTRUC (1948).

5. There is probably one more textual code, which is usually included under 'sound' (see, for example, BORDWELL and THOMPSON, 1990), but which performs an activity quite differentiated from narration and representation. We are referring to external or nondiegetic music, which seems to work in most films as a separate code.

6. 'Cameraman' would be inappropriate again because it refers to a profilmic event which has nothing to do with the text, unless we accept Genette's return to the centrality of the 'real author'.

7. The function of representation in film would probably come very close to the production of space and character, which Mieke Bal again includes in the story layer, making the application of Bal's theory to film even more problematic.

8. Apart from Bal and Genette's chapter on 'subjective narration', one of the best accounts of subjectivity in the novel is COHN's (1978).

9. BRANIGAN (1984: 76), for example, offers a brief list of different types of voice-over narration without any further discussion. The only exception I know is KOZLOFF's study of voice-over narration (1988).

10. BORDWELL (1985) rightly criticises what he calls the 'invisible observer' theories, which base their discussion of film narration on the position of the camera, since this element can be easily identified with the author. However, the fact that, as I have said, other elements are at work in the presentation of a film, does not mean that the position of the camera must not be taken into account at all. If our theory of textual focalisation is accepted, the textualised position of the external focaliser must be where the camera is.

11. The rest, on the other hand, seem to underline the position of the external focaliser and increase its omniscience. Such is the case of the match on action, crosscutting and analytical breakdown, among others. For a discussion of continuity editing, see BORDWELL and THOMPSON (1990: 218–30).

12. In the terms suggested in this essay, this type of shot proposes the simultaneity

in the film text of external and internal, and the fact that the latter becomes more important for the development of the narrative than the former.

References

ASTRUC, ALEXANDRE (1948), 'Naissance d'une nouvelle avant-garde: la caméra-stylo', *Écran français* No. 144 (30 Mar. 1948).

BAL, MIEKE (1985, 1980), *Narratology. Introduction to the Theory of Narrative,* trans. Christine van Boheemen (Toronto: University of Toronto Press).

BORDWELL, DAVID (1985), *Narration in the Fiction Film* (Madison: University of Wisconsin Press).

BORDWELL, DAVID and THOMPSON, KRISTIN (1990, 1979), *Film Art. An Introduction* (New York: Alfred A. Knopf).

BRANIGAN, EWARD R. (1984), *Point of View in the Cinema. A Theory of Narration and Subjectivity in Classical Film* (Berlin: Mouton).

COHN, DORRIT (1978), *Transparent Minds* (Princeton: Princeton University Press).

GENETTE, GÉRARD (1972), *Figures III* (Paris: Editions du Seuil).

—— (1982), *Nouveau discours du récit* (Paris: Editions du Seuil).

JOST, FRANÇOIS (1983), 'Narration(s): en deça et au delà', *Communications* 38.

KAWIN, BRUCE F. (1978), *Mindscreen: Bergman, Godard and First-Person Film* (Princeton: Princeton University Press).

KOZLOFF, SARAH (1988), *Invisible Storytellers. Voice-over Narration in American Fiction Film* (Berkeley: University of California Press).

MITRY, JEAN (1965), *Esthétique et psychologie du cinéma,* vol. II (Paris: Éditions Universitaires).

MONACO, JAMES (1981), *How to Read a Film* (New York: Oxford University Press).

15   Story World and Screen*

EDWARD BRANIGAN

In chapter 2 of *Narrative Comprehension and Film* Branigan considers
filmic narrative from the point of view of the spectators, analysing
the way in which they transform the two-dimensional sequence of
visual and aural effects on the screen into a three-dimensional
world, which he calls the 'story world'. Gérard Genette, in chapter
2 of his *Narrative Discourse*, had pointed out as a basic characteristic
of all narratives – whether aural, written or cinematographic – the
co-existence of a dual temporality: the time of the thing narrated,
or story time (the time of the signified); and the time of the narrating (the time of the signifier). Building on this, Branigan proposes
three dual frames of reference for narrative in film: the temporal,
the spatial and the causal. Each of these frames, Branigan contends,
is simultaneously at work on two levels – on the screen and in the
story world – producing two fundamental, but often divergent,
systems of space, time and causal interaction, which a theory of
narrative must be able to analyse.

Branigan further distinguishes between the diegetic and the nondiegetic parts of the story world, that is, between the collection of
sense data accessible to each character and those that are not
accessible to any of the characters. As he explains, the spectator's
organization of information into diegetic and nondiegetic story
worlds is a critical step in the comprehension of a narrative and
of the relationship of story events to our everyday world. Drawing
on cognitive psychology, Branigan differentiates two kinds of perception processes in the spectator watching a film: 'top-down' and
'bottom-up' processing. These processes yield different and often
conflicting interpretations of data which the spectator has to combine into a system. Branigan's contention is that the ongoing process of constructing and understanding a narrative consists of a
'moment by moment regulation of conflicts among competing spatial, temporal, and causal hypotheses'. He ends with the suggestion

---

*EDWARD BRANIGAN, *Narrative Comprehension and Film* (London: Routledge, 1992),
pp. 33–44, 230–5.

that the same kind of scheme may be successfully applied to the analysis of change in space. This suggestion remains undeveloped, however, as he reduces the notion of space to the binary opposition 'foreground/background'. Indeed, the main shortcoming of the analytical system he proposes is his simplistic, a priori assumption that 'virtually all phenomena [in the physical world] can be explained in terms of interactions between parts *taken two at a time*' (emphasis in the original).

Nevertheless, Branigan's efforts to systematize the spatial, temporal and causal frames of reference at work in filmic narrative and to tabulate the spectator's complex cognitive processes in the assimilation of on-screen data and of equivalent experiences which may not derive directly from screen constitute a productive alliance of narratology with cognitive psychology for the analysis of cinematographic narrative.

A preliminary delineation of narrative in film

Narrative in film rests on our ability to create a three-dimensional world out of a two-dimensional wash of light and dark. A bare facticity of graphics on the screen – size, color, angle, line, shape, etc. – must be transformed into an array of solid objects; and a texture of noise must be transformed into speech, music, and the sounds made by solid objects. Light and sound in narrative film are thus experienced in two ways: virtually unshaped *on* a screen as well as apparently *moving within*, reflecting and issuing from, a world which contains solid objects making sounds. Every basic spatial and temporal relationship, such as position and duration, thus has a double interpretation. A green circle might be seen to the *left* of a square in the same plane, or alternatively, it might seen to lie *behind* the square along a diagonal line to the left. In the latter interpretation, the circle may become a 'sphere,' the square a 'box,' and 'size' and 'color' will be adjusted according to our judgments about how distance and light are being represented in a given perspective system. Similarly, the green circle may appear for ten seconds on the screen but represent many hours of world time for the green sphere, especially if there is no other 'action' by which to gauge duration. Rudolf Arnheim asserts:

It is one of the most important formal qualities of film that every object that is reproduced appears simultaneously in two entirely different frames of reference, namely the two-dimensional and the three-dimensional, and that as one identical object it fulfills two different functions in the two contexts.[1]

The spectator, therefore, encounters at least two major frames of reference in film: the space and time of a *screen* as well as (a sample of) the space and time of a *story world*.[2] More than space and time, however, is at stake. Causality also has a double interpretation. Changes in light and sound patterns will be perceived in at least two ways: as motion across a screen and as movement among objects in a story world. Causality on a screen will involve patterns of a purely visual, phenomenal logic where, for example, one blob smashes into another but the resulting transformations in motion and color may not be analogous to the interactions of three-dimensional objects like billiard balls; the blobs may even 'pass through' each other on the screen. Bizarre pictorial compositions and animation are clear examples of on-screen causality. In short, light and sound create two fundamental systems of space, time, and causal interaction: on a screen and within a story world. One of the tasks of narrative is to reconcile these systems.

It seems likely, in fact, that more than two frames of reference are active in our comprehension of film. It has even been argued that there is a stage of visual processing located halfway between two and three dimensional perception which produces a $2\frac{1}{2}$ dimensional representation of space.[3] Clearly, major changes occur during the conversion from phenomenal appearances on the screen to functions in a story world. One of the essential tasks of a narrative theory is to specify the various stages through which we represent and comprehend a film as a narrative. On-screen patterns of light, sound, and motion do not denote and hence cannot be true or false; they are fully present and neither narrative nor fictive. Moreover, the time in which these patterns are present on the screen is determined initially by the film projector. By contrast, a story builds complex spatial and temporal contexts, makes references to things which are not present (and may not exist), and allows broad conclusions to be drawn about sequences of actions. Moreover, time in the world of the story may be quite different than the time of the projection of the film. For example, in *Letter from an Unknown Woman* (Ophuls, 1948) screen time is ninety minutes while the story covers three hours of an early morning during which a letter is read, and the letter, in turn, dramatizes events spanning fifteen years at the turn of the century in the world of Vienna.

Many concepts have been proposed to help describe how on-screen data is transformed through various spatial, temporal, and causal

schemes culminating in a perceived story world. The various stages
have been described with concepts like script, set decoration,
technology, technique, performance, material, shot, form, style, plot,
diegesis, code, narration, and referent. Since nonnarrative ways of
organizing data may coexist with narrative, one might also recognize
a conflict among discursive schemes, an 'excess' within the story.[4]
The processing of film data has an important effect on how a spectator
feels about the conceptual structures which are ultimately
constructed. Some of the metaphors offered by film theorists suggest
that our comprehension of film proceeds only forward, one step at
a time, and depends simply on local and immediate juxtapositions,
but other metaphors are less restrictive. Rudolf Arnheim speaks of
picture postcards in an album while Noël Burch speaks of picture
postcards suspended in a void, 'radically autonomous'.[5] Early in his
career Eisenstein argued that shots are perceived not next to each
another in a horizontal or vertical chain, but on top of each other in
collision.[6] Later he refined the idea to include layers of pictures
'rushing towards the spectator,' but not necessarily in a straight line.
He proposed that film data might be perceived as arranged vertically
in matrix form, exhibiting a multiplicity of criss-crossing
relationships in an instant.[7] Finally, the psychologist Julian Hochberg
mentions three types of perceptual analysis in film: simple summation,
directional patterns, and cognitive maps.[8] [. . .]

It will be useful now to separate the concept of 'story world' into
two parts: the diegetic and the nondiegetic. In talking about a 'story,'
we often refer to certain events which surround a character, events
which have already occurred, or might occur in a particular manner,
in a certain sequence and time span, and so forth. We understand
such events as occurring in a 'world' governed by a particular set
of laws. I will refer to that imagined world as the *diegesis*. The
spectator presumes that the laws of such a world allow many events
to occur (whether or not we see them), contains many objects and
characters, contains other stories about other persons, and indeed
permits events to be organized and perceived in nonnarrative ways.
The diegetic world extends beyond what is seen in a given shot and
beyond even what is seen in the entire film, for we do not imagine
that a character may only see and hear what we observe him or her
seeing and hearing. The diegesis, then, is the implied spatial,
temporal, and causal system of a character – a collection of sense
data which is represented as being at least potentially accessible to a
character.[9] A sound in a film, for example, is diegetic if the spectator
judges that it has been, or could have been, heard by a character.
However some on-screen elements (e.g., 'mood' music) are
*non*diegetic and addressed only to the spectator. These elements

are *about* the diegetic world of a character and are meant to aid the spectator in organizing and interpreting that world and its events. Nondiegetic elements are not accessible to any of the characters. The spectator's organization of information into diegetic and nondiegetic story worlds is a critical step in the comprehension of a narrative and in understanding the relationship of story events to our everyday world.

Let us now attempt a preliminary delineation of narrative in film. This definition will aid us in examining narrative comprehension more precisely and will also provide a basis for outlining five recent types of narrative theory, each of which stresses and interprets a different aspect of the narrative process.

Narrative is a way of comprehending space, time, and causality. Since in film there are at least two important frames of reference for understanding space, time, and causality, narrative in film is the principle by which data is converted from the frame of the *screen* into a *diegesis* – a world – that frames a particular *story*, or sequence of actions, in that world; equally, it is the principle by which data is converted from story onto screen. To facilitate analysis, narrative may be divided into a series of relationships. For example:

1 The relationship of diegesis and story may be analyzed with such narratological concepts as Todorov's 'transformations,' or a *narrative schema*. Which kinds of action sequences occurring in what kind of world will qualify as a narrative? For example, a narrative schema ('abstract,' 'orientation,' 'initiating event,' etc.) describes how a reader collects a series of episodes into a focused causal chain (as opposed to a 'heap,' 'catalogue,' 'unfocused chain,' etc.).

   Causal chains are not just sequences of paired events, but also embody a desire for pairing events and the power to make pairs. Narrative causes ('remote,' 'intervening,' 'enabling,' etc.) are thus principles of explanation which are derived from cultural knowledge as well as from physical laws. Narrative causality includes the human plans, goals, desires, and routines – realized in action sequences – which are encouraged, tolerated, or proscribed by a community.

2 The relationship of diegesis and screen may be analyzed with such concepts as script, set decoration, technology, technique, shot, form, style, material, and excess. The present chapter will demonstrate that these kinds of concept may be approached by

measuring their effects on a spectator's judgments about the
ordering of space, time, and causality on the screen and in
the diegesis.

3   The relationship of diegesis and what is external to it – the
nondiegetic – raises issues of *narration*: from what sort of 'other
world' has a diegesis been created, a character presented, events
told? What has been concealed, or excluded? And,
furthermore, how do we come to *believe* in a narrative diegesis
and relate it to our own world; that is, what is the nature of
fictional and non-fictional reference?

[. . .] First we must examine the relationship of diegesis and screen,
namely, how is data on the screen transformed into a story world?
In order to answer this question, a distinction will be made between
two types of perception operative in watching a film. These two
types of perception produce different kinds of hypotheses about
space, time, and causality. Distinguishing between them will allow
us to examine closely how a spectator makes separate use of
judgments about space, time, and causality, as well as how a
spectator may integrate these judgments to produce an overall
narrative rendering of experience.

Top-down perception

The movement from screen to story world does not proceed along a
smooth path and in only one direction. Many of our abilities are
brought to bear simultaneously on a film, producing at least some
conflict and uncertainty. As a first step toward unravelling some of
these abilities and specifying the kinds of conflicts that arise, I will
use a fundamental cognitive psychological distinction to divide
perception into two kinds of process according to the 'direction' in
which they work. Some perceptual processes operate upon data on
the screen in a direct, 'bottom-up' manner by examining the data in
very brief periods of time (utilizing little or no associated memory)
and organizing it automatically into such features as edge, color,
depth, motion, aural pitch, and so on. Bottom-up perception is serial
and 'data-driven,' and produces only short-range effects. Other
perceptual processes, however, are based on acquired knowledge and
schemas, are not constrained by stimulus time, and work 'top-down'
on the data, using a spectator's expectations and goals as principles
of organization. Top-down processes are indirect in the sense that
they may reframe data in alternative ways independently of the

stimulus conditions which govern the initial appearance of the data. Top-down processes must be flexible and general in order to be effective across a wide range of situations while allowing for (unpredictable) variations among specific cases. Top-down processes often treat data as an inductive sample to be projected and tested within a variety of parallel frames of reference while bottom-up processes are highly specialized and atomistic (e.g., detecting motion). Both kinds of process operate simultaneously on the data creating a variety of representations with varying degrees of compatibility.[10]

Because top-down processes are active in watching a film, a spectator's cognitive activity is not restricted to the particular moment being viewed in a film. Instead the spectator is able to move forward and backward through screen data in order to experiment with a variety of syntactical, semantic, and referential hypotheses; as Ian Jarvie notes, 'We cannot *see* movies without *thinking* about them.'[11] By experimenting with various methods for ordering data, the spectator creates spatial, temporal, and causal experiences which do not derive directly from screen time. Also critical in top-down processing are procedures which test the degree of 'progress' which has been made toward solving a perceptual problem. Such procedures are active, for example, when we search for the 'end' of a story. If we are unable to detect progress, we may begin to doubt the particular techniques we have been using, or even whether we have properly understood the goal. Because of the diversity of top-down and bottom-up processes which may be at work at a given moment in a text, perception as a whole is perhaps best thought of as a system which struggles to manage different and often conflicting interpretations of data.

In addition, the fact that comprehension may be divided into top-down and bottom-up kinds of activity helps explain some inconsistencies in the terminology employed by film writers. For example, some writers prefer to use the concept of 'voice' in film as a means to identify the source of words that are actually heard by a spectator while other writers prefer to apply the concept more broadly in order to include a number of top-down factors that influence a spectator's perception. Bill Nichols argues for an expansive notion of 'voice.'

[I]n the evolution of documentary [as a genre] the contestation among forms has centered on the question of 'voice.' By 'voice' I mean something narrower than style: that which conveys to us a sense of a text's social point of view, of how it is speaking to us and how it is organizing the materials it is presenting to us. In this

sense 'voice' is not restricted to any one code or feature, such as
dialogue or spoken commentary. Voice is perhaps akin to that
intangible, moire-like pattern formed by the unique interaction of
all a film's codes, and it applies to *all* modes of documentary.[12]

For Nichols, the concept of 'voice' is not confined to words literally
spoken, or written, nor confined to fictional narrative; instead, 'voice'
includes powerful, nonverbal patterns even in nonfiction
(documentary) films. Accordingly, the 'person' whose voice is
'heard' in a text may be a much more complex (invisible and
inaudible) entity than a voice-over narrator or someone being
interviewed. Thus Nichols's approach is well-suited to an analysis of
narration. [. . .] Film narration cannot be limited to, say, an explicit
commentary, or defined by literal, material, purely formal, stylistic,
technical, technological, or 'bottom-up' kinds of categories.
Narration, and narrative, are preeminently top-down phenomena that
require for their analysis the use of wide-ranging, complex concepts
like 'point of view,' or Nichols's 'social point of view.'

When we think of narrative as a general phenomenon that may
appear in many physical forms (conversation, pictures, dance,
music, etc.), we are thinking of it as a top-down cognitive effect.
Wallace Martin may put it too strongly when he says that 'narratives
may be the source of the varied visual resources of the movies, rather
than vice versa.'[13] Nevertheless, much can be learned by
concentrating on top-down processes in an attempt to isolate the
psychological conditions that allow narrative to be understood in
all media.

I wish to examine some of the top-down processes which seem to
be relevant to our comprehension of narrative. I will begin by
considering how our top-down search for a coherent causal system
helps to organize screen data into diegetic and nondiegetic story
worlds, each with a coherent temporal system. Later in the chapter, I
will consider how judgments about screen space are related to
judgments about story space and the causality of a story world. In
general, we will discover that conflicts arise between top-down and
bottom-up processing, between story and screen, and between the
diegesis and what seems external to it. Hence we will find that
the ongoing process of constructing and understanding a narrative is
perhaps best seen as the moment by moment regulation of conflicts
among competing spatial, temporal, and causal hypotheses.
'Narrative' in film is therefore the overall process as well as the
result of searching among hypotheses for an equilibrium, however
precarious.

Temporal and spatial order

There is a sequence in *The Lady from Shanghai* (Welles, 1948) where three distinct actions are intercut through fifteen shots in such a way that it appears that when a woman presses a button, a door flies open allowing a dying man to drag himself into a room; when she presses the button again, a car is sent speeding down a road as a truck pulls up to a stop sign; and, when she presses the button a final time, the car is sent crashing into the back of the truck as the two men in the car react with horror at their helpless condition. The problem for the spectator of this film is how to interpret these events which can have no causal connection and yet are presented *as if* they were causally connected so that it seems that pushing a button brings a dying man into a room and creates a car accident.[14] In effect, we are being asked to accept a special fiction ('as if') within an already fictional mystery story.

In order to solve this causal problem the spectator must evaluate the temporal relationships posed by the sequence. Four important principles of causal reasoning are that a cause must precede an effect, an effect cannot work backward in time to create a cause, certain patterns of *repetition* among events make a causal connection more likely (e.g., pushing a button three times . . .) and a prior event which is temporally or spatially more proximate to the outcome than others is more likely to be a cause of the outcome.[15] Many different sorts of temporal situations, bearing on our judgments of causality, may be created through the juxtaposition of spatial fragments from different shots. As Arnheim emphasized, 'the fact that two sequences follow each other on the screen does not indicate in itself that they should be understood as following each other in time.'[16] Thus before tackling the causal problem, we must briefly survey some of the possible temporal, and spatial, situations which may arise.

An extraordinary fact about the physical world is that virtually all phenomena can be explained in terms of interactions between parts *taken two at a time*. According to Marvin Minsky, 'One could conceive of a universe in which whenever three stars formed an equilateral triangle, one of them would instantly disappear – but virtually no three-part interactions have ever been observed in the physical world.'[17] I will assume that explanations of phenomena are constructed on this basis; specifically, that the spectator constructs temporal, spatial, and causal situations by assembling parts two at a time. Thus in figure 1 [p. 244], temporal situation AB_1 in the story is created by imagining a particular relationship between the durations of two on-screen spaces, A and B, resulting in such story relationships as temporal continuity, ellipsis, overlap, simultaneity, reversal, or distortion.

More specifically, these temporal relationships in the story may be described as follows:

B_1 represents the time of A as *continuing* into B such that the story order AB_1 is presented as identical to the screen order AB.

B_2 represents the time of A as continuing into B but with an initial *ellipsis* so that the screen order is interpreted as having omitted something from the story (which must be restored by the spectator's imagination); that is, the true order is: A, X, B_2, where X is not represented on the screen. If the ellipsis is large, but later disappears when completed by new screen events, then B_2 is a flashforward.

B_3 represents the time of A as continuing into B but only after an initial *overlap* in which there has been a partial replay of time already experienced in A.

B_4 represents a complete overlap with the time of A so that story event B is understood to be *simultaneous* with story event A even though B is seen to occur after A on the screen; that is, story time overrides the literal order on the screen.

B_5 represents an overlap with the time of A but with an initial brief jump back in time. This produces a fleeting but curious story time in which an effect (in A) has apparently been shown prior to its cause (in B). The spectator, in fact, is tempted to *mentally reverse* A and B_5 (creating a relation like A and B_3) in order to restore the forward arrow of time in which causes precede effects (i.e., prospective time). It is also possible that AB_5 may require the spectator to imagine an even earlier time (e.g., B_6) which is then taken as an explanation of A in the story – an implicit flashback – while B_5 continues to represent the 'present time' of A. Using Noël Burch's terms, I will refer to the AB_5 type of story order as a *retrospective* or retroactive story time.[18] Our usual expectation is prospective time – A *and so* B. Less usual is retrospective time – A *because of* B.

Here is an example of retrospective time: Shot A shows an object from a certain position, but then shot B shows a person looking at the object from that previous position. In this way, we discover that the object we saw in A *had already been seen* by a character (and in fact, without knowing it at the time, we were seeing how

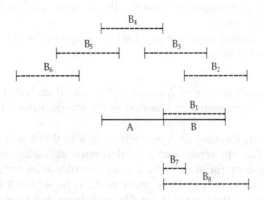

Figure 1 Story time

Graphic display of several varieties of story time created as a spectator relocates the on-screen time of spatial fragment B relative to the on-sceen time of spatial fragment A resulting in a new and imaginary temporal order in the story, relationship AB_n. Some of the new relationships that may be created include temporal continuity, ellipsis, overlap, simultaneity, reversal, and distortion. The general principles illustrated here for time may also be applied to describe the ordering of space into such patterns as chains, gaps, reversals, and distortions (see text).

that character saw the object). Thus with shot B we are forced to mentally readjust the order of events and reconceive shot A using the character as a new reference point, as a new condition for our seeing. We now conceive of the story event as composed of, first, a character who looks, followed by our view of what can be seen from that character's viewpoint. Part of shot B then comes to stand for either a literal, brief jump back in time, or else an approximation of what it would have looked like to have seen the character first looking. In any event, what is important is that the shots require the spectator to refigure the temporal scheme.

B_6 represents a time prior to A – a *past* time, or flashback, which requires the spectator to reorder story events and imagine other events which have been omitted and not seen on the screen between B_6 and A.

B_7 and B_8 represent temporal *distortions*. The on-screen duration of B (with respect to A!) is radically altered in such a way that it is not immediately clear what relationship with A is appropriate. For example, the duration of B may be compressed or expanded by running the film at a new speed, showing it backwards, repeating

B, showing alternative takes, omitting frames by step printing, using freeze frames, and so forth.[19] In these situations A and B do not seem commensurate and hence we cannot immediately decide what story order is appropriate. Also included in these categories is indeterminable time. For example, in Jean-Luc Godard's *Weekend* (1967) there is a shot (involving hippie-guerrillas) that is so carefully arranged that its time cannot be ascertained. In fact, the shot is a flashforward but it cannot be recognized as such until much later in the film when the event being depicted actually occurs! The shot is thus a retrospective, nonsubjective flashforward.

The above scheme is a way of talking generally about principles of temporal ordering. However, it also applies to principles of *spatial ordering*. Although my discussion of the particular causal problem of the car crash in *The Lady from Shanghai* will center on time, it should be evident that, in general, space is just as relevant to the solution of causal problems. Therefore I wish to indicate briefly how the above scheme may be interpreted as an overview of some spatial principles of ordering. The scheme is not meant to be restrictive but merely to provide a way of comparing various narrative theories each of which will use specialized terms to examine space and time in still finer detail.

In order to demonstrate how figure 1 may be applied to space, I will for the moment make an artificial, but simplifying assumption about space. I will assume that space comprises only two sectors: a foreground and a background. The question then becomes, how may we recognize a *change* in space? How may a given space 'connect to' and be related to another space to form a new ordered whole? For convenience I will also assume – as in the case of time – that the change is effected through the editing of shots even though the scheme applies to changes effected in other ways (e.g., through camera or character movement, sound, changes in lighting level). The result of these assumptions is that space may evolve in only three basic ways: a new background may appear with the old foreground; a new foreground may appear with the old background; or, both a new foreground and a new background may appear. In the first two cases, what is new is introduced in conjunction with what has already been seen (an old foreground, or else an old background). This means that spaces are being connected into a *chain*. In the third case (a new foreground and a new background) the relationship of the new space to the spaces which have already been seen is *open* and not yet defined; that is, there is a 'gap' of some type between new and old space. Such a gap is indicated in figure 1 by the gap between fragment A and fragment B_2. On the other hand, fragments B_1, B_3, and B_4 represent a new space which either adjoins, overlaps, or repeats an old space so as to compose a *chain* of spaces.

There is a special case of the open space $(A-B_2)$ which must be mentioned. When the new foreground is simply the old background and the new background is the old foreground, there has been no real change: foreground and background have simply been interchanged across the two shots. Space has been reversed, or mirrored between the shots. Fragments B_5 and B_6 are meant to represent this general class of *reverse angles* in film. A typical example is shot/reverse-shot editing which depicts a conversation between two characters by alternating shots taken over each character's shoulder.[20]

What can spatial 'reversals' like B_5 and B_6 mean in terms of the story world being created by the spectator from a series of on-screen spaces? David Bordwell offers a proposal:

> Shot/reverse-shot editing helps make narration covert by creating the sense that no important scenographic space remains unaccounted for. If shot two shows the important material outside shot one, there is no spatial point we can assign to the narration; the narration is always elsewhere, outside this shot but never visible in the next.[21]

In other words, when space is reversed we do not see a camera, sets, or technicians but only more diegetic space which seemingly is part of a consistent and unified group of spaces with no disturbing (causal) outside influences (e.g., by an 'author'). The new and larger space being represented through a reversal is an imaginary space – a diegetic space of the characters that is seemingly like itself in every direction.

There are, of course, degrees and kinds of chains, gaps, and reversals of space; and our recognition of the kinds will depend on the nature of other conventions governing, say, camera placement (for example, whether spaces are oriented toward a 180 degree axis of action). Connecting screen spaces to a pattern of story space does not prohibit also using gaps (B_2 and B_6), or other distortions (cf. B_7 and B_8), to create a story space which is *not* the sum of spatial fragments on the screen. Such a gap between screen and story space leads to degrees and kinds of 'impossible' space; that is, *to space which can not be justified as existing wholly within the diegesis*. Impossible space leads to perceptual problems of a new kind that force the spectator to reconsider prior hypotheses about time and causality.

[...]

Notes

1. RUDOLF ARNHEIM, *Film as Art* (Berkeley: University of California Press, 1957; first published in 1933), p. 59; see also pp. 12, 24–9.

2. On the distinction between screen and story world see, e.g., ALEXANDER SESONSKE, 'Cinema Space' in *Explorations of Phenomenology*, ed. David Carr and Edward S. Casey (The Hague: Martinus Nijhoff, 1973), pp. 399–409; HAIG KHATCHADOURIAN, 'Space and Time in Film,' *The British Journal of Aesthetics*, 27. 2 (Spring 1987): 169–77.

3. DAVID MARR, *Vision: A Computational Investigation into the Human Representation and Processing of Visual Information* (San Francisco: W. H. Freeman, 1982).

4. Kristin Thompson argues that 'A film depends on materiality for its existence; out of image and sound it creates its structures, but it can never make all the physical elements of the film part of its set of smooth perceptual cues. . . . [E]xcess arises from the conflict between the *materality* of a film and the unifying structures within it.' KRISTIN THOMPSON, 'The Concept of Cinematic Excess' in *Narrative, Apparatus, Ideology: A Film Theory Reader*, ed. Philip Rosen (New York: Columbia University Press, 1986), pp. 131–2 (Thompson's emphasis); see also pp. 133–5. The concept of excess is sometimes paired with its opposite, a lack of lacuna, especially in psychoanalytic theories of narrative.

5. NOËL BURCH, 'Carl Theodor Dreyer: The Major Phase' in *Cinema: A Critical Dictionary – The Major Film Makers*, vol. 1, ed. by Richard Roud (New York: The Viking Press, 1980), pp. 298–9; ARNHEIM, *Film as Art*, pp. 26–8.

6. SERGEI EISENSTEIN, 'A Dialectic Approach to Film Form' in *Film Form: Essays in Film Theory*, trans. by Jay Leyda (New York: Harcourt, Brace & World, 1949), pp. 49, 54–7.

7. SERGEI EISENSTEIN, *The Film Sense*, trans. by Jay Leyda (New York: Harcourt, Brace & World, 1947), pp. 74–81, 201–3. I have been somewhat free in interpreting Eisenstein's notions of vertical and polyphonic montage.

8. JULIAN HOCHBERG, 'Representation of Motion and Space in Video and Cinematic Displays', in *Handbook of Perception and Human Performance*, ed. Kenneth R. Boff, Lloyd Kaufman and James P. Thomas (New York: Wiley, 1986), pp. 22–58.

9. See EDWARD BRANIGAN, 'Diegesis and Authorship in Film,' *Iris* 7, 4. 2 (Fall 1986): 37–54.

10. The existence of bottom-up and top-down processes significantly alters the traditional distinction between perception and cognition. RAY JACKENDOFF, *Consciousness and the Computational Mind* (Cambridge, Mass.: MIT Press, 1987), pp. 271–2. For an account of film perception describing some of these processes, see HOCHBERG, 'Representation of Motion and Space', pp. 22–1 through 22–64 and VIRGINIA BROOKS, 'Film, Perception and Cognitive Psychology,' *Millennium Film Journal*, 14/15 (Fall/Winter 1984–5): 105–26. See generally DAVID BORDWELL's 'A Case for Cognitivism' in a special issue of *Iris* 9 devoted to 'Cinema and Cognitive Psychology,' 5. 2 (Spring 1989): 11–40.

11. IAN JARVIE, *Philosophy of the Film: Epistemology, Ontology, Aesthetics* (New York: Routledge & Kegan Paul, 1987), p. 130 (Jarvie's emphases).

12. BILL NICHOLS, 'The Voice of Documentary' in *Movies and Methods: An Anthology*, vol. 2, ed. Bill Nichols (Berkeley: University of California Press, 1985), pp. 260–1 (my emphases).

13. WALLACE MARTIN, *Recent Theories of Narrative* (Ithaca, NY: Cornell University Press, 1986), p. 144.

14. My discussion of this scene in *The Lady from Shanghai* is based on GEORGE M. WILSON's suggestive comments in *Narration in Light: Studies in Cinematic Point of View* (Baltimore: Johns Hopkins University Press, 1986), pp. 1–4, 10, 202–4. There are, however, many inaccuracies in Wilson's description of the shots and story events, including the number of shots and their order.

15. See MERRY BULLOCK, ROCHEL GELMAN, and RENEE BAILLARGEON, 'The Development of Causal Reasoning' in *The Development Psychology of Time*, ed. William J. Friedman (New York: Academic Press, 1982), pp. 210–15.

    Welles's 'impossible' causation in *The Lady from Shanghai* is achieved by bringing elements that are normally noncausal into proximity. Filmmakers like Bresson, Dreyer, Godard, Ozu and Straub and Huiller achieve similar effects by *separating* an actual cause from its effect thereby making connections and making (conventional) causality a problem.

16. ARNHEIM, *Film as Art*, p. 24.

17. MARVIN MINSKY, *The Society of Mind* (New York: Simon & Schuster, 1986), p. 329; cf. pp. 78, 149, 249.

18. NOËL BURCH, *Theory of Film Practice*, trans. Helen R. Lane (Princeton: Princeton University Press, 1981; originally published in French, 1969), pp. 12–14, 78–9.

19. In figure 1, I am treating Genette's concept of temporal 'frequency' – how often an event occurs on the screen as compared with how often it occurs in the story – as a special case of temporal 'order.' Thus the screen sequence, 'a-x^1-b-c-x^2,' would be analyzed by saying that 'x^2' occurs after 'c' on the screen but maps into the same position in the story as did 'x^1' which occurred between 'a' and 'b' on the screen. Note also that some effects of duration (e.g., rhythm) do not normally affect story order and hence are not included in figure 1.

20. Fragment B_5 in figure 1 would include over-the-shoulder shots because in such shots space is not exactly reversed, but instead includes some overlap between the two spaces. If the camera were turned on its axis exactly 180 degrees before the next shot, leaving neither an overlap nor a gap between the two spaces, the result would be a true reversal. It would be represented in figure 1 by a new line, like B_1, joining A but extending backwards. A true reversal is rare in classical narrative space perhaps because it may be difficult for a spectator to determine whether the new space is immediately adjacent to the old space or whether there is a *gap* between the spaces which is *not* visible (cf. A and B_6). This suggests that in classical narrative the most common articulation for space is a partial overlap (i.e., B_5 and B_3).

21. DAVID BORDWELL, JANET STAIGER, and KRISTIN THOMPSON, *The Classical Hollywood Cinema: Film Style & Mode of Production to 1960* (New York: Columbia University Press, 1985), chap. 5, 'Space in the Classical Film,' p. 59.

Part Five

Post-structuralist narratology

16 Reading for the Plot*

PETER BROOKS

In this excerpt from chapter 1 of *Reading for the Plot* (1984) Peter Brooks sets out to update and redefine the traditional concept of 'plot', fallen into disuse in the English-speaking world after the adverse criticism of such modernist critics as E. M. Forster. In line with French narratology, Brooks reiterates Aristotle's contention in the *Poetics* that plot, defined as 'the combination of the incidents, or things done in the story', is the most important element of narrative. He analyses various aspects of such concepts as the Russian formalist *'fabula'* and *'siuzhet'*, Gérard Genette's 'histoire' and 'discours' and Jonathan Culler's 'story' and 'discourse', concluding that a purely structuralist definition of plot would be restrictive and inadequate. In order to be explanatory, the analysis of plot – understood as the organizing line of a narrative – should be able to take account of intentionality. To this end, Brooks proposes a leap beyond formalism and specifically towards Freudian psychoanalysis, which is in line with much feminist criticism of the 1980s. In this connection it is interesting to point out the similarity between the title of chapter 2 of *Reading for the Plot*, 'Narrative Desire', and Teresa de Lauretis' 'Desire in Narrative', also published in 1984, which is reprinted as chapter 17 of this book. But whereas de Lauretis applies Freudian psychoanalysis to the desire of the woman spectator in film, Brooks's re-reading of Freud remains male-oriented. The main emphasis of his formulation lies in his conception of narrative as a psychological structuring device which governs both human behaviour and the definition of self.

I

[...]
'Reading for the plot,' we learned somewhere in the course of our

---

*PETER BROOKS, *Reading for the Plot: Design and Intention in Narrative* (Oxford: Clarendon, 1984), pp. 3–36, 325–30.

schooling, is a low form of activity. Modern criticism, especially in its Anglo-American branches, has tended to take its valuations from study of the lyric, and when it has discussed narrative has emphasized questions of 'point of view,' 'tone,' 'symbol,' 'spatial form,' or 'psychology.' The texture of narrative has been considered most interesting insofar as it approached the density of poetry. Plot has been disdained as the element of narrative that least sets off and defines high art – indeed, plot is that which especially characterizes popular mass-consumption literature: plot is why we read *Jaws*, but not Henry James. And yet, one must in good logic argue that plot is somehow prior to those elements most discussed by most critics, since it is the very organizing line, the thread of design, that makes narrative possible because finite and comprehensible. Aristotle, of course, recognized the logical priority of plot, and a recent critical tradition, starting with the Russian Formalists and coming up to the French and American 'narratologists,' has revived a quasi-Aristotelian sense of plot. [. . .]

There are evidently a number of different ways one might go about discussing the concept of plot and its function in the range of narrative forms. Plot is, first of all, a constant of all written and oral narrative, in that a narrative without at least a minimal plot would be incomprehensible. Plot is the principle of interconnectedness and intention which we cannot do without in moving through the discrete elements – incidents, episodes, actions – of a narrative: even such loosely articulated forms as the picaresque novel display devices of interconnectedness, structural repetitions that allow us to construct a whole; and we can make sense of such dense and seemingly chaotic texts as dreams because we use interpretive categories that enable us to reconstruct intentions and connections, to replot the dream as narrative. It would, then, be perfectly plausible to undertake a typology of plot and its elements from the *Iliad* and the *Odyssey* onward to the new novel and the 'metafictions' of our time.[1] Yet it seems clear also that there have been some historical moments at which plot has assumed a greater importance than at others, moments in which cultures have seemed to develop an unquenchable thirst for plots and to seek the expression of central individual and collective meanings through narrative design. From sometime in the mid-eighteenth century through to the mid-twentieth century, Western societies appear to have felt an extraordinary need or desire for plots, whether in fiction, history, philosophy, or any of the social sciences, which in fact largely came into being with the Enlightenment and Romanticism. As Voltaire announced and then the Romantics confirmed, history replaces theology as the key discourse and central imagination in that historical explanation becomes nearly a necessary factor of any thought about human society: the question of what we are typically must pass through the question of where we are, which in turn is interpreted to mean, how did we get to be there? Not only history but historiography, the philosophy of history, philology, mythography, diachronic linguistics, anthropology, archaeology, and evolutionary biology all establish their claim as fields of inquiry, and all respond to the need for an explanatory narrative that seeks its authority in a return to origins and the tracing of a coherent story forward from origin to present.

The enormous narrative production of the nineteenth century may suggest an anxiety at the loss of providential plots: the plotting of the individual or social or institutional life story takes on new urgency when one no longer can look to a sacred masterplot that organizes and explains the world. The emergence of narrative plot as a dominant mode of ordering and explanation may belong to the large process of secularization, dating from the Renaissance and gathering force during the Enlightenment, which marks a falling-away from those revealed plots – the Chosen People, Redemption, the Second Coming – that appeared to subsume transitory human time to the timeless. [. . .] By the end of the Enlightenment, there is no longer any consensus on this prediction, and no cultural cohesion around a point of fixity which allows thought and vision so to transfix time. And this may explain the nineteenth century's obsession with questions of origin, evolution, progress, genealogy, its foregrounding of the historical narrative as par excellence the necessary mode of explanation and understanding.

We still live today in the age of narrative plots, consuming avidly Harlequin romances and television serials and daily comic strips, creating and demanding narrative in the presentation of persons and news events and sports contests. [. . .] And yet, we know that with the advent of Modernism came an era of suspicion toward plot, engendered perhaps by an overelaboration of and overdependence on plots in the nineteenth century. [. . .] A reflection on plot as the syntax of a certain way of speaking our understanding of the world may tell us something about how and why we have come to stake so many of the central concerns of our society, and of our lives, on narrative.

II

[. . .]
Plot as it interests me is not a matter of typology or of fixed structures, but rather a structuring operation peculiar to those messages that

253

are developed through temporal succession, the instrumental logic of a specific mode of human understanding. Plot, let us say in preliminary definition, is the logic and dynamic of narrative, and narrative itself a form of understanding and explanation.

Such a conception of plot seems to be at least compatible with Aristotle's understanding of *mythos*, the term from the *Poetics* that is normally translated as 'plot.' It is Aristotle's claim that plot (*mythos*) and action (*praxis*) are logically prior to the other parts of dramatic fictions, including character (*ethos*). *Mythos* is defined as 'the combination of the incidents, or things done in the story,' and Aristotle argues that of all the parts of the story, this is the most important.[2] [...] Later in the same paragraph he reiterates, using an analogy that may prove helpful to thinking about plot: 'We maintain, therefore, that the first essential, the life and soul, so to speak, of Tragedy is Plot; and that the Characters come second – compare the parallel in painting, where the most beautiful colours laid on without order will not give one the same pleasure as a simple black-and-white sketch of a portrait.' Plot, then, is conceived to be the outline or armature of the story, that which supports and organizes the rest. From such a view, Aristotle proceeds to derive three consequences. First, the action imitated by the tragedy must be complete in itself. This in turn means that it must have a beginning, a middle, and an end – a point wholly obvious but one that will prove to have interesting effects in its applications. Finally, just as in the visual arts a whole must be of a size that can be taken in by the eye, so a plot must be 'of a length to be taken in by the memory.' This is important, since memory – as much in reading a novel as in seeing a play – is the key faculty in the capacity to perceive relations of beginnings, middles, and ends through time, the shaping power of narrative.

But our English term 'plot' has its own semantic range, one that is interestingly broad and possibly instructive. [...] Common to the original sense of the word is the idea of boundedness, demarcation, the drawing of lines to mark off and order. This easily extends to the chart or diagram of the demarcated area, which in turn modulates to the outline of the literary work. From the organized space, plot becomes the organizing line, demarcating and diagramming that which was previously undifferentiated. We might think here of the geometrical expression, plotting points, or curves, on a graph by means of coordinates, as a way of locating something, perhaps oneself. The fourth sense of the word, the scheme or conspiracy, seems to have come into English through the contaminating influence of the French *complot*, and became widely known at the time of the Gunpowder Plot. I would suggest that in modern literature this sense of plot nearly always attaches itself to the others: the organizing line of plot is more often than not some scheme or machination, a concerted plan for the accomplishment of some purpose which goes against the ostensible and dominant legalities of the fictional world, the realization of a blocked and resisted desire. Plots are not simply organizing structures, they are also intentional structures, goal-oriented and forward-moving.

Plot as we need and want the term is hence an embracing concept for the design and intention of narrative, a structure for those meanings that are developed through temporal succession, or perhaps better: a structuring operation elicited by, and made necessary by, those meanings that develop through succession and time. A further analysis of the question is suggested here by a distinction urged by the Russian Formalists, that between *fabula* and *sjužet*. *Fabula* is defined as the order of events referred to by the narrative, whereas *sjužet* is the order of events presented in the narrative discourse. [. . .] In the wake of the Russian Formalists, French structural analysts of narrative proposed their own pairs of terms, predominantly *histoire* (corresponding to *fabula*) and *récit*, or else *discours* (corresponding to *sjužet*). English usage has been more unsettled. 'Story' and 'plot' would seem to be generally acceptable renderings in most circumstances, though a structural and semiotic analysis will find advantages in the less semantically charged formulation 'story' and 'discourse.'[3]

'Plot' in fact seems to me to cut across the *fabula/sjužet* distinction in that to speak of plot is to consider both story elements and their ordering. Plot could be thought of as the interpretive activity elicited by the distinction between *sjužet* and *fabula*, the way we *use* the one against the other. To keep our terms straight without sacrificing the advantages of the semantic range of 'plot,' let us say that we can generally understand plot to be an aspect of *sjužet* in that it belongs to the narrative discourse, as its active shaping force, but that it makes sense (as indeed *sjužet* itself principally makes sense) as it is used to reflect on *fabula*, as our understanding of story. Plot is thus the dynamic shaping force of the narrative discourse. I find confirmation for such a view in Paul Ricœur's definition of plot as 'the intelligible whole that governs a succession of events in any story.' Ricœur continues, using the terms 'events' and 'story' rather than *fabula* and *sjužet*: 'This provisory definition immediately shows the plot's connecting function between an event or events and the story. A story is *made out of* events to the extent that plot *makes* events *into* a story. The plot, therefore, places us at the crossing point of temporality and narrativity. . . .'[4] Ricœur's emphasis on the constructive role of plot, its active, shaping function, offers a useful corrective to the structural narratologists' neglect of the dynamics of narrative and points us toward the reader's vital role in the understanding of plot.

[...]

Plot as a logic of narrative would hence seem to be analogous to the syntax of meanings that are temporally unfolded and recovered, meanings that cannot otherwise be created or understood. Genette's study of narrative discourse in reference to Proust leads him to note that one can tell a story without any reference to the place of its telling, the location from which it is proffered, but that one cannot tell a story without indications of the time of telling in relation to the told: the use of verb tenses, and their relation one to another, necessarily gives us a certain temporal place in relation to the story. Genette calls this discrepancy in the situation of time and place a 'dissymmetry' of the language code itself, 'the deep causes of which escape us.'[5] While Genette's point is valid and important in the context of linguistics and the philosophy of language, one might note that commonsensically the deep causes are evident to the point of banality, if also rather grim: that is, man is ambulatory, but he is mortal. [...]

Walter Benjamin has made this point in the simplest and most extreme way, in claiming that what we seek in narrative fictions is that knowledge of death which is denied to us in our own lives: the death that writes *finis* to the life and therefore confers on it its meaning. 'Death,' says Benjamin, 'is the sanction of everything that the story can tell.'[6] Benjamin thus advances the ultimate argument for the necessary retrospectivity of narrative: that only the end can finally determine meaning, close the sentence as a signifying totality. Many of the most suggestive analysts of narrative have shared this conviction that the end writes the beginning and shapes the middle: Propp, for instance, and Frank Kermode, and Jean-Paul Sartre, in his distinction between living and telling, argued in *La Nausée*. [...] We should here note that opposed to this view stand other analysts, such as Claude Bremond, or Jean Pouillon, who many years ago argued (as a Sartrean attempting to rescue narrative from the constraints Sartre found in it) that the preterite tense used classically in the novel is decoded by the reader as a kind of present, that of an action and a significance being forged before his eyes, in his hands, so to speak.[8] It is to my mind an interesting and not wholly resolvable question how much, and in what ways, we in reading image the pastness of the action presented, in most cases, in verbs in the past tense. [...] If the past is to be read as present, it is a curious present that we know to be past in relation to a future we know to be already in place, already in wait for us to reach it. Perhaps we would do best to speak of the *anticipation of retrospection* as our chief tool in making sense of narrative, the master trope of its strange logic. [. . .]

III

[. . .]

In an essay called 'Story and Discourse in the Analysis of Narrative,' Jonathan Culler has argued that we need to recognize that narrative proceeds according to a 'double logic,' in that at certain problematic moments story events seem to be produced by the requirements of the narrative discourse, its needs of meaning, rather than vice-versa, as we normally assume.[9] In other words, the apparently normal claim that *fabula* precedes *sjužet*, which is a reworking of the givens of *fabula*, must be reversed at problematic, challenging moments of narrative, to show that *fabula* is rather produced by the requirements of *sjužet*: that something must have happened because of the results that we know – that, as Cynthia Chase puts it about Daniel Deronda's Jewishness, 'his origin is the effect of its effects.'[10] Culler cautions critics against the assumption that these two perspectives can be synthesized without contradiction.

[. . .]

The irreconcilability of the 'two logics' points to the peculiar work of understanding that narrative is called upon to perform, and to the paralogical status of its 'solutions.' Let me restate the problem in this way: prior events, causes, are so only retrospectively, in a reading back from the end. In this sense, the metaphoric work of eventual totalization determines the meaning and status of the metonymic work of sequence – though it must also be claimed that the metonymies of the middle produced, gave birth to, the final metaphor. The contradiction may be in the very nature of narrative, which not only uses but *is* a double logic. The detective story, as a kind of dime-store modern version of 'wisdom literature,' is useful in displaying the double logic most overtly, using the plot of the inquest to find, or construct, a story of the crime which will offer just those features necessary to the thematic coherence we call a solution, while claiming, of course, that the solution has been made necessary by the crime. To quote Holmes at the end of another of his cases, that of 'The Naval Treaty': 'The principal difficulty in your case . . . lay in the fact of there being too much evidence. What was vital was overlaid and hidden by what was irrelevant. Of all the facts which were presented to us we had to pick just those which we deemed to be essential, and then piece them together in their order so as to reconstruct this very remarkable chain of events.'[11] Here we have a clear *ars poetica*, of the detective and of the novelist, and of the plotting of narrative as an example of the mental operation described by Wallace Stevens as 'The poem of the mind in the act of finding/What will suffice.'

It would be my further claim that narrative's nature as a contradictious double logic tells us something about why we have and need narrative, and how the need to plot meanings is itself productive of narrative. We may explore this proposition by way of [. . .] Rousseau's *Confessions,* and I shall use as my example from it the notorious episode that closes Book Two, the story of the stolen ribbon. Rousseau has been serving as a lackey in the household of Mme de Vercellis, and feeling that he [. . .] is out of his place, misplaced, and therefore ever on the lookout for some special mark of favor that would indicate that Mme de Vercellis knows he is destined for better things. But she dies without any recognition of Rousseau, and without any legacy. In the ensuing liquidation of her household, Rousseau steals a little pink and silver ribbon, which is found in his room. Asked where he got it, he lies and says that Marion, a young peasant girl serving as a cook, gave it to him. Confronted with Marion, who calmly denies the allegation, Rousseau persists in his account, which leads Marion to exclaim, 'You are making me very unhappy, but I wouldn't want to be in your place.'[12] In doubt as to the truth, the Comte de la Roque (Mme de Vercellis's heir) dismisses them both. Rousseau now goes on to image the probable future scenario of Marion's life: dismissed under the shadow of accusation, penniless, without recommendation or protection, what could become of her? Rousseau sketches with hypothetical certainty a career that would make her 'worse than myself,' that is, presumably, a prostitute. This cruel memory has continued to trouble him so that in his insomnias the figure of Marion comes to reproach him with the crime, as if it had been committed only yesterday, but he has never been able to bring himself to make a clean breast of it, even to his closest friend. In fact, the desire to deliver himself of the weight of this particular crime, he then tells us, contributed greatly to his decision to write his confessions.

The facts of the case and its consequences have thus far been presented by Rousseau the narrator in what he claims the reader cannot deny to be an open and straightforward confession. [. . .] Curiously, it was his friendship for her that caused the accusation. She was present in his thoughts, and he excused himself by way of the first object that occurred to him: 'je m'excusai sur le premier objet qui s'offrit.' This apparently gratuitous and aberrant choice of person to serve as victim – unsettling in its suggestion of random vectors of plot – then receives something closer to a motivation when Rousseau explains that he accused Marion of doing what he wanted to do: of having given him the ribbon since he intended to give it to her. Thus his *amitié* for Marion appears to partake of love, and he can imagine being the recipient of what he wanted to give, which allows of a further reversal when the love-offering is poisoned in its source: love veers to sadism. What prevents Rousseau from owning up and straightening out this tangled ribbon is not the fear of punishment but the fear of shame: 'I only saw the horror of being recognized, publicly declared, with myself present, thief, liar, false accuser.' As so often in the *Confessions*, it is the fear of judgment from the outside, judgment by those who cannot see the *dispositions intérieures*, that appears to motivate both bad behavior and the confession that such behavior necessitates: the fear of being judged as in a place where he does not belong produces both lies and confessions. [. . .]

Juxtaposed in the episode of the stolen ribbon as presented in the *Confessions* we have a straightforward account of narrative events, presented in their chronological order; a subsequent narrative of inner feelings and motives standing in stark contradiction to the narrative of events; a hallucinatory narrative of the hypothetical future of the other persona of the episode, Marion; and a narrative of the generation of the text of the *Confessions*, since the need to tell this story – or these stories – claims genetic force. Is there any way we can order these four elements in a logical discourse? Apparently not, since the very point of the discrepancy between the narrative of actions and narrative of internal dispositions is their fundamental lack of congruence, the inability of either ever fully to coincide with or explain the other. One could no doubt discover a motive of connection between the two through a psychoanalytic discourse: Rousseau provides a key for so doing when he introduces his desire for Marion into the scenario and suggests that somehow this desire produced effects opposite from what he intended, the subject and object of desire changed places, and love became sadistic. All this could be reconceptualized by way of Freud, most pertinently through the concept of denial, denegation. But to bring such a psychoanalytic discourse to bear would in fact be – given the nature of Freud's analyses of the problem – to add another layer of narrative, however illuminating, to those Rousseau has already piled up. It would not offer an escape from narrative.

Rousseau's narrative layerings suggest a failure to find a single answer to the question of where his proper *place* is, what his publicly declared name, rank, and character are to be. Always out of place, never coincident with his inner self in the eyes of others – and thus in his behavior – he is always going back over the traces of conduct and interior disposition, not to reconcile them – which is impossible – but to confess their irreconcilability, which generates Marion's future story and Rousseau's future confessions. In other words, the only ordering or solution to the problem in understanding Rousseau has set up here is more narrative. [. . .] To understand me, Rousseau says more than once in the *Confessions*, most impressively at the close of Book Four, the reader must follow me at every moment of my existence; and it will be up to the reader, not Rousseau, to assemble the elements of the narrative and determine what they mean. Thus what Rousseau must fear, in writing his *Confessions*, is not saying too much or speaking lies, but failing to say everything. In claiming the need to *tout dire*, Rousseau makes explicit that the contradictions encountered in the attempt to understand and present the self in all its truth provide a powerful narrative machine. Any time one goes over a moment of the past, the machine can be relied on to produce more narrative – not only differing stories of the past, but future scenarios and narratives of writing itself. There is simply no end to narrative on this model, since there is no 'solution' to the 'crime.'[13] The narrative plotting in its entirety is the solution, and since that entirety has no endpoint for the writing – as opposed to the biological – self, Rousseau is reduced to requesting the reader's permission to *make* an end here: 'Qu'il me soit permis de n'en reparler jamais.' [. . .]

If I emphasize plotting even more than plot, it is because the participle best suggests the dynamic aspect of narrative that most interests me: that which moves us forward as readers of the narrative text, that which makes us – like the heroes of the text often, and certainly like their authors – want and need plotting, seeking through the narrative text as it unfurls before us a precipitation of shape and meaning, some simulacrum of understanding of how meaning can be construed over and through time. I am convinced that the study of narrative needs to move beyond the various formalist criticisms that have predominated in our time: formalisms that have taught us much, but which ultimately – as the later work of Barthes recognized – cannot deal with the dynamics of texts as actualized in the reading process.
[. . .]

In the attempt to be beyond pure formalism – while never discarding its lessons – psychoanalysis promises, and requires, that in addition to such usual narratological preoccupations as function, sequence, and paradigm, we engage the dynamic of memory and the history of desire as they work to shape the recovery of meaning within time. Beyond formalism, Susan Sontag argued some years ago, we need an erotics of art.[14] What follows may be conceived as a

contribution to that erotics, or, more soberly, a reading of our
compulsions to read.

Notes

1. One of the ambitions of NORTHROP FRYE in *Anatomy of Criticism* (Princeton:
   Princeton University Press, 1957) is to provide such a typology in his *mythoi*.
   Yet there is in Frye a certain confusion between *mythoi* as plot structures and
   as myths or archetypes which to my mind makes his work less valuable than
   it might be.

2. ARISTOTLE, *Poetics*, trans. Ingram Bywater, in *Introduction to Aristotle*, ed.
   Richard McKeon (2nd edn; Chicago: University of Chicago Press, 1973), p. 678.

3. See SEYMOUR CHATMAN, *Story and Discourse* (Ithaca, NY: Cornell University
   Press, 1978) [and] ROBERT SCHOLES, *Structuralism in Literature* (New Haven:
   Yale University Press, 1974).

4. PAUL RICŒUR, 'Narrative Time,' in *On Narrative*, ed. W. J. T. Mitchell (Chicago:
   University of Chicago Press, 1981), p. 167.

5. GÉRARD GENETTE, 'Discours du récit,' in *Figures III* (Paris: Editions du Seuil,
   1972; English trans. Jane Lewin, *Narrative Discourse* (Ithaca, NY: Cornell
   University Press, 1980)), p. 228.

6. WALTER BENJAMIN, 'The Storyteller' [*Der Erzähler*], in *Illuminations*, trans.
   Harry Zohn (New York: Schocken Books, 1969), p. 94.

7. See FRANK KERMODE, *The Sense of an Ending* (New York: Oxford University
   Press, 1967); JEAN-PAUL SARTRE, *La Nausée* (Paris: Gallimard, 1947), pp. 59–60;
   SARTRE, *Les Mots* (Paris: Gallimard, 1968), p. 171.

8. JEAN POUILLON, *Temps et roman* (Paris: Gallimard, 1946). See also CLAUDE
   BREMOND, *Logique du récit* (Paris: Editions du Seuil, 1973).

9. JONATHAN CULLER, 'Story and Discourse in the Analysis of Narrative,' in *The
   Pursuit of Signs* (London: Routledge & Kegan Paul, 1981), p. 178.

10. CYNTHIA CHASE, 'The Decomposition of the Elephants: Double Reading *Daniel
    Deronda*,' *PMLA* 93, no. 2 (1978), p. 218.

11. SIR ARTHUR CONAN DOYLE, 'The Naval Treaty,' in *The Complete Sherlock Holmes*
    (New York: Doubleday, 1953), vol. 1, p. 540.

12. JEAN-JACQUES ROUSSEAU, *Confessions* (Paris: Bibliothèque de la Pléïade, 1959),
    p. 85.

13. On the 'text as machine' in Rousseau, and on the episode of the stolen ribbon
    as a whole, see the notable essay by PAUL DE MAN, 'The Purloined Ribbon,'
    in *Allegories of Reading* (New Haven: Yale University Press, 1979), pp. 278–301.
    While my use of the episode of the stolen ribbon is substantially different
    from de Man's, I am indebted to his remarkable analysis.

14. SUSAN SONTAG, *Against Interpretation* (New York: Farrar, Straus & Giroux, 1966),
    p. 14.

17 Desire in Narrative*

TERESA DE LAURETIS

Teresa de Lauretis' *Alice Doesn't: Feminism, Semiotics, Cinema* (1984) is a groundbreaking study in which, as the subtitle indicates, the author attempts to reconcile semiotics and feminist theory for the purpose of analysing narrative in general and film narrative in particular. In the excerpt reprinted below, taken from chapter 5, de Lauretis discards early structuralist studies, like those published in *Communications* no. 8, on the grounds of their incapacity to account for the structural connection between desire and narrative. Drawing on Roland Barthes' suggestion that there is a structural relationship between narrative and the Oedipus, de Lauretis sets out to analyse the anthropological and structural patterns of the myth, bringing together insights from Propp, Lévi-Strauss and Freud as well as from Christian Metz and Laura Mulvey, among others. Her theory therefore combines anthropological and historical data with structuralism, semiotics and feminist theory. De Lauretis' basic contention is that desire should not be analysed thematically, but structurally; that in fact (male) desire generates narrative and is at the heart of the multifarious versions of what she considers to be the only narrative plot: a hero's quest for fulfilment where woman is the coveted reward. De Lauretis agrees with Simone de Beauvoir's classic feminist denunciation of the construction of woman as 'other' in patriarchal culture and asks important questions about female subjectivity and its representation in narrative as well as about the female spectator's (and by extension, reader's) capacity to achieve a pleasurable identification with the protagonists. Earlier feminist criticism, such as Judith Fetterley's *The Resisting Reader* (1978), had already pointed out the exclusion of female desire from male narratives as well as from male critical theory. De Lauretis' most innovating contribution to film analysis is her contention that the process of identification of the female spectator involves not one but two simultaneous sets

*TERESA DE LAURETIS, *Alice Doesn't: Feminism, Semiotics, Cinema* (Bloomington: Indiana University Press, 1984), pp. 103–43, 200–7.

of identifying relations, one with the looks of the camera and of
the male characters, and the other with the image, the passive
body and landscape.

The question of desire

[...]

For feminist theory in particular, the interest in narrativity amounts
to a *theoretical return* to narrative and the posing of questions that
have been either preempted or displaced by semiotic studies. That
return amounts, as is often the case with any radical critique, to a
rereading of the sacred texts against the passionate urging of a
different question, a different practice, and a different desire. For if
Metz's work on *la grande syntagmatique* left little room for a
consideration of the working of desire in narrative structuration,
Barthes's discourse on the pleasure of the text, at once erotic and
epistemological, also develops from his prior hunch that a
connection exists between language, narrative, and the Oedipus.[1]
[...]

Oedipus's question then, like Freud's, generates a narrative, turns
into a quest. Thus not only is a question, as Felman says, always a
question of desire; a story too is always a question of desire.

But whose desire is it that speaks, and whom does that desire
address? The received interpretations of the Oedipus story, Freud's
among others, leave no doubt. The desire is Oedipus's, and though
its object may be woman (or Truth or knowledge or power), its term
of reference and address is man: man as social being and mythical
subject, founder of the social order, and source of mimetic violence;
hence the institution of the incest prohibition, its maintenance in
Sophocles' Oedipus as in Hamlet's revenge of his father, its costs and
benefits, again, for man. However, we need not limit our
understanding of the inscription of desire in narrative to the Oedipus
story proper, which is in fact paradigmatic of all narratives. [...]

The mythical subject

However varied the conditions of presence of the narrative form in
fictional genres, rituals, or social discourses, its movement seems to
be that of a passage, a transformation predicated on the figure of a
hero, a mythical subject. While this is already common knowledge,
what has remained largely unanalyzed is how this view of myth and
narrative rests on a specific assumption about sexual difference.

Narratology: An Introduction

[. . .]

In this mythical-textual mechanics, then, the hero must be male, regardless of the gender of the text-image, because the obstacle, whatever its personification, is morphologically female and indeed, simply, the womb. The implication here is not inconsequential. For if the work of the mythical structuration is to establish distinctions, the primary distinction on which all others depend is not, say, life and death, but rather sexual difference. In other words, the picture of the world produced in mythical thought since the very beginning of culture would rest, first and foremost, on what we call biology. Opposite pairs such as inside/outside, the raw/the cooked, or life/death appear to be merely derivatives of the fundamental opposition between boundary and passage; and if passage may be in either direction, from inside to outside or vice versa, from life to death or vice versa, nonetheless all these terms are predicated on the *single* figure of the hero who crosses the boundary and penetrates the other space. In so doing the hero, the mythical subject, is constructed as human being and as male; he is the active principle of culture, the establisher of distinction, the creator of differences. Female is what is not susceptible to transformation, to life or death; she (it) is an element of plot-space, a topos, a resistance, matrix and matter.

The distance between this view and Propp's is not merely 'methodological'; it is ideological. Suffice it to point out that in very similar terms René Girard interprets the Oedipus myth in its double link to tragedy and to sacrificial ritual, and defines the role of Oedipus as that of surrogate victim. Ritual sacrifice, he states, serves to reestablish an order periodically violated by the eruption of violent reciprocity, the cyclical violence inherent in 'nondifference,' or what Lotman calls 'non-discreteness.' By his victory over the Sphinx, Oedipus has crossed the boundary and thus established his status as hero. However, in committing regicide, patricide, and incest, he has become 'the slayer of distinctions,' has abolished differences and thus contravened the mythical order. [. . .] What is important here, for the purpose of our discussion, is the relation of mythical thought to the narrative form, the plot-text. As Girard states that tragedy must be understood in its mythological framework, which in turn retains its basis in sacrificial ritual or sacred violence, so does Lotman insist on the mutual influence of the two textual mechanisms, the mythical text and the plot-text. The Soviet scholar exemplifies their coexistence or interrelatedness in a great variety of texts from Shakespeare's *Comedy of Errors* to works by Dostoevsky, Tolstoy, and Pushkin, from Greek myths and Russian folktales to the *Acts of the Apostles*. He notes how, in spite of the fact that historically-specific ideas are transmitted by means of the linear plot mechanism, the mythical or eschatological schema continues to be imposed on the secular identity of literary characters; the recurrence in modern texts of themes like fall-rebirth, resurrection, conversion or enlightenment, bears witness to its presence. And further, this imposition achieves the effect of fashioning the ordinary man's individual, inner world on the model of the macrocosm, presenting the individual as a 'conflictingly organized collective.' Thus, he concludes, if 'plot represents a powerful means of making sense of life,' it is because plot (narrative) mediates, integrates, and ultimately reconciles the mythical and the historical, norm and excess, the spatial and temporal orders, the individual and the collectivity.

It is neither facile nor simply paradoxical, in light of such convincing evidence, to state that if the crime of Oedipus is the destruction of differences, the combined work of myth and narrative is the production of Oedipus.[2] The business of the mythical subject is the construction of differences; but as the cyclical mechanism continues to work through narrative – integrating occurrences and excess, modeling fictional characters (heroes and villains, mothers and fathers, sons and lovers) on the mythical places of subject and obstacle, and projecting those spatial positions into the temporal development of plot – narrative itself takes over the function of the mythical subject. The work of narrative, then, is a mapping of differences, and specifically, first and foremost, of sexual difference into each text; and hence, by a sort of accumulation, into the universe of meaning, fiction, and history, represented by the literary-artistic tradition and all the texts of culture. But we have learned from semiotics that the productivity of the text, its play of structure and excess, engages the reader, viewer, or listener as subject in (and for) its process. Much as social formations and representations appeal to and position the individual as subject in the process to which we give the name of ideology, the movement of narrative discourse shifts and places the reader, viewer, or listener in certain portions of the plot space. Therefore, to say that narrative is the production of Oedipus is to say that each reader – male or female – is constrained and defined within the two positions of a sexual difference thus conceived: male-hero-human, on the side of the subject; and female-obstacle-boundary-space, on the other.

If Lotman is right, if the mythical mechanism produces the human being as man and everything else as, not even 'woman', but non-man, an absolute abstraction (and this has been so since the beginning of time, since the origin of plot at the origin of culture), the question arises, how or with which positions do readers, viewers, or listeners identify, given that they are already socially constituted women and men? In particular, what forms of identification are possible, what

265

positions are available to female readers, viewers, and listeners?
This is one of the first questions to be asked or rearticulated by
feminist criticism; and this is where the work of people like Propp
and Freud must be seriously reconsidered.

[...]

Oedipus interruptus

[...]

To succeed, for a film, is to fulfill its contract, to please its audiences
or at least induce them to buy the ticket, the popcorn, the magazines,
and the various paraphernalia of movie promotion. But for a film to
work, to be effective, it *has* to please. All films must offer their
spectators some kind of pleasure, something of interest, be it a
technical, artistic, critical interest, or the kind of pleasure that goes
by the names of entertainment and escape; preferably both. These
kinds of pleasure and interest, film theory has proposed, are closely
related to the question of desire (desire to know, desire to see), and
thus depend on a personal response, an engagement of the
spectator's subjectivity, and the possibility of identification.

The fact that films, as the saying goes, speak to each one and to
all, that they address spectators both individually and as members
of a social group, a given culture, age, or country, implies that certain
patterns or possibilities of identification for each and all spectators
must be built into the film. This is undoubtedly one of the functions
of genres, and their historical development throughout the century
attests to the need for cinema to sustain and provide new modes of
spectator identification in keeping with social changes. Because films
address spectators as social subjects, then, the modalities of
identification bear directly on the process of spectatorship, that is to
say, the ways in which the subjectivity of the spectator is engaged in
the process of viewing, understanding (making sense of), or even
seeing the film.

If women spectators are to buy their tickets and their popcorn, the
work of cinema, unlike 'the aim of biology,' may be said to require
women's consent; and we may well suspect that narrative cinema in
particular must be aimed, like desire, toward seducing women into
femininity. What manner of seduction operates in cinema to procure
that consent, to engage the female subject's identification in the
narrative movement, and so fulfill the cinematic contract? What
manner of seduction operates in cinema to solicit the complicity of
women spectators in a desire whose terms are those of the Oedipus?
In the following pages I will be concerned with female spectatorship,

and in particular the kinds of identification available to women
spectators and the nature of the process by which female subjectivity
is engaged in narrative cinema; thus I will reconsider the terms or
positionalities of desire as constituted in cinema by the relations of
image and narrative.

The cinematic apparatus, in the totality of its operations and effects,
produces not merely images but imaging. It binds affect and
meanings to images by establishing terms of identification, orienting
the movement of desire, and positioning the spectator in relation to
them.

[...]

The look of the camera (at the profilmic), the look of the spectator
(at the film projected on the screen), and the intradiegetic look of
each character within the film (at other characters, objects, etc.)
intersect, join, and relay one another in a complex system which
structures vision and meaning. [...] Cinema 'turns' on this series of
looks, writes Heath, and that series in turn provides the framework
'for a pattern of multiply relaying identifications'; within this
framework occur both 'subject-identification' and 'subject-process.'[3]
'It is the place of the look that defines cinema,' specifies Mulvey, and
governs its representation of woman. The possibility of shifting,
varying, and exposing the look is employed both to set out and to
contain the tension between a pure solicitation of the scopic drive
and the demands of the diegesis; in other words, to integrate
voyeurism into the conventions of storytelling, and thus combine visual
and narrative pleasure. The following passage refers to two particular
films, but could easily be read as paradigmatic of the narrative film
in general:

> The film opens with the woman as object of the combined gaze of
> spectator and all the male protagonists in the film. She is isolated,
> glamorous, on display, sexualised. But as the narrative progresses
> she falls in love with the main male protagonist and becomes his
> property, losing her outward glamorous characteristics, her
> generalised sexuality, her show-girl connotations; her eroticism is
> subjected to the male star alone.[4]

If the female position in narrative is fixed by the mythical mechanism
in a certain portion of the plot-space, which the hero crosses or
crosses to, a quite similar effect is produced in narrative cinema by
the apparatus of looks converging on the female figure. The woman
is framed by the look of the camera as icon, or object of the gaze: an
image made to be looked at by the spectator, whose look is relayed

by the look of the male character(s). The latter not only controls the events and narrative action but is 'the bearer' of the look of the spectator. The male protagonist is thus 'a figure in a landscape,' she adds, 'free to command the stage . . . of spatial illusion in which he articulates the look and creates the action' (p. 13). The metaphors could not be more appropriate.

In that landscape, stage, or portion of plot-space, the female character may be all along, throughout the film, representing and literally marking out the place (to) which the hero will cross. There she simply awaits his return like Darling Clementine; as she indeed does in countless Westerns, war, and adventure movies, providing the 'love interest,' which in the jargon of movie reviewers has come to denote, first, the singular function of the female character, and then, the character itself.[5] Or she may resist confinement in that symbolic space by disturbing it, perverting it, making trouble, seeking to exceed the boundary – visually as well as narratively – as in film noir. Or again, when the film narrative centers on a female protagonist, in melodrama, in the 'woman's film,' etc., the narrative is patterned on a journey, whether inward or outward, whose possible outcomes are those outlined by Freud's mythical story of femininity. In the best of cases, that is, in the 'happy' ending, the protagonist will reach the place (the space) where a modern Oedipus will find her and fulfill the promise of his (off-screen) journey. Not only, then, is the female position that of a given portion of the plot-space; more precisely, in cinema, it figures the (achieved) movement of the narrative toward that space. It represents narrative closure.
[. . .]

If narrative is governed by an Oedipal logic, it is because it is situated within the system of exchange instituted by the incest prohibition, where woman functions as both a sign (representation) and a value (object) for that exchange. And if we remark Lea Melandri's observation that the woman as Mother (matter and matrix, body and womb) is the primary measure of value, 'an equivalent more universal than money,' then indeed we can see why the narrative image on which the film, any film, can be represented, sold, and bought is finally the woman.[6] What the promotion stills and posters outside the cinema display, to lure the passers-by, is not just an *image of woman* but the image of her narrative position, the *narrative image* of woman – a felicitous phrase suggestive of the join of image and story, the interlocking of visual and narrative registers effected by the cinematic apparatus of the look. In cinema as well, then, woman properly represents the fulfillment of the narrative promise (made, as we know, to the little boy), and that representation works to support the male status of the mythical subject. The female position,

produced as the end result of narrativization, is the figure of
narrative closure, the narrative image in which the film, as Heath
says, 'comes together.'

With regard to women spectators, therefore, the notion of a passage
or movement of the spectator through the narrative film seems
strangely at odds with the theories of narrative presented so far. Or
rather, it would seem so if we assumed – as is often done – that
spectators naturally identify with one or the other group of text-
images, one or the other textual zone, female or male, according to
their gender. If we assumed a single, undivided identification of each
spectator with either the male or the female figure, the passage
through the film would simply instate or reconfirm male spectators
in the position of the mythical subject, the human being; but it
would only allow female spectators the position of the mythical
obstacle, monster or landscape. How can the female spectator be
entertained as subject of the very movement that places her as its
object, that makes her the figure of its own closure?

Clearly, at least for women spectators, we cannot assume
identification to be single or simple. For one thing, identification is
itself a movement, a subject-process, a relation: the identification (of
oneself) with something other (than oneself). In psychoanalytic
terms, it is succinctly defined as the 'psychological process whereby
the subject assimilates an aspect, property or attribute of the other
and *is transformed*, wholly or partially, after the model the other
provides. It is by means of a series of identifications that the
personality is constituted and specified.'[7] This last point is crucial,
and the resemblance of this formulation to the description of the
apparatus of the look in cinema cannot escape us. The importance of
the concept of identification, Laplanche and Pontalis insist, derives
from its central role in the formation of subjectivity; identification is
'not simply one psychical mechanism among others, but the
operation itself whereby the human subject is constituted' (p. 206).
To identify, in short, is to be actively involved as subject in a process,
a series of relations; a process that, it must be stressed, is materially
supported by the specific practices – textual, discursive, behavioral
– in which each relation is inscribed. Cinematic identification, in
particular, is inscribed across the two registers articulated by the
system of the look, the narrative and the visual (sound becoming a
necessary third register in those films which intentionally use sound
as an anti-narrative or de-narrativising element).

Secondly, no one can really *see* oneself as an inert object or a
sightless body; neither can one see oneself *altogether* as other. One
has an ego, after all, even when one is a woman (as Virginia Woolf
might say), and by definition the ego must be active or at least

fantasize itself in an active manner. Whence, Freud is led to postulate, the phallic phase in females: the striving of little girls to be masculine is due to the active aim of the libido, which then succumbs to the momentous process of repression when femininity 'sets in.' But, he adds, that masculine phase, with its libidinal activity, never totally lets up and frequently makes itself felt throughout a woman's life, in what he calls 'regressions to the fixations of the pre-Oedipus phases.' One can of course remark that the term 'regression' is a vector in the field of (Freud's) narrative discourse. [. . .]

The point, however, is made – and it is relevant to the present discussion – that 'femininity' and 'masculinity' are never fully attained or fully relinquished: 'in the course of some women's lives there is a repeated alternation between periods in which femininity or masculinity gain the upper hand.'[8] The two terms, femininity and masculinity, do not refer so much to qualities or states of being inherent in a person, as to positions which she occupies in relation to desire. They are terms of identification. And the alternation between them, Freud seems to suggest, is a specific character of female subjectivity. Following through this view in relation to cinematic identification, could we say that identification in women spectators alternates between the two terms put in play by the apparatus: the look of the camera and the image on the screen, the subject and the object of the gaze? The word alternation conveys the sense of an either/or, either one or the other at any given time (which is presumably what Freud had in mind), not the two together. The problem with the notion of an alternation between image and gaze is that they are not commensurable terms: the gaze is a figure, not an image. We see the image; we do not see the gaze. To cite again an often-cited phrase, one can 'look at her looking,' but one cannot look at oneself looking. The analogy that links identification-with-the-look to masculinity and identification-with-the-image to femininity breaks down precisely when we think of a spectator alternating between the two. Neither can be abandoned for the other, even for a moment; no image can be identified, or identified with, apart from the look that inscribes it as image, and vice versa. If the female subject were indeed related to the film in this manner, its division would be irreparable, unsuturable; no identification or meaning would be possible. This difficulty has led film theorists, following Lacan and forgetting Freud, practically to disregard the problem of sexual differentiation *in the spectators* and to define cinematic identification as masculine, that is to say, as an identification with the gaze, which both historically and theoretically is the representation of the phallus and the figure of the male's desire.[9]

That Freud conceived of femininity and masculinity primarily in narrative rather than visual terms (although with an emphasis on sight – in the traumatic apprehension of castration as punishment – quite in keeping with his dramatic model) may help us to reconsider the problem of female identification. Femininity and masculinity, in his story, are positions occupied by the subject in relation to desire, corresponding respectively to the passive and the active aims of the libido. They are positionalities within a movement that carries both the male child and the female child toward one and the same destination: Oedipus and the Oedipal stage. That movement, I have argued, is the movement of narrative discourse, which specifies and even produces the masculine position as that of mythical subject, and the feminine position as mythical obstacle or, simply, the space in which that movement occurs. Transferring this notion by analogy to cinema, we could say that the female spectator identifies with both the subject and the space of the narrative movement, with the figure of movement and the figure of its closure, the narrative image. Both are figural identifications, and both are possible at once; more, they are concurrently borne and mutually implicated by the process of narrativity. This manner of identification would uphold both positionalities of desire, both active and passive aims: desire for the other, and desire to be desired by the other. This, I think, is in fact the operation by which narrative and cinema solicit the spectators' consent and seduce women into femininity: by a double identification, a surplus of pleasure produced by the spectators themselves for cinema and for society's profit.

[...]

Notes

1. ROLAND BARTHES, *The Pleasure of the Text*, trans. Richard Miller (New York: Hill & Wang, 1975).

2. Cf. MIA CAMPIONI and ELIZABETH GROSS, 'Little Hans: The Production of Oedipus,' in *Language, Sexuality and Subversion*, ed. Paul Foss and Meaghan Morris (Darlington, Australia: Feral Publications, 1978), pp. 99–122.

3. STEPHEN HEATH, *Questions of Cinema* (Bloomington: Indiana University Press, 1981), pp. 119–20. 'The shift between the first and second looks sets up the spectator's identification with the camera (rigorously constructed, placing heavy constraints, for example, on camera movement). The look at the film is an involvement in identifying relations of the spectator to the photographic image (the particular terms of position required by the fact of the photograph itself), to the human figure presented in image (the enticement and the necessity of a human presence "on the screen"), to the narrative which gives the sense of the flow of photographic images (the guide-line for the spectator through the film, the ground that must be adopted for its intelligible reception). Finally, the looks of the characters allow for the establishment of

the various "point of view" identifications (the spectator looking with a character, from near to the position of his or her look, or as a character, the image marked in some way as "subjective" ' (p. 120).

4. LAURA MULVEY, 'Visual Pleasure and Narrative Cinema,' *Screen* 16.3 (Autumn 1975): 13. In this connection should be mentioned the notion of a 'fourth look' advanced by Willemen: a form of direct address to the viewer, an 'articulation of images and looks which brings into play the position and activity of the viewer ... When the scopic drive is brought into focus, then the viewer also runs the risk of becoming the object of the look, of being overlooked in the act of looking. The fourth look is the *possibility* of that look and is always present in the wings, so to speak.' (PAUL WILLEMEN, 'Letter to John,' *Screen* 21.2 (Summer 1980): 56.)

5. See CLAIRE JOHNSTON, 'Women's Cinema as Counter-Cinema,' in *Notes on Women's Cinema*, ed. Claire Johnston (London: SEFT, 1974), p. 27; and PAM COOK and CLAIRE JOHNSTON, 'The Place of Women in the Cinema of Raoul Walsh,' in *Raoul Walsh*, ed. Phil Hardy (Edinburgh: Edinburgh Film Festival, 1974).

6. LEA MELANDRI, *L'infamia originaria* (Milan: Edizioni L'Erba Voglio, 1977), see notes 16 and 30 of chapter 1.

7. J. LAPLANCHE and J.-B. PONTALIS, *The Language of Psycho-Analysis*, trans. Donald Nicholson-Smith (New York: Norton, 1973), p. 205; my emphasis.

8. SIGMUND FREUD, 'Femininity,' in *The Standard Edition of the Complete Psychological Works of Sigmund Freud*, ed. James Strachey (London: Hogarth Press, 1955), vol. 22, p. 131.

9. See JACQUELINE ROSE, 'The Cinematic Apparatus: Problems in Current Theory' in *The Cinematic Apparatus*, ed. Teresa de Lauretis and Stephen Heath (London: Macmillan; New York: St. Martin's Press, 1980), pp. 172–86. See also HEATH, 'Difference,' *Screen* 19.3 (Autumn 1978): 50–112.

18 The Value of Narrativity in the Representation of Reality*

HAYDEN WHITE

Starting from the Barthesean proposition that narrative 'is simply there like life itself . . . international, transhistorical, transcultural' (1977: 79), Hayden White sets out to analyse the value attached to narrativity in three forms of historical representation of reality: annals, chronicle and historical narrative. Following Hegel, White associates the development of historical narrative with the conflict created by the construction of a system of morality or human law and the historian's desire to endow events recounted with a manifest moral meaning or purpose. This moralizing intent forces the historian to confer some kind of 'authority' on the description of events, to impose on them a plot structure and to provide a closure for the otherwise open-ended and amoral historical data. White's article undermines the traditional assumption that historical narrative is superior to annals and chronicles and puts in question its purported objectivity; for, as he contends, the 'value attached to narrativity in the representation of real events arises out of a desire to have real events display the coherence, integrity, fullness, and closure of an image of life that is and can only be imaginary'. In this light, the idea that history is truthful and objective and literature subjective and false becomes doubtful: history is presented as one among many kinds of narrative discourse, and as such subjective, provisional, partial and incomplete, a human construction whose validity depends on the social conventions and authority under which it is written.

Hayden White's approach to history is an instance of the application of the post-structural and deconstructive methods to non-fictional discourse. The issues he raises are highly polemical, dealing as they do with the central assumptions of Western culture concerning discursive strategies. White's works analyse history as narrative and rhetoric, not as a transparent, neutral mapping of reality.

*Reprinted from W. J. T. Mitchell (ed.), *On Narrative* (Chicago: University of Chicago Press, 1981), pp. 1–23. First publ. in *Critical Inquiry* 7.1 (1980): 5–29.

To raise the question of the nature of narrative is to invite reflection on the very nature of culture and, possibly, even on the nature of humanity itself. So natural is the impulse to narrate, so inevitable is the form of narrative for any report of the way things really happened, that narrativity could appear problematical only in a culture in which it was absent – absent or, as in some domains of contemporary Western intellectual and artistic culture, programmatically refused. As a panglobal fact of culture, narrative and narration are less problems than simply data. As the late (and already profoundly missed) Roland Barthes remarked, narrative 'is simply there like life itself . . . international, transhistorical, transcultural.'[1] Far from being a problem, then, narrative might well be considered a solution to a problem of general human concern, namely, the problem of how to translate *knowing* into *telling*,[2] the problem of fashioning human experience into a form assimilable to structures of meaning that are generally human rather than culture-specific. We may not be able fully to comprehend specific thought patterns of another culture, but we have relatively less difficulty *understanding* a story coming from another culture, however exotic that culture may appear to us. As Barthes says, 'narrative . . . is *translatable* without fundamental damage' in a way that a lyric poem or a philosophical discourse is not.

This suggests that far from being one code among many that a culture may utilize for endowing experience with meaning, narrative is a metacode, a human universal on the basis of which transcultural messages about the nature of a shared reality can be transmitted. Arising, as Barthes says, between our experience of the world and our efforts to describe that experience in language, narrative 'ceaselessly substitutes meaning for the straightforward copy of the events recounted.' And it would follow, on this view, that the absence of narrative capacity or a refusal of narrative indicates an absence or refusal of meaning itself.

But what *kind* of meaning is absent or refused? The fortunes of narrative in the history of historical writing give us some insight into this question. Historians do not *have* to report their truths about the real world in narrative form; they may choose other, non-narrative, even anti-narrative, modes of representation, such as the meditation, the anatomy, or the epitome. Tocqueville, Burckhardt, Huizinga, and Braudel to mention only the most notable masters of modern historiography, refused narrative in certain of their historiographical works, presumably on the assumption that the meaning of the events with which they wished to deal did not lend itself to representation in the narrative mode. They refused to tell a story about the past, or, rather, they did not tell a story with well-marked beginning, middle, and end phases; they did not impose upon the processses that interested them the *form* that we normally associate with storytelling. While they certainly *narrated* their accounts of the reality that they perceived, or thought they perceived, to exist within or behind the evidence they had examined, they did not *narrativize* that reality, did not impose upon it the form of a story. And their example permits us to distinguish between a historical discourse that narrates, on the one side, and a discourse that narrativizes, on the other; between a discourse that openly adopts a perspective that looks out on the world and reports it and a discourse that feigns to make the world speak itself and speak itself *as a story.*

The idea that narrative should be considered less as a *form* of representation than as a *manner of speaking* about events, whether real or imaginary, has been recently elaborated within a discussion of the relationship between 'discourse' and 'narrative' that has arisen in the wake of structuralism and is associated with the work of Jakobson, Benveniste, Genette, Todorov, and Barthes. Here narrative is regarded as a manner of speaking characterized, as Genette expresses it, 'by a certain number of exclusions and restrictive conditions' that the more 'open' form of discourse does not impose upon the speaker.[3] [...]

This distinction between discourse and narrative is, of course, based solely on an analysis of the grammatical features of two modes of discourse in which the 'objectivity' of the one and the 'subjectivity' of the other are definable primarily by a 'linguistic order of criteria.' The subjectivity of the discourse is given by the presence, explicit or implicit, of an 'ego' who can be defined 'only as the person who maintains the discourse.' By contrast, 'the objectivity of narrative is defined by the absence of all reference to the narrator.' In the *narrativizing* discourse, then, we can say, with Benveniste, ' "Truly there is no longer a 'narrator.' The events are chronologically recorded as they appear on the horizon of the story. Here no one speaks. The events seem to tell themselves." '[4]

What is involved in the production of a discourse in which 'events seem to tell themselves,' especially when it is a matter of events that are explicitly identified as 'real' rather than 'imaginary,' as in the case of historical representations?[5] In a discourse having to do with manifestly imaginary events, which are the 'contents' of fictional discourses, the question poses few problems. For why should not imaginary events be represented as 'speaking themselves'? Why should not, in the domain of the imaginary, even the stones themselves speak – like Memnon's column when touched by the rays of the sun? But *real* events should not speak, should not tell themselves. Real events should simply be; they can perfectly well serve as the *referents* of a discourse, can be spoken about, but they should not pose as the *tellers* of a narrative. The lateness of the invention of historical discourse in human history, and the difficulty of sustaining it in times of cultural breakdown (as in the early Middle Ages) suggest the *artificiality* of the notion that *real* events could 'speak themselves' or be represented as 'telling their own story.' Such a fiction would have posed no problems before the distinction between real and imaginary events was imposed upon the storyteller; storytelling becomes a problem only *after* two orders of events dispose themselves before him as possible components of his stories and his storytelling is compelled to exfoliate under the injunction to keep the two orders unmixed in his discourse. What we call 'mythic' narrative is under no obligation to keep the two orders of events distinct from one another. Narrative becomes a *problem* only when we wish to give to *real* events the *form* of story. It is because real events do not offer themselves as stories that their narrativization is so difficult.

What is involved, then, in that finding of the 'true story,' that discovery of the 'real story' within or behind the events that come to us in the chaotic form of 'historical records'? What wish is enacted, what desire is gratified, by the fantasy that *real* events are properly represented when they can be shown to display the formal coherency of a story? In the enigma of this wish, this desire, we catch a glimpse of the cultural function of narrativizing discourse in general, an intimation of the psychological impulse behind the apparently universal need not only to narrate but to give to events an aspect of narrativity.

Historiography is an especially good ground on which to consider the nature of narration and narrativity because it is here that our desire for the imaginary, the possible, must contest with the imperatives of the real, the actual. If we view narration and narrativity as the instruments by which the conflicting claims of the imaginary and the real are mediated, arbitrated, or resolved in a discourse, we begin to comprehend both the appeal of narrative and the grounds for refusing it. If putatively real events are represented in a non-narrative form, what kind of reality is it that offers itself, or is conceived to offer itself, to perception? What would a non-narrative representation of historical reality look like?

Fortunately, we have examples aplenty of representations of historical reality which are non-narrative in form. Indeed, the official wisdom of the modern historiographical establishment has it that there are three basic kinds of historical representation, the imperfect 'historicality' of two of which is evidenced in their failure to attain to full narrativity of the events of which they treat. These three kinds are: the annals, the chronicle, and the history proper. Needless to say, it is not narrativity alone which permits the distinction among the three kinds, for it is not enough that an account of events, even of past events, even of past real events, display all of the features of narrativity in order for it to count as a proper history. In addition, professional opinion has it, the account must manifest a proper concern for the judicious handling of evidence, and it must honor the chronological order of the original occurrence of the events of which it treats as a baseline that must not be transgressed in classifying any given event as either a cause or an effect. But by common consent, it is not enough that a historical account deal in real, rather than merely imaginary, events; and it is not enough that the account in its order of discourse represent events according to the chronological sequence in which they originally occurred. The events must be not only registered within the chronological framework of their original occurrence but narrated as well, that is to say, revealed as possessing a structure, an order of meaning, which they do *not* possess as mere sequence.

The annals form, needless to say, completely lacks this narrative component, consisting only of a list of events ordered in chronological sequence. The chronicle, by contrast, often seems to wish to tell a story, aspires to narrativity, but typically fails to achieve it. More specifically, the chronicle usually is marked by a failure to achieve narrative *closure*. It does not so much conclude as simply terminate. It starts out to tell a story but breaks off *in medias res*, in the chronicler's own present; it leaves things unresolved or, rather, leaves them unresolved in a story-like way. While annals represent historical reality *as if* real events did not display the form of story, the chronicle represents it *as if* real events appeared to human consciousness in the form of *unfinished* stories.

Official wisdom has it that however objective a historian might be in his reporting of events, however judicious in his assessment of evidence, however punctilious in his dating of *res gestae*, his account remains something less than a proper history when he has failed to give to reality the form of a story. Where there is no narrative, Croce said, there is no history,[6] and Peter Gay, writing from a perspective that is directly opposed to the relativism of Croce, puts it just as starkly: 'Historical narration without analysis is trivial, historical analysis without narration is incomplete.'[7] Gay's formulation calls up the Kantian bias of the demand for narration in historical representation, for it suggests, to paraphrase Kant, that historical narratives without analysis are empty, while historical analyses without narrative are blind. So, we may ask, what kind of insight does narrative give into the nature of real events? What kind of blindness with respect to reality does narrativity dispell?

In what follows I will treat the annals and chronicle forms of historical representation not as the 'imperfect' histories they are conventionally conceived to be but rather as particular products of possible conceptions of historical reality, conceptions that are alternatives to, rather than failed anticipations of, the fully realized historical discourse that the modern history form is supposed to embody. This procedure will throw light on the problems of both historiography and narration alike and will illuminate what I conceive to be the purely conventional nature of the relationship between them. What will be revealed, I think, is that the very distinction between real and imaginary events, basic to modern discussions of both history and fiction, presupposes a notion of reality in which 'the true' is identified with 'the real' only insofar as it can be shown to possess the character of narrativity.

When we moderns look at an example of a medieval annals, we cannot but be struck by the apparent naiveté of the annalist; and we are inclined to ascribe this naiveté to the annalist's apparent refusal, inability, or unwillingness to transform the set of events ordered vertically as a file of annual markers into the elements of a linear/horizontal process. In other words, we are likely to be put off by the annalist's apparent failure to see that historical events dispose themselves to the percipient eye as 'stories' *waiting to be told*, waiting to be narrated. But surely a genuinely historical interest would require that we ask not how or why the annalist failed to write a 'narrative' but rather what kind of notion of reality led him to represent in the *annals form* what, after all, he took to be real events. If we could answer this question, we might be able to understand why, in our own time and cultural condition, we could conceive of narrativity itself as a problem.

[...]

If we grant that this discourse unfolds under a sign of a desire for the real, as we must do in order to justify the inclusion of the annals form among the types of historical representation, we must conclude that it is a product of an image of reality in which *the social system*, which alone could provide the diacritical markers for ranking the importance of events, is only minimally present to the consciousness of the writer or, rather, is present as a factor in the composition of the discourse only by virtue of its absence. Everywhere it is the forces of disorder, natural and human, the forces of violence and destruction, which occupy the forefront of attention. The account deals in *qualities* rather than *agents*, figuring forth a world in which things *happen to* people rather than one in which people *do* things. [...]

What is lacking in the list of events to give it a similar regularity and fullness is a notion of a social center by which both to locate them with respect to one another and to charge them with ethical or moral significance. It is the absence of any consciousness of a *social* center that prohibits the annalist from ranking the events which he treats as elements of a historical field of occurrence. And it is the absence of such a center that precludes or undercuts any impulse he might have had to work up his discourse into the form of a narrative. [...]

All this suggests to me that Hegel was right when he opined that a genuinely historical account had to display not only a certain form, that is, the narrative, but also a certain content, namely, a political-social order.[8] [...]

Hegel insists that the proper subject of such a record is the state, but the state is to him an abstraction. The reality which lends itself to narrative representation is the *conflict* between desire, on the one side, and the law on the other. Where there is no rule of law, there can be neither a subject nor the kind of event which lends itself to narrative representation. This proposition could not be empirically verified or falsified, to be sure; it rather enables a presupposition or hypothesis which permits us to imagine how both 'historicity' and 'narrativity' are possible. It also authorizes us to consider the proposition that neither is possible without some notion of the legal subject which can serve as the agent, agency, and subject of historical narrative in all of its manifestations, from the annals through the chronicle to the historical discourse as we know it in its modern realizations and failures.

The question of the law, legality, or legitimacy does not arise in those parts of the *Annals of Saint Gall* which we have been considering; at least, the question of *human* law does not arise. [...] The coming of the Saracens is of the same moral significance as Charles' fight against the Saxons. We have no way of knowing whether the annalist would have been impelled to flesh out his list of events and rise to the challenge of a narrative representation of those events if he had written in the consciousness of the threat to a specific social system and the possibility of anarchy against which the legal system might have been erected. But once we have been alerted to the intimate relationship that Hegel suggests exists between law, historicality, and narrativity, we cannot but be struck by the frequency with which narrativity, whether of the fictional or the factual sort, presupposes the existence of a legal system against or on behalf of which the typical agents of a narrative account militate. And this raises the suspicion that narrative in general, from the folktale to the novel, from the annals to the fully realized 'history,' has to do with the topics of law, legality, legitimacy, or, more generally, *authority*. [. . .]

Interest in the social system, which is nothing other than a system of human relationships governed by law, creates the possibility of conceiving the kinds of tensions, conflicts, struggles, and their various kinds of resolutions that we are accustomed to find in any representation of reality presenting itself to us as a history. Perhaps, then, the growth and development of historical consciousness which is attended by a concomitant growth and development of narrative capability (of the sort met with in the chronicle as against the annals form) has something to do with the extent to which the legal system functions as a subject of concern. If every fully realized story, however we define that familiar but conceptually elusive entity, is a kind of allegory, points to a moral, or endows events, whether real or imaginary, with a significance that they do not possess as a mere sequence, then it seems possible to conclude that every historical narrative has as its latent or manifest purpose the desire to *moralize* the events of which it treats.

[. . .]

Does it follow that in order for there to be a narrative, there must be some equivalent of the Lord, some sacred being endowed with the authority and power of the Lord, existing in time? If so, what could such an equivalent be?

The nature of such a being, capable of serving as the central organizing principle of meaning of a discourse that is both realistic and narrative in structure, is called up in the mode of historical representation known as the chronicle. By common consensus among historians of historical writing, the chronicle form is a 'higher' form of historical conceptualization and represents a mode of historiographical representation superior to the annals form. Its superiority consists, it is agreed, in its greater comprehensiveness, its organization of materials 'by topics and reigns,' and its greater narrative coherency. The chronicle also has a central subject, the life of an individual, town, or region, some great undertaking, such as a war or crusade, or some institution, such as a monarchy, episcopacy, or monastery. The link of the chronicle with the annals is perceived in the perseverance of the chronology as the organizing principle of the discourse, and, so we are told, this is what makes the chronicle something less than a fully realized 'history.' Moreover, the chronicle, like the annals but unlike the history, does not so much 'conclude' as simply terminate; typically it lacks closure, that summing up of the 'meaning' of the chain of events with which it deals that we normally expect from the well-made story. The chronicle typically promises closure but does not provide it – which is one of the reasons that the nineteenth-century editors of the medieval chronicles denied them the status of genuine histories.

Suppose that we look at the matter differently. Suppose that we do not grant that the chronicle is a 'higher' or more sophisticated representation of reality than the annals but is merely a *different* kind of representation, marked by a desire for a kind of order and fullness in an account of reality that remains theoretically unjustified, a desire that is, until shown otherwise, purely gratuitous.
[. . .]

In order for an account of the events to be considered a historical account, however, it is not enough that they be recorded in the order of their original occurrence. It is the fact that they *can* be recorded otherwise, in an order of narrative, that makes them at once questionable as to their authenticity and susceptible to being considered tokens of reality. In order to qualify as 'historical,' an event must be susceptible to at least two narrations of its occurrence. Unless at least two versions of the same set of events can be imagined, there is no reason for the historian to take upon himself the authority of giving the true account of what really happened. The authority of the historical narrative is the authority of reality itself; the historical account endows this reality with form and thereby makes it desirable, imposing upon its processes the formal coherency that only stories possess.

The history, then, belongs to the category of what might be called the 'discourse of the real,' as against the 'discourse of the imaginary' or the 'discourse of desire.' The formulation is Lacanian, obviously, but I do not wish to push the Lacanian aspects of it too far. I merely wish to suggest that we can comprehend the appeal of historical discourse by recognizing the extent to which it makes the real desirable, makes the real into an object of desire, and does so by its imposition, upon events that are represented as real, of the formal coherency that stories possess. Unlike the annals, the reality that is represented in the historical narrative, in 'speaking itself,' speaks *to* us, summons us from afar (this 'afar' is the land of forms), and displays to us a formal coherency that we ourselves lack. The historical narrative, as against the chronicle, reveals to us a world that is putatively 'finished,' done with, over, and yet not dissolved, not falling apart. In this world, reality wears the mask of a meaning, the completeness and fullness of which we can only *imagine*, never experience. Insofar as historical stories can be completed, can be given narrative closure, can be shown to have had a *plot* all along, they give to reality the odor of the *ideal*. This is why the plot of a historical narrative is always an embarrassment and has to be presented as 'found' in the events rather than put there by narrative techniques.

The embarrassment of plot to historical narrative is reflected in the all but universal disdain with which modern historians regard the 'philosophy of history,' of which Hegel provides the modern paradigm. This (fourth) form of historical representation is condemned because it consists of nothing but plot; its story elements exist only as manifestations, epiphenomena, of the plot structure, in the service of which its discourse is disposed. Here reality wears a face of such regularity, order, and coherence that it leaves no room for human agency, presenting an aspect of such wholeness and completeness that it intimidates rather than invites to imaginative identification. But in the plot of the philosophy of history, the various plots of the various histories which tell us of merely regional happenings in the past are revealed for what they really are: images of that authority which summons us to participation in a moral universe that, but for its story form, would have no appeal at all.

This puts us close to a possible characterization of the demand for closure in the history, for the want of which the chronicle form is adjudged to be deficient as a narrative. The demand for closure in the historical story is a demand, I suggest, for moral meaning, a demand that sequences of real events be assessed as to their significance as elements of a *moral* drama.

[. . .]

We can perceive the operations of moral consciousness in the achievement of narrative fullness in an example of late medieval historiography, the *Cronica* of Dino Compagni, written between 1310 and 1312 and generally recognized as a proper historical narrative.[9] Dino's work not only 'fills in the gaps' which might have been left in an annalistic handling of its subject matter (the struggles between the Black and White factions of the dominant Guelf party in Florence between 1280 and 1312) and organizes its story according to a well-marked ternary plot structure; it also achieves narrative fullness by explicitly invoking the idea of a social system to serve as a fixed reference point by which the flow of ephemeral events can be endowed with specifically moral meaning. In this respect, the *Cronica* clearly displays the extent to which the chronicle must approach the form of an allegory, moral or anagogical as the case may be, in order to achieve *both* narrativity and historicality.

It is interesting to observe that as the chronicle form is displaced by the proper history, certain of the features of the former disappear. First of all, no explicit patron is invoked: Dino's narrative does not unfold under the authority of a specific patron, as Richerus' does;

instead, Dino simply asserts his right to recount notable events (*cose notevoli*) which he has 'seen and heard' on the basis of a superior capacity of foresight. 'No one saw these events in their beginnings [*principi*] more certainly than I,' he says. His prospective audience is not, then, a specific ideal reader, as Gerbert was for Richerus, but rather a *group* that is conceived to share his perspective on the true nature of all events: those citizens of Florence who are capable, as he puts it, of recognizing 'the benefits of God, who rules and governs for all time.' At the same time, he speaks to another group, the depraved citizens of Florence, those who are responsible for the 'conflicts' (*discordie*) that had wracked the city for some three decades. To the former, his narrative is intended to hold out the hope of deliverance from these conflicts; to the latter, it is intended as an admonition and a threat of retribution. The chaos of the last ten years is contrasted with more 'prosperous' years to come, after the emperor Henry VII has descended on Florence in order to punish a people whose 'evil customs and false profits' have 'corrupted and spoiled the whole world.'[10] What Kermode calls 'the weight of meaning' of the events recounted is 'thrown forward' onto a future just beyond the immediate present, a future fraught with moral judgment and punishment for the wicked.[11]

The jeremiad with which Dino's work closes marks it as belonging to a period before which a genuine historical 'objectivity,' which is to say, a secularist ideology, had been established – so the commentators tell us. But it is difficult to see how the kind of narrative fullness for which Dino is praised could have been attained without the implicit invocation of the moral standard that he uses to distinguish between those real events worthy of being recorded and those unworthy of it. [...]

It is this moralistic ending which keeps Dino's *Cronica* from meeting the standard of a modern, 'objective' historical account. Yet it is this moralism which alone permits the work to end or, rather, to *conclude* in a way different from the way that the annals and the chronicle forms do. But on what other grounds could a narrative of real events *possibly* conclude? When it is a matter of recounting the concourse of real events, what other 'ending' could a given sequence of such events have than a 'moralizing' ending? What else could narrative closure consist of than the *passage* from one moral order to another? I confess that I cannot think of any other way of 'concluding' an account of *real* events; for we cannot say, surely, that any sequence of real events actually comes to an end, that reality itself disappears, that events *of the order of the real* have ceased to happen. Such events could only have seemed to have ceased to happen when meaning is shifted, and shifted by narrative means, from one physical or social space to another. Where moral sensitivity is lacking, as it seems to be in an annalistic account of reality, or is only potentially present, as it appears to be in a chronicle, not only meaning but the means to track such shifts of meaning, that is, narrativity, appears to be lacking also. Where, in any account of reality, narrativity is present, we can be sure that morality or a moralizing impulse is present too. There is no other way that reality can be endowed with the kind of meaning that both displays itself in its consummation and withholds itself by its displacement to another story 'waiting to be told' just beyond the confines of 'the end.'

What I have been working around to is the question of the *value* attached to narrativity itself, especially in representations of reality of the sort which historical discourse embodies. [. . .] It is the historians themselves who have transformed narrativity from a manner of speaking into a paradigm of the form which reality itself displays to a 'realistic' consciousness. It is they who have made narrativity into a value, the presence of which in a discourse having to do with real events signals at once its objectivity, its seriousness, and its realism.

I have sought to suggest that this value attached to narrativity in the representation of real events arises out of a desire to have real events display the coherence, integrity, fullness, and closure of an image of life that is and can only be imaginary. The notion that sequences of real events possess the formal attributes of the stories we tell about imaginary events could only have its origin in wishes, daydreams, reveries. Does the world really present itself to perception in the form of well-made stories, with central subjects, proper beginnings, middles, and ends, and a coherence that permits us to see 'the end' in every beginning? Or does it present itself more in the forms that the annals and chronicle suggest, either as mere sequence without beginning or end or as sequences of beginnings that only terminate and never conclude? And does the world, even the social world, ever really come to us as already narrativized, already 'speaking itself' from beyond the horizon of our capacity to make scientific sense of it? Or is the fiction of such a world, a world capable of speaking itself and of displaying itself as a form of a story, necessary for the establishment of that moral authority without which the notion of a specifically social reality would be unthinkable? If it were only a matter of realism in representation, one could make a pretty good case for both the annals and chronicle forms as paradigms of ways that reality offers itself to perception. Is it possible that their supposed want of objectivity, manifested in their failure to narrativize reality adequately, has nothing to do with the modes of perception which they presuppose but with their failure to represent the *moral* under the aspect of the *aesthetic*? And could we answer that question without giving a narrative account of the history of objectivity itself, an account that would already prejudice the outcome of the story we would tell in favor of the *moral* in general? Could we ever narrativize *without* moralizing?

Notes

1. ROLAND BARTHES, 'Introduction to the Structural Analysis of Narratives,' *Image, Music, Text*, trans. Stephen Heath (New York, 1977), p. 79.
2. The words 'narrative,' 'narration,' 'to narrate,' and so on derive via the Latin *gnārus* ('knowing,' 'acquainted with,' 'expert,' 'skilful,' and so forth) and *narrō* ('relate,' 'tell') from the Sanskrit root *gnâ* ('know'). The same root yields γνώριμος ('knowable,' 'known'): see EMILE BOISACQ, *Dictionnaire étymologique de la langue grecque* (Heidelberg, 1950), under the entry for this word. My Thanks to Ted Morris of Cornell, one of our great etymologists.
3. GÉRARD GENETTE, 'Boundaries of Narrative,' *New Literary History* 8.1 (Autumn 1976): 11.
4. EMILE BENVENISTE as quoted by Genette, 'Boundaries of Narrative,' p. 9. Cf. BENVENISTE, *Problems in General Linguistics*, trans. Mary Elizabeth Meek (Coral Gables, Fla., 1971), p. 208.
5. See LOUIS O. MINK, 'Narrative Form as a Cognitive Instrument,' and LIONEL GOSSMAN, 'History and Literature,' in *The Writing of History: Literary Form and Historical Understanding*, ed. Robert H. Canary and Henry Kozicki (Madison, Wis., 1978), with complete bibliography on the problem of narrative form in historical writing.
6. I discuss Croce in *Metahistory: The Historical Imagination in Nineteenth Century Europe* (Baltimore: Johns Hopkins University Press, 1973), pp. 381–5.
7. PETER GAY, *Style in History* (New York, 1974), p. 189.
8. G. W. F. HEGEL, *The Philosophy of History*, trans. J. Sibree (New York, 1956), pp. 60–1.
9. *La cronica di Dino Compagni delle cose occorrenti ne'tempi suoi e La canzone morale Del Pregio dello stesso autore*, ed. Isidore Del Lungo, 4th edn rev. (Florence, 1902). Cf. HARRY ELMER BARNES, *A History of Historical Writing* (New York, 1962), pp. 80–1.
10. Ibid. p. 5: my translations.
11. See FRANK KERMODE, *The Sense of an Ending: Studies in the Theory of Fiction* (Oxford, 1967), chap. 1.

19 Line*

J. HILLIS MILLER

In this excerpt from *Ariadne's Thread* J. Hillis Miller refocuses the
traditional analysis of narrative plot by exploring the concept of
'narrative line'. Going back to etymological and mythical definitions, Miller forcefully unravels the extraordinary complexity
and intrinsically oxymoronic quality of a concept that informs
every single stage of the narrative function. As he explains, the
very linearity of the material act of writing is counterbalanced by
the necessary iteration of alphabetical symbols and interruptions
in the flow of ink on the blank page, so that the line is both
a thread and a labyrinth, simultaneously moving forwards and
backwards and incessantly begging for new nuances of meaning
in a wealth of repetitive echoes.

By means of intense and subtle analysis Miller demonstrates
how the relationships of meaning within a narrative line are based
on catachresis – that is, on constant displacement of meaning from
one sign to another. His contention is that narrative allegorizes
meaning, constantly deferring the possibility of unequivocal
expression. In this sense, we can say that the subtler the analysis,
the less neat and simple the narrative line.

Miller's approach is both a development of narratology in the
wide sense of theoretical work on narrative and a critique of some
of the simplistic assumptions of early structuralist theories. Along
with other critics of the 'deconstructive school' like Paul de Man,
Miller contends that the formalist notion of a science of literature
is a contradiction in terms because, as Paul de Man argues in 'The
Resistance to Theory' (1982), 'the grammatical decoding of a text
leaves a residue of indetermination that has to be, but cannot be,
resolved by a grammatical means, however extensively conceived.'
A great deal of earlier narratological work would be for de Man
or Miller an attempt at a 'grammatical decoding' of texts which
disregards the hermeneutic function of reading, a mechanical

---

*J. HILLIS MILLER, *Ariadne's Thread: Story Lines* (New Haven: Yale University Press
1992), pp. 1–25.

approach which cannot claim to reach the 'determining figural dimensions' of a text.

[...] How should the critic thread her or his way into the labyrinthine problems of narrative form, and in particular into the problem of repetition in fiction? The line of the line itself? The motif, image, concept, or formal model of the line, however, far from being a 'clue' to the labyrinth, turns out [...] to be itself the labyrinth. To follow the motif of the line will not be to simplify the knotted problems of narrative form but to retrace the whole tangle from the starting place of a certain point of entry.
[...]
To begin at the beginning with the physical aspects of the book, the novel as book, its conditions of production and use. The linearity of the written or printed book is a puissant support of logocentrism. The writer, Walter Pater or Elizabeth Gaskell, George Eliot or Charles Dickens, sits at a desk and spins out on the page a long thread or filament of ink. Word follows word from the beginning to the end. The manuscript is set for printing in the same way, whether letter by letter, by linotype, or from tape by computer. The reader follows, or is supposed to follow, the text in the same way, reading word by word and line by line from the beginning to the end. This linearity is broken, in the Victorian novel for example, only by the engravings that juxtapose 'illustrations' in another medium to the continuous flow of printed words, or by anything in the words on the page which in one way or another says, see page so and so. An example of this is the repetition from one place to another of the same word, phrase, or image. The physical, social, and economic conditions of the printing and distribution of Victorian books, that is, the breaking of the text into numbered or titled parts, books, or chapters, and publication in parts either separately or with other material in a periodical, interrupts this linearity but does not transform it into something else. The text of a Victorian novel, to remain with that as prime example for the moment, with its divisions into chapters and parts, is like bits of string laid end to end in series. Its publication in parts over a period of time that, in the case of Dickens's big novels, was almost two years in length, only emphasizes this linearity. Publication in parts gives that linearity an explicitly temporal dimension, a dimension already present in the time it takes to follow a novel word by word, line by line, page by page. Victorian readers had to read one part of *Bleak House* and then, after an interval, the next part, and so on. The spurious instantaneous unity or simultaneity of the single volume held in one's hand was further broken by the fact that Victorian novels, even when their scattered

parts were gathered in volume form, were often printed in two, three, or even four volumes. The linearity of a novel is always temporal. It is an image of time as a line. Martin Heidegger, in *Sein und Zeit* and elsewhere, has shown how all the language of temporality is contaminated by spatial terms. From Aristotle on, according to Heidegger, this spatializing of time has reinforced the systematic assumptions of logocentric metaphysics. More recently, Paul Ricœur, in *Temps et récit*, has explored the relation between notions of time in Aristotle and St. Augustine and forms of narrative coherence in our tradition.[1] One must distinguish sharply, however, between effects of discontinuity, spaces or hiatuses between segments of a narrative line, and true disturbances of the line that make it curve back on itself, recross itself, tie itself in knots. Those spaces may have a powerful effect, in one way or another, on the meaning, but they are not in themselves forms of repetition breaking linearity.

[. . .]

The image of the line, it is easy to see, cannot be detached from the problem of repetition. Repetition might be defined as anything that happens to the line to trouble its straightforward linearity: returnings, knottings, recrossings, crinklings to and fro, suspensions, interruptions. As Ruskin says in *Fors Clavigera*, the Daedalian labyrinth, made from a single thread or path curved and recurved, may serve as a model for everything 'linear and complex' since. The phrase is an oxymoron. It names a line that is not simply linear, not a straightforward movement from beginning to middle to end. In what follows, I shall explore the way linear terminology and linear form used to discuss realistic fiction subverts itself by becoming 'complex' – knotted, repetitive, doubled, broken, phantasmal.

To put down first, pell-mell, like the twisted bits of string in the pockets of the narrator of *Cranford*, some line images as they are associated with narrative form or with the everyday terminology of storytelling: narrative line, life line, by-line, main line, drop me a line, 'break up their lines to weep,' linotype, what's my line?, genealogical line, genetic strain, affiliation, defile, thread of the story, ficelle, lineaments, crossroads, impasse, dénouement, cornered, loose thread, marginal, trope, chiasmus, hyperbole, crisis, double bind, tie that binds, circulation, recoup, engraving, beyond the pale, trespass, crossing the bar, missing link, marriage tie, couple, coupling, copulation, plot, double plot, subplot, spin a yarn, get an angle on, the end of the line.

It may be possible gradually to untwist these hanks, to lay them end to end in a neat series, to make an orderly chain of them, knot added to knot in macramé, or to crochet them into a fabric making a visible figure, a figure in the carpet. Initially to be emphasized is how rich and complex is the family of terms involving the line image – figures of speech, idioms, slang, conceptual words, or narrative motifs like Hercules at the crossroads. Dozens of examples spring to mind in proliferating abundance, like a tangled skein of yarn bits. This is especially the case if the line is extended slightly to include the adjacent figures of cutting, weaving, and setting limits, drawing boundary lines. How can one find the law of this tangled multitude or set limits to it? The notions of legislation (imposed from without or found within) and of boundary are themselves already images of the line. (*Lex* is from the root *lege*, to collect. It is the same root as that for *logic* and *coil*.) The thing to be defined enters into and contaminates the definer, according to a recurrent aporia.

One can see that the line image, in whatever region of narrative terms it is used, tends to be logocentric, monological. The model of the line is a powerful part of the traditional metaphysical terminology. It cannot easily be detached from these implications or from the functions it has within that system. Narrative event follows narrative event in a purely metonymic line, but the series tends to organize itself or to be organized into a causal chain. The chase has a beast in view. The end of the story is the retrospective revelation of the law of the whole. That law is an underlying 'truth' that ties all together in an inevitable sequence revealing a hitherto hidden figure in the carpet. The image of the line tends always to imply the norm of a single continuous unified structure determined by one external organizing principle. This principle holds the whole line together, gives it its law, controls its progressive extension, curving or straight, with some *arché*, *telos*, or ground. Origin, goal, or base: all three come together in the gathering movement of logos. *Logos* in Greek meant transcendent word, speech, reason, proportion, substance, or ground. The word comes from *legein*, to gather, as in English collect, legislate, legend, or coil.

What is the status of these etymologies? Identification of the true meaning of the word? Some original presence rooted in the ground of immediate experience, physical or metaphysical? By no means. They serve rather to indicate the lack of enclosure of a given word. Each word inheres in a labyrinth of branching interverbal relationships going back not to a referential source but to something already, at the beginning, a figurative transfer, according to the Rousseauistic or Condillacian law that all words were originally metaphors. The searcher through the labyrinth of words, moreover, often encounters for a given word not a single root, but rather forks in the etymological line leading to bifurcated or trifurcated roots or to that philologist's confession of archeological ignorance: 'Origin unknown.' No reason (that I can see) prevents there being bends or absolute breaks in the etymological line. The realm of words is a free country. Or is it? No reason (that I can see) forbids deploying a given sound or sign to uses entirely without affiliation to its figurative roots. Or is this impossible? What coercion does the word itself, as a material base, exert over the range of meanings one can give it? Can one bend, but not break, the etymological line? In any case, the effect of etymological retracing is not to ground the word solidly but to render it unstable, equivocal, wavering, groundless. All etymology is false etymology, in the sense that some bend or discontinuity always breaks up the etymological line. If the line suggests always the gatherings of the word, at the same time, in all the places of its use, the line contains the possibility of turning back on itself. In this turning it subverts its own linearity and become repetition. Without the line there is no repetition, but repetition is what disturbs, suspends, or destroys the line's linearity, like a soft wintry aurora playing behind its straightforward logic.

Linear terminology describing narrative tends to organize itself into links, chains, strands, figures, configurations, each covering one of the topographical regions I have identified as basic to the problematic of realist fiction: time, character, the narrator, and so on. To identify line terminology used for stories, bit of string by bit of string, will be to cover the whole ground, according to the paradox of Ariadne's thread. That thread maps the whole labyrinth, rather than providing a single track to its centre and back out. The thread is the labyrinth and at the same time it is a repetition of the labyrinth.

The bits of string I have gathered may be organized in nine areas of linear terminology.

First come the physical aspects of writing or of printed books: letters, signs, hieroglyphs, folds, bindings, and margins, as well as letters in the sense indicated in the phrase 'drop me a line.'

A second region of linear terminology involves all the words for narrative line or diegesis: dénouement, curve of the action, turn of events, broken or dropped thread, line of argument, story line, figure in the carpet – all the terms, in short, assuming that narration is the retracing of a story that has already happened. Note that these lines are all figurative. They do not describe the actual physical linearity of lines of type or of writing. Nor do most of them even describe the sequence of chapters or episodes in a novel. Most name rather the imagined sequence of the events narrated.

A third topic is the use of linear terms to describe character, as in the phrases 'life line,' or 'what's my line?' Physiognomy is the reading of character from facial lineaments. The word *character* itself is a figure meaning the outward signs in the lines on a person's face of his inward nature. A character is a sign, as in the phrase 'Chinese written character.'

A fourth place is all the terminology of interpersonal relations: filiation, affiliation, marriage tie, liaison, genetic or ancestral line, and so on. One cannot talk about relations among persons without using the line images.

Another region is that of economic terminology. The language of interpersonal relations borrows heavily from economic words, as in 'expense of spirit in a waste of shame,' or when one says 'pay him back' or 'repay him with interest' or speaks of someone as 'out of circulation.' Many, if not all, economic terms involve linear imagery: circulation, binding promise or contract, recoup, coupon, margin, cutback, line your pockets, on the line (which means ready for immediate expenditure), currency, current, and pass current.

Another area of narrative terminology involves topography: roads, crossroads, paths, frontiers, gates, windows, doors, turnings, journeys, narrative motifs like Oedipus murdering Laius at the place where three roads cross or Hercules at the crossroads.

Another topic for investigation is illustrations for novels. Most nineteenth-century novels were of course illustrated by etchings or engravings, that is, by pictures printed from plates incised with lines. Ruskin in *Ariadne Florentina* (1873–75) has investigated this use of the line to make a repeatable design.[2]

Another region for investigation is figurative language in the text of a novel. The terminology for figures of speech is strongly linear, as when one speaks of tropes, of topoi, of chiasmus, of ellipsis, of hyperbole, and so on.

A final topos in the criticism of fiction is the question of realistic representation. Mimesis in a 'realistic' novel is a detour from the real world that mirrors that world and in one way or another, in the cultural or psychic economy of production and consumption, leads the reader back to it.

Each of these topological areas invites separate discussion. The image, figure, or concept of the line threads its way through all the traditional terms for storywriting or storytelling. Line images make the dominant figure in this particular carpet. The peculiarity of all these regions of criticism is that there are no terms but figurative ones to speak of any of them. The term *narrative line*, for example, is a catachresis. It is the violent, forced, or abusive importation of a term from another realm to name something which has no proper name. The relationship of meaning among all these areas of terminology is not from sign to thing but a displacement from one sign to another sign that in its turn draws its meaning from another figurative sign, in a constant displacement. The name for this displacement is allegory. Storytelling, usually thought of as the putting into language of someone's experience of life, is in its writing or reading a hiatus in that experience. Narrative is the allegorizing along a temporal line of this perpetual displacement from immediacy. Allegory in this sense, however, expresses the impossibility of expressing unequivocally, and so dominating, what is meant by experience or by writing. My exploration of the labyrinth of narrative terms is in its turn to be defined as a perhaps impossible search for the center of the maze, the Minotaur or spider that has created and so commands it all.

The reasons for this impossibility may be variously formulated. Perhaps it might be better to say, since what is in question here is the failure of reason, that the inability of the mind to reach the center of narrative's maze and so dominate it may be encountered from various directions. One way is in the blind alley reached when any term or family of terms is followed as far as it will go as a means of talking about objective aspects of specific novels. No one thread (character, realism, interpersonal relation, or whatever) can be followed to a central point where it provides a means of overseeing, controlling, and understanding the whole. Instead it reaches, sooner or later, a crossroad, a blunt fork, where either path leads manifestly to a blank wall. This double blind is at once the failure to reach the center of the labyrinth and at the same time the reaching of a false center, everywhere and nowhere, attainable by any thread or path. These empty corridors are vacant of any presiding Minotaur. The Minotaur, as Ruskin saw, is a spider, Arachne-arachnid who devours her mate, weaver of a web that is herself. This ubiquitous figure both hides and reveals an absence, an abyss.

The impasse in the exploration of a given novel or a given term in narrative criticism occurs differently in each case, yet in each case it is experienced as something irrational, alogical. The critic suffers a breakdown of distinctions – for example, that between figurative and literal language, or between the text and that extratextual reality the text mirrors, or between the notion that the novel copies something and the notion that it makes something happen. The critic may be unable to decide, of two repeating elements, which is the original of which, which the 'illustration' of the other, or whether in fact they repeat or are rather heterogeneous, inassimilable to a single pattern, whether they are centered, double-centered, or acentric. The critic may be unable to tell whether a given textual knot is 'purely verbal' or has to do with 'life.' The reader may experience the impossibility of deciding, in a given passage, who is speaking, the author, the narrator, or the character, where or when, and to whom. Such a passage in its undecidability bears the indelible traces of being a written document, not something that could ever be spoken by a single voice and so returned to a single *logos*. Always, in such passages, something is left over or missing, something is too much or too little. This forbids imputing the language back to a single mind, imagined or real. In one way or another the monological becomes dialogical, the unitary thread of language something like a Möbius strip, with two sides and yet only one side. An alternative metaphor would be that of a complex knot of many crossings. Such a knot may be in one region untied, made unperplexed, but only at the expense of making a tangle of knotted crossings at some other point on the loop. The number of crossings remains stubbornly the same.

The critic, in a further frustration, may experience the impossibility of detaching a part of narrative form from the whole knot of problems and so understanding that. He cannot separate one piece and explore it in isolation. The part/whole, inside/outside division breaks down. The part turns out to be indistinguishable from the whole. The outside is already inside. Character in the novel, for example, may not be defined without talking about interpersonal relations, about time, about figures of speech, about mimesis, and so on.

The critic may also experience the impossibility of getting outside the maze and seeing it from without, giving it its law or finding its law, as opposed to trying to reach a commanding center by exploration from within. Any terminology of explication is already folded into the text the critic is attempting to see from without. This is related to the impossibility of distinguishing analytical terminology, the terms the critic needs to interpret novels, from terminology used inside the novels themselves. Any novel already interprets itself. It uses within itself the same kind of language, encounters the same impasses, as are used and encountered by the critic. The critic may fancy himself safely and rationally outside the contradictory language of the text, but he is already entangled in its web. Similar blind forks or double binds are encountered in the attempt to develop a general 'theoretical' terminology for reading prose fiction and, on the other hand, in the attempt to eschew theory, to go to the text itself and, without theoretical presuppositions, to explicate its meaning.

Criticism of a given novel or body of novels should therefore be the following of one or another track until it reaches, in the text, one or another of these double blinds, rather than the attempt to find a presupposed unity. Such a unity always turns out to be spurious, imposed rather than intrinsic. This can be experienced, however, only through the patient work of following some thread as far, deep into the labyrinth of the text, as it will go. Such an effort to read is not the 'deconstruction' of a given novel. It is rather a discovery of the way the novel deconstructs itself in the process of constructing its web of storytelling. These blind alleys in the analysis of narrative may not by any means be avoided. They may only be veiled by some credulity making a standing place where there is an abyss – for example, in taking consciousness as a solid ground. The thinly veiled chasm may be avoided only by stopping short, by taking something for granted in the terminology one is using rather than interrogating it, or by not pushing the analysis of the text in question far enough so that the impossibility of a single definitive reading emerges.

The impasse of narrative analysis is a genuine double blind alley. It results first from the fact that there is in no region of narrative or of its analysis a literal ground – in history, consciousness, society, the physical world, or whatever – for which the other regions are figures. The terminology of narrative is therefore universally catachresis. Each is a trope breaking down the reassuring distinction between figure and ground, base of so much theoretical seeing.

The other fork of this double blind is the fact that the terminology of narrative may by no effort be compartmentalized, divided into hanks of different colored thread. The same terms must be used in all regions. All the topoi overlap. Neither the critic nor the novelist can, for example, talk about sexual relations without at the same time using economic terminology (getting, spending, and so on), or without talking about mimetic representations (reproduction), or about topography (crossings), and in fact about all the other topics of narrative. The language of narrative is always displaced, borrowed. Therefore any single thread leads everywhere, like a labyrinth made of a single line or corridor crinkled to and fro.

Take, as an example of this, the letter X. It is a letter, a sign, but a sign for signs generally and for a multitude of relations involving ultimately interchanges among all nine of my places. X is a crossroads, the figure of speech called chiasmus, a kiss, a fish, Christ, the cross of the crucifixion, an unknown in mathematics, the proofreader's sign for a broken letter, a place marked on a map (X marks the spot), an illustration (as when we say, 'See figure X'), the signature of an illiterate person, the sign of an error or erasure ('crossed out'), the indication of degrees of fineness (as in the X's on a sack of flour or sugar), the place of encounters, reversals, and exchanges, the region of both/and or either/or ('She is my ex-wife'), the place of a gap, gape, or yawning chasm, the undecidable, the foyer of genealogical crossings, the sign of crossing oneself, of the X chromosome, of crisis, of the double cross, of star-crossed lovers, of cross-examination, or cross-stitching, of cross-purposes, of the witch's cross, of the criss-cross (originally Christ-cross), and of the cross child. X is, finally, the sign of death, as in the skull and crossbones, or the crossed-out eyes of the cartoon figure who is baffled, unconscious, or dead: X X. In all these uses, the 'ex' means out of, beside itself, displaced. The real and visible rises, exhales, from the unreal, or does the unreal always appear as the intervening veil or substitute for the absent real, as, in stanza 18 of Wallace Stevens's 'Man with the Blue Guitar,' daylight comes 'Like light in a mirroring of cliffs,/Rising upward from a sea of ex.'[3]

Daylight, the visible and nameable, is always doubly derived, secondary. It rises from the sea and then is further displaced by its mirroring from the cliffs in a wandering like that of all those terms I have been examining. This movement makes the source itself unreal, a sea of ex. Stevens speaks, in section 13 of 'An Ordinary Evening in New Haven,' of the approach of night, from which the light comes and to which it returns, as 'the big X of the returning primitive.'[4] The real and the unreal, the metaphorical and the literal, the figure and the ground, constantly change places, in oscillating chiasmus, for 'ex'ample in Stevens's contradictory explanation of 'sea of ex' in his letters. To Renato Poggioli he wrote: 'A sea of ex means a purely negative sea. The realm of has-been without interest or provocativeness.' To Hy Simons: 'Sea of Ex. The imagination takes us out of (Ex) reality into a pure irreality. One has this sense of irreality often in the presence of morning light on cliffs which then rise from a sea that has ceased to be real and is therefore a sea of Ex.'[5] Which is unreal, which real, the sea or the light? It cannot be decided. Whatever one sees is unreal and creates as its ground a phantasmal real, which becomes unreal in its turn when one turns to it.
[...]

Notes

1. See PAUL RICŒUR, *Temps et récit*, vol. *1* (Paris: Editions du Seuil, 1983), pp. 19–84; RICŒUR, *Time and Narrative*, vol. *1*, trans. Kathleen McLaughlin and David Pellauer (Chicago: University of Chicago Press, 1984), pp. 5–51.
2. I investigate this region of narrative criticism in a book entitled *Illustration* (Cambridge University Press, 1992).
3. WALLACE STEVENS, 'The Man with the Blue Guitar,' in *The Collected Poems of Wallace Stevens* (New York: Alfred A. Knopf, 1954), p. 175.
4. STEVENS, 'An Ordinary Evening in New Haven,' in *Collected Poems*, p. 274.
5. *The Letters of Wallace Stevens*, ed. Holly Stevens (New York: Alfred A. Knopf, 1966), pp. 783, 360.

Notes on Authors

MIEKE BAL (1946) was a member of the Institute of Comparative Literature, University of Utrecht and teaches at present at the Department of Foreign Languages, Literature and Linguistics at the University of Rochester. Her books include *Narratologie: Essais sur la signification narrative dans quatre romans modernes* (1977); *De theorie van vertellen en verhalen* (1978), translated as *Narratology: Introduction to the Theory of Narrative* (1985); and *Lethal Love: Feminist Literary Readings of Biblical Love Stories* (1987). She has also edited *Mensen van papier: over personages in de literatuur* (1979) and coedited (with Inge E. Boer) *The Point of Theory: Practices of Cultural Analysis* (1994).

ROLAND BARTHES (1915–1980) graduated in Classics (1939) and Grammar and Philology (1943). He taught for a short period in Bucharest and worked at the Centre National de la Recherche Scientifique (1952–59) and was Chef de Travaux at the École Pratique des Hautes Études. From 1976 he held the first Chair of Semiology at the Collège de France. Some of his many influential books are *Le Degré zéro de l'écriture* (1953), translated as *Writing Degree Zero* (1967); *Mythologies* (1957), translated as *Mythologies* (1972); *Eléments de sémiologie* (1964), translated as *Elements of Semiology* (1967); *Essais critiques* (1964), translated as *Critical Essays* (1972); *S/Z* (1970), translated as *S/Z* (1974); *Le Plaisir du texte* (1973), translated as *The Pleasure of the Text* (1975); *Roland Barthes* (1975), translated as *Roland Barthes by Roland Barthes* (1977); *Fragments d'un discours amoureux* (1977), translated as *A Lover's Discourse: Fragments* (1978); *Image-Music-Text* (ed. Stephen Heath, 1977).

WAYNE C. BOOTH (1921) was Dean of the College and George M. Pullman Distinguished Service Professor of English at the University of Chicago (1962–91). He won the Christian Gauss Award (Phi Beta Kappa) in 1962 and the David H. Russell Award for Distinguished Research (National Council of Teachers of English) in 1966 for *The Rhetoric of Fiction* (1961; 2nd. ed. 1983). He is also the author of *Now Don't Try to Reason with Me: Essays and Ironies for a Credulous Age* (1970); *Modern Dogma and the Rhetoric of Assent* (1974); *A Rhetoric of Irony* (1974); *Critical Understanding: The Powers and Limits of Pluralism* (1979); and *The Company We Keep: An Ethics of Fiction*. He has edited *The Knowledge Most Worth Having* (1967); and has been the coeditor of the journal *Critical Inquiry* from 1974.

EDWARD BRANIGAN (1945) is Professor and Chair of the Film Studies Program at the University of California, Santa Barbara. He is the author of *Point of View in the Cinema: A Theory of Narration and Subjectivity in Classical Film* (1984); and *Narrative Comprehension and Film* (1992), as well as general editor (with Charles Wolfe) of the American Film Institute Readers series.

CLAUDE BREMOND (1929) has been Chef de Travaux at the École Pratique des Hautes Études (Paris). He has written *Logique du récit* (1973) and has coedited (with Jacques Berlioz and Cathérine Velay-Vallantin) *Formes médiévales du conte merveilleux* (1989);

Mille et un contes de la nuit (with Jamel Eddine Bencheikh, André Miquel Bencheikh and James Eddine) (1991); and *Thematics: New Approaches* (with Joshua Landy and Thomas Pavel) (1995).

PETER BROOKS (1938) is Distinguished Tripp Professor of the Humanities at Yale University, and Director of the Whitney Humanities Center and Chairman of the French Department at Yale. He is the author of *The Novel of Worldliness* (1969); *The Melodramatic Imagination* (1976); Reading for the Plot: Design and Intention in Narrative (1984); and *Body Work: Objects of Desire in Modern Narrative* (1993). He has edited *The Child's Past* (1972); and coedited *Man and His Fictions* (1973) and *The Lesson of Paul de Man* (1985).

JONATHAN CULLER (1944) has been Professor of English and Comparative Literature since 1977 and Director of the Society for the Humanities at Cornell University since 1984. He studied at Harvard and St. John's College (Oxford), and was Fellow and Director of Studies in Modern Languages at Selwyn College (Cambridge), and Lecturer in French and Tutor at Brasenose College (Oxford). His books include *Flaubert: The Uses of Uncertainty* (1974); *Structuralist Poetics: Structuralism, Linguistics, and the Study of Literature* (1975); *Ferdinand de Saussure* (1976); *On Deconstruction: Theory and Criticism after Structuralism* (1982); *Roland Barthes* (1983); *The Pursuit of Signs: Semiotics, Literature, Deconstruction* (1983); and *Framing the Sign: Criticism and its Institutions* (1988).

CELESTINO DELEYTO (1959) is senior lecturer of film and literature at the University of Zaragoza (Spain). He is the editor of *Flashbacks: Re-Reading the Classical Hollywood Cinema* (1992). Besides his work on literature, he has published articles on Almodóvar, Saura, Woody Allen and Hollywood film in *Film Criticism* and several Spanish and British journals. He is currently working on the narrative representation of gender relationships in Hollywood films.

GÉRARD GENETTE (1930) is Director of Studies at the École des Hautes Études en Sciences Sociales in Paris. He is the author of many outstanding books on literary theory and narratology, including *Figures I, II, III* (1966, 1969, 1972), translated in part as *Narrative Discourse* (1980) and *Figures of Literary Discourse* (1982); *Mimologiques: voyages en Cratylie* (1976); *Introduction à l'architexte* (1979); *Palimpsestes: la littérature au second degré* (1982); *Nouveau discours du récit* (1983), translated as *Narrative Discourse Revisited* (1988); *Seuils* (1987); *Fiction et diction* (1991); and *L'œuvre de l'art* (1994). He has also edited *Esthétique et poétique* (1992).

WALKER GIBSON (1919) has been a professor of English at the University of Massachusetts at Amherst. He was president of the National Council of Teachers of English and a consultant for the US Office of Education. He is the author of *Come as You Are* (1958); *The Limits of Language* (1962); *Tough, Sweet and Stuffy: An Essay on Modern American Prose Styles* (1966); *Persona: A Style Study for Readers and Writers* (1969) and (with William Lutz) of *Doublespeak: A Brief History, Definition, and Bibliography, with a List of Award Winners* (1991). He has coedited *The Play of Language* (1971).

ALGIRDAS-JULIEN GREIMAS (1917–1992), of Lithuanian origin, was born in Tula (Russia). He obtained his *doctorat ès lettres* at the Sorbonne in 1949 and taught in Alexandria, Ankara, Istanbul and Poitiers before he became Directeur d'études at the École Pratique des Hautes Études (VIᵉ section) in 1965. His writings include *Sémantique structurale: Recherche de méthode* (1966); *Du sens* (1970); *Maupassant: La sémiotique du texte* (1976); *Sémiotique: Dictionnaire raisonné de la théorie du langage* (with J. Courtés, 1979); *Sémiotique des Passions: Des états de chose aux états d'âme* (with Jacques Fontanille, 1991). He also edited *Essais de sémiotique poétique* (1972).

Narratology: An Introduction

LINDA HUTCHEON (1947) was Professor of English at McMaster University (Hamilton) until 1988 and is now Professor of English and Comparative Literature at the University of Toronto. She is the author of several books on narrative and postmodernism, including *Narcissistic Narrative: The Metafictional Paradox* (1980); *Formalism and the Freudian Aesthetic: The Example of Charles Mauron* (1984); *A Theory of Parody: The Teachings of 20th-Century Art Forms* (1985); *The Canadian Postmodern: A Study of Contemporary English-Canadian Fiction* (1988); *A Poetics of Postmodernism* (1988); *The Politics of Representation in Canadian Art and Literature* (1988); *The Politics of Postmodernism* (1989); *Splitting Images: Contemporary Canadian Ironies* (1991); and *Irony's Edge: The Theory and Politics of Irony* (1994). She has also edited *Double Talking: Essays on Verbal and Visual Ironies in Canadian Contemporary Art and Literature* (1992).

TERESA DE LAURETIS is Professor of the History of Consciousness at the University of California, Santa Cruz. She is editor of *Queer Theory: Lesbian and Gay Sexualities* (special issue of *differences*, 1981) coeditor (with Stephen Heath) of *The Cinematic Apparatus* (1980) and the author of *La sintassi del desiderio* (1976), *Umberto Eco* (1981), *Alice Doesn't: Feminism, Semiotics, Cinema* (1984), *Technologies of Gender: Essays on Theory, Film and Fiction* (1987) and *The Practice of Love: Lesbian Sexuality and Perverse Desire* (1994).

J. HILLIS MILLER (1928) taught at Johns Hopkins University until 1972, then for fourteen years at Yale where he was the Frederick W. Hilles Professor of English and Comparative Literature. In 1986 he became Distinguished Professor of English and Comparative Literature at the University of California, Irvine. He has been the President of the MLA and is perhaps best known as a founding member of the so-called Yale School of deconstruction. He holds an honorary degree from the University of Zaragoza (Spain). His numerous works developing a phenomenological and (later) deconstructive approach to literary narrative include *The Form of Victorian Fiction* (1967); *Fiction and Repetition* (1982); *Hawthorne and History: Defacing It* (1991); *Ariadne's Thread: Story Lines* (1992); and *Topographies* (1994).

GERALD PRINCE (1942) is Professor of French at the University of Pennsylvania. His most significant publications are *Métaphysique et technique dans l'œuvre romanesque de Sartre* (1968); *A Grammar of Stories: An Introduction* (1973); *Narratology: The Form and Functioning of Narrative* (1982); *A Dictionary of Narratology* (1988); and *Narrative as Theme: Studies in French Fiction* (1992). He has coedited (with Warren Motte) *Alternatives* (1993).

PAUL RICŒUR (1913) was the Dean of the Faculty of Letters and Human Sciences at the University of Paris X (Nanterre) for many years and was later appointed the John Nuveen Professor Emeritus in the Divinity School, the Department of Philosophy, and the Committee on Social Thought at the University of Chicago (1984). He is the author of many books on hermeneutics. Among the most relevant for literary theory are *De l'interpretation: Essai sur Freud* (1965), translated as *Freud and Philosophy: An Essay on Interpretation* (1970); *La métaphore vive* (1975), translated as *The Rule of Metaphor: Multi-Disciplinary Studies in the Creation of Meaning in Language* (1978); *Interpretation Theory: Discourse and the Surplus of Meaning* (1976); *Être, essence et substance chez Platon et Aristote* (1982); *Temps et récit I, II, III* (1983, 1984, 1985), translated as *Time and Narrative, vols. 1, 2, 3* (1984, 1986, 1988); *Lectures on Ideology and Utopia by Paul Ricœur* (edited by George H. Taylor, 1986); *From Text to Action: Essays in Hermeneutics* (1991).

F. K. STANZEL (1923) has taught at the Universities of Harvard, Cambridge and Graz (Austria), where he became Professor of English in 1962. He became Emeritus Professor in 1993. He is the author of *Die typischen Erzählsituationen im Roman* (1955), translated as *Narrative Situations in the Novel* (1971), *Typische Formen des Romans*

(1964); *Theorie des Erzählens* (1979), translated as *A Theory of Narrative* (1984), and *Linguistische und literarische Aspekte des erzählenden Diskurses* (1984).

MEIR STERNBERG is Professor of Poetics and Comparative Literature at Tel Aviv University. He is the author of *Expositional Modes and Temporal Ordering in Fiction* (1978) and *The Poetics of Biblical Narrative* (1985), and has contributed numerous articles on narratology to *Poetics Today* and other critical journals.

HAYDEN WHITE (1928) has taught at the Universities of Rochester, California (Los Angeles) and the Wesleyan University. He is Presidential Professor of Historical Studies at the University of California, Santa Cruz. His books include *The Uses of History* (1968); *Metahistory: The Historical Imagination in Nineteenth-Century Europe* (1973); *Tropics of Discourse: Essays in Cultural Criticism* (1978); and *The Content of the Form: Narrative Discourse and Historical Representation* (1987).

Select Bibliography and Further Reading

The following bibliographies include mostly general studies of theoretical issues in narrative. No attempt has been made to include information on specific narrative genres (the novel, autobiography, etc.) or on theoretical issues which are not intrinsically narratological (reflexivity, intertextuality, or general literary theory). Some of the titles listed contain extensive additional bibliographies on narrative theory (e.g. Booth's *Rhetoric of Fiction*, Genette's *Narrative Discourse Revisited* and Martin's *Recent Theories of Narrative*). Readers will find additional references in the notes.

Narratology: general

ARISTOTLE. *The Poetics*. Trans. W. Hamilton Fyfe. In *Aristotle: The Poetics. 'Longinus': On the Sublime. Demetrius: On Style*. Cambridge, Mass.: Harvard University Press, 1927.

BAKHTIN, M. M., and PAVEL N. MEDVEDEV. *The Formal Method in Literary Scholarship: A Critical Introduction to Sociological Poetics*. 1928. Trans. Albert J. Wehrle. Cambridge, Mass.: Harvard University Press, 1985.

BAL, MIEKE. *Narratologie: Essais sur la signification narrative dans quatre romans modernes*. Paris: Klincksieck, 1977.

—— *Narratology: Introduction to the Theory of Narrative*. 1978. Trans. Christine van Boheemen. Toronto: University of Toronto Press, 1985.

BARTHES, ROLAND. 'Introduction to the Structural Analysis of Narratives.' *Image, Music, Text*. Ed. and trans. Stephen Heath. New York: Hill & Wang, 1977, pp. 79–117.

BARTHES, ROLAND, et al. *Poétique du récit*. Paris: Seuil, 1977.

BONHEIM, HELMUT. *Literary Systematics*. Cambridge: Brewer, 1990.

BROOKS, CLEANTH, and ROBERT PENN WARREN. *Understanding Fiction*. 1943. Englewood Cliffs, NJ: Prentice Hall, 1959.

CHATMAN, SEYMOUR. *Story and Discourse: Narrative Structure in Fiction and Film*. Ithaca, NY: Cornell University Press, 1978.

—— *Coming to Terms: The Rhetoric of Narrative in Fiction and Film*. Ithaca, NY: Cornell University Press, 1991.

COHAN, STEVEN, and LINDA M. SHIRES. *Telling Stories: A Theoretical Analysis of Narrative Fiction*. New York: Routledge, 1988.

DOLEŽEL, LUBOMÍR. *Narrative Modes in Czech Literature*. Toronto: University of Toronto Press, 1973.

FEHN, ANN, INGEBORG HOESTEREY, and MARIA TATAR, eds. *Neverending Stories: Toward a Critical Narratology*. Princeton: Princeton University Press, 1992.

FERRARA, FERNANDO. 'Theory and Model for the Structural Analysis of Fiction.' *New Literary History* 5.2 (1974): 245–68.

FLUDERNIK, MONIKA. *The Fictions of Language and the Language of Fiction*. London: Routledge, 1993.

—— *Towards a 'Natural' Narratology*. London: Routledge, 1996.

FRYE, NORTHROP. *Anatomy of Criticism: Four Essays*. Princeton: Princeton University Press, 1957, pp. 263–8, 303–15.

GENETTE, GÉRARD. *Figures of Literary Discourse*. Trans. Alan Sheridan. New York: Columbia University Press, 1982.

—— *Narrative Discourse*. Trans. Jane E. Lewin. Ithaca, NY: Cornell University Press, 1980.

—— *Narrative Discourse Revisited*. Trans. Jane E. Lewin. Ithaca, NY: Cornell University Press, 1988.

—— *Fiction et diction*. Paris: Seuil, 1991.

HAMBURGER, KÄTE. *The Logic of Literature*. Trans. Marilynn J. Rose. Bloomington: Indiana University Press, 1973.

HARDEE, A. MAYNOR, and G. HENRY FREEMAN, eds. *Narratology and Narrative*. (French Literature Series.) Amsterdam: Rodopi, 1990.

HARDY, BARBARA. *Tellers and Listeners: The Narrative Imagination*. New York: Humanities Press, 1975.

HÉNAULT, ANNE. *Les enjeux de la sémiotique, 2: Narratologie, sémiotique générale*. Paris: Presses Universitaires de France, 1983.

HOFFMAN, MICHAEL, and PATRICK MURPHY, eds. *Essentials of the Theory of Fiction*. Durham, NC: Duke University Press, 1988.

JAHN, MANFRED, and ANSGAR NÜNNING. 'Narratology'. *European English Messenger* 2.2 (1993): 24–9.

KNIGHT, DIANA. 'Structuralism I: Narratology. Joseph Conrad, *Heart of Darkness*.' In *Literary Theory at Work: Three Texts*. Ed. Douglas Tallack. London: Batsford, 1987, pp. 9–28.

KUMAR, SHIV, and KEITH McKEAN, eds. *Critical Approaches to Fiction*. New York: McGraw-Hill, 1965.

LÄMMERT, EBERHARD. *Bauformen des Erzählens*. Stuttgart: Metzler, 1955.

LANSER, SUSAN SNIADER. *The Narrative Act: Point of View in Prose Fiction*. Princeton: Princeton University Press, 1981.

LEFEBVE, MAURICE-JEAN. *Structure du discours de la poésie et du récit*. Neuchâtel: La Baconnière, 1971.

LEMON, LEE T., and MARION J. REIS, eds. *Russian Formalist Criticism: Four Essays*. Lincoln: University of Nebraska Press, 1965.

LODGE, DAVID. *The Language of Fiction*. London: Routledge, 1984.

MARTIN, WALLACE. *Recent Theories of Narrative*. Ithaca, NY: Cornell University Press, 1986.

On Narrative and Narratives. New Literary History 6, 11 (Winter 1975, Spring 1976).

Poetics Today 1 and 2 (1980, 1981). Issues devoted to narratology.

Poetics Today 11, 12 (Summer and Winter 1990, Fall 1991). 'Narratology revisited.'

POZUELO YVANCOS, JOSÉ MARÍA. *Del formalismo a la neorretórica*. Madrid: Taurus, 1988.

—— *Poética de la ficción*. Madrid: Síntesis, 1993.

PRINCE, GERALD. *Narratology: The Form and Functioning of Narrative*. Berlin: Mouton, 1982.

—— *A Dictionary of Narratology*. University of Nebraska Press, 1988.

REID, IAN. *Narrative Exchanges*. London: Routledge, 1992.

RICŒUR, PAUL. *Time and Narrative, vol. 1*. Trans. Kathleen McLaughlin and David Pellauer. Chicago: University of Chicago Press, 1984.

—— *Time and Narrative, vol. 2*. Trans. Kathleen McLaughlin and David Pellauer. Chicago: University of Chicago Press, 1985.

—— *Time and Narrative, vol. 3*. Trans. Kathleen Blamey and David Pellauer. Chicago: University of Chicago Press, 1988.

RIEHLE, W., H. FOLTINEK and W. ZACHARASIEWICZ, eds. *Tales and 'Their Telling*

Difference': Zur Theorie und Geschichte der Narrativik. Festschrift zum 70. Geburtstag von Franz K. Stanzel. Heidelberg: Winter, 1993.

RIMMON-KENAN, SHLOMITH. *Narrative Fiction: Contemporary Poetics.* New York: Methuen, 1983.

SCHOLES, ROBERT, and ROBERT KELLOGG. *The Nature of Narrative.* London: Oxford University Press, 1966.

SEGRE, CESARE. *Le strutture e il tempo.* Turin: Einaudi, 1976.

—— *Avviamento all'analisi del testo letterario.* Turin: Einaudi, 1985.

SHERER, PETER, and JOSEPH STERNBERG. *Narrative Style.* Dubuque, IA: Kendall-Hunt, 1986.

SHKLOVKSI, VIKTOR. *O teorii prozy.* 2nd edn. Moscow: Federatsia, 1927.

STANZEL, FRANZ. *Narrative Situations in the Novel: Tom Jones, Moby-Dick, The Ambassadors, Ulysses.* 1955. Trans. James P. Pusack. Bloomington: Indiana University Press, 1971.

—— *A Theory of Narrative.* 1979. Trans. Charlotte Goedsche. Cambridge: Cambridge University Press, 1984.

STURGESS, PHILIP J. M. *Narrativity: Theory and Practice.* Oxford: Clarendon, 1992.

TODOROV, TZVETAN. 'Categories of the Literary Narrative.' Trans. Ann Goodman. *Film Reader* 2 (1977): 19–37.

—— *The Poetics of Prose.* Trans. Richard Howard. Ithaca, NY: Cornell University Press; Oxford: Blackwell, 1977.

TOMASHEVSKI, BORIS. 'Thematics.' 1925. Select. and trans. of *Teorija literatury.* In Lemon and Reis, 61–98.

TOOLAN, MICHAEL J. *Narrative: A Critical Linguistic Introduction.* London: Routledge, 1988.

—— *The Stylistics of Fiction: A Literary-Linguistic Approach.* London: Routledge, 1990.

USPENSKI, BORIS. *A Poetics of Composition.* Berkeley: University of California Press, 1973.

VILLANUEVA, DARÍO. *Comentario de textos narrativos: la novela.* Gijón: Júcar; Valladolid: Aceña, 1989.

WEBER, JEAN JACQUES. *Critical Analysis of Fiction: Essays in Discourse Stylistics.* Amsterdam: Rodopi, 1992.

Action, agents and narrated world

BAAK, J. J. VAN. *The Place of Space in Narration: A Semiotic Approach to the Problem of Literary Space. With an Analysis of the Role of Space in I. E. Babel's Konarmija.* Amsterdam: Rodopi, 1983.

BOHEEMEN, CHRISTINE VAN. 'The Semiotics of Plot: Toward a Typology of Fictions.' *Poetics Today* 3.4 (1982): 89–96.

BREMOND, CLAUDE. *Logique du récit.* Paris: Seuil, 1973.

BURKE, KENNETH. *A Grammar of Motives.* Los Angeles: University of California Press, 1969.

CASERIO, ROBERT L. 'Story, Discourse, and Amglo-American Philosophy of Action.' *The Journal of Narrative Technique* 17.1 (1987): 1–11.

CHAMBERS, ROSS. *Story and Situation: Narrative Seduction and the Power of Fiction.* Manchester: Manchester University Press, 1984.

CHATMAN, SEYMOUR. 'On the Formalist-Structuralist Theory of Character.' *Journal of Literary Semantics* 1 (1972): 57–79.

CROSMAN, JOHN D., ed. *Narrative Syntax: Traditions and Reviews.* Athens: Scholars Press.

CULLER, JONATHAN. 'Fabula and Sjuzhet in the Analysis of Narrative.' *Poetics Today* 1.3 (1980): 27–37.

Diacritics 7 (Spring 1977). Issue on Bremond and Greimas.

DIJK, TEUN A. VAN. 'Action, Action Description, and Narrative.' *New Literary History* 6.2 (1975): 273–94.

—— 'Narrative Macro-Structures: Logical and Cognitive Foundations.' *Poetics and Theory of Literature* 1 (1976): 547–68.

—— 'Philosophy of Action and Theory of Narratives.' *Poetics* 5 (1976).

—— *Macrostructures*. Hillsdale, NJ: Erlbaum, 1980.

DIPPLE, ELIZABETH. *Plot*. London: Methuen, 1970.

DOLEŽEL, LUBOMÍR. 'Towards a Structural Theory of Content in Prose Fiction.' In *Literary Style*. Ed. Seymour Chatman. London: Oxford University Press, 1971, pp. 95–110.

—— 'Narrative Modalities.' *Journal of Literary Semantics* 5.1 (1976): 5–14.

—— 'Narrative Worlds.' In *Sound, Sign, and Meaning*. Ed. L. Matejka. Ann Arbor: University of Michigan Press, 1976, pp. 524–33.

—— 'Narrative Semantics.' *Poetics and Theory of Literature* 1 (1976): 129–51. Rpt. in *Sound, Sign, and Meaning: Quinquagenary of the Prague Linguistic Circle*. Ed. Ladislav Matejka. University of Michigan, 1976: 542–52.

—— 'A Scheme of Narrative Time.' In *Semiotics of Art: Prague School Contributions*. Ed. L. Matejka and I. Titunik. Cambridge, Mass.: MIT Press, 1976, pp. 209–17.

—— 'Extensional and Intensional Narrative Worlds.' *Poetics* 8 (1978): 193–211.

—— 'Narrative, Semantics and Motif Theory.' *Studia Poetica* 2. Ed. Karol Csúri. Szeged: Josef Attila Tudomanyegyetem, 1980.

DUNDES, ALAN. *The Morphology of North American Indian Folktales*. Helsinki: Suomalainen Tiedeakatemia, 1964.

ELSBREE, LANGDON. *The Rituals of Life: Patterns in Narratives*. New York: Associated Faculty Presses, 1982.

EWEN, JOSEPH. *Character in Narrative*. Tel Aviv: Sifri'at Po'alim, 1980.

FÜGER, WILHELM. 'Zur Tiefenstruktur des Narrativen. Prolegomena zu einer generativen "Grammatik" des Erzählens.' *Poetica* 5 (1972): 268–92.

GARVEY, JAMES. 'Characterization in Narrative.' *Poetics* 7 (1978): 63–78.

GELLEY, ALEXANDER. 'The Represented World: Towards a Phenomenological Theory of Description in the Novel.' *Journal of Aesthetics and Art Criticism* 37 (1979): 415–22.

GREIMAS, A.-J. 'Narrative Grammar: Units and Levels.' *Modern Language Notes* 86 (1971): 793–806.

—— 'Elements of a Narrative Grammar.' *Diacritics* 7 (1977): 23–40.

—— *Structural Semantics: An Attempt at a Method*. Trans. Daniele McDowell, Ronald Schleifer, and Alan Velie. Introd. Ronald Schleifer. Lincoln: University of Minnesota Press, 1983.

GREIMAS, A.-J., and J. COURTÉS. *Sémiotique: Dictionnaire raisonné de la théorie du langage*. Paris: Hachette, 1979.

—— 'The Cognitive Dimension of Narrative Discourse.' *Greimassian Semiotics. New Literary History* 20 (Spring 1989): 563–79.

HAMON, PHILIPPE. 'Pour un statut sémiologique du personnage.' *Littérature* 6 (1972). Rev. edn. in Barthes et al., *Poétique de récit*. Paris: Seuil, 1977, pp. 115–80.

HOFFMAN, GERHARD. *Raum, Situation, erzählte Wirklichkeit*. Stuttgart: Metzler, 1978.

IHWE, J. F. 'On the Foundations of a General Theory of Narrative Structure.' *Poetics* 3 (1972): 5–14.

JOHNSON, NANCY S., and JEAN M. MANDLER. 'A Tale of Two Structures: Underlying and Surface Forms in Stories.' *Poetics* 9 (1980): 51–86.

JOLLES, ANDRÉ. *Einfache Formen: Legende, Sage, Mythe, Rätsel, Spruch, Kasus, Memorabile, Märchen, Witz*. 1929. 2nd edn Halle: Niemeyer, 1956.

KRISTEVA, JULIA. *Le texte du roman*. The Hague: Mouton, 1970.

LEONDAR, BARBARA. 'Hatching Plots: Genesis of a Storymaking.' In *The Arts and Cognition*. Ed. David Perkins and Barbara Leondar. Baltimore: Johns Hopkins University Press, 1977.

LOTMAN, IURI. 'The Origin of Plot in the Light of Typology.' Trans. Julian Graffy. *Poetics Today* 1.1/2 (1979): 161–84.

MARGOLIN, URI. 'Structuralist Approaches to Character in Narrative: The State of the Art.' *Semiotica* 75/76 (1989): 1–24.

MATHIEU, MICHEL. 'Analyse du récit (I). La structure des histoires.' *Poétique* 30 (1977): 226–42 (Bibliography).

MEEHAN, JAMES. 'Tale-Spin.' In *Inside Computer Understanding: Five Programs Plus Miniatures*. Hillsdale, NJ: Erlbaum, 1981, 197–226.

MUDRICK, MARVIN. 'Character and Event in Fiction.' *Yale Review* 50 (1961): 202–18.

PAVEL, THOMAS G. *The Poetics of Plot: The Case of English Renaissance Drama*. Minneapolis: University of Minnesota Press, 1985.

—— *Fictional Worlds*. Cambridge, Mass.: Harvard University Press, 1986.

PLANALP, SALLY. 'Scripts, Story Grammars, and Casual Schemas.' In *Contemporary Issues in Language and Discourse Processes*. Ed. Donald G. Ellis and William A. Donohue. Hillsdale, NJ: Erlbaum, 1986.

PRINCE, GERALD. *A Grammar of Stories: An Introduction*. The Hague: Mouton, 1973.

—— 'What is the Story in Narratology?' *James Joyce Quarterly* 18 (1981): 277–85.

PROPP, VLADIMIR. *Morphology of the Folktale*. 1927. Trans. Laurence Scott. 2nd edn, rev. and ed. Louis A. Wagner, introd. Alan Dundes. Austin: University of Texas Press, 1968, 1988.

REVZIN, I. I. and O. G. REVZINA. 'Toward a Formal Analysis of Plot Construction.' In *Semiotics and Structuralism: Readings from the Soviet Union*. Ed. Henryk Baran. White Plains, NY: Arts and Sciences, 1976, pp. 244–56.

RONEN, RUTH. 'Space in Fiction.' *Poetics Today* 7.3 (1986): 421–38.

RUMELHART, DAVID. 'Notes on a Schema for Stories.' In *Representation and Understanding*. Ed. Daniel Bobrow and A. Collins. New York: Academic Press, 1975, pp. 211–36.

SUVIN, DARKO. 'Can People be (Re)Presented in Fiction? Toward a Theory of Narrative Agents and a Materialist Critique beyond Technology or Reductionism.' In *Marxism and the Interpretation of Culture*. Ed. Lawrence Grossberg and Cary Nelson. Urbana: University of Illinois Press, 1988: 663–96.

TODOROV, TZVETAN. *Grammaire du Décaméron*. The Hague: Mouton, 1969.

VESELOVSKI, A. N. *Poetika siuzhetov*. In A. N. Veselovski, *Sobranie Sochinenii* 2:1 (Petersburg, 1913): 1–133.

WRIGHT, GEORG HENRIK VON. *Norm and Action*. London: Routledge, 1963.

—— *An Essay in Deontic Logic and the General Theory of Action*. Amsterdam: North Holland, 1968.

Story, structure, point of view

BAL, MIEKE. 'The Narrating and the Focalizing: A Theory of the Agents in Narrative.' *Style* 17 (1983): 234–69.

—— 'Notes on Narrative Embedding.' *Poetics Today* 2 (1981): 41–59.

—— 'The Laughing Mice, or: On Focalization.' *Poetics Today* 2 (1981): 202–10.

BAQUERO GOYANES, MARIANO. *Estructuras de la novela actual*. Madrid: Castalia, 1989.

BERENDSEN, MARJET. 'The Teller and the Observer: Narration and Focalization in Narrative Texts.' *Style* 18.2 (1984): 140–56.

BLIN, GEORGES. *Stendhal et les problèmes du roman*. Paris: Corti, 1954.

BONHEIM, HELMUT. *The Narrative Modes: Techniques of the Short Story*. Cambridge: Brewer, 1982.

BORDWELL, DAVID. *Narration in the Fiction Film*. Madison: University of Wisconsin Press, 1985.

BRINTON, LAURE. ' "Represented Perception": A Study in Narrative Style.' *Poetics* 9 (1980): 363–81.

BRODSKY, CLAUDIA J. *The Imposition of Form: Studies in Narrative Representation and Knowledge*. Princeton, NJ: Princeton University Press, 1987.

BRONZWAER, W. J. M. *Tense in the Novel: An Investigation of Some Potentialities of Linguistic Criticism*. Groningen: Walters-Noordhof, 1970.

BROOKE-ROSE, CHRISTINE. *A Rhetoric of the Unreal: Studies in Narrative and Structure, Especially of the Fantastic*. Cambridge: Cambridge University Press, 1981.

BUELL, LAWRENCE. 'Observer-Hero Narrative.' *Texas Studies in Literature and Language* 21 (1979): 93–111.

CHAMBERLAIN, DANIEL FRANK. *Narrative Perspective in Fiction: A Phenomenological Mediation of Reader, Text, and World*. Toronto: University of Toronto Press, 1990.

CHATMAN, SEYMOUR. *Story and Discourse: Narrative Structure in Fiction and Film*. Ithaca, NY: Cornell University Press, 1978.

CORDESSE, GÉRARD. 'Narration et focalisation.' *Poétique* 76 (1988): 487–98.

CRANE, R. S. 'The Concept of Plot and the Plot of *Tom Jones*.' In *Critics and Criticism: Essays in Method*. Ed. R. S. Crane. Abridged edn. Chicago: University of Chicago Press, 1957, pp. 62–93.

DÄLLENBACH, LUCIEN. *The Mirror in the Text*. Trans. Jeremy Whiteley and Emma Hughes. Oxford: Polity Press, 1989.

EDMISTON, WILLIAM F. 'Focalization and the First-Person Narrator: A Revision of the Theory.' *Poetics Today* 10 (1989): 729–44.

EHRLICH, SUSAN. *Point of View: A Linguistic Analysis of Literary Style*. London: Routledge, 1990.

FEHR, BERNARD. 'Substitutionary Narration and Description: A Chapter in Stylistics.' *English Studies* 20 (1938): 97–107.

FERGUSON, SUZANNE. 'The Face in the Mirror: Authorial Presence in the Multiple Vision of Third-Person Impressionist Narrative.' *Criticism* 21 (1979): 230–50.

FLEISCHMAN, SUZANNE. *Tense and Narrativity: From Medieval Performance to Modern Fiction*. London: Routledge, 1990.

FONTANILLE, J. *Les Espaces subjectifs: Introduction à la sémiotique de l'observateur (discours-peinture-cinéma)*. Paris: Hachette, 1989.

FOWLER, ROGER. *Linguistics and the Novel*. 1977. London: Methuen, 1985.

FRANK, JOSEPH. 'Spatial Form in Modern Literature.' *Sewanee Review* 53 (1945).

FRIEDMAN, MELVIN J. *Stream of Consciousness: A Study of Literary Method*. New Haven: Yale University Press, 1955.

FRIEDMAN, NORMAN. 'Forms of the Plot.' *Journal of General Education* 8.4 (1955): 241–53.

—— 'Point of View in Fiction: The Development of a Critical Concept.' *PMLA* 70 (1955): 1160–84.

GALVÁN, FERNANDO, AÍDA DÍAZ BILD, TOMÁS MONTERREY and MANUEL BRITO. *Ensayos sobre metaficción inglesa*. Universidad de La Laguna: Secretariado de Publicaciones, 1994.

GARCÍA LANDA, JOSÉ ANGEL. 'Enunciación, ficción y niveles semióticos en el texto narrativo.' *Miscelánea* 15 (1994): 263–300.

GEE, JAMES PAUL, and FRANÇOIS GROSJEAN. 'Empirical Evidence for Narrative Structure.' *Cognitive Science* 8 (Jan.-Mar. 1984): 59–85.

GENETTE, GÉRARD. *Narrative Discourse*. Trans. Jane E. Lewin. Ithaca, NY: Cornell University Press, 1980.

GROETHUYSEN, B. 'De quelques aspects du temps: Notes pour une phénoménologie du récit.' *Recherches philosophiques* 5 (1935–6): 139–95.

GUILLÉN, CLAUDIO. 'On the Concept and Metaphor of Perspective.' In Guillén, *Literature as System*. Princeton: Princeton University Press, 1971.

HAMON, PHILLIPE. 'What Is a Description?' In *French Literary Theory Today*. Ed. T. Todorov. Cambridge: Cambridge University Press, 1982, pp. 147–78.

—— *Introduction à l'analyse du descriptif*. Paris: Hachette, 1981.

Narratology: An Introduction

HANSEN, UFFE. 'Segmentierung narrativer Texte: zum Problem der Erzählperspektive in der Fiktionsprosa.' *Text und Kontext* 3.2 (1975): 3–48.

HEATH, STEPHEN. 'Narrative Space.' *Screen* 17.3 (1976): 68–112.

HENDRICKS, WILLIAM O. *Essays on Semiolinguistics and Verbal Art.* The Hague: Mouton, 1973.

HERMAN, DAVID. 'Hypothetical Focalization.' *Narrative* 2.3 (1994): 230–53.

HOLLOWAY, JOHN. *Narrative and Structure: Exploratory Essays.* Cambridge: Cambridge University Press, 1979.

HUTCHEON, LINDA. *Narcissistic Narrative: The Metafictional Paradox.* 1980. New York: Methuen, 1984.

IBSCH, ELRUD. 'Historical Changes of the Function of Spatial Description in Literary Texts.' *Poetics Today* 3.4 (1982): 98–113.

JEFFERSON, ANN. *The Nouveau Roman and the Poetics of Fiction.* Cambridge: Cambridge University Press, 1980.

KAHLER, ERICH. *The Inward Turn of Narrative.* Trans. Richard Winston and Clara Winston. With a Foreword by Joseph Frank. Princeton, NJ: Princeton University Press, 1973.

KERMODE, FRANK. *The Sense of an Ending: Studies in the Theory of Fiction.* Oxford: Oxford University Press, 1967.

KITTAY, JEFFREY. 'Descriptive Limits.' *Yale French Studies* 61 (1981).

KLAUS, PETER. 'Description and Event in Narrative.' *Orbis Litterarum* 37 (1982): 211–16.

KLOEPFER, ROLF. 'Dynamic Structures in Narrative Literature.' *Poetics Today* 1 (1980): 51–86.

LABOV, WILLIAM. *Language in the Inner City.* University Park: University of Pennsylvania Press, 1972.

LABOV, WILLIAM and JOSHUA WALETZKY. 'Narrative Analysis: Oral Versions of Personal Experience.' In *Essays on the Verbal and Visual Arts.* Ed. Jane Helm. Seattle: University of Washington Press, 1967, pp. 12–45.

LETHCOE, RONALD JAMES. 'Narrated Speech and Consciousness.' Diss. University of Wisconsin, 1969.

LINTVELT, JAAP. *Essai de typologie narrative: Le 'point de vue'. Théorie et analyse.* Paris: Corti, 1981.

Littérature 38 (May 1980). 'Le décrit.'

LOTMAN, IURI. 'Point of View in a Text.' *New Literary History* 6 (1975): 339–52.

LUBBOCK, PERCY. *The Craft of Fiction.* London: Cape, 1921.

LUDWIG, OTTO. 'Formen der Erzählung.' *Otto Ludwigs gessamelte Schriften.* Ed. A. Stern. Leipzig: Grunow, 1891. Vol. 6, pp. 202–6.

LUKÁCS, GEORG. 'Narrate or Describe?' In Lukács, *Writer and Critic.* London: Merlin, 1978, pp. 110–48. Trans. of 'Erzählen oder Beschreiben?' 1936.

MACAULEY, ROBIE, and GEORGE LANNING. *Technique in Fiction.* New York: Harper, 1964.

MARTÍN JIMÉNEZ, ALFONSO. *Tiempo e imaginación en el texto narrativo.* Universidad de Valladolid, 1993.

MILLER, J. HILLIS. 'Ariadne's Thread: Repetition and the Narrative Line.' In *Interpretation of Narrative.* Ed. Mario J. Valdés and Owen Miller. Toronto: University of Toronto Press, 1978, pp. 148–66.

—— 'Narrative Middles: A Preliminary Outline.' *Genre* 11.3 (1978): 375–87.

—— 'The Problematic of Ending in Narrative.' *Nineteenth-Century Fiction* 33 (1978): 3–7.

—— *Fiction and Repetition.* Cambridge, Mass.: Harvard University Press, 1982.

MÜLLER, GUNTHER. 'Erzählzeit und erzählte Zeit.' *Festschrift für Kluckhorn.* 1948. Repr. in Gunther Müller, *Morphologische Poetik.* Ed. Elena Müller. Tübingen: Niemeyer, 1968, pp. 195–212.

NELLES, WILLIAM. 'Getting Focalization into Focus.' *Poetics Today* 11 (Summer 1990): 365–82.

NUTTALL, A. D. *Openings*. Oxford: Oxford University Press, 1991.

PASCAL, ROY. 'Tense and the Novel.' *Modern Language Review* 57 (1962): 1–11.

PETSCH, ROBERT. *Wesen und Formen der Erzählkunst*. Halle, 1934.

POUILLON, JEAN. *Tiempo y novela*. 1948. Buenos Aires: Paidós, 1970. Trans. of *Temps et roman*. Paris: Gallimard, 1946.

PRINCE, GERALD. *Narratology: The Form and Functioning of Narrative*. Berlin: Mouton, 1982.

RABKIN, ERIC S. *Narrative Suspense: 'When Slim Turned Sideways . . .'* Ann Arbor, Mich: University of Michigan Press, 1973.

—— 'Spatial Form and Plot.' *Critical Inquiry* 4.2 (1977): 253–70.

RICARDOU, JEAN. *Problèmes du nouveau roman*. Paris: Seuil, 1967.

—— 'Time of the Narration, Time of the Fiction.' *James Joyce Quarterly* 16 (1979): 7–15.

RICHTER, DAVID H. *Fable's End: Completeness and Closure in Rhetorical Fiction*. Chicago: University of Chicago Press, 1974.

RICŒUR, PAUL. 'Structure, Word, Event.' Trans. Robert D. Sweeny. *Philosophy Today* 12 (1968): 62–75.

—— 'Narrative Time.' *Critical Inquiry* 7 (1980): 169–90.

RIQUELME, JOHN PAUL. 'Dual Reflections on Transparency: Consciousness in Fiction.' *Comparative Literature Studies* 17.2 (1981): 155–67.

ROSSUM-GUYON, FRANÇOISE VAN. 'Point de vue ou perspective narrative: théories et concepts critiques.' *Poétique* 7 (1970): 476–97.

RYDING, WILLIAM M. *Structure in Medieval Narrative*. The Hague: Mouton, 1971.

SCHMID, WOLF. *Der Textaufbau in den Erzählungen Dostoevskijs*. Munich: Fink, 1973.

SEGRE, CESARE. *Le strutture e il tempo*. Turin: Einaudi, 1976.

—— *Avviamento all'analisi del testo letterario*. Turin: Einaudi, 1985.

SHKLOVSKI, VIKTOR. 'On the Connection between Devices of Syuzhet Construction and General Stylistic Devices.' *Twentieth Century Studies* 7–8 (1972): 54–61.

SMITH, BARBARA HERRNSTEIN. *Poetic Closure: A Study of how Poems End*. Chicago: University of Chicago Press, 1978.

SMITTEN, JEFFREY R., and ANN DAGHISTANY, eds. *Spatial Form in Narrative*. Ithaca, NY: Cornell University Press, 1981.

SPIELHAGEN, FRIEDRICH. *Beiträge zur Theorie und Technik des Romans*. Leipzig: Staackmann, 1883.

STERNBERG, MEIR. *Expositional Modes and Temporal Ordering in Fiction*. Baltimore: Johns Hopkins University Press, 1978.

—— 'Telling in Time (I): Chronology and Narrative Theory.' *Poetics Today* 11 (Winter 1990): 901–48.

—— 'Telling in Time (II): Chronology, Teleology, Narrativity.' *Poetics Today* 13.3 (1992): 463–540.

STEVICK, PHILIP. *The Chapter in Fiction: Theories of Narrative Division*. Syracuse, NY: Syracuse University Press, 1970.

TODOROV, TZVETAN. 'The Two Principles of Narrative.' *Diacritics* 1 (Fall 1971): 37–44.

TORGOVNICK, MARIANNA. *Closure in the Novel*. Princeton: Princeton University Press, 1981.

TYNIANOV, YURI. 'Plot and Story-Line in the Cinema.' *Russian Poetics in Translation* 5 (1978): 20–1.

VAN BOHEEMEN-SAAF, CHRISTINE. *Between Sacred and Profane: Narrative Design and the Logic of Myth from Chaucer to Coover*. New York: Humanities Press, 1987.

VANCE, EUGENE. *From Topic to Tale: Logic and Narrativity in the Middle Ages*. Minneapolis: University of Minnesota Press, 1987.

VITOUX, PIERRE. 'Le jeu de la focalisation.' *Poétique* 51 (1982): 355–64.

VOLEK, EMIL. *Metaestructuralismo: Poética moderna, semiótica narrativa y filosofía de las ciencias sociales*. Madrid: Fundamentos, 1985.

WARD, J. A. *The Search for Form: Studies in the Structure of James's Fiction.* Chapel Hill: University of North Carolina Press, 1967.

WAUGH, PATRICIA. *Metafiction: The Theory and Practice of Self-Conscious Fiction.* London: Routledge, 1984.

WEIMANN, ROBERT. 'Point of View in Fiction.' In *Preserve and Create: Essays in Marxist Criticism.* Ed. Gaylord C. LeRoy and Ursula Beitz. New York: Humanities Press, 1973, pp. 54–75.

WEINRICH, HARALD. *Tempus: Besprochene und erzählte Welt.* Stuttgart: Kohlhammer, 1964.

WILSON, GEORGE M. *Narration in Light: Studies in Cinematic Point of View.* Baltimore: Johns Hopkins University Press, 1986.

WOLFSON, NESSA. 'Tense-Switching in Narrative.' *Language and Style* 14 (1981): 226–31.

Yale French Studies 61 (1981). 'Towards a Theory of Description.'

Text, voice, narrative pragmatics

ADAMS, JON K. *Pragmatics and Fiction.* Amsterdam: Benjamins, 1985.

ADORNO, T. W. 'La situation du narrateur dans le roman contemporain.' In Adorno, *Notes sur la littérature.* 1958. Trans. Sybille Muller. Paris: Flammarion, 1984, pp. 37–45.

AYALA, FRANCISCO. *La estructura narrativa y otras experiencias literarias.* Barcelona: Crítica, 1984.

BAKHTIN, MIKHAIL. *The Dialogic Imagination.* Ed. Michael Holquist. Trans. Caryl Emerson and Michael Holquist. Austin: University of Texas Press, 1981.

—— *Problems of Dostoevski's Poetics.* Minneapolis: University of Minnesota Press, 1984.

BALLY, CHARLES. 'Le style indirect libre en français moderne.' *Germanisch-Romanische Monatschrift* 4 (1912): 549–56, 597–606.

BANFIELD, ANN. *Unspeakable Sentences.* New York: Routledge, 1982.

BARNES, TREVOR, and JAMES S. DUNCAN. *Writing Worlds: Discourse, Text and Metaphor in the Representation of Landscape.* London: Routledge, 1991.

BELLOS, DAVID. 'Narrative and Communication.' *Signs of Change* 3 (1978): 34–52.

BENJAMIN, WALTER. 'The Storyteller.' In Benjamin, *Illuminations.* Trans. Harry Zohn. New York: Schocken Books, 1969, pp. 83–110.

BIALOSTOSKY, DON H. 'Dialogics, Narratology, and The Virtual Space of Discourse.' *The Journal of Narrative Technique* 19.1 (1989): 167–73.

BICKERTON, DEREK. 'Modes of Interior Monologue: A Formal Definition.' *Modern Language Quarterly* 28 (1967): 229–39.

BONHEIM, HELMUT. *The Narrative Modes: Techniques of the Short Story.* Cambridge: Brewer, 1982.

BOOTH, WAYNE C. *The Rhetoric of Fiction.* Chicago: University of Chicago Press, 1961. 2nd edn. Harmondsworth: Penguin, 1983.

BOWLING, L. E. 'What Is the Stream of Consciousness Technique?' *PMLA* 65 (1950): 333–45.

CEBIK, L. B. *Fictional Narrative and Truth: An Epistemic Analysis.* Langam, Md.: University Presses of America, 1984.

CHAMPIGNY, ROBERT. *Ontology of the Narrative.* The Hague: Mouton, 1972.

CHATMAN, SEYMOUR. 'The Structure of Narrative Transmission.' In *Style and Structure in Literature.* Ed. Roger Fowler. Ithaca, NY: Cornell University Press, 1975, pp. 213–57.

—— 'Characters and Narrators: Filter, Center, Slant, and Interest-Focus.' *Poetics Today* 7 (1986): 189–204.

CHRISTENSEN, INGER. *The Meaning of Metafiction: A Critical Study of Selected Novels by Sterne, Nabokov, Barth and Beckett*. Bergen: Universitetsforlaget, 1981.

COHN, DORRIT. *Transparent Minds: Narrative Modes for Presenting Consciousness in Fiction*. Princeton: Princeton University Press, 1978.

—— 'Signposts of Fictionality: A Narratological Perspective.' *Poetics Today* 11.4 (1990): 775–804.

COSTE, DIDIER. *Narrative as Communication*. Minneapolis: University of Minnesota Press, 1989.

DAHL, LIISA. *Linguistic Features of the Stream-of-Consciousness Techniques of James Joyce, Virginia Woolf and Eugene O'Neill*. Turku: Turun Yliopisto, 1970.

DILLON, GEORGE L., and FREDERICK KIRCHOFF. 'On the Form and Function of Free Indirect Style.' *Poetics and Theory of Literature* 1 (1976): 431–40.

DOLEŽEL, LUBOMÍR. 'The Typology of the Narrator: Point of View in Fiction.' In *To Honor Roman Jakobson*. The Hague: Mouton, 1967. Vol. 1, pp. 541–52.

DUJARDIN, EDOUARD. *Le Monologue intérieur*. Paris: Messein, 1931.

EBINE, HIROSHI. 'The Duality of Omniscient Narration.' *Studies in English Literature* 50 (1974): 245–57.

EDMISTON, WILLIAM F. 'Focalization and the First-Person Narrator: A Revision of the Theory.' *Poetics Today* 10 (1989): 729–44.

EPSTEIN, E. L. 'The Irrelevant Narrator: A Stylistic Note on the Place of the Author in Contemporary Technique of the Novel.' *Language and Style* 2 (1969): 92–4.

ESPINOLA, JUDITH C. 'The Nature, Function and Performance of Indirect Discourse in Prose Fiction.' *Speech Monographs* 41 (1974): 193–204.

EWEN, JOSEPH. 'Writer, Narrator and Implied Author.' *Ha-Sifrut* 18–19 (1974): 137–73.

FLUDERNIK, MONIKA. *The Fictions of Language and the Language of Fiction*. London: Routledge, 1993.

FOSTER, DENNIS. *Confession and Complicity in Narrative*. Cambridge: Cambridge University Press, 1987.

FOWLER, ROGER. 'How to See Through Language: Perspective in Fiction.' *Poetics* 1 (1982): 213–35.

—— *Linguistic Criticism*. Oxford: Oxford University Press, 1986.

FRIEDEMANN, KÄTE. *Die Rolle des Erzählers in der Epik*. Berlin, 1910. Rpt. Darmstadt: Wissenschaftliche Buchgesellschaft, 1965.

GELLEY, ALEXANDER. *Narrative Crossings: Theory and Pragmatics in Prose Fiction*. Baltimore: Johns Hopkins University Press, 1987.

GENETTE, GÉRARD. *Narrative Discourse*. Trans. Jane E. Lewin. Ithaca, NY: Cornell University Press, 1980.

—— *Narrative Discourse Revisited*. Trans. Jane E. Lewin. Ithaca, NY: Cornell University Press, 1988.

—— 'Fictional Narrative, Factual Narrative.' *Poetics Today* 11.4 (1990): 755–74.

—— *Fiction et diction*. Paris: Seuil, 1991.

GLOWINSKI, MICHAL. 'On the First-Person Novel.' *New Literary History* 9 (1977): 103–14.

GUIRAUD, PIERRE. 'Modern Linguistic Looks at Rhetoric: Free Indirect Style.' In *Patterns of Literary Style*. Ed. J. Strelka. University Park: Pennsylvania State University Press, 1971, pp. 77–89.

HARTLEY, L. G. 'The Sacred River, Stream of Consciousness: The Evolution of a Method.' *Sewanee Review* 39 (1931): 80–9.

HEPPENSTALL, RAYNER. 'Stream of Consciousness.' In Heppenstall, *The Fourfold Tradition*. London: Barrie and Rockliff, 1961, pp. 132–59.

HERNADI, PAUL. 'Dual Perspective: Free Indirect Discourse and Related Techniques.' *Comparative Literature* 24 (1972): 32–43.

HUMPHREY, ROBERT. *Stream of Consciousness in the Modern Novel*. Berkeley: University of California Press, 1954.

HUTCHISON, CHRIS. 'The Act of Narration: A Critical Survey of Some Speech-Act Theories of Narrative Discourse.' *Journal of Literary Semantics* 13 (1984): 3–35.

ISER, WOLFGANG. 'Narrative Strategies as a Means of Communication.' In *Interpretation of Narrative*. Ed. Mario J. Valdes and Owen J. Miller. Toronto: University of Toronto Press, 1978.

JEFFERSON, ANN. 'The Place of Free Indirect Discurse in the Poetics of Fiction: With Examples from Joyce's "Evelina".' *Essays in Poetics* 5 (1980): 36–47.

KAYSER, WOLFGANG. 'Qui raconte le roman?' In Barthes et al., *Poétique du récit*. Paris: Seuil, 1978, pp. 59–84.

KRYSINKI, WLADIMIR. 'The Narrator as a Sayer of the Author: Narrative Voices and Symbolic Structures.' *Strumenti Critici* 2 (1977): 44–89.

LE GUIN, URSULA K. 'It Was a Dark and Stormy Night; or, Why Are We Huddling about the Campfire?' *Critical Inquiry* 7.1 (1980): 191–9.

LEECH, GEOFFREY N., and MICHAEL H. SHORT. *Style in Fiction: A Linguistic Introduction to English Fictional Prose*. London: Longman, 1981.

LIPS, MARGUERITE. *Le style indirect libre*. Paris: Payot, 1926.

LLOYD, GENEVIEVE. *Being in Time: Selves and Narrators in Philosophy and Literature*. London: Routledge, 1993.

MARGOLIS, JOSEPH. 'The Logic and Structures of Fictional Narrative.' *Philosophy and Literature* 7.2 (1983): 162–81.

MARTÍNEZ BONATI, FÉLIX. *La ficción narrativea (su lógica y ontología)*. Murcia: Secretariado de Publicaciones de la Universidad de Murcia, 1992.

MATHIEU, MICHEL. 'Analyse du récit (II). Le discours narratif.' *Poétique* 30 (1977): 243–59 (Bibliography).

MCHALE, BRIAN. 'Free Indirect Discourse: A Survey of Recent Accounts.' *Poetics and Theory of Literature* 3 (1978): 249–87.

MILLER, J. HILLIS. 'Three Problems of Fictional Form: First-Person Narration in *David Copperfield* and *Huckleberry Finn*.' *Experience in the Novel: Selected Papers from the English Institute*. Ed. Roy Harvey Peace. New York: Columbia University Press, 1968.

NÜNNING, ANSGAR. *Grundzüge eines kommunikantionstheoretischen Modells der erzählerischen Vermittlung: Die Funktionen der Erzählinstanz in den Romanen George Eliots*. Trier: Wissenschaftlischer Verlag, 1989.

PASCAL, ROY. *The Dual Voice: Free Indirect Speech and Its Functioning in the Nineteenth-Century European Novel*. Manchester: Manchester University Press, 1977.

PAVEL, THOMAS G. 'Literary Narratives.' In *Discourse and Literature*. Ed. T. A. van Dijk. Amsterdam: John Benjamins, 1985, pp. 85–103.

PELC, JERZY. 'On the Concept of Narration.' *Semiotica* 5 (1971): 1–19.

PHELAN, JAMES. *Worlds from Words: A Theory of Language in Fiction*. Chicago: University of Chicago Press, 1981.

POUILLON, JEAN. *Temps et roman*. Paris: Gallimard, 1948.

PRINCE, GERALD. 'Notes toward a Characterization of Fictional Narratees.' *Genre* 4.1 (1971): 100–6.

—— 'On Readers and Listeners in Narrative.' *Neophilologus* 55 (1971): 117–22.

PYWOWARCZYK, MARY ANN. 'The Narratee and the Situation of Enunciation: A Reconsideration of Prince's Theory.' *Genre* 9 (1976): 161–77.

RAUH, GISA. *Linguistische Beschreibung deiktischer Komplexität in narrativen Texten*. Tübingen: TBL-Narr, 1978.

ROJAS, MARIO. 'Tipología del discurso del personaje en el texto narrativo.' *Dispositio* 5–6 (1980–1) 19–55.

ROMBERG, BERTIL. *Studies in the Narrative Technique of the First-Person Novel*. Stockholm: Almquist and Wiksell, 1962.

ROMERA, ANTONIO R. 'El monólogo silente en Galdós y en Joyce.' *Atenea* 257–8 (1946): 373–9.

RON, MOSHE. 'Free Indirect Discourse, Mimetic Language Games and the Subject of Fiction.' *Poetics Today* 2 (1981): 17–39.

Ross, Donald, Jr. 'Who's Talking? How Characters Become Narrators in Fiction.' *Modern Language Notes* 91 (1976): 1222–42.

Routley, Richard. 'The Semantical Structure of Fictional Discourse.' *Poetics* 8 (1979): 3–30.

Rubin, Louis D., jun. *The Teller in the Tale*. Seattle: University of Washington Press, 1967.

Ruin, Inger. 'Narrative Modes and Linguistic Form: A Case Study in Fictional Discourse.' *Stockholm Papers in English Language and Literature* 3 (1982): 18–53.

Rush, Jeffrey S. 'Lyric Oneness: The Free Syntactical Indirect and the Boundary between Narrative and Narration.' *Wide Angle* 8 (1986): 27–33.

Ryan, M. L. 'The Pragmatics of Personal and Impersonal Fiction.' *Poetics* 10 (1981): 517–39.

Sallenave, Danièle. 'A propos du "monologue intérieur" lecture d'une théorie.' *Littérature* 5 (1972): 62–87.

Simpson, Paul. *Language, Ideology, and Point of View*. London: Routledge, 1993.

Steinberg, Edwin R., ed. *The Stream of Consciousness Technique in the Modern Novel*. Port Washington, NY: Kennikat, 1979.

Tacca, O. *Las voces de la novela*. 3rd edn. Madrid: Gredos, 1985.

Tamir, Nomi. 'Personal Narrative and Its Linguistic Foundations.' *Poetics and Theory of Literature* 1 (1976): 403–29.

Thibault, Paul. 'Narrative Discourse as a Multi-Level System of Communication: Some Theoretical Proposals Concerning Bakhtin's Dialogic Principle.' *Studies in Twentieth Century Literature* 9 (1984): 89–117.

Tillotson, Geoffrey. *Thackeray the Novelist*. Cambridge: Cambridge University Press, 1954.

Tillotson, Kathleen. *The Tale and the Teller*. London: Rupert Hart-Davis, 1959.

Vera Luján, A. 'El concepto de "texto" en la semiología de la narración.' In *Anales de la Universidad de Murcia. Letras* 41.1–2 (1983): 3–30.

Voloshinov, V. N. *Marxism and the Philosophy of Language*. Trans. Ladislav Matejka and I. R. Titunik. Cambridge, Mass.: Harvard University Press, 1986.

Warhol, Robyn R. *Gendered Interventions: Narrative Discourse in the Victorian Novel*. New Brunswick: Rutgers University Press, 1990.

Weissman, Frida S. *Du monologue intérieur à la sous-conversation*. Paris: Nizet, 1978.

Yacobi, Tamar. 'Narrative Structure and Fictional Meditation.' *Poetics Today* 8 (1987): 335–72.

Reading

Barthes, Roland. *S/Z*. Paris: Seuil, 1970. Trans. Richard Miller. Preface by Richard Howard. New York: Hill & Wang, 1974.

Branigan, Edward. *Narrative Comprehension and Film*, London: Routledge, 1992.

Brooks, Peter. *Reading for the Plot: Design and Intention in Narrative*. Oxford: Clarendon Press, 1984.

Chamberlain, Daniel Frank. 'Narrative Perspective in the Reading Experience.' In Chamberlain, *Narrative Perspective in Fiction*. Toronto: University of Toronto Press, 1990, pp. 161–4.

D'Sonza, Dinesh. 'Response.' *Narrative* 2.3 (1994): 268–9.

Dijk, T. A. van, and W. Kintsch. 'Cognitive Psychology and Discourse: Recalling and Summarizing Stories.' In *Current Trends in Text Linguistics*. Ed. W. U. Dressler. Berlin: De Gruyter, 1978, pp. 61–80.

Eco, Umberto. *The Role of the Reader*. London: Hutchinson, 1983.

Harweg, Roland. 'Präsuppositionen und Rekonstruktion. Zur Erzählsituation in Thomas Manns *Tristan* aus textlinguistischer Sicht.' In *Textgrammatik: Beiträge* zur *Problem der Textualität*. Ed. Michael Schecher and Peter Wunderli. Tübingen: Niemeyer, 1975, pp. 166–85.

ISER, WOLFGANG. *The Implied Reader. Patterns of Communication in Prose Fiction from Bunyan to Beckett*. Baltimore: Johns Hopkins University Press, 1974. Trans. of *Der Implizite Leser: Kommunikationsformen des Romans von Bunyan bis Beckett*. Munich: Fink, 1972.

KERMODE, FRANK. *The Genesis of Secrecy: On the Interpretation of Narrative*. Cambridge, Mass.: Harvard University Press, 1979.

KINTSCH. W., and T. A. VAN DIJK. 'Comment on se rappelle et on résume de histoires.' *Langages* 40 (1975): 98–116.

LANGELLIER, KRISTIN. 'A Phenomenology of Narrative in Performance.' In *Phenomenology in Rhetoric and Communication*. Ed. Stanley Deetz. Washington, DC: University Press of America for the Center for Advanced Research in Phenomenology, 1981, pp. 83–90.

MANDLER, JEAN MATER. *Stories, Scripts, and Scenes: Aspects of Schema Theory*. Hillsdale, NJ: Erlbaum, 1984.

—— 'On the Psychological Reality of Story Structure.' *Discourse Processes* 10 (Jan.–Mar. 1987): 1–29.

MARIN, LOUIS, *The Semiotics of the Passion Narratives*. Trans. Alfred M. Johnson, Jr. Pittsburgh: Pickwick, 1980.

PEARSE, JAMES A. 'Beyond the Narrational Frame: Interpretation and Metafiction.' *Quarterly Journal of Speech* 66 (1980): 73–84.

PHELAN, JAMES. *Reading People, Reading Plots*. Chicago: University of Chicago Press, 1979.

PLEH, CSABA. 'On Formal- and Content-Based Models of Story Memory.' In *Literary Discourse: Aspects of Cognitive and Social Psychological Approaches*. Ed. Laszlo Halasz. New York: Walter de Gruyter, 1987.

RABINOVITZ, PETER. *Before Reading: Narrative Conventions and the Politics of Interpretation*. Ithaca, NY: Cornell University Press, 1987.

RUTHROF, HORST. *The Reader's Construction of Narrative*. London: Routledge, 1981.

SARBIN, THEODORE R. *Narrative Psychology: The Storied Nature of Human Conduct*. New York: Praeger, 1986.

STEIN, NANCY L. 'The Comprehension and Appreciation of Stories: A Developmental Analysis.' In *The Arts, Cognition and Basic Skills*. Ed. Stanley S. Madeja. St Louis: Cemrel, 1978.

SZANTO, GEORGE. *Narrative Tastes and Social Perspectives: The Matter of Quality*. New York: St Martin's Press, 1987.

THORNDYKE, P. W. 'Cognitive Studies in Comprehension and Memory of Narrative Discourse.' *Cognitive Psychology* (1977): 77–110.

TOMPKINS, JANE P., ed. *Reader-Response Criticism*. Baltimore: Johns Hopkins University Press, 1980.

Interdisciplinary narratology

ALPHEN, ERNST VAN. 'The Narrative of Perception and the Perception of Narrative.' *Poetics Today* 11.3 (1990): 483–510.

APPLEBEE, ARTHUR N. *The Child's Concept of Story: Ages Two to Seventeen*. Chicago: University of Chicago Press, 1978.

ARMSTRONG, NANCY and LEONARD TENNENHOUSE. 'History, Poststructuralism, and the Question of Narrative.' *Narrative* 1.1 (1993): 45–58.

BARRY, JACKSON G. 'Narratology's Centrifugal Force: A Literary Perspective on the Extensions of Narrative Theory.' *Poetics Today* 11 (1990): 295–307.

BORDWELL, DAVID. *Narration in the Fiction Film*. Madison: University of Wisconsin Press, 1985.

BRANIGAN, EDWARD. *Narrative Comprehension and Film*. London: Routledge, 1992.

CALVO GONZÁLEZ, JOSÉ. *El discurso de los hechos: Narrativismo en la interpretación operativa*. Madrid: Tecnos, 1993.

CASERIO, ROBERT L. ' "A Pathos of Uncertain Agency": Paul de Man and Narrative.' *Journal of Narrative Technique* 20.2 (1990): 195–209.

CASSELL, JUSTINE, and DAVID MCNEILL. 'Gesture and the Poetics of Prose.' *Poetics Today* 12.3 (1991): 375–404.

CERVELLINI, M. 'Focalizzacione e manifestacione pittorica.' *Estudios semióticos* 1 (1984): 39–59.

CHAMBERS, ROSS. 'Narrative and Other Triangles.' *The Journal of Narrative Technique* 19.1 (1989): 31–48.

CHATMAN, SEYMOUR. *Coming to Terms: The Rhetoric of Narrative in Fiction and Film*. Ithaca, NY: Cornell University Press, 1991.

CORNIS-POPE, MARCEL. 'Poststructuralist Narratology and Critical Writing: A *Figure in the Carpet* Textshop.' *Journal of Narrative Tehcnique* 20.2 (1990): 245–65.

Critical Inquiry 7 (Autumn 1980). 'On Narrative.'

CRUZ RODRÍGUEZ, MANUEL. *Narratividad: La nueva síntesis*. Barcelona: Península, 1986.

DANTO, ARTHUR C. *Narration and Knowledge*. Including *Analytical Philosophy of History*. New York: Columbia University Press, 1985.

DAVIS, ROBERT CON, ed. *Lacan and Narration: The Psychoanalytic Difference in Narrative Theory*. Baltimore: Johns Hopkins University Press, 1983.

DE LAURETIS, TERESA. 'Desire in Narrative.' In de Lauretis, *Alice Doesn't: Feminism, Semiotics, Cinema*. Bloomington: Indiana University Press, 1984, pp. 103–57.

DEHN, NATALIE. 'Story Generation after TALE-SPIN.' *Proceedings of the Seventh IJCAI* (1981): 16–18.

DIAWARA, MANTHIA. 'Oral Literature and African Film: Narratology in Wend Kuuni.' *Présence Africaine* 142 (1987): 36–49.

FREEMAN, MARK. *Rewriting the Self: History, Memory, Narrative*. London: Routledge, 1993.

GOFFMAN, ERVING. *Frame Analysis: An Essay on the Organization of Experience*. Cambridge, Mass.: Harvard University Press, 1974.

GONZÁLEZ REQUENA, JESÚS. 'Enunciación, punto de vista, sujeto.' *Contracampo* 42 (1987): 6–41.

GÜLICH, ELISABETH, and UTA M. QUASTHOFF. 'Narrative Analysis.' In *Handbook of Discourse Analysis 2: Dimensions of Discourse*. Ed. Teun A. van Dijk. New York: Academic Press, 1985.

—— 'Narrative Analysis: An Interdisciplinary Dialogue.' *Poetics* 15 (1986): 1–2.

HASLETT, BETT. 'A Developmental Analysis of Children's Narratives.' In *Contemporary Issues in Language and Discourse Processes*. Ed. Donald G. Ellis and William A. Donohue. Hillsdale, NJ: Erlbaum, 1986.

HIRSCH, MARIANNE. *The Mother/Daughter Plot: Narrative, Psychoanalysis, Feminism*. Indianapolis: Indiana University Press, 1989.

HOFFMAN, JOHN C. *Law, Freedom and Story: The Role of Narrative in Therapy, Society and Faith*. New York: Humanities Press, 1986.

JAMESON, FREDRIC. *The Political Unconscious: Narrative as a Socially Symbolic Act*. Ithaca, NY: Cornell Unviersity Press, 1981.

KOZLOFF, SARAH RUTH. 'Narrative Theory and Television.' In *Channels of Discourse: Television and Contemporary Criticism*. Ed. Robert C. Allen. Chapel Hill: University of North Carolina Press, 1987.

LONGHURST, DEREK. *Gender, Genre, and Narrative Pleasure*. London: Routledge, 1991.

MANDLER, JEAN MATER. *Stories, Scripts and Scenes: Aspects of Schema Theory*. Hillsdale, NJ: Erlbaum, 1984.

——, 'On the Psychological Reality of Story Structure.' *Discourse Processes* 10 (Jan.–Mar. 1987): 1–29.

McKnight, Edgar V. *Meaning in Texts: the Historical Shaping of a Narrative Hermeneutics*. Philadelphia: Fortress, 1978.

Meaney, Geraldine. *(Un)like Subjects: Women, Theory, Fiction*. London: Routledge, 1993.

Mellard, James M. *Doing Tropology: Analysis of Narrative Discourse*. Urbana: University of Illinois Press, 1987.

Miller, D. A. *Narrative and Its Discontents: Problems of Closure in the Traditional Novel*. Princeton: Princeton University Press, 1981.

Miller, J. Hillis. 'Narrative and History.' *English Literary History* 41 (1974): 455–73.

—— 'Ariachne's Broken Woof.' *Georgia Review* 31 (1977).

—— 'From Narrative Theory to Joyce; from Joyce to Narrative Theory.' In *The Seventh of Joyce*. Ed. Bernard Benstock. Bloomington: Indiana University Press; Brighton: Harvester, 1982.

—— *Ariadne's Thread: Story Lines*. New Haven: Yale University Press, 1992.

Miller, Nancy K. 'Emphasis Added: Plots and Plausibilities in Women's Fiction.' *PMLA* 96 (1981). Repr. in *The New Feminist Criticism*. Ed. Elaine Showalter. New York: Pantheon, 1985, pp. 339–60.

Mink, Louis O. 'Narrative Form as a Cognitive Instrument.' In *The Writing of History: Literary Form and Historical Understanding*. Ed. Robert H. Canary and Henry Kozicki. Madison, Wisc.: University of Wisconsin Press, 1978, pp. 129–49.

Mitchell, Juliet. 'Femininity, Narrative and Psychoanalysis.' In *Feminist Literary Theory: A Reader*. Ed. Mary Eagleton. Oxford: Blackwell, 1986, pp. 100–3.

Mitchell, W. J. T., ed. *On Narrative*. Chicago: University of Chicago Press, 1981.

Morey, Miguel. *El orden de los acontecimientos: Sobre el saber narrativo*. Barcelona: Península, 1988.

Nash, Christopher, ed. *Narrative in Culture: Storytelling in the Sciences, Philosophy, and Literature*. London: Routledge, 1989.

Nelson, Paul, *Narrative and Morality: A Theological Inquiry*. University Park: Pennsylvania State University Press, 1987.

Norris, Christopher. 'Narrative Theory or Theory-as-Narrative: The Politics of "Post-Modern" Reason.' In Norris, *The Contest of Faculties: Philosophy and Theory after Deconstruction*. London: Methuen, 1985.

Poetics 15 (April 1986). 'Narrative Analysis: An Interdisciplinary Dialogue.'

Ryan, M. L. 'Stacks, Frames and Boundaries, or Narrative as Computer Language.' *Poetics Today* 11 (Winter 1990): 873–99.

—— *Possible Worlds, Artificial Intelligence and Narrative Theory*. Bloomington: Indiana University Press, 1991.

Sarbin, Theodore R., ed. *Narrative Psychology: The Storied Nature of Human Conduct*. New York: Praeger, 1986.

Schafer, Roy, *Narrative Actions in Psychoanalysis*. Worcester, Mass.: Clark University Press, 1981.

Scollon, R., and S. Scollon. *Narrative, Literacy and Face in Interethnic Communication*. Norwood, NJ: Ablex, 1981.

Siegle, Robert. *The Politics of Reflexivity: Narrative and the Constitutive Poetics of Culture*. Baltimore: Johns Hopkins University Press, 1986.

Smith, Joseph H. and Humphrey Morris, eds. *Telling Facts: History and Narration in Psychoanalysis*. Baltimore: Johns Hopkins University Press, 1992.

Spence, Donald. *Narrative Truth and Historical Truth: Meaning and Interpretation in Psychoanalysis*. New York: Norton, 1982.

Stein, Nancy L., and Christine G. Glenn. 'Children's Concept of Time: The Development of a Story Schema.' In *The Developmental Psychology of Time*. Ed. William J. Friedman. New York: Academic Press, 1982.

Tolton, C. D. E. 'Narration in Film and Prose Fiction: A *mise au point*.' *University of Toronto Quarterly* 53.3 (1984): 264–82.

Turner, Victor. 'Social Dramas and Stories about Them.' *Critical Inquiry* 7 (1980): 141–68.

WHITE, HAYDEN. 'The Narrativization of Real Events.' *Critical Inquiry* 7 (Summer 1981): 793–8.

WICKER, BRIAN. *The Story-Shaped World: Fiction and Metaphysics: Some Variations on a Theme.* London: Athlone, 1975.

WINNETT, SUSAN. 'Coming Unstrung: Women, Men, Narrative, and Principles of Pleasure.' *PMLA* 105 (May 1990): 505–18.

On narratological theories

ALDRIDGE, A. O. 'Shifting Trends in Narrative Criticism.' *Comparative Literature Studies* 6 (Sept. 1969): 225–9.

BAL, MIEKE. 'The Point of Narratology.' *Poetics Today* 11.4 (1990): 727–54.

BRONZWAER, W. J. M. 'Mieke Bal's Concept of Focalization.' *Poetics Today* 2.2 (1981): 193–201.

BROOKE-ROSE, CHRISTINE. 'Whatever Happened to Narratology?' *Poetics Today* 11.2 (1990): 283–94.

BUDNAKIEWICZ, THÉRÈSE. 'A Conceptual Survey of Narrative Semiotics.' *Dispositio* 3.7–8 (1978): 189–217.

CHATMAN, SEYMOUR. 'What Can We Learn from Contextualist Narratology?' *Poetics Today* 11.2 (1990): 309–28.

GENETTE, GÉRARD. *Narrative Discourse Revisited.* Trans. Jane E. Lewin. Ithaca, NY: Cornell University Press, 1988.

GIRARD, RENÉ. 'French Theories of Fiction, 1947–1974.' *Bucknell Review* 22.1 (1976): 117–26.

GÜNTHERT, GEORGES. 'Vicisitudes de la semiótica y de la narración en el ámbito del hispanismo internacional (1980/89).' *Epos* 6 (1990): 533–44.

KURODA, S.-Y. 'Reflections on the Foundation of Narrative Theory from a Linguistic Point of View.' In *Pragmatics of Language and Literature.* Ed. Teun A. van Dijk. Amsterdam: North Holland, 1976, pp. 107–40.

MARTIN, WALLACE. *Recent Theories of Narrative.* Ithaca, NY: Cornell University Press, 1986.

MINER, EARL. 'Narrative.' In Miner, *Comparative Poetics: An Intercultural Essay on Theories of Literature.* Princeton: Princeton University Press, 1990, pp. 135–212.

MOSHER, HAROLD F. 'A New Synthesis of Narratology.' *Poetics Today* 1.3 (1980): 171–86.

—— 'Recent Studies in Narratology.' *Essays on Language and Literature* 17 (1981): 88–110.

—— 'Current Trends in Narratology.' *Critical Texts* 1 (1982): 1, 15–20.

RIMMON-KENAN, SHLOMITH. 'A Comprehensive Theory of Narrative: Genette's *Figures III* and the Structuralist Study of Fiction.' *Poetics and Theory of Literature* 1 (1976): 33–62.

RONEN, RUTH. 'Paradigm Shift in Plot Models: An Outline of the History of Narratology.' *Poetics Today* 11 (Winter 1990): 817–42.

RYAN, M. L. 'Linguistic Models in Narratology: From Structuralism to Generative Semantics.' *Semiotica* 28 (1979): 127–55.

SMITH, BARBARA HERRNSTEIN. 'Narrative Versions, Narrative Theories.' *Critical Inquiry* 7 (1980): 213–36.

SOSNOSKI, JAMES J., 'Story and Discourse and the Practice of Literary Criticism: "Araby", a Test Case.' *James Joyce Quarterly* 18.3 (1981): 255–65.

STRIEDTER, JURIJ. 'The Russian Formalist Theory of Prose.' *Poetics and Theory of Literature* 2 (1977): 429–70.

WOOD, DAVID, ed. *On Paul Ricœur: Narrative and Interpretation.* London: Routledge, 1992.

Index

Index

Index